KEIM'S HISTORY

OF

JESUS OF NAZARA.

VOL. V.

THE HISTORY

OF

JESUS OF NAZARA,

FREELY INVESTIGATED

IN ITS CONNECTION WITH THE NATIONAL LIFE OF ISRAEL,
AND RELATED IN DETAIL.

BY

DR. THEODOR KEIM.

TRANSLATED BY ARTHUR RANSOM.

VOL. V.

WIPF & STOCK · Eugene, Oregon

Wipf and Stock Publishers
199 W 8th Ave, Suite 3
Eugene, OR 97401

The History of Jesus of Nazara, Volume Five
Freely Investigated in its Connection with
the National Life of Israel, and Related in Detail
By Keim, Theodor and Ransom, Arthur
ISBN 13: 978-1-5326-1595-5
Publication date 12/9/2016
Previously published by Williams and Norgate, 1881

TRANSLATOR'S NOTE.

CIRCUMSTANCES over which I had no control are responsible for the delay that has taken place in the translation of this volume. The next—and last—volume is being proceeded with as rapidly as possible, and its publication may confidently be expected early next year. That volume will contain a copious Index of the whole work; and the large mass of valuable historical and literary information contained in both the text and the notes will be thus made readily accessible to the student.

Great care has been taken, in this as in the previous volumes, to make the translation correct. If, however, students should discover or have reason to suspect any error, they would oblige by drawing my attention to it before the whole of the next volume has left the press, that such error, if serious, may be corrected.

ARTHUR RANSOM.

BEDFORD, *May*, 1881.

TABLE OF CONTENTS.

FIRST PART.

	PAGE
THE MESSIANIC PROGRESS TO JERUSALEM	1
I.—THE JOURNEY TO THE FEAST	1
A. Peræa	1
B. Judæa and Jericho	21
C. A Day at Jericho	47
II.—THE ENTRY INTO JERUSALEM	65
A. From Jericho to Bethphage	65
B. The Johannine Christ at Bethany	72
C. The Jubilant Recognition of the Messiah	88
D. The Lord of the Temple	113
III.—THE DECISIVE STRUGGLE	132
A. The Assailants	133
B. The Tempters	155
C. The Last Disclosures and Announcement of Woe upon the System	190
IV.—THE FAREWELL	225
A. On the Mount of Olives	225
B. At Bethany	247
C. At Jerusalem. The Last Supper	275

First Part.

THE MESSIANIC PROGRESS TO JERUSALEM.

DIVISION I.—THE JOURNEY TO THE FEAST.

A.—PERÆA.

AFTER the official announcement of the first of Nisan, the moon of blossoms and of Easter, had been carried from Jerusalem throughout the land with haste and jubilation, because in two weeks Easter would have come, Jesus set out from Galilee, probably on the first day after the Sabbath, viz. Sunday the third of April, A.D. 35. He found himself, perhaps to his own astonishment, in the midst of a festival caravan.[1] This was not, however, the stream of festival visitants from Galilee, which as a rule flowed specially full and strong, nay, menacing to the rulers of Jerusalem, to this spring feast, to the most venerable and the most eminent of all the Jewish festivals. Jesus made a practice of withdrawing himself from the masses in order to secure liberty and rest; and he avoided them on this occasion in particular, when the menaces of his foes, the estrangement of the unstable populace, and the seriousness of his decisive course, imposed

---

[1] The announcement of the new moon, and of the first of Nisan, by fire signals, later by messengers, see *Rosh hashanah*, 1, in Lightfoot, p. 201; and Friedlieb, *Archäolgie der Leidensgesch.*, 1843, p. 43. The chronology will be treated of in a separate section.

solitude upon him.¹ If, in view of the great train of followers who accompanied him, we were to think of a marching forth of Jesus at the head of the Galilean people as a necessary moral and indeed also material commencement of his Messiahship in Jerusalem, we should be trifling not only with the immediate testimony of our documents, but also with all the facts, great and small, of the history of Jesus from Galilee to Jerusalem, and with the whole character of his life.² It will suffice here to point out that the very road which Jesus chose proved his entire renunciation of any attempt to excite a movement of the masses between Galilee and Jerusalem.

The retinue of Jesus rather consisted exclusively of a part of that body of adherents that afterwards, in the apostolic period, constituted the church of Galilee.³ If we yielded to the first impression produced by our Gospels, we should suppose it was only the Twelve who followed him.⁴ We have, however, incidental intimations that those who accompanied him were much more numerous, even if we deduct the people that sought out and accompanied him after his entrance into Judæa and Jericho.⁵ All the Gospels mention a numerous company of Galilean women, among whom appear in particular Mary Magdalene, Mary of James, Joanna, and Salome. But Luke, at the entry into the Holy City and at the scene in Golgotha, knows also of a mass of disciples and acquaintances, of whom it is true he mentions only one by name, the Clopas who was probably the father of the second James among the Twelve, and the husband of the

---

[1] That Jesus joined the Galilean festival caravan is thought even by Neander, pp. 465, 467; Strauss, *New Life of Jesus*, Eng. trans., I. p. 383. On the crowding to the Easter festival, above, I. p. 303. Also Irenæus, 2, 22, 3. Magnitude of the caravans, Tholuk, *Glaubw.* p. 215.

[2] Comp. the Fragmentist, *Von d. Zweck Jesu u. s. Jünger*, pp. 140 sqq. Geiger, *Judenth.* I. pp. 115 sqq.

[3] This Galilean church is first seen in 1 Cor. xv. 6, and by name, Acts ix. 31.

[4] Matt. xix. 10, 13, 23, 25, 28, xxi. 1 sqq.; Luke xxii. 28.

[5] Matt. xix. 2 (according to verse 1, already in the Judæan territory, against Hilg. *Zeitschrift*, 1868, pp. 22, 43), xx. 17, 29, xxi. 8 sqq.

above-mentioned second Mary.[1] Though we may have to subtract something from the account by Luke, since the mythical narratives of the seventy disciples whom Jesus chose besides the Twelve, and of the one hundred and twenty adherents who formed the first Christian community immediately after the departure of Jesus, have probably magnified his numbers; yet, on the other hand, the retinue of Galilean women remains untouched, whilst at the same time the accompaniment of a—though smaller—number of men and youths belonging to the outer circles of disciples is not only very probable in and of itself, but is also directly established by certain indications in the oldest Gospel.[2] If there were needed a proof that Jesus had no intention of seeking to influence Jerusalem and the hierarchy there, and of compelling Messianic success by the aid of Galilee or even merely of his own most trusty adherents from Galilee, the proof would in fact be found in this very retinue. He invited no one to accompany him to Jerusalem, certainly not the women who could not strengthen, nor support, nor dignify, nor commend him. He left his friends behind in their home, in order to implicate none but himself in the decisive struggle; but he could not turn away his most intimate adherents if they of their own free will determined to accompany him and to share his entry into Jerusalem—his triumphs as they hoped, his fatal destiny as he feared.

The road which Jesus chose was an unfrequented one. Not merely the shortest, but also the most frequented way from Galilee to Jerusalem led directly southwards through the heart of the country west of the Jordan, through southern Galilee and Samaria. The Jewish historian expressly says that it was the

[1] Matt. xxvii. 55, xxviii. 1; Luke xix. 37, xxiii. 49, xxiv. 10, 13, 18; Mark xv. 40 sq. Clopas, above, III. p. 274.

[2] Comp. Matt. xix. 21, 29 sq., xx. 17. James, the brother of Jesus, was not among those who accompanied, although in 1 Cor. xv. 7, as well as in the Gospel of the Hebrews, he is cited as witness of the resurrection. The appearance in question was in Galilee (see Resurrection); and had it been in Jerusalem, the still unbelieving brother need not—according to John vii. 3 sqq.—have gone up to Jerusalem with Jesus. There can be no reference to the mother of Jesus.

custom of the Galileans, when they went to the festivals in the Holy City, to take the road through the country of the Samaritans. In three days, he remarks elsewhere, it was possible to reach Jerusalem from Galilee by this route.[1] From Capernaum it was twelve, from Nazara six, leagues to Ginæa and the Samaritan frontier; six leagues further lay Sichem, nearly twelve further lay Jerusalem; and thus it was possible to exchange the view of the lake for that of the temple by a journey of thirty leagues.[2] But our most reliable sources tell us that Jesus passed into the Judæan frontier from the other side of Jordan, that is, instead of taking the direct southerly way west of the Jordan, he took the south-easterly and more circuitous way through Peræa beyond the Jordan, and finally re-crossed to the west bank of that river.[3] Indeed, we can understand why he took this course. He thus not merely gave expression to his antipathy to Samaria, which district he had previously expressly closed to the mission of his disciples and which he now himself avoided; but he also here enjoyed the advantage of the quietest, most secure, and least observed route of travel. On this by-way he was disturbed by none of those evil-disposed and contentious Samaritans who so often filled the journeys of the Galilean festival-pilgrims with obstacles and annoyances. Here the quiet and the *incognito* of his journey were broken by no Galilean festival-trains, with their confusion and noise and the *abandon* of their humour and their jubilant singing, nor even by the inquisitive and obtrusive populations of southern Galilee and northern Judæa. And the remoteness afforded protection against tetrarchical attacks, even though the way, with the whole of Peræa, was under the rule of Antipas.[4]

[1] Jos. *Ant.* 20, 6, 1; *Vita*, 52.

[2] According to Van de Velde. Comp. above, II. p. 1. Ginæa (Dshenin), Jos. *Ant.* 20, 6, 1; *B. J.* 2, 12, 3; 3, 3, 4.

[3] Matt. xix. 1; Mark x. 1. See below. Correct definition of Peræa as country *beyond* Jordan, Pliny, *H. N.* 5, 15: Peræa asperis dispersa montibus et a ceteris Judæis Jordane amne discreta.

[4] The caravans of the Galileans, and the sanguinary conflicts with the Samaritans close by Ginæa, Jos. *Ant.* 20, 6, 1; comp. *Vita*, 52. Other evil deeds of the Samaritans, *Ant.* 18, 2, 2. Lightfoot, p. 201 (deceptive fire-signals of the new moon).

The sparsely populated and little frequented Jordan valley on other occasions served as a means of escape from difficulties and perplexities. The Roman general Vitellius, in the spring of 37, when he purposed to help the tetrarch Antipas against the Arabs, marched his troops along "the Great Plain" of the Jordan, because the Jews had forbidden an army with heathen standards to pass through their country.[1]

Without doubt, Jesus went directly from Capernaum eastward, at once over the lake and over the river that flowed through the lake, in order thus at a stroke to escape the populous district of southern Galilee and to get out of sight of the court. Journeying still a few leagues on the banks of his favourite lake, he entered upon the thirty-leagues-long Jordan valley between Tarichæa-Hippos and Jericho, and left behind him all the charms, all the life and social intercourse of Galilee, and with it the greater part of his own history. The middle and lower Jordan valley offered a direct contrast to the landscapes amongst which Jesus had hitherto moved between the Jordan sources and Capernaum. The plains on both sides of the Jordan were dry and treeless; both ranges of flanking hills presented barren and shapeless outlines; the heat was oppressive, and the dazzling reflection of the sunlight from limestone hills was intolerable; while houses and villages were rare both in the plain and on the ridges of the hills. Naturally in the summer heat of the deep cleft the trees and bushes were burnt up, and there prevailed a heavy sultriness in the air which was fatal to the health of man and beast. To judge from the vivid description by Dixon, the feet became as burning coals on the hot sand, the temples throbbed painfully, the tongue became swollen and inflamed, the lips blistered, the eyes blinked and closed themselves before the unbearable light. But the Jordan, rushing onward among green bushes through its hundred windings in the narrow fifty-foot-deep river-bed, the steep incline of which fell a thousand feet, and the numerous

---

[1] Jos. *Ant.* 18, 5, 3. "The Great Plain" here simply the plain of the Jordan (above, II. p. 235), comp. *B. J.* 4, 8, 2. Comp. Vespasian's march, *ib.* 4, 8, 1.

streams and brooks—from the Hieromiax (Yarmuk) at Gadara to the Jabbok (Wady Serka) in the latitude of Sichem, and to Wady Sheriah at Jericho—which pierce the monotonous hills right and left, and call forth a southern vegetation of palms, olives, and vines, lent to the district a scanty adornment, and presented at spots rest and variety to the eye, chiefly at that very time of the year when everywhere the copious waters were rushing in wild and noisy tumult, and the cooler air awoke and protected the beautiful tints of spring.[1] Unfortunately there remains no notice of this Peræan journey of Jesus, beyond a colourless sentence; but we can surmise that four or five days were consumed before the arrival in the district of Jericho ended the fatigues which must have attended the condition of the roads in the spring, the dangerous fording of the torrents, and the want of provisions and lodgings, the procuring of which had as usual been left to the disciples.[2] One of the few inhabited places which Jesus passed was directly over against Scythopolis on the southern frontier of Galilee, situated high upon the hill, that "well-watered" city of Decapolis, Pella, in which a generation later, in the stormy time of the Jewish wars, the community of the Messiah found its safety.[3]

This Peræa journey of Jesus is not altogether unchallenged. It is true that the language of Matthew and Mark, although somewhat obscure, excludes every other explanation.[4] On the

---

[1] Comp. Jos. *B. J.* 3, 3, 3, and generally above, II. pp. 234, 235. W. H. Dixon's *Holy Land*.

[2] The danger of the torrents in the spring, Joshua iii. 15, and above, *l. c.* note. Provisions, comp. Matt. xvi. 5; Luke ix. 52, x. 1. Day's journey of the caravans, from 6 to 12 leagues, average 7 to 8; comp. Winer, *Tagreise*.

[3] P. aquis dives, Pliny, *H. N.* 5, 16.

[4] The expression in Matt. xix. 1 does not require elucidation from Mark (x. 1), since a misunderstanding is quite impossible; for even admitting it possible that the Gospel was written in Pella, the author can neither (with Delitzsch, Köstlin) wish to say that Judæa lay to him beyond the Jordan (for he assumes the contrary, iv. 25), nor that a part of Judæa lay in Peræa (against iv. 25), but simply that the "coming" to Judæa took place (Lig., Fr., Mey., Strauss) via trans amnem (beeber hajarden, πέραν LXX.). In Mark, not only is the reading διὰ (A) a correction, but also καὶ (Sin. BCL), the former almost better than the latter, since the latter is very liable to be

other hand, the third of the Synoptics very strikingly substitutes for the Peræan journey a Samaritan one. According to Luke's extremely obscure report of the journey, Jesus did not cross the Jordan at all, but, following the custom of the Galileans, he left the southern frontier of Galilee at the village Ginæa (now Dshenin), and traversed entirely or in part the Samaritan territory. And indeed there is much to support the former, and much more to support the latter, supposition.[1] According to the former supposition, we must think of Jesus as making a day's journey in Samaria as far as Sichem, and then, instead of pressing forward in a southerly direction, at once taking the south-easterly road, a seven leagues' walk along which would bring him to the Jordan valley, whereas in Matthew's account—he would find a less frequented route.

misunderstood. Equivalent to that in Matthew is the reading in Mark, Cod. Bez., St. Gall., It., Vulg., and other versions. Weisse, p. 432 (comp. Scholt. *Joh.* p. 73), dreams of a mutilation of Mark by Matthew, and then doubts (p. 433)—as Paulus dreamt of a brief journey to the temple dedication—whether this Peræan route ended at Jerusalem, and not again in Galilee. Caspari, pp. 77, 143, 153, 159 sq., is in favour of restoring the "Judæa beyond Jordan" (after Kuin., Grätz; comp. Ptol. 5, 16, 9), and understands thereby Golan (!). He says there was no road there at all (but comp. Jos. *Ant.* 14, 3, 4; *B. J.* 4, 8, 1; and Van de Velde); and nothing is said of crossing the Jordan! Even Hilgenfeld, *Zeitschrift*, 1868, p. 22, influenced by De Wette's untenable linguistic objections, thinks that at least the original text of Matthew might have reckoned Peræa as belonging to Judæa!

[1] Luke ix. 52, xiii. 22, xvii. 11. The expression in xvii. 11, διὰ μέσου Σ. κ. Γ., may mean either "through the midst," or "through the boundaries between Samaria and Galilee." The former explanation would (against Fr. and De Wette, who thought of the journey from north to south) be possible only if Jesus had travelled northwards instead of southwards, for then Galilee would have come after Samaria; thus also, in effect, Paulus and Olsh. admit. The second explanation is altogether untenable, at least in the form hitherto given it (Grot., Wetst., Schl., Meyer, Bl., Hofm.), viz., that Jesus travelled between the boundaries of Samaria and Galilee from west to east towards the Jordan (Wetst., towards Scythopolis); for, after a previous visit to Samaria in ix. 52, he could not with any reason in xvii. 11 appear afresh upon the northern frontier, or regard the little excursion of four or five leagues from Ginæa (Jos. *Ant.* 20, 6, 1) to the Jordan valley as a great journey, indeed as a journey towards Jerusalem. On the other hand, unless we prefer to believe in Luke's perfect innocence of geography, the boundaries between Samaria and Galilee from north to south in the Jordan valley may be thought of, if it be but admitted that Luke included Peræa in Galilee, as in point of fact the whole principality of Antipas, including Peræa, is often called simply Galilee: comp. only Luke himself, iii. 1, and Jos. *Ant.* 18, 5, 4 (against 17, 8, 1; 17, 11, 4; 18, 7, 1. See above, IV. p. 218, note 1. Vespasian's march from Neapolis past Kuriut (near Shiloh) to Jericho, *B. J.* 4, 8, 1, was analogous.

He would then press towards Archelais and Jericho in the south, but without crossing the Jordan, remaining on the west bank, and passing first through the desert valley district between Samaria and Galilee, more correctly Peræa, then through the more cultivated Judæan country. But this route, although the most rational expedient we can find for Luke, is altogether unworthy of acceptance, quite apart from the unhistorical object aimed at by the Pauline Luke of showing us Jesus in the "way of the Gentiles," and from the mythical and unskilful distribution of the material among the stages of the journey. Indeed, it is in the highest degree improbable that Jesus, in the situation in which he was, should so openly traverse the populous region of south Galilee, that he should enter Samaria at all, towards which he felt a personal antipathy, and where at any rate he could do nothing to further his pressing Jewish aims; moreover, if he had entered Samaria, it is highly improbable he should pay but a hurried visit, and then forsake the Samaritan highway in order to withdraw to the remote Jordan valley.[1] The whole of this representation can be explained only from the unhappy crossing of two views. On the one side, it was sought to show that Jesus, instead of avoiding Samaria, made a solemn progress through it; on the other, that he remained as near as possible to the route of historical tradition, not through Samaria, but through Peræa. Hence arose the representation that he entered Samaria but did not traverse the whole of it; that he visited the Jordan, and reached Jerusalem by way of Jericho, and not of Sichem, Sophna, Bethel, and Ramah. There is no need here to speak of the historical errors in the fourth Gospel, which knows nothing at all of the

---

[1] Even Weisse, pp. 433 sq., Strauss, *New Life of Jesus*, Eng. trans., I. p. 301, Scholten, *Joh.* p. 272, Hausr. p. 385 (above, III. p. 136), do not know how to handle critically the Samaritan journey in Luke. Schenkel, in his *Charakterbild*, pp. 151 sqq., still more in the article *Jesus* in *Bibel-Lexikon*, has been the most strongly influenced by the description of Luke and John. He holds that in Matthew and Mark there is here a great gap which Luke's zealous investigation has filled in; and that there was a ministry of several months in Samaria, Peræa, and Judæa, with visits to Jerusalem, whilst at the same time it is admitted that Jesus had been already indicted in Galilee for not paying the temple tribute. *But that was only just before Easter.*

historical Easter journey of Jesus from Galilee to Jerusalem, because it has already long since established Jesus at Jerusalem. This subject can be deferred till we come to the entry into Jerusalem; but we may here mention that Jesus' brief sojourn in Peræa, which in the fourth Gospel precedes the resurrection of Lazarus, bears a similar relation to the narratives of Matthew and Mark as does the brief residence in the city of Ephraim, which follows that resurrection, to the Samaritan journey in Luke, since Ephraim lay in the neighbourhood of Bethel, a little nearer to Jerusalem, on the highway between Sichem and the Holy City.[1] Herein, however, John makes the mistake of thinking that Luke's Samaritan journey went southwards from Sichem. The main point is, that we take note how one account ever stands in connection with the other, and how every fresh unhistorical deviation seeks to establish its probability by a correct or incorrect attachment to earlier accounts.

With the Samaritan journey there is intimately connected, in Luke, a very unhistorical view of the whole character of this expedition to Jerusalem. The narrative of a Samaritan journey is, namely, the immediate consequence of the erroneous notion that Jesus took a missionary journey, in his old manner, from Galilee to Jerusalem; and more exactly still, it is the conse-

---

[1] John x. 40, and xi. 54. As to the position of Ephraim (Sin., L., It., Vulg., Ephrem) there may be a doubt (Eus. 8 Roman miles, Jerome 20, from Jerusalem, but Larsow and Parthey, p. 196, now read 20 also in Eusebius); yet not only does Eusebius know most distinctly that Jerusalem is near (κώμη μεγίστη περὶ τὰ ὅρια Αἰλίας; Jerome: villa prægrandis Ephræa), but Josephus also, *B. J.* 4, 9, 9 (comp. 2 Chron. xiii. 19, where, instead of Ephron, there is Ephrain in the Keri), makes it quite certain that the little town (πολίχνιον) lay south of Akrabe, Gophna, and Bethel, in the neighbourhood of the last town which was three or four leagues from Jerusalem, and on the highway to Jerusalem. Ewald renounces the attempt to fix the locality, p. 502; Furrer, *Bedeut. der bibl. Geogr.* p. 21, looks for the place in Wady Farah, two leagues and a half from Jerusalem, and is at least much more nearly correct than Caspari, who thinks (p. 158) of the place El Fariah, two leagues north-east of Sichem, about fifteen leagues from Jerusalem. But even Wady Farah lies much too far to the east. Späth, in Hilg.'s *Zeitschrift*, 1868, p. 339, explains the presence of the name in John as having reference to the earliest prophecies, particularly Hosea's. In fact, it is but a step to regard it as representative of the rejected and ultimately won (Hosea i. 11) country of the Ten Tribes and of the Samaritans; comp. above, II. p. 349 : Messias filius Ephraim.

quence of the desire—as pious as it was ardent—to represent him as the director, indeed as the first pioneer, of the Pauline mission to the Gentiles.

The very plan of Jesus naturally excluded any missionary activity by the way. His one goal was Judæa and Jerusalem; his means to his end was a quiet journey; his time was limited. Easter was at the door, and the country between middle Galilee and Jerusalem was so great, the towns and villages, even those merely which were close to the highway, were so many, that an Easter journey could not suffice for even the most superficial mission.[1] Thus the very way which he took, the route along the plain of the Jordan—as solitary as had been, a little before, the route to the sources of the Jordan—showed a renunciation of missionary work on the journey. Finally, the more faithful sources, Matthew yet more plainly than Mark, prove that everything was quiet in Peræa; that even in the immediate neighbourhood of Jerusalem, in Jericho and Bethany, Jesus did not by any means volunteer to preach; that it was simply the flocking together of the people from the time of his approach to the Judæan frontier at Jericho which led to several works of healing, speeches, and replies, as he went.[2] But in Luke, though Jesus has his face directed towards Jerusalem, and it is several times remarked that he passed through towns and villages on his way to Jerusalem, yet the preaching and healing in the presence of

---

[1] Even Weizsäcker (as Neander, p. 440; Schenkel, *Bibel-Lexikon*, III. p. 288; Hausrath, pp. 433 sq.) finds, p. 513, that in Mark x. 1, not a journey, but a sojourn in Judæa and Peræa, is referred to. How many are the ways of harmonistics!

[2] In Matt. xix. 1, 2, the flocking of the multitudes to Jesus is evidently placed on the frontier of Judæa reached from Peræa (see above, p. 2, n. 5). The chief definition of locality contained in the expression "there," used concerning the people, has reference to the entry into Judæa, and to that Peræa was only the route and the means. This distinction between Peræa and Judæa is perfectly intelligible. Hence Ewald, p. 504 (comp. Gess, p. 112), has completely misunderstood the narrative when he places the subsequent incidents, including that of the rich young man, in the period of the departure from Galilee. Even Mark here proves him to be in error. Mark x. 1 agrees with Matt., if we drop the καί. If we retain it, then the flocking of the people to Jesus is transferred to Peræa. And at any rate the report of a teaching by Jesus "as he was wont," is an unhistorical generalization.

multitudes of people so far predominates, that the Galilean ministry is completely outdone in both extent and character, particularly in the copiousness of the doctrinal utterances. The movement of the journey is altogether stopped, and the narrator endeavours to remove the impression of a complete standstill by introducing artificially and violently, yet without any convincing force, repeated scattered notes in which he asserts that the journey was resumed and continued.[1] Indeed, Luke not only gives a copiousness of detailed facts which stay the journey and show the mission to be in full activity, but he expressly represents Jesus as intending to carry on the mission work, for he shows a fresh and extensive selection of seventy disciples, who were to preach the gospel at the various stages of the journeys as Jesus' forerunners, and were to confirm their preaching by healings.[2] Hence we must infer that this Evangelist aimed not only at creating in this journey to Jerusalem a quiet place for the great mass of material of the sayings and doings of Jesus which he possessed over and above his predecessors in this history-writing, and which in truth belonged either to Galilee or to Jerusalem; but that he intended to give to this travelling ministry the importance of a new great mission, penetrating the whole land and complementing what had gone before, the completing and the crowning of the work of the seventy forerunners.[3]

But the special object of introducing this travelling mission was its Samaritan, its Gentile-favouring, its Pauline character. Hence, in the first place, the passage through a part of the

---

[1] Allusions to the journey, Luke ix. 51, xiii. 22, xvii. 11. Comp. above, I. p. 102. According to Schleiermacher, *Luk.* p. 161, he has mixed up several journeys (comp. even Strauss, *New Life of J.*, Eng. trans., I. p. 301); according to the artificial interpretation of Meyer and others, Jesus, after the experience in ix. 52, postponed his entry into Samaria until xvii. 11.

[2] Luke x. 1.

[3] That the fragments in question belong to the Galilean or Jerusalemite ministry of Jesus, is seen, not only in the parallel passages of the other Gospels, particularly of Matthew, but also in the contents of so many of the fragments, as Luke xiii. 1, 31, 34, or even ix. 57, x. 25, xi. 14, 29, 37—53, xii. 1, xiii. 10, 23, xiv. 1, 7, xv. 2, xvi. 14, xvii. 20, xviii. 9.

Samaritan territory. Hence the revelation of the spirit of forbearance and of unconquerable human love to the very first Samaritan village, to the village which, with a narrowness equal to that of the Jewish fanaticism of the Twelve, refused hospitality to the pilgrims to Jerusalem. The sons of thunder, James and John, who in the angry spirit of Elijah would have called down fire from heaven upon the godless—doing, but in a religious way, very much like the people of Galilee, who were accustomed to set fire to the villages of the Samaritans—are said to have been put to shame by the reproof: "Know ye not what spirit ye are of?"[1] In the same connection falls another toleration-utterance of Jesus, spoken to the second son of thunder, John, with reference to his zeal against an exorcist, who indeed used the name of Jesus, but did not follow him: "Hinder it not, for he who is not against us is for us!"[2] Hence again, together with toleration, we have a profound and loving recognition of the moral, nay, of the religious, equality of those despised Samaritans. A parable holds up as a model of neighbourly love the Samaritan who binds up the wounds of his Jewish brother, the victim of robbers between Jerusalem and Jericho, passed by with indifference by priest and Levite; and a narrative of fact shows, out of ten lepers cleansed, nine ungrateful Jews and one grateful Samaritan.[3] Hence, on the other side, the combating and rejecting the Scribes and Pharisees, the Jewish people, Jerusalem: another sign that the kingdom of God, in fulfilment of Jesus' menace in his initial sermon at Nazara, is, from the commencement of the fatal journey, seriously, and as much as in the apostolic time after Stephen's

---

[1] Luke ix. 52—56. The best established reading of the oldest codices wants the addition, οὐκ οἶδ. οἵου πνεύμ.; this is therefore a good gloss out of 1 Kings xix. 11 sqq. (comp. Numb. xiv. 24): οὐκ ἐν τῷ πνεύμ. ὁ κύριος. Just so it is no injury to the MS. to strike out in verse 54 the appeal of the Zebedeans to Elijah (after 2 Kings i. 10, 12), and in verse 56 the addition about saving (from xix. 10). The incendiarism of the Galileans, Jos. *Ant.* 20, 6, 1, comp. 12, 4, 1.

[2] Luke ix. 49; Mark ix. 38.

[3] Luke x. 25, 30. Comp. also the Prodigal Son, xv. 11 sqq. See above, IV. p. 7.

death, offered to the Gentiles.¹ When we review the whole of this representation, there can remain no doubt that the solemn and so fully reported sending forth of the seventy disciples at the beginning of the Samaritan journey, signifies not merely the extension and intensifying of the mission, but essentially a mission to the Gentiles, as moreover the number seventy is best explained from the number of the seventy nations reckoned by the Jews: thus, twelve Apostles for the twelve tribes of Israel, and seventy for the nations of the earth, their first fruit being the Samaritan people on the way to Jerusalem.² The addresses of Jesus himself, which he is said to have delivered on this occasion, are quite full of this sense. To the Seventy, and not to the Twelve, Jesus commits, according to Luke, the great harvest of the world; them he bids—without respect to Jewish prohibitions of food, particularly in relation to the Gentiles—to eat and drink what was offered them in the houses they entered

---

¹ Luke x. 13, 21, 25, xi. 14 sqq., 37—54, xii. 54, xiii. 1 sqq., 10 sqq., 23 sqq., &c. Comp. the Synopsis at end of Vol. I. In the Acts, the hitherto completely overlooked turning-point is not immediately Stephen (Lekebusch), but Acts ix. 31.

² The number seventy is overwhelmingly attested against seventy-two (*Recogn.* 1, 40, B D, It., Vulg.). (These various readings also in the number of the Mosaic elders, see Lightfoot, p. 518, hence also of the seventy translators and the seventy Synedrists.) Prototypical of this favourite number of the Hebrews, seventy (comp. Gen. xlvi. 27; Ex. xv. 27; Judges i. 7, ix. 2; 2 Kings x. 6; Jer. xxv. 11, &c.; also Jos. *B.J.* 2, 20, 5, *Vita*, 11, 14; and Wetst.), are partly the seventy elders of Moses, Ex. xxiv. 1, 9, Numbers xi. 16, to which the seventy Synedrists have reference; partly, the nations of the earth (Japhetites 14, Hamites 30, Semites 26) in the lists of the nations in Gen. x., and of whom Jewish tradition counted seventy, *Jon.* Gen. xi. 7, xxviii. 3; *Gem. Sanh.* 17, 1; Clem. *Hom.* 18, 4, *Recogn.* 2, 42; Epiph. *Haer.* 51, 7. Compare the seventy Gentile shepherds (chiefly representative of seventy periods), Book of Enoch 80, and Dillm. p. 265. See also Eisenmeng. II. p. 736; Bertholdt, pp. 162, 186; Winer, *Erde* and *Synedrium*. Theophyl. and others thought of Ex. xv. 27. The Jewish mixed tradition is remarkable, that the seventy Synedrists understood the seventy languages of the nations, *Sanh. l. c.* Jesus' seventy disciples might remind us (thus *Recogn.* 1, 40, comp. Neander, Meyer, Gess) of the elders of Moses (comp. Ex. xviii. 17 sqq.), because of Luke x. 2; but evidently the preponderant thought—as not only Strauss, Baur, De Wette, Bleek, Hilg., Volkm., but even Olsh. and Pressensé, find —is, according to the whole context, that of the extra-Israelitish nations. Formerly Strauss (*L. J.*, 4th ed., I. pp. 594 sqq.) left both explanations open; but he now (*New Life of J.*, Eng. trans., I. p. 379) admits that Luke's source might have thought of the elders, Luke of the nations. Similarly Bleek, II. p. 150. Neander, p. 405, undecided.

on their mission; and in allusion to their field of labour, he utters the "Woe" concerning the former Jewish fields of labour, Chorazin, Bethsaida, Capernaum.[1] Their success also far outdoes that of the Twelve. Even the demons, over which the Twelve had so little power, are subject to the Seventy; they overthrow in a decisive manner Satan, the prince of the heathen gods, and whom Jesus sees powerless under their ministry, falling dethroned from heaven.[2] In recompence, he gives them power and authority over serpents and scorpions, to tread victoriously under foot the whole brood of the heathen devil-world; and, what is more, he gives them the assurance that their names are written in the Book of Life. For himself, he now for the first time experienced the ecstatic feeling which prompted him to magnify the Father's mode of revelation, his own personal exaltation with the Father, and the glory of those who had lived to see that time and him.[3] There then follows a new address to the disciples, whom Luke at any rate misunderstands to be the Seventy. He therein points beyond their work to one greater than they are, to the great Paul, who was to utter yet more openly and more widely what they had here and there spoken in darkness and in the ear and in the room, and even before magistrates and authorities, and before Roman governors.[4]

[1] Luke x. 1 sqq.
[2] Luke x. 17 sqq. Comp. Is. xiv. 12; Book of Enoch 90, &c.; Rev. xii. 9. Also Bertholdt, p. 186: Scias, esse 70 principes atque unicuique populo unum princ. ex his 70 contigisse. (Quite similarly, *Recogn.* 2, 42.) Sunt autem sub potestate Sammaelis. Comp. above, II. pp. 312 note 2, 317 note 1. See the commentaries for the fanciful dreams of seeing the fall of Satan in the circumstances mentioned in Matt. xii. 29 (Gess), in the temptation (Lange), or indeed in the incarnation, nay, the pre-existence of Jesus (from the Fathers down to Hofmann and Stier). Vision, Weisse, II. p. 146. The correct meaning also in Neander, p. 408 (seeing in spirit, without a vision), and Weiss, *N. T. Theol.* p. 78. Ewald, p. 436, and others represent the passage as addressed to the Twelve.
[3] Luke x. 19 sqq. Comp. Is. xliii. 2; Ezek. ii. 6; Dan. iii. 27, vi. 22; Rev. ii. 11; Mark xvi. 18. Miraculous passing of the Israelites over serpents and scorpions which are compelled to make themselves into a bridge, told by the Rabbis; see Wetst. p. 721. Names in the Book of Life, Ex. xxxii. 32; Dan. xii. 1; Book of Enoch 104; Rev. iii. 5, xiii. 8, xvii. 8, xx. 12, xxi. 27; Phil. iv. 3.
[4] Luke xii. 1 sqq.

It only remains to be asked whether all this is credible? This question must be met by an unqualified negation. Jesus did not pass through Samaria; he passed through Peræa. Jesus did not pronounce any definite sentence concerning the admission of the Samaritans and the Gentiles: he was then on his way to Jerusalem, there to decide solemnly the Jewish question. And his Apostles afterwards remembered merely that they were to go to the people, to Israel; they knew nothing about a previous mission by Jesus to either the Gentiles or the Samaritans, otherwise they would not have been obliged to obtain authority for such a mission direct from heaven.[1] Not one of these incidents is trustworthy in detail.[2] Instead of the sentence, " He that is not against us is for us," the opposite is better attested, "He that is not for me is against me."[3] The demand of the sons of Zebedee for fire to come down upon a Samaritan village was never made, and it exhibits a vainglorious sense of power which none of the disciples ever possessed. It is purposely ascribed to the "sons of thunder," in order to give prominence to the antipathy to the Gentiles felt by the first Apostles, and also to emphasize the difference between Elijah and Jesus, the Old Testament and the New.[4] The beautiful parable of the Good Samaritan—doubly beautiful because it exhibits the neighbour not merely externally, but also internally in the man—is artificially tacked on to a notoriously simpler controversy of Jesus at Jerusalem.[5] The incident of the ten lepers is an artificial imitation, here of the incident of the one leper, there of that of Naaman the Syrian, which also occurred in the

[1] Acts x. 10 sqq., 36, 42.

[2] Against Strauss, *New Life of J.*, Eng. trans., I. pp. 301 sq., 355.

[3] Against Luke ix. 50 and Mark ix. 40, see Matt. xii. 30, but also Luke xi. 23. The incident also reminds us of Numb. xi. 28 sq.; and those who cast out devils in the name of Jesus belong for the most part to the apostolic and a later period, Acts xix. 13.

[4] On the other hand, Weisse, II. p. 144.

[5] Luke x. 25, comp. Matt. xix. 16, specially xxii. 35 (Mark xii. 28), which latter conversation is wanting in the parallel passage in Luke. It is at once noticed that Jesus never elsewhere spoke against priests and Levites, but against Scribes. The turn given to the word "neighbour" in x. 29 and 36 is wonderfully fine. Some suspicion also in Neander, p. 492; Weisse, I. p. 147.

neighbourhood of Jericho.[1] The sending forth of the seventy disciples has no historical attestation whatever; not one of the other Gospels, not even Mark, nor John, nor even the Acts of the Apostles—which in its Pentecost miracle makes the Twelve speak the languages of all nations—contains a trace of it. Ecclesiastical tradition is perplexed about it, and can do no more than invent fables.[2] Looked at more closely, the incident resolves itself into impossibilities. How could these seventy—in reality the precursors of the messengers of the journey and death of Ignatius and Peregrinus—have been as mechanically as superfluously sent, two and two, to different stations as far as Jerusalem? How could they have returned all together at the same time from the most remote stations? How could they, in such a brief span of time, have done so many works? How could Jesus have ascribed to them an importance far beyond that of the Twelve, whilst they afterwards sank back into obscurity, and even the laudatory reporter could not give the name of one of the seventy, who were in fact the vague symbols of the seventy nations? Even the utterances to the seventy sink back into nothingness. The only novelty in these utterances is Jesus' words of greeting to the returning men; and the whole address bears the stamp of the apocryphal and fanciful exagge-

[1] Luke xvii. 12 and v. 12 (Matt. viii. 2). Then also 2 Kings v. 1 sqq., where we must remember that Elijah was in Gilgal (iv. 38), *i.e.* between Jordan and Jericho, just as now Jesus was before Jericho. Of parabolical origin, Strauss, *L. J.*, 4th ed., II. p. 53; Weisse, II. p. 173; Hase, p. 167. On the other hand, Neander, p. 436.

[2] See the fables out of Clem. *Hypotyp.* V. in Eusebius 1, 12, concerning the names of the seventy,—Barnabas, Sosthenes, Kephas in Antioch (Gal. ii. 11), Matthias, and Joseph Barsabba, Thaddæus, and James (1 Cor. xv. 7). Then the great list in *Chron. Pasch.*, ed. Dind., I. pp. 400 sqq. Whilst in the beginning of the agitation against Matthew, Schulz and Schneck. accused Matthew of ignorance of the seventy, the position of the seventy is now rather almost entirely overthrown by criticism. Strauss, De Wette, Theile, Baur, Hilg., Volkmar, Br. Bauer, have rejected them. Ewald (pp. 392, 428) and Weizs. (p. 211) adopt this standpoint. The seventy are defended by Ebr., Olsh., Tholuck, Krabbe, Meyer, Neander, Bleek, Gess, and others; even by Hase, Weisse, Schenkel. But comp. only Neander (p. 405), Bleek (p. 149), Weisse (I. p. 405), to see how weak is the defence which does not seriously defend either the number, the special mission, or the addresses. Schleiermacher had already found no permanent organization (pp. 373, 379); and Hase allowed them to sink back into nothingness on account of absence of significance.

ration of a later time. Or is any one disposed to believe that Jesus found the conqueror of Satan in the seventy and not in himself, and that he seriously said he saw Satan fall from heaven, where he never looked for him, and where he was sought by, at most, the Jews and the Revelation of John?[1] All the other passages are artificially and inappropriately dragged in from the mission address to the Twelve or from other places, and the prophecy about Paul is an arbitrary application of an utterance addressed to the Twelve and concerning the Twelve.[2] Thus nothing is left of the whole mission; and the only question that can remain open is, whether Luke fabricated these incidents for himself, or whether—as is more probable—he found them already existing disconnectedly in his later sources of Ebionite and Samaritan-Christian origin.[3]

As is wont to happen, this unhistorical and late report has had superimposed upon it a still later, more exaggerated, and more comprehensive one. According to the fourth Gospel, it was not at the close of his ministry, but in the very beginning of it, that Jesus "must needs" make a journey through Samaria,

[1] And even Mark xvi. 18 is apocryphal. Jesus himself the conqueror over Satan, Matt. xii. 29. Satan not in heaven, Matt. xii. 29, xvi. 18. Comp. above, p. 14, note 2. In Rev. xii. 9, the fall of Satan from heaven is joined on to the entry of the Messiah into heaven. Then begins his fury upon earth through the agency of the Roman domination. Homiletically we can derive a meaning from this fall of Satan by means of the disciples, so far as the kingdom of God appears guaranteed by the extension of the single personality of Jesus into an actual human community; even historically, so far as the apostolic period completed the fall of the evil one; but this narrative is not historically a part of the life of Jesus.

[2] Comp. above, I. pp. 112 sq., and what is said on the missionary addresses in Vol. III. The reference to Paul, Luke xii. 2 sq.; Matt. x. 26 sq.

[3] Luke's style of representation, from ix. 51 onwards, favours the assumption of Hebraistic sources; but the question remains open whether these were simply Jewish-Ebionite with reference to the Twelve (as already concerning x. 17—20 the reference to the Twelve has been often supposed to be), or specially Gentile-favouring Samaritan, which the number of the seventy would in particular lead us to assume. Schleierm., Bleek, Ewald, had already shown themselves indisposed to recognize the seventy (see above, p. 16, note 2); the criticism in Baur's *Ev.* pp. 498 sqq., has disposed of them. A hitch in this criticism is the feeble opinion of Strauss (*New Life of J.*, Eng. trans., I. p. 301) that the Samaritan ministry according to Luke may possibly be as well founded as the purely Israelitish one of Matthew.

18   THE JOURNEY TO THE FEAST.

only in the reverse direction, from Judæa to his Galilean fatherland.[1] It is the famous conversation with the Samaritan woman of which we are thinking, beginning with Jesus' request for a drink of water, and rising to its climax in the revelation of the prophet and finally of the Messiah, who declared to the woman her sins, and to Samaria, as to Israel, the temporary duration of its religion, the substitution of the religion of spirit and truth for the material temple-service; and leading up to conversions on a large scale, brought about—unlike those of Jerusalem and Galilee—without miracles, in the town of Sychar, the neighbour and in reality the representative of Sichem, the old and renowned metropolis of the country where formerly the patriarchs, later the kings of the northern secession kingdom, dwelt, and where later still the spurious Samaritan temple had stood.[2] This district—according to Furrer's expression, "a pearl of scenery"—is correctly and finely described. There is Jacob's Well, a hundred feet deep, the water still occasionally springing forth, scarcely

---

[1] John iv. 4 sqq.

[2] Sychar, John iv. 5 (Jerome reads Sichem), is generally regarded as a satirical allusion to Sichem, with a suggestion of *shikkor* (drunken), Isaiah xxviii. 1 sqq., or of *sheker* (lie), Hab. ii. 18. Thus already Reland (shikkor) and Lightf. (sheker), and many recent critics, not merely Hilg., Scholt., Späth, Furrer, but also Hengst., Olsh., Wies., Credner, Lücke. Let the reader remember the easy interchange of the liquids *m* and *r*. But it is remarkable that this transformation, in the word Sichem at least, does not occur elsewhere (Συχὲμ, Σιχὲμ, Σίκιμα). On the other hand, Hug., Luther, Licht., Ewald, Meyer, Del., Casp., assume a Sychar, a different town from Sichem. In fact, the Talmud has a Suchar and a well of Suchar (Wies. *Syn.* p. 256, after Lightf. p. 586); and Walcott, *Bibl. S.* 1843, I. p. 74, and Rosen. *Zeitschr. deutschmorg Ges.* 1860, II. pp. 334 sqq. (comp. Casp. pp. 106 sq.), point to the village El-Askar, which lies a short quarter of a league north of Jacob's Well and Joseph's tomb, and a league from Sichem eastwardly (at the southern foot of Ebal). Eus., *Onom.*, already indicates that: Sychar πρὸ τῆς νέας πόλεως, although he also again says of Sichem, ἐν προαστείοις νέας πόλεως (p. 346). These notices are not to be overlooked, and the similarity of Sychar, Suchar, Askar, is striking. We must assume either that Sychar (differently from Neapolis, Nablus) received and perpetuated the name of the ancient Sichem, or that it had previously been an independent place separated from Sichem. But the Evangelist seems to have mentioned this place and not Sichem, since (1) he found the meaning of the word (*sheker*, comp. iv. 18, 22) specially striking; (2) he did not wish to assert the conversion of the chief city itself by Jesus (comp. Acts viii. 5); and (3) he nevertheless reminded every one acquainted with the Old Testament of Sichem, by the name, by Jacob's Well, and by Joseph's tomb.

more than half a league to the south-east of the well-watered valley of Sichem, and to the right of the highway that runs from south to north. There is the rocky head of Gerizim, distant about 800 feet up a steep ascent to the left of the highway and well, from the latter of which is visible the site of the temple that was destroyed by the Jewish king John Hyrcanus; and on the east is the smiling and waving corn country of Mokhnah. But correctly and grandly as the district is depicted, and, still more, instructively and triumphantly as the new religion of Jesus and of the children of God is described, this incident is nevertheless not literally true; and it is not the intention of the author himself to convince us of the literal character of the narrative, but only to excite a strong belief in the founder of the spiritual, eternal and world-dominating faith.[1] Otherwise he would not have taken the liberty of satirically giving the name of the obscure little town of Sychar as representative of Sichem and of the Samaritan spurious religion, of transforming the five gods of the ancestors of the Samaritans allegorically into five husbands, the present god—half Jehovah, half Zeus—into the sixth husband or lover of the Samaritan woman, i.e. of the district, and of depicting the Samaritan woman herself—who in this as in other respects is completely fictitious—as both wanton and pious, superficial and profound, as a convicted sinner, and yet as one to whom the loftiest and most spiritual utterances are addressed. Finally, he would not have made the Samaritan harvest—which is expressly placed in the future, in the apostolic period, and did not now come to pass—appear in a vivid manner as already present, as a personal work of Jesus, nay, as a quenching the thirst of the land with living water at the very hour in which, later, the life of the word streamed from the Crucified One.[2] If

---

[1] Comp. Robinson, III.; Ritter, XVI. pp. 654 sqq.; Furrer, *Wand.* pp. 230 sqq.; *Bedentung bibl. Geogr.* p. 22; Casp. pp. 105 sqq. See also above, II. p. 259.

[2] Sychar=Sheker, Hab. ii. 18; comp. Ecclus. l. 26. The five men, above, 1. p. 159. Weak objection by Gess, p. 11. The Rabbis also complain of the idola Cuthæorum, Lightf. p. 314. Similarly Hilg., Scholt., and even (retaining the fact) Hengst. The harvest, future, iv. 35; comp. Acts viii. 5 sqq. Present, iv. 39 sqq. The hour of

to the above we add all the other palpable difficulties, great and small, of the literal narrative—of which difficulties the lofty and exaggerated revelation of Jesus to the unintelligent, sinful, sensual woman of Samaria is by no means the least—and the evident connection of this new exaltation of Jesus' career with the Luke-exaltation, it is really not necessary to spend many words to show that Jesus did missionary work in Samaria neither at the beginning nor at the end of his ministry, that he never represented the Samaritan and the Jewish worship as of equal worth, and that—Stephen and Mark notwithstanding—he never, either in public utterances or in the presence of his disciples only, announced the definitive end of the national worship.[1] Let him who will find fault when history frees itself of this narrative; in truth, only those can escape the stumbling-block of the narrative and accept it heartily who dissever it from the life of the Lord and give up its literal accuracy, and who conceive it as a later and impressive description of the conquest of the world by Christianity, under the figure of the Master himself, who was the leader and procurer of that victory.[2]

watering (comp. above, II. pp. 334 sq.), the sixth, iv. 6 sqq.; comp. xix. 14, 34, and xii. 20 sqq.

[1] To the difficulties in detail belong also (1) the improbability of fetching water from Jacob's Well, since Sichem is full of springs (eighteen wells, Furrer, *Bed.* p. 23), and Askar (Sychar) has the spring Askar in close proximity on the north (Casp. p. 107); (2) the improbability of thirst in the winter instead of in the summer, about January (iv. 35), as also Furrer (Meyer, Sevin, mention December) remarks, whilst Casp., p. 108, thinks of the end of May (harvest time) ! (3) the pretended request of Jesus for water (iv. 7 ; comp. verses 31 sq.) ; (4) the superiority of not only Jesus but also his disciples to the prevailing prejudice against the Samaritans (iv. 9 ; comp. Lightf. p. 614), iv. 8, 31.—The occurrence of Luke (Gospel, and Acts viii. 5) is brought to mind not only by the Samaritan journey generally, but also by the picture of the harvest, Luke x. 2 ; John iv. 35. The fall of the temple, after Acts vii. 48 and (itself after the passage in the Acts) Mark xiv. 58. The drawing of water and the request for water remind us of Gen. xxiv. 11 sqq.; 1 Sam. ix. 11 ; 1 Kings xvii. 10.

[2] Contrary to these certain results of criticism, Schenkel (p. 174) still finds the seal of credibility in the incident. Rénan knows that Jesus possessed divers disciples in Sichem, and indeed that Josephus has spoken of Hellenist ones !

B.—JUDÆA AND JERICHO.

The uniformity of the quiet pilgrimage of Jesus to Jerusalem was first broken in upon at the lower Jordan, when he entered the frontiers of Judæa, on Thursday, the 7th of April. At a point not far to the south-west of the ancient town of the Gadites, Beth Nimrah (Talmudic, Nimrin), in the neighbourhood of the Jordan, the Peræan route joins at a sharp angle the route from Gilead, which reaches the Jordan from the north-east, from Ramoth Gilead and Gerasa, traversing the hilly district by the valley of Wady Shaib. The route then crosses the Jordan, which is here ninety feet from bank to bank, goes through Wady Nawaimeh into the Judæan territory, and in two or three leagues brings the traveller to the fine old city of Jericho, the capital of the tribe of Benjamin. The splendour of the river banks, with the lush young green of spring and the jubilant songs of the nightingales, soon disappears; but after a fresh brief experience of desert sandy country, the perpetual paradise of the western Jordan pastures is reached. Jericho, by the Greeks called Jerikûs ['Ιεριχοῦς], at present the insignificant little village of Eriha, with its dozen round huts, its ruins, and thorn hedges, still has its green, well-watered, mildly warm oasis, more than a league broad, in the midst of the sand and the heat, and close under the lofty protecting wall of the western bare and jagged and awe-inspiring limestone hills, which, "theatrically" arranged in a moon-like crescent, seem to guard the approach to the stronghold of Israel, Jerusalem.[1] Gardens, and woods of fig-sycamores

[1] The region between the Jordan and Jericho desert, Jos. *B.J.* 4, 8, 3; comp. Furrer, *Wand.* pp. 153 sqq.; also Dixon. The distance from the Jordan, see above, II. p. 234 (in Van de Velde, the above measurements). Extent of the oasis: 70 *stadia* long, 20 broad, Jos. *B.J.* 4, 8, 3. 100 long, Strabo, 16, 2. 200 *jugera*, Just. 36, 3. A league and more in circumference at present, Furrer, p. 151. Description of the springs, Josephus, *l. c.*; Furrer, p. 150. The mildness of the temperature mentioned by others besides Josephus, particularly Just. 36, 3: tepidi æris natur. quædam et perpetua apricitas. The theatre of hills, Jos. *B.J.* 4, 8, 2; comp. Strabo and Just. Ruins, see below, p. 23, note 5.

and tall palm-trees of every kind, and a lower growth of odorous roses and of valuable but now vanished balsam, spice, and cotton plants, surrounded the "city of palms," along with the luxuriant, early-ripening corn-fields that supplied to the house of God the first fruits for Easter, and the moist, rich meadows bedecked with flowers, a land of booty for the bees and a treasure-house of the most famous honey.[1] This fortunate, incomparable, "divine" landscape, with its miraculous blessing of the well of Elisha, and with its prodigious return even for the smallest amount of tillage, Josephus has praised almost more than the charms of Gennesar; and after Moab, Ammon, and Amalek had left off suing for its favours, the Syrians, then Cleopatra, the queen of Egypt, and later Greek and Roman historiographers, geographers, and poets, cast envious glances at this pearl of the Jews and of king Herod.[2] Moreover, Jericho was the key of the whole land, from south to north, from west to east, a highway of commerce, a rendezvous of Israel; and was therefore guarded by castles and camps in the periods of the Syrians, of the Hasmonæans, of the Herods and the Romans.[3] The last princes had also vied with each other in costly buildings, since they were fond of transferring the official residence hither, in spring and autumn, from the harsh and barren Jerusalem. The Hasmonæans had here their palace, which was last inhabited by Alexandra, the mother-in-law of Herod the Great.[4] Splendid large ponds surrounded the castle, in which the terrible Idumæan, in the midst of sport, took the life of his young

---

[1] See the fine descriptions in Jos. *B. J.* 4, 8, 3; 1, 6, 6; 1, 18, 5; *Ant.* 14, 4, 1; 15, 4, 2. Strabo; Just.; Pliny, *H.N.* 5, 15, briefly: Hiericuntem palmetis consitam, fontibus irriquam. The roses, Ecclus. xxiv. 14. City of palms, Deut. xxxiv. 3; Judges i. 16, iii. 13. The name Jericho, either City of the Moon or City of Fragrance.

[2] The most highly favoured and most divinely fruitful region, Jos. *B. J.* 4, 8, 3. Comp. Horace. Ep. II. 2, 184. Comp. my article *Herodes* in *Bibel-Lex.* III. p. 30. Moab, Judges iii. 13. The fertility was dependent not only on the Elisha spring (2 Kings ii. 18 sqq.), but also on the more northerly Duk-spring, and on Wady Kelt.

[3] Place of meeting, comp. Jos. *Ant.* 17, 6, 3, 5; *B. J.* 4, 8, 1. Castles, camps, 1 Macc. xvi. 15, ix. 50; Jos. *Ant.* 14, 15, 3; *B. J.* 1, 21, 4; 4, 9, 1; 5, 2, 3. Strabo, 16, 2 (castles Thrax and Taurus); comp. Winer, and Furrer (*Bibel-Lex.*) on Jericho.

[4] Jos. *Ant.* 15, 3, 3; *B.J.* 1, 21, 4. Comp. 1 Macc. ix. 50.

brother-in-law, the high-priest Aristobulus, Alexandra's son.[1] This crime did not frighten him away; he merely built at a distance from the now haunted castle a new one that was still more beautiful and commodious. He also built a splendid theatre, and an enormous hippodrome, in which, on the eve of his death, he was able to keep confined the nobility of the whole country. He himself died in the palace at Jericho.[2] Archelaus rebuilt the palace yet more beautifully after it had been plundered and burnt in the disturbances which followed the death of Herod; he enlarged the gardens and the palm groves, to which he conducted fresh water-courses.[3] Thanks to nature, situation, and the kings, Jericho shook off the curse of Joshua—who, at the taking possession of the country, had strictly forbidden the rebuilding of this city—and became great and rich, so that from the time of Herod the Great the whole neighbourhood, from the fortress Kypros, south of Jericho, to Phasaelis and Archelais on the north, and even the wilderness, became full of villages and cultivated fields.[4] This prosperity continued even under the Romans. Already under Gabinius temporarily the fourth among the five chief cities of the land, under the emperors Jericho became the central point of a toparchy to which, after the fall of Jerusalem—which also had a third revival—belonged the first position in the Judæan south.[5]

There is no doubt that Jesus's little caravan took breath again in the neighbourhood of Jericho, after the toils of the inhospi-

---

[1] Jos. *Ant.* 15, 3, 3. Above, I. p. 250.

[2] Jos. *B. J.* 1, 21, 4; *Ant.* 17, 6, 3, 5; 17, 8, 2. Above, I. p. 253.

[3] Jos. *Ant.* 17, 10, 6; 17, 13, 1.

[4] Large and rich city, Jos. *Ant.* 14, 15, 3; *B. J.* 4, 8, 2. Strabo, 16, 2. Just. 36, 3. The curse, Joshua vi. 26; comp. Judges iii. 13. Cultivation of the whole district, Jos. *Ant.* 16, 5, 2.

[5] Jos. *Ant.* 14, 5, 4. Toparchy, *B. J.* 3, 3, 5. Prosperity at the time of Pliny, the first toparchy, Pliny, 5, 15. Eus. *Onom.* 234: καταβλη θ. αὐτῆς ἐπὶ τ. πολιορκ. Ιερ. (comp. *B. J.* 4, 8, 2) ἑτέρα ἐκ τρίτου συνέστη πόλις. It was still standing at the time of Eusebius and Jerome. By the side of it, ruins of two older cities. At the present time are to be seen a number of ruins, notably a rectangular tower (Dixon), which is said to be the house of Zacchæus.

table journey, and under the influence of a landscape which bore such a conspicuous resemblance to the Gennesar district. Moreover, they now found not only hospitality, but also sympathy and appreciation. The reputation of the Prophet of Galilee had long since reached even here. Indeed, individuals had sought him out in Galilee itself; and though most of the people did not know him, they were anxious to see him; and his companions were not reticent, but told of his works and whispered his intentions. Silent as death about the Peræan journey, the Gospels become eloquent from this point onwards; and the minutiæ as well as the general contents of their communications lend to their narration the impress of truth. They show us the multitudes of men that flocked to Jesus from the Judæan frontiers, would-be followers and controversial Pharisees who addressed him. They mention in a general way healings or doctrinal addresses, but particularly vivacious conversations with the disciples. And they do this in such a way that we can plainly see how, among the springs, the palms, and men, in proximity to the place where John baptized, and in proximity to Jerusalem, there again sprang up in him and in his disciples the elasticity and joyousness of spirit which had been lost.

Jesus certainly did not here utter any popular addresses like those he delivered in Galilee, although Mark relates that he taught according to his wont.[1] Conversational intercourse, brief occasional thoughtful remarks, would naturally be called forth by the sympathetic attitude of the population; but a missionary preaching, properly so called, is altogether excluded, although we may surmise that, at least in the neighbourhood of Jerusalem, Jesus, either by way of prudent initiative, or in consequence of the support which he now began to receive from the crowds of people that flocked to him, as well as with a retrospective reference to the associations of the place where he was baptized, organized, improvised a Messianic movement by introducing the old watchword. And if we recognize this passage, why not the

[1] Mark x. 1 (Matt. xix. 1 sq.).

whole,—the great mission of Luke between Galilee and Jerusalem? But as the mission is an empty phantom as far as Jericho, so is it also between Jericho and Jerusalem. No Matthew, no Mark, knows anything whatever of the popular addresses, or indeed is able to report any detail; and everything harmonizes with the report that Jesus passed through the magnificent Jericho almost without any halt, therefore certainly without any great missionary work, in order to find his mission in Jerusalem, and there alone.[1]

It would be a useless labour to challenge in detail the order of sequence of the occurrences from the Jordan to Jerusalem. We might, for example, find that a disputation with the Pharisees makes its appearance at the entrance-gate of Judæa, placed there by the writer almost intentionally in order that it might stand as border-watcher of the holy region, and as forerunner of the approaching life-and-death struggle.[2] Yet we should not overlook that the sympathetic thronging of the people around him—which itself, again, explains the Pharisaic opposition—is perhaps only prematurely stated and in too strong language, that the order of sequence is not artificial, and that on the whole one's doubts are satisfactorily met by the close unanimity of the three earlier Gospels, which commences just at this point, as well as by the undeniable simplicity and naturalness of their miracle-less narratives,—both evidences of a fixed, unhesitating, early tradition, closely connected with Jesus' fate at Jerusalem and his exhibition of the fullest resignation.[3]

[1] Matt. xix. 2 mentions only healings, no addresses to the people; Mark x. 1, the addresses to the people, but indefinitely. Weizs. p. 513 (see above, p. 10, note 1) would, with others, gather from Mark x. 1 a protracted sojourn in Judæa and Peræa.

[2] Matt. xix. 3 (Mark x. 2).

[3] Thronging of the people in Matt. xix. 2, yet more strongly than Mark. x. 1. Recently Volkmar has found in the narratives which precede the entry into Jerusalem nothing but more or less unhistorical doctrinal pictures of the true religion : (1) honour paid to woman (by a no longer barbarian marriage law), (2) believing disposition (the child), (3) all-surrendering love (the youth), (4) true hope, which does not seek for everything in the future (Peter), (5) ministering love and its greatness (the sons of Zebedee). The arbitrary character of this purely factual series of divisions is at once seen, since the respective details are loosely connected, and there does not exist a

THE JOURNEY TO THE FEAST.

Thus we begin the entrance into the Jewish land, the crossing the Jordan, with the innocent and lovely picture of the Jewish parents who bring their infants to Jesus that he—as did the Scribes and synagogue-rulers—might lay his hands upon them and pray over them.[1] In Luke, where the Pharisees are wanting, this incident is placed in the first position; in Matthew and Mark, at least in the second, and is so narrated that in Matthew it happens on the highway, and in Mark in the first hospitable house of the Jewish district. And it is quite characteristic that in Judæa, as in Galilee, the wives, the mothers, although not expressly mentioned, chiefly and first apply to the man of religion, the new prophet, encouraged by the crowd of women in his retinue, and still more by the loving spirit which they discover in the countenance and in the words of Jesus. It is characteristic also that these mothers, indifferent to the great questions which are about to be opened for them and the whole nation at Jerusalem, content themselves with a blessing for the darlings of their hearts and homes; and that Jesus himself begins his ministry in the south with an exhibition of the profound affectionateness which he had not even yet lost, and with an act of blessing. We must not fear that this incident is merely a duplicate tradition of that of the Galilean child whom Jesus placed in the midst of the jealous disciples, introduced here with the view of representing Jesus, on his entrance into the holy country, as the bringer of blessing to the nation, or—since the nation rejected him—to the coming generation.[2] For the account

---

rational ground for treating of the axioms of the true religion *outside* of the gates of Jerusalem. Particularly is No. 1 no leading proposition of Jesus', which could come in the series before No. 2; No. 3 shows at first the very opposite, and would therefore be a very poor example; 3 and 5 coincide in idea, and ought not to be separated by 4; and who can find in 4 the hope that is partly withdrawn from the future life? Hilg., 1868, p. 24, also schematizes: (1) sanctity of marriage, (2) children born to married persons, (3) possession! Strauss, 4th ed., I. p. 645, intimates that one detail (the marriage controversy) points rather to Jerusalem.

[1] Matt. xix. 13; Luke xviii. 15; Mark x. 13. The benedictions in the synagogue, Buxt. *Synag.* p. 138.

[2] Matt. xviii. 2.

JUDÆA AND JERICHO. 27

is too ingenuous, the event is too probable, the words of Jesus are too profoundly significant and new. As formerly Gehazi, the servant of Elisha, wished to repulse the Shunammite woman when she seized the feet of the prophet and strove for help for the dead child, so the disciples, partly in order to guard the rest of their Master, and partly in the haughty elevation of feeling excited by their kingly projects at Jerusalem, chid the bringers of the infants, who, as well as those whom they protected in their arms, were of little importance to the disciples.[1] But mildly as Elisha, and not merely, like him, out of compassion for the petitioners, but also out of love for the children both in their own persons and as symbols, Jesus uttered the noble words: "Let the little children come to me, and prevent them not, for of such"—that is, of persons with such dispositions—"is the kingdom of heaven." And laying his hands upon them, nay, according to Mark taking them in his arms and blessing them, he at one and the same time made the parents happy, and put to shame the disciples who had once more forgotten the child-way to the kingdom of heaven.[2]

But the gentle could be harsh, the pliant unbending, when principle and not the heart had to speak. On the very threshold of the Jewish territory the Pharisees met him. They could hardly have been intentionally placed in his way as advanced posts, as guards to cover Jericho and Jerusalem. It might indeed have been already known in Jerusalem that he was coming to the feast; but his route no one could have known, particularly if he went through Peræa. Either these Pharisees were themselves

---

[1] 2 Kings iv. 27. As the persons chidden, Mark points to the (οἱ) bearers of the infants, Luke leaves it indefinite, Matt. favours the chiding of the children.

[2] Luke and Mark (according to Weisse, I. p. 564, better) have here the addition which is wanting to them in the passage corresponding to Matt. xviii. 3 (comp. above, III. p. 105, IV. p. 335), although it is more needful there than here, where it is wanting in Matthew. The likeness of condition (Matt. xix. 14) does not refer (Bengel, De Wette; comp. above, IV. p. 336, note 2) to physical age, but, as in Matt. xviii. 3 sqq., to the mental *habitus* (Wetstein). Laying on of hands effective benediction, comp. Gen. xxvii. 4, 12 sqq., xlviii. 14. For the genuineness of the passage, Strauss, I. p. 725.

pilgrims to the feast on the much-frequented road, perhaps in the direction from Peræa, or they were dwellers in the district, perhaps of Jericho, since there was no part of the country where Pharisees were not. They longed to engage in conflict with the man who broke the ordinances, as all the country knew, who was nevertheless a favourite with the people, and who was now in a conspicuous manner enthusiastically greeted even in Judæa,—they longed to engage in a conflict with this man which should either destroy or unmask him. It had been remarked that in Galilee Jesus had rejected legal divorce when referring to Antipas' second marriage, though the question of divorce had not then been discussed with any particular earnestness.[1] What he had said in the Sermon on the Mount against the Pharisaic legalism had thus, at least in fragments, escaped from the smaller circle of the disciples to the knowledge of the general public; or he had not withheld from the people his dislike to an ordinance that ploughed such deep furrows in the whole civil and domestic life, and undermined all sincerity and all modesty and all love.[2] Thus with this one discovery, which had luckily rewarded their painstaking whilst there was so much else to find out and to censure, they accosted him, and temptingly asked, as if they wished now first to hear or indeed to learn, and with the genuinely Pharisaic trifling: "Is it permitted to a man to put away his wife?"[3]

[1] Ewald (p. 504) thinks of the marriage of Antipas as giving rise to the controversy. But that was not, properly speaking, a divorce (Jos. *Ant.* 18, 5, 1), and the scandal lay not in the separation, but in the fresh marriage. Among the Jews divorces were frequent. Finally, we cannot speak of a contemporaneousness of the Antipas incident and the last preaching of Jesus (comp. Matt. xiv. 3 sqq.).

[2] Comp. above, III. p. 308 sq.

[3] Matt. xix. 3; Mark x. 2. Mark gives the original form of the question, since he has not the addition of Matthew, divorce for every cause, or on every ground. In itself this brutal extension of the freedom of divorce would be quite possible, quite Jewish (comp. Jos. *Ant.* 4, 8, 23: $\kappa\alpha\theta'$ $\mathring{\alpha}\varsigma$ $\delta\eta\pi\sigma\tau'$ $o\mathring{v}\nu$ $a\mathring{\iota}\tau\mathring{\iota}\alpha\varsigma$. $\pi o\lambda\lambda a\mathring{\iota}$ δ' $\mathring{a}\nu$ $\tau o\mathring{\iota}\varsigma$ $\mathring{a}\nu\theta\rho\acute{\omega}\pi o\iota\varsigma$ $\tau o\iota a\mathring{\upsilon}\tau a\iota$ $\gamma\acute{\epsilon}\nu o\iota\nu\tau o$). But since the concession by Jesus of divorce in case of fornication (Matt. xix. 9, opp. Mark x. 11 sq.) is not probable (above, III. p. 309), but that general postulate of the Jews stands in evident relation to this limited concession of Jesus, the former falls with the latter. Comp. Weisse, I. p. 562. Moreover, Pharisaic Judaism was factually united against Jesus *only* in this, that it permitted divorce *at all*, by no means that it permitted *every* kind of divorce. By the latter

Jesus, as quickly self-possessed and mentally strong as he ever was and must be against such sudden attacks, turned to the decisive and impartial testimony of Scripture; though not to the commands of Moses, which here as nowhere else failed to support him, but to the venerable introduction of the books of Moses, the history of the creation, which proclaimed the divine and eternal law of marriage, and to the commentary which that history found in the words of the first man, really in the words of God. "Have you not read," said he to the Scribes, in a manner which put them to the blush, "that the Creator from the beginning created them male and female? And that he said, For this cause shall a man leave his father and his mother, and shall cleave unto his wife, and they two shall be one flesh?[1] Wherefore they are no more two, but one flesh. What therefore God has joined together, let not a man part asunder." In point of fact, this grasp of the A B C of the natural creation, this most convincing apology of marriage, is here equally fine with the passing from nature to Scripture by a simple quotation concerning the things of the primitive age, and, in the other place, with the acute reflection on the nature of marriage, and finally with the concise, nervous conclusion concerning divine will and human caprice. And this humanity of Jesus overcomes with victorious weapons the impress of the profound and controversial spirit by the recognition of an earthly ordinance with which his personal life, nay, his inclinations and his principles, had nothing to do.

But his citations had not convinced, had not even touched, the Pharisees. They had Moses on their side; with an easy triumph they adduced the name about which he had been silent, since he had appealed against the ancient to what was more ancient. "Why then did Moses command to give a writing of

question, therefore, with reference to which the teachers themselves were divided, Jesus could not have been tempted. This "temptation" (Matt.) Neander has groundlessly denied (p. 440).

[1] Gen. i. 27. The words of Adam, Gen. ii. 23 sq. "The two" does not stand in the Hebrew, but only (in the interest of monogamy) in the LXX., which Paul also follows, 1 Cor. vi. 16.

divorcement and to put her away?"[1] Now Moses stood against Jesus; and Jesus for the first time was placed in the dilemma which compelled him—perhaps not merely externally by word and explanation, but also mentally in his reflection, in his judgment, in his principle—either to sacrifice Moses, or to hold him fast as he had always held him fast, and had designated his teaching the indissoluble word of God, in opposition to the ordinances which he—Jesus—tore in pieces. Vigorous controversy was of a like service to him as disputation to Luther; he was necessitated either to stand still with his principles, or distinctly and boldly at the most dangerous moment, under the eyes of Jerusalem, to go further, even to the denial of what he had hitherto, without severe consistency but piously, held fast and wished to hold fast, although, when more closely looked at, it contradicted his principle. Thus did Jesus, for the first time, arrive at the point of repudiating Moses,—he found it necessary and he yielded reluctantly. He might have broken off the point of the contradiction, if he, with the letter itself of Moses in his hand—which permitted divorce on account of only infamous acts—had branded the frivolity of his opponents who permitted divorce "for every cause;" and had he thus answered, as Matthew gives it, that he recognized divorce in a qualified manner, namely divorce on account of adultery, then he must have adopted this plan of procedure.[2] But he, stricter than his successors in the Church,

---

[1] Deut. xxiv. 1. Form of bill of divorce, see above, III. p. 310, note 1; Jos. *Ant.* 4, 8, 23.

[2] Matt. xix. 9: μὴ ἐπὶ πορνείᾳ should be struck out, after Mark x. 11, and agreeably with the remarks in Vol. III. *l. c.*, and above, p. 28. This erasure appears here the more necessary because Jesus' entire answer insists on the law of marriage absolutely and without any exceptions, as definitely (verses 6—8) as it does universally (verse 9), and would be fundamentally weakened by the admission of exceptions; because the great alarm of the disciples (Matt. xix. 10)—who were deprived of every loophole of possibility of divorce only by Shammæan views— can be only thus explained; because, finally, Paul, in 1 Cor. vii. 11, is not acquainted with this qualification. Textually, the addition is open to no suspicion; it is only the connection which shows plainly that it is a correction of the later Church with its allowance of divorce, an allowance which certainly gradually became too lax, though justified on the ground of concrete conditions. Hug, Grätz, Weisse, and others, recognized the doubtful character of the addition, which Meyer defended.

would have no divorce of any kind; and since he would have none, he was compelled to give a direct contradiction to Moses. The Scriptures made his task the easier because here Scripture stood against Scripture—nay, Moses against Moses, to whom, according to Jewish opinion, the first book belonged as much as the second; and because he believed himself able to show that Moses' bill of divorcement in the last of the books of Moses was the fruit of that yielding to the stubbornness of the national character which he could prove in so manifold a manner from the rest of the history of Moses. "Because Moses"—he said, courageously and without long deliberation—"having regard to your hardness of heart, suffered you to put away your wives! But from the beginning it was not so! But I say unto you, whosoever puts away his wife and marries another, commits adultery; and he who marries a divorced woman commits adultery."[1] Doubtless the Pharisees regarded their cause as won by this solution of his difficulty; Jesus had declared himself against Moses; he had cut himself loose from the national institutions and from the nation by setting up his "I" against the "You." Here was a point discovered on which he could in fact be indicted before the Sanhedrim.[2] *We* are able to see that the bearing of this sentence was certainly infinite; that having made this one breach in the Law, it was easy to widen the breach in every direction, and to refer the whole of the ceremonial and sacrificial worship of Moses to compliance with the materialistic longings of the people; and that not only Jesus' opponents, but also his Church, which renounced the Law of Moses, might rejoice in the brave act of the Master, who both overthrew the edifice of Pharisaism and also began the work of loosening and even of tearing away the stones with which Moses built.[3] Only we should not forget

---

[1] Comp. Matt. v. 32; Luke xvi. 18. Hardness of heart, comp. Deut. x. 16; Is. xlviii. 4; Ez. iii. 7; Zech. vii. 12. In the Rabbis often, jezer hara. $ἀπ' ἀρχῆς =$ rishonah.

[2] Here is the only point where the Johannine expression, "your Law," finds support.

[3] Montanus based his theory upon this sentence, Tert. *Mon.* 14. Comp. Acts vii. 48 sqq.

that even here he was actuated by a fervent piety, and that he, compelled thus to act in this one point, did not complete the overthrow of the whole either in avowal or in deed; that, in the historical limitation of his task, he remained a preacher of Moses to the end. He was a destroyer of Moses in the way of principle and its destructive consequences, only as Socrates was a destroyer of the worship of his fatherland; and those Gospel Scriptures which, like Mark and John, and Mark in particular, in this very incident loudly and for a purpose announce the absolute and radical breach of Jesus with the prescribed ordinances, have recorded rather the belief of their time than that of Jesus.[1]

The conversation of Jesus with the Pharisees was recalled in the circle of the disciples, after the former had left the place. "If the case of the man be so with his wife"—said they to him on the way, and not exactly in a house, as Mark, according to his wont, describes it—"then it is not advisable to marry."[2] We see from this expression that these disciples themselves still strongly sympathized with the Pharisaic and general Jewish view of the easy separability of married persons; and that, they themselves being for the most part married, it fell heavily upon their hearts to be tied up to the existing marriage under all circumstances,— an anxiety which more plainly than all shows that Jesus softened his vigorous statement by no exception, not even by the most conciliating exception of the wife's adultery, which the later

---

[1] The secondary character of Mark, as to this narration, which is naturally not admitted by Volkmar, has been made prominent by Bleek (II. p. 261). What is most important is, that Mark makes Jesus provoke the conflict with Moses (x. 3), which is quite unhistorical, nay, is impossible; for Jesus did not intentionally create the critical situation; he was in reality driven into contradiction against Moses, in the course of discussion, by the objection of his opponents (Matt. xix. 7). Who does not further perceive the secondary character of Mark, in the mixing up by Mark of the two utterances in Matt. xix. 4 sqq. and 7 sqq., in the introduction of the passage of Scripture as a saying of Jesus (Mark x. 7), in the introduction of the conversation in the house (x. 10), in the divorce of the woman from the man, which is quite un-Jewish (Greco-Roman, see Wetst. on 1 Cor. vii. 13), and is without any justification from Jos. *Ant.* 15, 7, 10 (Salome's bill of divorce against Costobarus), and 1 Cor. vii. 10, 13? The historical inappropriateness in Mark x. 12, even Volkmar is compelled to admit.

[2] The house, in Mark ii. 1, 15, iii. 19, vii. 17, 24, ix. 28, x. 10.

Church, and first of all our Matthew, introduced.[1] This anxious appeal of the disciples does not at all give us a right to ask why it did not make itself heard earlier, when similar propositions were enounced in the Sermon on the Mount, and whether perhaps those propositions of the Sermon on the Mount are not to be regarded, on this very ground, as mere duplicates of the current events which were so full of life. Without that Sermon on the Mount, to the nucleus of which these propositions belong, our present incident, this disputation, could not well have occurred. The objection of the disciples was not, however, uttered on that former occasion, and it was now uttered the rather because the question was now for the first time thoroughly canvassed on its own merits, so as to produce a strong and permanent impression.[2] Jesus answered the objection in a noteworthy manner—in Matthew at least, whilst Mark prudently avoids the difficult words. He confirms not only, as in Mark, the indissolubility of marriage—where Mark, with his western marriage law, used an altogether unhistorical formula—but also in a surprising manner the conclusion of the disciples concerning the unadvisability of marriage.[3] The surprise is double: first he appears to give an unqualified sanction to this carnally anxious conclusion, and then suddenly gives another turn to the subject; and secondly, in this fresh turn, he seems to overthrow his own carefully considered and correct view of the nature of the creation and of the sanctity of marriage. " Not all men," answered Jesus, "receive the proposition; but they to whom it is given.

[1] Divorce after adulterium, *Pastor of Hermas*, 2, 4. Further help, with many consequences, given in 1 Cor. vii. 15.

[2] Matt. v. 32 and xix. 3 sqq. are seen to be independently original, notwithstanding all their relationship. See above, III. p. 310.

[3] Mark x. 11 sq., and above, p. 32, n. 1. Matt. xix. 12 sq. The words here, "not all give room to (accept or understand) this saying," has no reference whatever to the saying in verse 9 about the indissolubility of marriage (Hofm.), but to that of the disciples in verse 10 about abstinence from marriage (thus most critics); for what follows does not treat of non-dissolubility or dissolubility, but *only* of abstinence; wherefore Bengel, De Wette, Bleek, have referred "this saying" even less to the words of the disciples than to the following abstinence doctrine of Jesus himself, which, however, is not correct.

For there are"—said he, in a genuinely Jewish mode of speaking —"eunuchs who were so born from their mothers' womb; and there are eunuchs who were made such by men; and there are eunuchs who have made themselves such for the sake of the kingdom of heaven. Let him receive it who is able to receive it."[1]

Thus, in a bold paradox, he gave assent to the proposition of the disciples, that marriage was not advisable. But that which they, apparently with his approval, had ingeniously arrived at with a view of adapting the difficult moral command to their sensual needs, was for him the stepping-stone to a demand which represented the renunciation, and indeed the unqualified renunciation, of marriage as a moral sacrifice and not as a sensual alleviation. From the natural and the artificial suppression of the sexual function, he distinguished that of moral purpose; he spoke of the renunciation of marriage for the kingdom of heaven's sake, which one and another—he did not mean any Essene, but most probably particular prophets, the Baptist and himself—had already made.[2] We do not see here plainly what he understood by renunciation "for the kingdom of heaven's sake;" and we still less plainly see how he was able to harmonize such an absolute renunciation of marriage with his emphatic assertion of the law of marriage. Did he contradict himself? or did he, like his Apostle Paul, hold that marriage was good, but celibacy better, purer, more perfect? Did he connect this latter idea with his saying at Jerusalem, that at the resurrection, at the consummation of the creation and of the kingdom of heaven, men would not marry,

---

[1] The Rabbis also distinguish seris (eunuchus) chammah (solis, naturæ), seris adam (per homines); and the former is also called saris bide shamaim (eunuch of God). Self-eunuchization is spoken of in *B. Sohar* with reference to Isaiah lvi. 3, and it is said of the Scribes: qui semet ipsos castrant per integros sex dies hebdomadis legique incumbunt, nocte vero sabb. demum rei uxoriæ operam dant, Schöttgen, p. 159.

[2] He was not thinking of the Essenes, since they had nothing to do with the kingdom of heaven. The prophets were at least the preparers of the kingdom. John might for his part remain unmarried for reasons of purification (Matt. xi.); but Jesus credited him with *his* higher conception, particularly here where he treats him as the ideal of Israel.

but would lead a life like that of the angels?[1] But this obscure, easily misunderstood passage, which the great Church teacher Origen, in the days of his first youthful love to the Lord, is said to have interpreted and acted upon literally, gains clearness as soon as we look at it in its own context.[2] The energetic defender of the will of God in the creation could not have supplementarily cast upon Him the shadow of physical impurity, as if God, like Moses, had for a long time shown indulgence to the sensuousness which, however, He had himself created. The lively, joyous, unquestioning usufructuary of the gifts of nature and of God could cast a stone at none of these gifts. The preacher of the virtues of the spirit and the will could build a virtue upon no act or omission of nature. But when he calls John and himself patterns of those who had made themselves eunuchs for the kingdom of heaven's sake, and when he requires his disciples to forsake houses and wives for the kingdom of heaven's sake, it becomes to us positively intelligible what he means by the severe solitary sentence in which expositors have thought to detect an Essene view of the universe or an obscure utterance of Jesus against himself.[3] The moral zeal for the kingdom of heaven, for the undivided life in God and in the cause, in the great task, of God, demands first of all the possessing what one has as if one had it not; and he imposes the actual not-having upon individuals in isolated cases. But this not-having is no command, and it is not even commended except to the most intimate circle of disciples; it is the voluntary act, nay the divine gift, of individuals who derive from themselves the impulse thus to be, or who are conscious of the power to imitate the life of the Master

---

[1] Matt. xx. 30; 1 Cor. vii. 1 sqq. Neander (p. 442), Weisse (II. p. 104), and naturally Volkmar (p. 483), actually contest the connection with the former speech.

[2] Redepenning, *Origen*, I. p. 144. An evil-disposed opponent might appeal to the Gospel of the Egyptians (see above, I. p. 44).

[3] Matt. xix. 27 sqq. Not only Gfrörer, but even Strauss (4th ed., I. p. 646) and Hilgenfeld (1868, p. 24), have thought of Essenism. Weisse (II. p. 104): sacerdotal tone of mind. More correctly, with emphasis on the practical task, Neander, p. 443; Witt. p. 187.

at his slightest hint, and to be free of the world in their spiritual activity.[1] Thus he remained in harmony with himself. He proclaimed marriage to be the ordinance of the race, and celibacy for the kingdom's sake to be an exceptional gift and achievement of few. The strict but wise Master led his disciples as far as to the dispensing with earthly good, but not a line further towards the renouncing of it; for he imposed no new unnatural yoke like that of the Pharisees. Hence a very few, and perhaps even those not without misunderstanding, have followed him in the virtue which he proclaimed as an exception and not as the rule.[2]

The scene of conflict with the Pharisees was soon after followed by a more friendly encounter. The contradicted sign in Israel repelled Pharisees, and by it Pharisees were attracted. A young man educated in Pharisaic principles, attracted both by the gentle personal character of Jesus and by his theory and advocacy of the kingdom, approached him with one of those questions such as the Baptist in that very region had heard out of so many mouths and hearts—with the question of confidence in the new Teacher in Israel and of distrust of the way of righteousness which he had hitherto trodden: "Teacher, what good thing shall I do that I may have eternal life?" or, according to the later and once more ingeniously contrived report of Luke and Mark, more flatteringly: "Good Teacher, what shall I do that I may have eternal life?"[3] According to all these authors, Jesus

---

[1] Since Jesus by no means made celibacy a rule, and yet (Matt. xix. 10) adopted the proposition, "it is not profitable to marry," this proposition therefore plainly carries with it the sense of that which is of special moral advantage, and not of that which is necessary to moral health.

[2] The myth of John the virgin, see above, III. p. 262, note 4, based chiefly on the Essene view of Rev. xiv. 4. Montanism in error, Tert. *Monog.* 3: Dominus spadonibus aperit regna cœlorum ut et ipse spado. Origen, see above, p. 35.

[2] Matt. xix. 16; Luke xviii. 18; Mark x. 17. Similar questions (Luke iii. 10) among the Rabbis. *Berach.* Wetstein, p. 449: Rabbi, doce nos viam ad vitam æternam. *Ib.* p. 450: quid debeo facere et faciam? The designation of the questioner as young man in Matt. xix. 22 (in Luke ἄρχων, in Mark only εἷς) is quite correct, although Weisse and Holtzmann explain it as a transposition from verse 20, and Neander introduces an elderly synagogue overseer (p. 446); not only is the whole impression that of an eager and immature young man, but in all the Gospels the com-

objected that the claim to be the "Good," in the more correct construction of Matthew, the oracle of the Good, was an invasion of the sovereign right of God. "One is the Good, God;" but goodness in life was the long since fixed command of that One. In harmony with himself, and, one might almost say, with a certain intentional reference to previous events, he here pointed again to those moral commands of Moses, which he never attacked, even though he attacked the bill of divorce: "Thou knowest the commands, Thou shalt not kill, nor commit adultery, nor steal, nor bear false witness; thou shalt honour father and mother, love thy neighbour as thyself."[1] In this straightforward answer he again revealed the great Teacher who

mandment to obey parents is placed before the person in question. As here Matthew is censured, but unjustly, so in the yet much weightier point of the young man's question and Jesus' answer. There are here two distinct conceptions, one represented by Matthew, the other by Luke and Mark; whilst the Gospel of the Hebrews seeks to connect the two by the aid of the weak invention of two rich men. On Marcion, comp. Zeller, in *Theol. Jahrb.* 1851, p. 334. In Matthew the attested reading, often amalgamated with Luke and Mark, is: $διδασκ., τί αγ.$, &c. $Τί με ἐρωτᾷς περὶ τοῦ ἀγαθοῦ; εἷς ε. ὁ ἀγ.$ The conception in Luke and Mark, see in Tischendorf. Even Bleek (comp. Neander, Weisse, Schenkel, Holtzm.) and Hilgenfeld are inclined to prefer Luke and Mark here, since at any rate Matt. can be better explained from Luke and Mark, than *vice versa*. Gess (p. 113) is for both answers! The general opinion is, that Matthew did not wish to allow Jesus' goodness to be denied. This is the reverse of fact, for this denial exists in the form given by Matt. xix. 17, and the construction in Luke and Mark is explicable out of this very form. But what is decisive is: (1) the title "*Good* Rabbi" was *absolutely* unknown among the Jews. See Lightfoot, p. 554, who did not find it anywhere in the whole Talmud. It is a Greco-Roman, not a Jewish, style of title. (2) The Matthew form is more difficult and more vigorous, the other is smoother and more characterless, as every one can see. In the second century, certainly, this reading was generally preferred; comp. Volkmar, *Marcion*, p. 86. Besides, the secondary character of the two later writers is otherwise easily discovered; comp. only xix. 17, 19, 21, 23—26. The representation in the text above, that Jesus is treated as oracle of what is good, is exposed to the objection of Meyer, that the emphasis falls only on the good and not on Jesus ($με$, not $ἐμέ$). But $εἷς$!

[1] Jesus refers mainly to the two tables of the Law, Laws 6—9 and 5. Luke and Mark place adultery before murder = LXX., Vat. Ex. xx. 13 sqq. Comp. Vat. Deut. v. 17; Romans xiii. 9; Anger, I. p. 18; Hilgenfeld, p. 25. Mark adds $μὴ ἀποστερήσῃς$, probably after Ex. xx. 17 (tenth commandment), not (Meyer) from Deut. xxiv. 14 ($οὐκ ἀπαδικήσεις μισθὸν$). The concluding injunction to love our neighbours, Levit. xix. 18 (also Matt. xxii. 39), only in Matthew and the Gospel of the Hebrews (comp. Hilg. 1868, p. 25), but scarcely (as Origen already thought) a mere addition, since it forms the appropriate transition to the injunction to give away goods to our fellow-men.

needed not to build his religion either upon the overthrow of Moses or upon the setting aside of the most elementary rules of morality by what was high-sounding and out of the way. On the contrary, the simplest, the most self-evident, but by the Pharisees most abused rule, the love of parents, the love of mankind, what in fact was most generally current, nearest, most natural,—that was the virtue which he preached and insisted upon, and proclaimed to be the inheritor of the loftiest promises and blessings. But to the young Pharisee this virtue seemed too conventional, too insignificant; with self-gratulation and self-righteousness, but also with a high-soaring belief in the necessity of a loftier performance, he answered: "All this I observed. In what am I still lacking?"[1]

Jesus was, doubtless, not inclined to endorse this strong belief in the factual fulfilment of the so-called ordinary duties, when he had just before insisted upon that fulfilment as something great, eternal, and never completed; and he was doubtless in a position, by a few questions, to make experience the means of moderating the feeling of self-satisfaction in this respect. But since the young man preferred extraordinary virtue to ordinary, Jesus, with a quick, pedagogic mastery of the situation, offered him what was extraordinary, a means of incontrovertibly proving his asserted unbounded love of his fellows, in order thereby to sober his impetuous nature, and to humble the feeling of strength which was not sufficient to accomplish the great and therefore also not the small: "If thou wilt be perfect"—spoke he, half in earnest, but half also by way of accommodating himself to the questioner—"go, sell what thou hast, give to the poor,

---

[1] ἐκ νεότ. μου, from youth onwards, well established only in Luke and Mark, wanting in Matthew in Sin. B D L. Hilgenfeld retains it. Luke and Mark may have introduced it from Matt. xix. 22. The belief in the complete fulfilment of the Law (above, III. p. 97, note 3) often in the Talmud: Abraham, Moses, Aaron, integram legem observarunt. Among the Rabbis also: R. Chanina and others boast totam legem observasse ab Aleph usque ad Tau. Schöttgen, p. 160. The question, τί ἔτι ὑστερῶ, only in Matthew; on the other hand, Luke and Mark interweave it into Jesus' answer. Comp. *Aruch*, f. 127, 4: num reliquum est mihi aliquod officium? Schöttgen, p. 161. Also Wetstein, p. 450.

and thou shalt have a treasure in the heavens; and come, follow me!"[1] Upon this superabundantly zealous young man he imposed an obligation such as he had never imposed upon his adherents, upon his Apostles. Of them he had indeed demanded the following and the forsaking, but by no means the selling all and giving it away. And upon the young man he imposed an obligation, the extraordinary character of which seemed to be in direct contradiction to the ordinary duties which he had previously named, and chiefly with that of obedience to parents. It may be doubted whether Jesus was in earnest in the imposition of this obligation and in insisting upon compliance with his command, or whether it was not rather his intention to humble the young man, who might become his disciple on confessing his weakness. But since the requirement of Jesus is much too definitely expressed to allow of such a doubt; since, moreover, he afterwards loudly complained of the lack of the spirit of self-sacrifice on the part of the rich; since, also, he elsewhere commends the renunciation of the earthly for the kingdom of God's sake, as an ideal which, though he imposed it upon no one, he held up before all; on these accounts, we must hold that he was in earnest in his requirement, and we must admit that this was his right when met by a feeling of self-satisfaction which must either be shattered or, by an actual sacrifice unto blood, must at once gain justification and purification and reach the longed-for perfection.[2] To the young man, however, the test which he

---

[1] According to Matt. xix. 21 (comp. Luke xviii. 22, Mark x. 21: one thing more remains to thee). In Mark x. 21, indeed, it is said: Follow, bearing the cross. The treasures in heaven are similarly acquired according to the Rabbis and Luke xii. 33. Acquired by striving after righteousness, Matt. vi. 19, 33. See above, III. pp. 30 sq. Alms to the poor is often enjoined by the Jews. *Soh. Gen.* in Schöttgen, p. 162: divitias homini dat ideo, ut pauperes alat. *Avod. Sar.* f. 64, 1: vendite omnia, quæ habetis (and then become a proselyte), Wetstein, p. 451.

[2] Hilgenfeld (1868, pp. 25 sqq.) makes an attack that is altogether out of date against the canonical Matthew, commending in its place the Gospel of the Hebrews (comp. Hilg. *N. T.* 16, 25), which Neander (p. 449) had already justly rejected, and which knows nothing of a perfection by way of the opus operatum and of the thereby acquired treasures in heaven, a representation worthy of the Shepherd. He pays as little regard to the singularity of the case (Weisse, I. p. 565) as to the related passages,

himself had challenged proved too severe. On the one hand, he was powerfully drawn by the good and great Teacher and by an innate leaning towards the ideal; on the other hand, he was attracted by the realism of his actual riches. And the riches conquered; he went away, though, it is true, with the conscience-wound of a heart perturbed by the sense of bann and of weakness, perturbed by the loss of the Master and of the ideal.

This conversation had its reverberations in the circle of the disciples. And Jesus himself—even though he did not, as Mark represents, conceive an affection for the young man at the first glance, and on his bold assertion of his self-satisfaction and self-confidence—was much too strongly moved by this tragedy of a human history, unlike any he had before witnessed, by this descent from high to low, from noble to ignoble, not to have allowed his sympathy and his thoughts to accompany the sorrowful retreat of the sorrowing man.[1] "Verily, I say unto you"— spoke he to the desciples—"that a rich man shall enter into the kingdom of heaven with bitter pains.[2] Again I say unto you, it is less difficult for a camel to go through a needle's eye than a rich man into the kingdom of God."[3] This strong and, in its form, genuinely Oriental expression of Jesus shocked the disciples, in

---

Matt. v. 48, v. 12, vi. 1 sqq., 20. He also thinks that Peter's question, xix. 27, was not possible if Jesus had previously spoken of a heavenly treasure!

[1] Mark x. 21.

[2] According to Matt. xix. 23 (comp. Luke xviii. 24; Mark x. 23). Luke, the man of the kingdom of the present, has "enter into," instead of "shall enter into."

[3] Difference of expression in the three. In Matt. xix. 24, β. οὐρ., Or., Patr.; θεοῦ, Sin. B C D (more difficult, see above, Vol. III. p. 48, note 3). Comp. Rabbis: camelus saltat in cabo (smallest corn-measure). Non ostendunt elephamtem incedentem per foramen acus. Introducere eleph. per for. a. = impossibilia. Lightfoot, p. 347; Schöttgen, p. 163; Wetstein, p. 451. Celsus (6, 16), in fact, charges Jesus with having borrowed this speech (as well as others, *e. g.* that about smiting the cheek, 7, 58) from Plato. For similar sentiment, comp. Matt. vii. 13; thus already Origen, 15, 20. Erroneous explanation, which makes a thick rope ($\kappa\acute{\alpha}\mu\iota\lambda o\varsigma$) out of "camel," or a small gate out of the "needle's eye." The saying of Jesus repeated in the Koran, chap. vii. 38: non ingredientur paradisum, donec transeat camelus foramen acus. The Gospel of the Hebrews represents the figurative speech as solemnly addressed to Peter: Simon fili Johanne (sitting next to Jesus), facilius est, &c. (Hilg. *Hebr.-Ev.* 17); plainly because Peter then (Matt. xix. 27) takes up the word.

Mark, where Jesus is represented as repeating and, by his imagery, intensifying even doubly and trebly his proposition, which he accompanied by a significant glance around him. The disciples themselves were naturally out of well-to-do houses; and at one blow they saw themselves and half Galilee—as previously on the question of marriage—now cut off from entrance into the long-coveted kingdom.[1] "Who then can be saved?" cried they to Jesus, not unbelievingly, but half despairingly, in a way which sets at rest every doubt whether they themselves and the most important of Jesus' adherents belonged to the beggars or to the possessors of property in Galilee.[2] With a look that was appropriate to the personal reference of the question, Jesus answered out of the depth of his infinite faith in God, and in the words of God himself once heard by Abraham and Sarah: "With men this is impossible, but with God all is possible."[3] Thus he, after his own manner, as the strong one whose strength was rooted in God alone, took away all human self-confidence, by sealing with his assenting testimony the factual impotence of the young man and the desponding anxiety of the disciples, while he set the minds of the disciples at rest without making them self-secure, by permitting them to believe in the gift of God which had hitherto broken in them the ban of possession, and would do it in them and others even to the great deciding point of all things.

The appeasement of their anxiety and the recognition of Jesus did them more than sufficient service. The dejected were again encouraged; the saved of God recalled, with something of petty jealousy, their human contributions towards their salvation. Most of all it became clear to them, when they had overcome the

---

[1] Mark x. 23—26. On the other hand, there falls upon Mark the *gravamen* that he, in x. 24, speaks not of the rich, but of those that trust in what they possess (above, Vol. I. p. 123); but, according to Sin. B Δ It., these words fall away altogether, and there stands only, How hard it is to enter into the kingdom of God!

[2] Similar question, Numbers xxiv. 23.

[3] Gen. xviii. 14; Luke i. 37. The Platonist Celsus adds (5, 24), that to God the natural and the rational alone are possible.

first alarm caused by Jesus' utterance about the rich, that their contributions could be regarded as the right, sound, and gratifying antithesis to the non-following of the rich; although they did not reflect that they had merely left their goods, and had neither sold nor given them away. With this faith grew their claims; and with the nearer approach of the kingdom of heaven, of which Jesus had again reminded them, grew their selfish longings. The conjecture that the claim made by Peter—narrated by the three Evangelists immediately after the incident of the young man—could not in reality have followed the deep humiliation of the young man and of the disciples, is overborne by the perception that the mental revulsion of the disciples from dismay to bold importunity is thoroughly psychological, although it is anything but noble religiously.[1] "Behold," Peter briskly began, "*we* have left all and followed thee!" This was spoken in a tone which showed that at any rate he wished to say what Matthew makes him say: "What, then, shall we have?"[2] Jesus received him in a marvellous manner. Upon the man who had so suddenly grown again self-satisfied, nay exacting, he might appropriately have enforced the lost moral of the occurrence of the day, just as on one occasion, according to Luke, he corrected the mistaken wish of the disciples, who, as the wages of their ploughing and pasturing, longed to sit at meat as well-deserving, though in truth unprofitable, servants.[3] But no. He, who insisted upon human weakness and the divine gift, nevertheless knew how to respect human achievements, and was ready to prize them doubly, since the case of the young man showed him the significance of the sincere and faithful adherence of his disciples, and the journey to

---

[1] Matt. xix. 27; Luke xviii. 28; Mark x. 28. Hilgenfeld (1868, pp. 25 sqq.) thinks that, particularly after the mention of treasure in heaven (Matt. xix. 21), Peter's question was impossible. But the disciples' giving away was differently conceived from that of the young man; and Peter, if he appropriated the treasure in heaven to himself, was interested in knowing of what it consisted. Indeed, the treasure must come upon earth, see above, III. p. 53, note 1.

[2] Weisse, I. p. 567: Peter was concerned rather about his soul!

[3] Luke xvii. 7.

Jerusalem demanded the steeling of its persistence. He therefore took the course of first encouraging, not humbling, and of then allowing the admonition to modesty to follow the promises. "Verily, I say unto you"—thus he began, in words that would comfort, elevate, and inspirit—" that ye, my followers, in the renovation of things, when the Son of Man sits down on the throne of his glory, shall yourselves also sit upon twelve thrones as judges of the twelve tribes of Israel.[1] And every one that has left brothers or sisters, or father or mother, or children, or land or houses, for my name's sake, shall receive manifold, and shall inherit eternal life." For this is the genuine utterance, which has been preserved in its purity by Matthew alone; whilst Luke and Mark, at a later period which had almost given up an expectation of Jesus' coming again, have consoled the faithful with the mediocre gains of the present time, afterwards crowned by eternal life.[2]

[1] This passage only in Matt. xix. 28, and indeed (against Neander, p. 451) quite correctly, since even the following shows a distinction between the Apostles and the wider circle of disciples. Luke and Mark have only the general promise of Jesus, which follows. We might find the reason in antipathy to the anticipation of material presence, which antipathy is to be found in Luke xviii. 29, and Mark x. 30. Yet Luke has the passage in question, in his sources, inappropriately at the Last Supper, xxii. 28 sqq.; but Mark lets it go entirely, for the above reason (comp. Mark ix. 1). The renovation of things (palingenesis) only here (comp. Matt. xvii. 11; Acts i. 6, iii. 21), except in the Epistle of Titus, iii. 5 (bath of the second-birth); it corresponds to the Old Testament shub, heshib, chiddesh (subst., besides chadashot, Is. xlii. 9, preferably shubah or teshubah), comp. Ezekiel xvi. 55; Nahum ii. 3; Mal. iv. 6; Dan. ix. 25. In Ezekiel, shub lekadmato (to its origin). The idea is, theocratic renovation of the world, Matt. v. 5 (in Eng. version), not exactly by a new heaven and a new earth (Is. lxv. 17, lxvi. 22; Book of Enoch 45, 91; Rev. xxi. 1; Rom. viii. 19; 2 Peter iii. 13), or by resurrection, of which there is no trace in the Gospels. See above, IV. pp. 294 sq. Among the Greeks, also by Philo and Josephus, mention often made of restoration of possessions, fatherland, life, the world; παλ. πατρίδος, Jos. Ant. 11, 3, 9; comp. Wetst. and Grimm. Thrones of the Apostles sitting in judgment (who also rule, Grot., Kuinöl, Neander, p. 451; Colani, p. 63; Gess, p. 149), comp. Daniel vii. 22; Wisdom, iii. 8; Book of Enoch 61 sqq., 108; 1 Cor. vi. 2; Rev. xx. 4. *Shem. rabb.* s. 5: sedere faciet sanctus seniores Israelis sicut in semicirculo, ipse iis præsidens sicut pater synedrii et judicabunt nationes mundi. Lightfoot, p. 611. Later, there was shown at least the episcopal throne of James, Eus. 7, 19. Throne of glory particularly often in the interpolated Book of Enoch, 45 sqq., 55, 60. Rationalistic treatment of the throne, Neander, p. 451; Weisse, II. p. 106; Schenkel, p. 215; Gess, p. 115, obscure until the fulfilment.

[2] The same lost seven objects stand in Matthew and Mark, only Mark, with Luke, unskilfully places house first and land last. Luke has only five objects, yet factually

THE JOURNEY TO THE FEAST.

After Jesus had promised to the Twelve participation in the Messianic judgment of Israel and of the twelve tribes who were to be again restored by this judgment,—and after he had promised to those other followers by whom he was surrounded, the copious —although not, in the sense of Mark, materially literal—restitution of all temporal losses, with the addition of the eternal, i.e. the endless, blissful life of the resurrection, he then added to the royal gift the sobering warning, and in a masterly manner, in one address—preserved in its entirety only by Matthew—he suppressed the sense of security, the sense of merit acquired by works, and the feeling of jealousy.[1] "But," he said, "there will be many first last, and last first."[2] He had recourse to parable,

---

more, since he condenses parent and family from four into two, and adds wife. More important, however, is the difference that Luke and Mark place the manifold recompence (Mark, hundred-fold) in *this* world, and distinguish therefrom the future world with eternal life. But the present is not yet to them the Messianic period proper, which stood to them in the *obscure distance*, whilst Matthew (also their own sources) means this; but to Luke and Mark it is the current pre-Messianic time; wherefore Mark, in an arbitrary addition, introduces persecutions, by which he points to Nero, Domitian, and indeed also Trajan. Comp. above, IV. p. 295. According to Schenkel (*Bibel-Lex.* III. p. 299), the sentences in Mark are genuine. Volkmar, also, does not see in Mark and Luke the juvenility of this teaching about the present world; Matthew is the stiff Jewish man of the transcendental. On the rich compensation, comp. Is. lxi. 7 (twofold). Similarly, *Targ.* Cant. viii. 7: duplum in sec. fut.

[1] In a repulsive manner, Mark (he alone) represents that the literal, sensibly individual restoration of what was lost was placed in prospect, certainly not in an eschatological relation, but—in the immanent development of the kingdom which, as that which is certain, Jesus himself shall enjoy and give—in antithesis to what is obscure and uncertain (x. 30). Volkmar derives this from Paul, 1 Cor. iii. 22; 2 Cor. vi. 10! But Paul is more ideal in his immanence doctrine.

[2] This addition is in Matt. xix. 30 (explained xx. 16); Mark x. 31; Luke, not here, but xiii. 30 (with reference to the Gentiles). Naturally there is also lacking in Luke the parable, which is altogether unsuitable for Paul (1 Cor. xv. 10; Luke xii. 3); and Mark readily follows him, although the short passage (x. 31) then remains essentially obscure. Volkmar would derive the parable from Mark xii. 1. Weisse, II. p. 107, is nearer the truth. Yet he (I. p. 567), like De Wette, Neander, Strauss, questions the connection of the sentence with the following parable. The proposition itself has many parallels, though that does not give us the right to make Matthew or Mark dependent upon them. Book of Enoch 103, 11 (Is. ix. 14): we hoped to be the head, and we were the tail. 4 Esdras v. 42: sicut non novissimorum tarditas, sic nec priorum velocitas. Barnabas 6 : τὰ ἔσχ. ὡς τὰ πρῶτα (Matt. xii. 45). Talmud: superiores inferius et inf. superius. *Tauch.* f. 3, 1 : Deus ultimos ponit in loco primorum. Schöttgen, p. 164. Wetst. p. 453. Hilgenfeld, p. 32.

to the kingdom-parable of the householder, or God, who, from early morning onwards, hires workmen for his vineyard, and agrees with them for the good wages of a *denarius* or franc a day. At the first, the third, the sixth, the ninth, and the eleventh hours, from six in the morning till five in the evening—we may say, to the ringing in of the evening rest—he seeks day labourers, whom, from nine o'clock onwards, he finds in numbers in the market-place, and sends the unoccupied into his vineyard. The payment begins at six in the evening. The steward, the Messiah, is expressly charged to pay the last first, the first last. The first murmur, not merely because the workmen of an hour are paid first, but also because they receive equally high wages, whilst *they*—the first—have borne the burden of the day and the heat. But as to the first, the householder appeals to the contract; and as to the work of the last and the unamiable ill-feeling of the first, he appeals to his right and to his goodness. This parable—which, with most striking resemblances, occurs also among the Jews—must not be misunderstood.[1] Without doubt, the payment does not appear simply as a gratuitous reward, but also as a wage for work; and the reward to those that began first appears literally as not a gratuitous one, but altogether as a wage for work. But since actually a very small minority of the labourers bear the whole burden of the day, and a large majority only a part of that burden, and yet are equally rewarded and rewarded first of all, the meaning of the whole parable, corresponding to the general view of Jesus and the necessary rejection of the Jewish claim of the disciple, is that of reward above merit, without merit, the reward of God by grace.[2] It would be a mistake to suppose that, in the calls to labour extending through the

---

[1] Exactly similar parables, Lightfoot, p. 347; Schöttgen, pp. 164 sqq.; Wetstein, p. 455. Day's wage a denarius among Jews and Gentiles, Wetst. p. 453. Soldiers had less, Tac. *Ann.* 1, 17. Hillel, only half a denarius, above, I. p. 349. Idle, Ex. v. 17. Heat, Gen. xviii. 1, xxxi. 40. At the eleventh hour it was customary to prepare for rest, without thinking any more of labour or fighting, Jos. *B. J.* 6, 2, 8.

[2] Matt. xx. 16, the words, "many called, few chosen," are a later interpolation. Tischendorf, after Sin. B L Z sah. copt. Nevertheless, retained by Hilg. p. 31.

hours of a day, Jesus was looking towards a great and extensive future development of his Church, in which the Apostles and the first followers only represented the sixth hour, in contrast to the later Apostle Paul, or indeed to the Gentiles.[1] This application is to-day possible and useful; but in point of fact, Jesus referred primarily altogether to the past, to the hitherto gradual gathering of his circle of disciples, and to the claims of those disciples. Thus understood, the utterance of Jesus throws a new light upon Peter's question as well as upon the claims of the Twelve generally, and, finally, upon Jesus' promise of thrones. Since Peter — in Matthew significantly called *the first*—gave prominence to the fact that he and others had followed Jesus from the beginning, he asked for, not only a reward, but a title of precedence before the mass of adherents, before the later followers, both in and out of the circle of Apostles. It was an ambition similar to that exhibited before the departure from Galilee, and just after that departure on the route to Jerusalem. Again, since Jesus placed the followers on an equality in importance and reward, he plainly proved that, in the face of the preferences to which he had given expression in Galilee, and even now in the promise of thrones to the Twelve, he firmly regarded at the same time all his adherents as essentially equal. They were to be equal in their gains, equal also—as was taught a moment later in the words to the sons of Zebedee—in the rights and claims of the

[1] The temporal succession which is represented in the first and the last (but as such does not exclude a difference of rank, of which De Wette and Hilgenfeld think) does not refer primarily to the Jews and Gentiles (Jerome, Theophyl., Grot., Strauss, Hilg., Volkmar), which is simply not indicated by the connection and subject (we need only recal the similar Jewish sayings), but—as Weizs. in particular sees—to the earlier and later disciples of Jesus. For the Gentile-favouring reference of the section, Hilgenfeld urges that a work wage is given to the first called merely (xx. 2); but to the later ones (verses 4 and 5) only an indefinite assurance; to the last called (according to the latest reading of Tischendorf, verse 7, where the clause corresponding to verse 4 is left out), no assurance at all (comp. among the Jews: pretium laboris non indicavit. Schöttgen, pp. 167 sq.). It may be the Jews who work according to contract and wage, and the Gentiles who work for favour (Hilg. 1868, pp. 30 sqq.). This is mere refinement, for verses 4, 5, 7, essentially correspond to the standpoint of the contract in verse 2. Hilgenfeld would withdraw this section from the "original manuscript," and give it to the Gentile-favouring Evangelist.

life of fellowship. These views were not altogether harmonious; but it is very finely seen how he repeatedly sought to combine the equilibrium of essential equality with the pre-eminence which individuals naturally acquired by their achievements and their mental superiority. He did this, indeed, not merely for the purpose of suppressing accidentally present sentiments of pride, but in the exercise of the authority inherent in the dignity and lofty position of his human personality, an authority which he necessarily derived from his conception of God and of man.

C.—A Day at Jericho.

Passing through the first localities on the western bank of the Jordan, they gradually drew near to Jericho. The ascent of the road, the approach to the populous city, vividly suggested to Jesus the last end of the last station, the speedy entry into Jerusalem. Mark has exhibited some artistic skill in so grouping the individual scenes that he places the conversation with the Pharisees at the crossing of the Jordan into Judæa, the children in the first hostel, the rich young man at the moment of departure from the house, the thoughts about Jerusalem when Jesus had again set forth on the highway.[1] Only the artificiality of the drawing has been already detected; and there is an entire absence of probability in the description of the further progress, in which Jesus is made to go on in advance, with the pomp of a hero, just like a Roman, while the disciples followed with astonishment and fear.[2] This is ingenious fiction which excellently well accords with the heroic and mysterious Mark-picture, but with no reality; for the disciples, on the contrary, had no

[1] Mark x. 2, 10, 13, 17, 32.
[2] Mark x. 32. According to Volkmar (p. 468), some had even remained behind (comp. John vi. 66). But nothing of this stands in the passage; prominence is given to the fear of those who were following only in order to introduce the taking to himself of the anxious Twelve (verse 32).

presentiment of anything dreadful as to Jesus, but only of good.[1] All three Evangelists agree that, on the way, Jesus, in conformity with a well-known Jewish fondness for certain numbers, uttered his last and third anticipation of death prior to the entry into Jerusalem. "Behold, we go up to Jerusalem," spake he to the Twelve, taking them aside as his confidants and commissaries, "and the Son of Man will be delivered to the high-priests and Scribes; and they will condemn him to death and deliver him to the Gentiles, to mock, to scourge, and to crucify; and on the third day he will rise again."[2] The announcement of his passion which he here gave was the most detailed of all.[3] He now prospectively recognized that he should die after a trial, and after being delivered by the Sanhedrim to the Romans. In point of fact, however, he had already thus pictured his destiny in Galilee, when he thought of the Sanhedrists and of crucifixion. Nothing remains to be said here concerning the historical character of these utterances in general; and the conversation with the sons of Zebedee, immediately afterwards, may be taken to prove, by its undoubted genuineness, that Jesus was silently thinking of the cross, even though, in his blessing of the children, in parable, conversation, and controversy, he confirmed the mental quiet and mental peace of Galilee. But exception can be taken to the details, and an extension of the standpoint of fulfilment can be admitted; and thus one may—to say nothing more of the announcement of the resurrection—be inclined to

---

[1] The non-understanding of the disciples is certainly omitted by Mark at the third announcement of death, x. 34 (comp. Luke xviii. 34); whereon Volkmar (p. 499) lays special stress, saying that here is an advance upon ix. 32. Whence should this come? and how strongly do x. 28, 35, xi. 9, &c., speak against this advance! The mysterious Christ, above, I. p. 124.

[2] Matt. xx. 17; Luke xviii. 31; Mark x. 32.

[3] Hilgenfeld (1868, p. 33) finds in this third announcement nothing new, and regards it as an addition by the Evangelist, like the second. See above, IV. p. 307. On the other hand, Renan thought that Jesus, after the preceding presentiments, now for the first time definitely announced his death. Again, Steinmeyer (*Leidensgesch.* 1868, pp. 61 sq.) consistently asserted, in disposing of the climax depicted above, IV. p. 298, note 1, that the resolve was involved in the incarnation.

A DAY AT JERICHO.

question or to erase all the minutiæ of the description of Roman maltreatment, including the mocking and scourging, particularly the unaccountable spitting in Luke and Mark.[1]

To how small an extent were his disciples able to accommodate themselves to these gloomy prospects, even allowing for exaggeration in the assertion which Luke makes, with a triple reference, that they understood nothing of all he said, nothing of the fulfilments of the prophets' predictions, to which Jesus, according to Luke's statement, appealed like a dogmatist.[2] They understood that he spoke of dying, as is plainly shown by the subsequent conversation with the sons of Zebedee; but they failed to realize the horrible thought of death, because their ear and heart were almost exclusively fixed upon the ideas of life and glory which had now for a long time occupied their fancy and fired their enthusiasm, and which had been revived by Jesus again and again, as previously in the promise to the Twelve, so now again at the close of the announcement of the passion.[3] Even now Jesus had placed before their eyes as something final and near, not his resurrection, but his Messianic glorification; and consequently, against the will of Jesus and certainly not through any fault of his, the enthusiastic fancies of the disciples acquired fresh strength. Nay, what Jesus said about the thrones of the Apostles, dissociated from its solemn and warning context, became the frame-work which was clothed with the foliage and gorgeous blossoms of a materially ambitious expectation. James and John, the sons of Zebedee, the sons of thunder, and, with Peter, favourites of Jesus, at once communicated to their

---

[1] Similarly Weisse, I. p. 568. The simplest account in Matthew. Peculiar to Luke is (1) the initial pointing to the fulfilment of Scripture, comp. Luke xxii. 37; (2) the silence about the Sanhedrim, the immediate delivery to the Gentiles; (3) the intensifying of the maltreatment (four details, spitting in addition); (4) the non-understanding of the disciples. Peculiar to Matthew is the crucifying instead of the slaying. Mark follows Matthew chiefly; but he has spitting and slaying, like Luke. Comp. above, IV. pp. 273 sq., 306 sqq.

[2] Luke xviii. 31, 34. Matthew and Mark are silent about the impression.

[3] Similarly also Volkmar, p. 500: they thought to be able to leap into glory without suffering.

mother Jesus' renewed utterance about the future, the near and rapidly approaching fulfilment. What they themselves longed for, their mother longed for still more ardently; and what they had not the courage to ask, especially after the recent exhibition of jealousy by the disciples and Jesus' words of reprimand, the mother undertook to ask, as one who stood more removed, who was older, and yet was also an adherent and friend of Jesus.[1]

So, like Bathsheba of old going to David on Solomon's behalf, Salome went to Jesus with her two sons. There was no time to be wasted, and timid reticence was brought to an end by the march of events. Salome bowed herself before Jesus, and her bearing or her words showed that she wished to make a request.[2] "What wilt thou?" spoke Jesus. She answered, "Say that these my two sons may sit, one on thy right, and the other on thy left, in thy kingdom."[3] Her faith in the Messiah, therefore,

---

[1] Matt. xx. 20; Mark x. 35. Luke, following his sources, gives a similar controversy at the Last Supper, where, however, it does not fit (Strauss, Neander), xxii. 24. According to Volkmar (p. 501), he wished to screen the pillars, in order the better to introduce his Paulinism, just as in ix. 21. But he was not really so careful to screen them, comp. only ix. 49, 54, xii. 3. And why Luke more careful to screen them than Matthew? According to Mark, the two Apostles appealed directly to Jesus, without their mother; and Schulz, Schenkel, and Volkmar, consider this the original form of the narrative, confirmed by the direct censure of the two sons of Zebedee by Jesus and by the other Apostles. But Mark could have fabricated his altered representation directly out of the latter circumstance (as Meyer and Bleek also see). Matthew's representation is psychologically much more likely to be true (also Neander, Strauss, Weisse); such a request the two could not venture upon themselves,—they would be prevented by a feeling of shame before Jesus and their fellow-apostles; but an interceding mother could present it. But Mark allowed the mother to disappear so much the more readily because he would not accept any guardianship over the Apostles, and wished to give emphasis to their correction. There is certainly a striking similarity between the scene in Matt. and that in 1 Kings i. 15 (Greek text). But even if there were an external imitation here, Matthew is factually independent. Strauss is sceptical as to the position of the incident, 4th ed., I. p. 724.

[2] On Salome, see above, III. p. 262. Mark has not a bowing down, on the other hand a distorted form of the request (x. 35), in which he wished perhaps to depict the perplexity of the sons of Zebedee.

[3] The places of honour, comp. 1 Sam. xxiii. 17. Jos. *Ant.* 6, 11, 9: Jonathan, at Saul's table, on the right, Abner on the left. The Rabbis place the Messiah on the right hand of God, Abraham on the left, Aaron on the right of Moses, Gamaliel the elder on the right of his son, the Sanhedrists on the left, the queen on the right of the throne of Pharaoh, the daughter on the left. Wetstein, p. 456.

was strong, firm as a rock; a word by the man whom she revered, loved, and the two thrones, or rather seats of honour, of her darlings were secured. And how appropriate, how readily self-suggesting was the distribution: two throne companions, two firstlings, two bosom friends, two vigilant spirits of fire, two children of one womb! Peter himself, the only rival, must have acknowledged that this arrangement was very seemly, and that the exclusion of one of the brothers would be unseemly and cruel. It is true, Salome asked a great deal, and much more than the John of the Revelation, sharing the kingdom fraternally with the others, claimed for himself.[1] The mental sobriety and moral strictness of Jesus quickly overthrew the well-arranged plan. Turning from the mother, he at once addressed himself to her sons, because to him the disciples were more intimate, more responsible, and more important, and because he could perceive, as did afterwards the ten, that they were the silent authors of the thought expressed by their mother. The fact that Jesus thus directly addressed himself to the sons, explains the inferior reading of Mark, who makes the sons appeal to Jesus themselves, and without their mother's support. "Ye know not what ye ask," said Jesus, pointing out to them at the same time, as the way to the throne of God, holy sacrifices of which they had not thought. It was *his* way, his Messiah-way, to which he looked forward and in which he believed, the way through suffering, but which also led to the throne. He saw plainly that whoever wished to sit near him on the throne must participate in his sufferings; and he could not doubt that the wish was coloured by gay tints of childish fancy that would fade before the stern severity of what was required. "Can ye drink of the cup, the cup of suffering, of which I am about to drink? Can ye"—at least thus runs the later Christian formula—"be baptized with the baptism with which I shall be baptized?"[2] A unanimous

---

[1] Rev. i. 6, 9, iii. 21. According to Volkmar (p. 500), just this longing for supremacy was here symbolized.

[2] Matthew has only the cup; Mark has the baptism as well. The latter is most probably taken from the address in Luke xii. 50, and has given occasion to the late

"We can," was the answer of the sons of thunder, an answer which Jesus probably so much the less expected because the brothers' anticipation of the throne had betrayed no serious reflection upon the dark point in the future. But these choleric men were prepared, in their longing for the crowns and also out of love to their Master, to decide with a sudden resolve to tread even the path of suffering of which until then they had scarcely heard, and in which they had not hitherto believed. Now would Jesus not be compelled to award them the thrones? Certainly, to judge from the introduction to his answer; but an inner scruple restrained him from going further than he had already gone in this province of hopes and expectations, from crowning uncertain and actually unfulfilled promises with the highest gifts, and still more from anticipating by human thoughts or arrangements, future events which were still secrets in the mind of God. In this connection, the difference between the judicial thrones of the Twelve and the thrones of supremacy of the two, as well as between prospective enjoyment and actual donation, must not be overlooked. Thus he promised to them what the immediate future must certainly bring; what he was ever anew requiring of his followers; what they themselves had so solemnly accepted and applauded, certainly not as end but simply as means, as the thoroughfare, as the way to the throne, whilst the stern and reproving Master seemed to give prominence to the harsh means as an end in itself, to the bitter transition as the final issue—for he on his own part promised nothing beyond. But he placed the thrones in the hand of God, as he owed it to God to do, and also to the beloved disciples whom he was anxious to lead on and up to the highest aims, not by encouraging in them

---

conception of martyrdom, lavacrum sanguinis (comp. Tert. *Scorp.* 12). In Matthew, the baptism has forced its way into late codices (against Sin. B D L Z). Baptism, as such, first became a most important element in the consciousness of the apostolic times; comp. Rom. vi. 3, Rev. vii. 14; yet the John-baptism had importance enough for Jesus and his adherents. On the chalice (Kos), comp. Is. li. 17; Jer. xxv. 15, xlix. 12; Ps. lxxv. 8; Rev. xiv. 10, &c.; Matt. xxvi. 39, 42. Even in the classics, Tib. 1, 6, 14: tristia cum multo pocula felle bibit. Wetst. p. 457.

a comfortable and indolent sense of security, but by awakening their hope and inciting them to action. " My cup shall ye indeed drink ; but to sit down on my right and my left—it is not mine to give this, but—for whom it is prepared."[1] Undoubtedly Jesus had not in view—as the Church at times has supposed—a later and much later martyrdom of the two brothers, which, as to James, is with certainty historically attested, and which occurred tolerably early, nine years after the departure of Jesus. His whole perspective was just at this time a very near, a very narrow one. He thought chiefly of a participation by the sons of thunder in his sufferings or even in his death at Jerusalem, a participation which perhaps, as in the case of Peter, occurred only in words, and the non-occurrence of which Jesus himself, a few days later, could take account of in Jerusalem.[2]

[1] Matthew adds: by my Father. Similarly, Matt. xxv. 34. Perplexity of Weisse, I. p. 570, Gess. p. 117, on account of the reticence of Jesus, opp. xvi. 27, xix. 28, xxv. 34.

[2] Comp. Matt. xxvi. 31; Luke xxii. 31 sq. The martyrdom of James, Acts xii. 2. The martyrdom of John is first mentioned, by Georg. Hamartolos, in the ninth century, with a reference to our passage, but also on the ground of the second book of Papias. See Nolte, *Kath. Quartalschrift*, 1862, p. 466, and Hilgenfeld's *Zeitschrift*, 1865, p. 78, 1868, p. 34; also Holtzmann's article *Johannes* in *Bibel-Lexikon*, III. p. 333. On the other hand, Polycrates, Irenæus, and Tertullian, assume his natural death (Polycrates ap. Eus. 3, 31; 5, 24. Irenæus, 2, 22, 5, &c. Tertullian, *Anim.* 50); and Origen (*In Matth.* t. XVI. 6) is reminded by our passage simply of the Roman banishment to Patmos. The belief in the oil-martyrdom of John (Tert. *Præsc.* 36) was at the same time developed on the basis of our passage and of Rev. i. 9 ; and yet more literally does the belief in drinking poison without harm ($\pi\rho\alpha\xi$. Ιω. 10 sq.; comp. Fabric. *C. A. N. T.* I. p. 576) remind us of our passage (comp. Mark xvi. 18); the earlier tradition represents others as thus drinking (Barsabbas, Pap. ap. Eus. 3, 39). Comp. Hilg. *l. c.* The account of Georgius Hamartolos (Παπ. ὁ Ἱεραπ. ἐπίσκ. αὐτόπτης τούτου γενόμενος ἐν τῷ δευτέρῳ λόγῳ τ. κυριακ. λογίων φάσκει, ὅτι ὑπὸ Ἰουδαίων ἀνῃρέθη, &c.) I would, for my part, with Holtzmann, apply to the historical John, not only because it evidently puts an end to the Ephesian illusions and unpleasantly fulfils Steitzen's hope (*Stud.* 1868, pp. 487 sqq.) of fresh documents for the Ephesian Zebedean, but because of the exact citation and title of book (Holtzm.), because of the inconceivability of a confounding of the Apostle with John Presbyter, since Georgius confounds the teacher of Papias with the Apostle (Παπίας αὐτόπτης τούτου γενόμενος), while on the other hand the sources leave no doubt about the natural death of the Presbyter (above, I. p. 222); finally, because of the tangible fact that the martyrdom of John had, from the time of Irenæus and Polycrates, been suppressed by confounding the Apostle with the living Presbyter. And a noteworthy *ancient* support is given to the report of Papias by Heracleon, who is able to reckon as Apostles that did not suffer

The ambition of the two brothers excited a commotion which must have broken the calm of the sacred journey of the Lord, if he had not in the midst of it taken his stand against those who began it, and if he had not, by the glorious words of his cordially tender and intellectually conclusive rejoinder, in a conciliatory manner, quieted the billows which agitated the circle of the disciples as well as our minds. The ten other disciples subsequently learnt something of this secret transaction of the sons of Zebedee with Jesus. Not only Peter, but the rest also were sorely hurt by the vaingloriousness of the two; and they seemed to be fully justified in this by the equality they derived from Jesus, by the promise of the twelve thrones, and by the parable of the twelve day-labourers; whilst the old childish jealousy, bursting forth afresh at every provocation, showed that in truth they were not defending the principle of equality so much as the passion of personal ambition which they shared with the sons of Zebedee. Hence, in Jesus' absence, there passed from one to another reproaches, justifications, and refutations.[1] Then Jesus, inwardly sorrowing over the perversity of his followers, as well as over the profanation of the profoundest principles that underlay his life and his death, called them to him. In the face of the endless repetition of the inconsistent conflicts which threatened the character and the future of his cause, he found the words which, in severity yet in love, described the true nature of his community, and the peculiar character of the new kingdom as distinguished from the earthly kingdoms, and with an incontrovertible logic based the character of his kingdom upon

---

martyrdom only Matthew, Philip, and Thomas (Clem. *Strom.* 4, 9, 73). The historical situation of this death is to be found in the persecutions before the destruction of Jerusalem, Eus. 3, 5. An invention by Papias, on the basis of our passage, Matt. xx., is altogether excluded by the traditional standpoint of the man. Hilgenfeld abides by his scepticism (as might be expected, since he still does not see the confounding of the two Johns). With equal arbitrariness, Hilgenfeld asserts that Matt. xx. 23 must have been written before the death of John, as Volkmar (p. 500) after that death. Wittichen (*Idee des Menschen*, p. 149) speaks of a self-deception of Jesus concerning the martyrdom of John.

[1] Matt. xx. 24; Mark x. 41; comp. Luke xxii. 24.

his personal vocation and ministry. "Ye know that the rulers of the nations use force against them, and that the great exercise authority over them.[1] Not so shall it be among *you;* but he who will be great among you, let him be your minister, and he who will be first among you, let him be your servant; even as the Son of Man came not to be ministered unto, but to minister and to give up his life a ransom in the place of many."[2] This was an utterance out of the fulness of his life, out of the heart of his principles. And by overthrowing, as pagan in character, the ludicrous and cheap fancy-thrones of the Twelve, and supplying their place by a demand for a ministering self-sacrifice on behalf of the brethren, of humanity, he struck a firm, sharp, penetrating blow with the lance of truth, and toppled over even those thrones which, in an Old Testament spirit and with an Oriental symbolism, he was still inconsistently wishful to retain for the Messiah and the Messiah's associates. The latest criticism has raised not many objections to the whole of this narrative, a narrative the genuineness of which is most evident in its lowly and lofty human features. Only the memorable reference to the death of atonement for many—this "dogmatic atonement theory" —is vigorously attacked by Baur and his followers. For the present, let it suffice to answer that Jesus a moment later, namely at the Last Supper, exhibited the same new conception of his death, and that the word "ransom" was suggested to him by the very general designation of the just then paid and much talked-of temple-tax.[3]

[1] Mark, οἱ δοκοῦντες ἄρχειν = they who are accounted to rule (Gal. ii. 9). Thus also Bleek and Winer.

[2] Comp. *Juchas.* 36, 1: mortuus est magn. discip. numerus ob non exhibitum inter se mutuum officium. Lightfoot, p. 319. *Kidd.* f. 32, 2: R. Elieser, R. Joshua, R. Zadok, were ministered to by R. Gamaliel, for he stood; they lay and received their drink from him: invenimus majorem, qui ministri officio functus est, Wetst. p. 458.

[3] Baur, *N. T. Theol.* p. 100; comp. Volkmar, p. 501 (the vicarious idea post-Pauline!), and Hilg. p. 34, who is more conservative, not questioning the essential originality of the passage. Baur even thought that the word did not harmonize at all with this otherwise so simple exhortation to humility and the spirit of self-sacrifice. Schenkel (pp. 217 sq.) thinks of a freeing from the bondage of the letter and of the hierarchy. On the λύτρον ἀντὶ πολλῶν (kopher, comp. Book of Enoch, 98; Wünsche,

They now entered Jericho, where Jesus wished to take up his quarters for the day.[1] The distance to Jerusalem was too great and required too much exertion to be completed at once ; moreover, two Gospels speak expressly of a departure from Jericho with the accompaniment of a great multitude. The latter fact itself suggests a sojourn and a becoming known. Finally, Luke specially refers to Jesus' quarters for the night.[2] Unfortunately Matthew and Mark give nothing concerning this sojourn; they content themselves with describing the departure. On the other hand, Luke's description of the entry, though in a high degree vivid, graphic, and indeed instructive, is nevertheless imperfectly attested.[3] According to Luke, the progress of Jesus through this great city was beset by dense masses of people, by whom the streets through which he passed were in particular crowded, and among whom the cry ran from mouth to mouth, "Jesus the Nazarene!"[4] Even the chief publican Zacchæus (a name frequent among the Jews) was driven into the streets by his strong desire to see Jesus.[5] Jericho was naturally, on account of its size and

p. 17), see not only Matt. xvi. 26 and xxvi. 28, but also the designation of the temple-tax in Exodus xxx. 12 (Matt. xvii. 27), λύτρα τῆς ψυχῆς; and Philo, *De Mon.* 2, 2, 224 (Wetst. p. 439), αἱ εἰσφοραὶ λύτρα προσονομάζονται.

[1] According to Schenkel (*Bibel-Lex.* III. p. 291), Jesus, during his sojourn of several months in Judæa, took up his station chiefly in Jericho. In the *Charakterbild* (p. 179), Bethany was the central point. Weizs. (pp. 512 sqq.) makes the sojourn in Jerusalem between the Feast of Tabernacles and the last Easter to be only a transitory one; Jesus was in Judæa and Peræa (Mark x. 1), and a series of passages in the Synoptics themselves point to the south (pp. 307 sqq.). Consequently also Holtzmann (II. p. 371), Sevin (pp. 7 sq.), postulate a longer ministry in Judæa, or (according to Weisse, I. pp. 299, 429), in Jerusalem, without which everything would stand in the air. Rather these opinions stand in the air, because there is no space for such a sojourn!

[2] Matt. xx. 29; Mark x. 46; Luke xviii. 35, xix. 5.   [3] Luke xix. 1 sqq.

[4] Not, as Ewald says (p. 507), on entering, outside the gate; and quite as little at the other end, Bleek, II. p. 286.

[5] S(z)akkai, Ezra ii. 9; Neh. vii. 14; Jos. *Vita*, 46. The Rabbis thus name the father of R. Jochanan, and Lightfoot (p. 555) is almost inclined to identify this man who had grown old in piety with our Zacchæus. Ἀρχιτελώνης, that is the man placed immediately over the tax-gatherers, one of those that were next to the Roman tax-farmer, publicanus (Meyer, Bleek). Wetstein thinks groundlessly of a Roman knight, after Jos. *B. J.* 2, 14, 9. In Clem. *Hom.* 2, 1, &c., *Rec.* 1, 72 sq., 2, 19, Zacchæus appears later at Cæsarea. The Zacchæus Tower, on the north of the existing village (200 inhabitants), not until the twelfth century. See Arnold on Jericho.

its position, on the highway of Lower Jordan; it was on the frontier of Roman Judæa, on the side of the tetrarchy of Peræa; and for these reasons, as well as because of its valuable and quite unique productions, it was a main centre for the publicans. Thus it could not be wanting even in chief publicans.¹ But Zacchæus was too small of stature to see over the crowds. His zeal led him to get ahead of the crowd, and to climb a fig-mulberry tree, a tree which still forms fine shady avenues in Oriental cities.² Jesus approached, saw the man in the tree, and not only measuring his faith by his deed, but immediately looking through him even to the discerning of his name, bespoke, without further introduction—a Cæsar in knowledge and conquest—Zacchæus as his host, crying out to him, "Zacchæus, come down quickly, for to-day must I abide at thy house." Zacchæus hastened down and gladly received Jesus under his roof, whilst a murmur of discontent spread among the people : "He is gone to dwell with a man that is a sinner."³ So much the more did Zacchæus—a worthy rival of his father, Rabbi Zeira, and of other publicans who had become famous through their works and their piety—zealously strive, as the unworthy host of the Prophet of Galilee, to be justified; his great guest and the mortifying popular mistrust called for a great penitential sacrifice. Placing himself before the Lord, he said solemnly and earnestly: "Behold, the half of my goods, Lord, give I to the poor; and if I have taken anything from any one fraudulently, I restore it (according to the Law itself) four-fold."⁴ The publican's

---

¹ Strabo, 16, 2. Just. 36, 3: quod (opobals.) in his tantum region. gignitur.

² Furrer, *Wand.* p. 151. "He went before" will best bear the above meaning. It might also mean, "he went up a tree standing just opposite." The sycamore can hardly have reference to the sycophancy of the publicans, comp. Luke iii. 13 sq. It is at home in the lowlands, and Palestine was full of the splendid, lofty, wide-spreading tree, Winer. It is comical that Ewald (p. 507) thinks of a low tree.

³ On account of Luke xix. 11, 28, Olsh. and Schl. would postpone these aspersions and sayings to the next day, that of the departure. This is evidently contrary to the author; rather is the passage, verses 11 sqq., too closely connected with what precedes it (Bleek, p. 288).

⁴ Zeira, Lightfoot, p. 296 ; compare the publican John in Cæsarea, Jos. *B. J.* 2, 14, 4. The four-fold, Ex. xxii. 1 (four-fold), 4 (two-fold); Numbers v. 7 (the

gift was followed by the Lord's reward, an announcement of salvation for the house, an announcement which included an honourable recognition of the publican and a vindication of himself on account of his—thus evidently blessed—entry into the publican's house: "To-day is salvation come to this house, inasmuch as he also is a son of Abraham; for the Son of Man came to seek and to save the lost."[1] Notwithstanding all its probableness and the absence of the miraculous, and notwithstanding the germ-utterance which seems to form the original close of the original whole, many doubts rise up against this incident. The silence of the other Gospels, the extravagance of the concourse of people, the improbability that a man of wealth and position should climb a tree, the inconsiderateness, the imprudence of deliberately entering the house of a publican in opposition to the sentiments of the uncultured people who are represented as being thereby much offended and yet holding fast to their enthusiastic faith in the Messiah,—these are some of the suspicious circumstances. Others are, the glimmer of miracle in Jesus' inexplicable, or only in Luke intelligible, knowledge of the name and character of the publican, who until that hour had been a perfect stranger to him; and finally, though not the last, the easy explicability of a later origin of the whole narrative, which Luke evidently derived from his Ebionite Gospel.[2] The thronging into the city is, even to the trees that adorned the way, a copy partly of the exit from the same place, partly of the entry

---

whole and a fifth). Rabbis, a fifth of what is gained to the poor. Lightfoot, p. 556; comp. p. 296. Formula of giving to the poor, *ib.* Severe judgment: gravis est poenit. exactorum, foeneratorum; restituere tenentur. Schöttgen, p. 308; comp. Hosea xii. 9. Punishment in Roman law, see Wetstein, p. 784.

[1] Son of Abraham, as Luke xiii. 16, not only in the sense of national descent, but also of moral worth (Bleek), which, however, is not far removed from the Pauline Abrahamism (paganism, Rom. iv.) of which Tertullian, Cyprian, Chrysostom, and recently Volkmar, think. Comp. below.

[2] According to Paulus, some one named the man to Jesus (and certainly described him as well); according to Meyer, Jesus was in some way personally known; according to Neander and Bleek, one or the other of these suppositions is the true explanation; Weisse, II. p. 176, is vague; Olshausen and Strauss are more correct in thinking of miraculous knowledge.

into Jerusalem; the obnoxious visit to the publican, together with Jesus' germ-utterance, is a repetition of the historical meal at a publican's house, and of Jesus' justification on that occasion. The man who was "short of stature," however, is scarcely Paul the Apostle, at the same time the representative of heathenism, but he is one of the believing little ones who could not be lost and were not to be despised; and Zacchæus, the host and giver of alms, is—even to the name Zakkai, i.e. the pure—the practical example of the sentiment ascribed to Jesus by the Ebionites, "Give the contents of your dishes, full of plunder, as alms; behold! then all is *pure* to you."[1] Finally, we can plainly detect the intentional antithesis of the despised publican and haughty Jerusalem: the former has recognized the day of his visitation, the latter has not. Certainly both are artificial, for the words which Jesus utters weeping, and by which he declares to Jerusalem the futility of his visit, betray their own unhistorical character as readily as does the address to Zacchæus.[2]

Better attested than Jesus' entry into Jericho is his departure thence on the morning of Friday, the 8th of April. But we must not here be influenced by Luke, who reverses the order of events and converts the solemn departure into an entry, so that the remarkable occurrence which marked the departure, the healing of the blind of Jericho, is transferred to the entry. And he does this, not on the ground of any deviation of ancient tradition, but

---

[1] The crowd, Matt. xx. 29; comp. xxi. 8. Publicans' meal, Matt. ix. 10. The lost, xviii. 12 sqq. (xviii. 11 in the received text=Luke xix. 10). Zacchæus (Strauss, *New Life of Jesus*, Eng. trans., II. p. 137; Volkmar, p. 505) did not represent heathenism any more than did the woman in Luke xiii. 16; on the contrary, he was a Jew, as his name shows, and he made Jewish satisfaction (Köstlin, p. 228). The Ebionite Gospel does not concern itself at all with heathens. It has long since been shown (above, III. p. 268) that it is a mistake to think the publicans were heathens. It is very remarkable that even Volkmar has not thought of Paul (1 Cor. xv. 9). S(z)akkai means the pure; comp. Luke xi. 41 (Matt. xxiii. 26). Thus Zacchæus purified himself first by giving the unrighteous mammon to the poor, and then by restitution to the defrauded.

[2] One must be blind not to recognize the parallelism between xix. 5 sqq. and xix. 41—44. Doubt against Zacchæus, not even in Strauss, *l. c.* (comp. Haus. p. 435); faintly expressed in Weisse, II. p. 176.

simply for a reason which partly existed already for his late source, viz., in order to introduce the taking up quarters with Zacchæus by an indispensable concourse of people, and the concourse of people by an indispensable miracle, and finally the further progress to Jerusalem by a parable of greater importance than the healing of the blind.[1] The rest of the journey from Jericho is in the highest degree remarkable. It was marked throughout by the popular sympathy and the popular ovation which Luke has drawn somewhat prematurely, and has not quite happily prefaced by Jesus' visit to the house of the publican. A great crowd of people accompanied Jesus from Jericho; and the entry into Jerusalem at the head of a numerous company sufficiently proves that at Jericho we have to do, not with merely an honourable escort for a short distance, but with a formal accession to the festival caravan to Jerusalem. But since Jesus did not join the Jerichotic festival caravan—to do which would have been repulsive to him—but the multitude followed him and afterwards took part in the Messianic festival rejoicings of the Galileans, we here suddenly gain an unexpected occupation for the day of repose at Jericho, and a great light upon the significant turn which matters began to take on this 7th of April. Jesus' brief sojourn in Jericho sufficed, in the space of one day, to call forth that sympathetic interest in the Messiah which the quiet preparatory work of Jesus in Galilee had not succeeded in evoking in a year. And his one day's sojourn did this through the fame which had preceded him, by the impression produced by his person and words, most of all by the assertions of his Galilean adherents, who were less disposed than ever to conceal their glowing anticipations here among the people of the hot plain, a people warm-blooded, ever longing for excitement, and now agitated and inspired by the kindling festival gladness, a people, moreover, dwelling where there lingered the strongest vibrations of the recent Johannine watchword. The general excitement

---

[1] Luke xviii. 35—xix. 11. Grotius perverts the approach to Jericho (xviii. 35) to proximity while departing from that city (Bleek, II. p. 284).

would further be increased by the festival pilgrims who flocked thither from without.[1] The strongest evidence for this unanticipated mighty movement of the people is the healing of the blind, which is transferred to this point by three Gospels.[2] Two blind men, beggars according to Luke and Mark, sat by the wayside, and with a loud voice appealed to the passer-by, who they were told was Jesus.of Nazara: "Jesus, Son of David, have mercy upon us!" The people bade them be silent, but they cried the louder; upon which Jesus called to them and asked what their petition was. "Rabbuni, to see!" was the answer. Then Jesus said to them, "Go; your faith has saved you!" The blind saw and—the most eloquent proofs of Jesus' Messiahship—joined the train. This occurrence at once gives rise to many doubts by the numerous differences between the three Gospels. Here there are two blind; in Luke and Mark, only one, and he a beggar. Here the cure is effected by a command, there by a comforting address, and there again by touching. The descriptive Mark knows the name of the blind man, Bartimæus, that is, the son of the blind— forsooth, a double miracle; and he can tell of his joyful casting away his garment and springing up as soon as he learns from the people the sweet news of Jesus' concession.[3] In fact, the reflec-

---

[1] The Jerichotes fond of change and commotion, Jos. *Ant.* 17, 10, 2; 20, 5, 1; 20, 8, 10. The distinction between them and the Jews recognized by Strabo, 16, 2, who refers to mixed races that inhabited Galilee, Jericho, Philadelphia and Samaria. He speaks here of an Egyptian-Arabian-Phœnician mixture. Dixon testifies to a striking distinctiveness even in the present inhabitants of Eriha, and speaks of people of small stature with moon-faces, mild and cheerful women. Neander (p. 467) represents Jesus as going with the common caravan.

[2] Matt. xx. 29; Luke xviii. 35; Mark x. 46. See also the parallel passage in Matt. ix. 27, with the remarkable difference of secrecy there enjoined and publicity here (Paulus).

[3] The most important difference lies in the number, and the singular charge against Matthew has become stereotyped, viz., that he doubles the number of the sick, which is in general not capable of proof, and in the incident of the Gadarenes is disposed of in his favour. And here the duality (which is nothing wonderful in itself) is resolved into unity by the later Gospels, notably by Luke, who has shaped out of the two historical figures of the sojourn in Jericho two new ones, a blind man and an unclean-clean man (Zacchæus). Mark followed Luke, but, without adopting Zacchæus, gave expression to the duality, in so far as he introduced in a certain sense two blind men, father

tion readily suggests itself that the solemn moment itself is exceptionally favourable to the introduction of a mythical narrative. We may simply fix our attention upon the necessity that Jesus, since from the time of his reaching Jericho he is the ostensible Messiah, must fulfil in a material manner the words of Isaiah, "the blind see." Or (with Origen) we may take a sublimer flight, and call in the aid of the explanation that, on his departure from Jericho, Jesus went, not directly and with a spring to the heathen, as Volkmar supposes, but to the blind and to the leaders of the blind at Jerusalem, whom he was able and wishful to make to see, as his deed shows, and whom he could make not to see until they, blind with reference to his first entry, should recognize him when he came again.[1] On these grounds, a full certainty as to this narrative is not to be attained. And in order to become still further reconciled to such a conception, it is only necessary, when following Jesus from Jericho, to think of the blind and lame in the temple at Jerusalem, whom Jesus is said to have healed; since this miraculous ministry at Jerusalem, reported by Matthew alone in untenable generality, remains

and son. Formerly help was foolishly sought (even by Neander, pp. 466 sq.) in the assumption that Jesus had healed a man both at his entry and at his departure, and that Matthew had placed the two together; Strauss, 4th ed., II. p. 56; Bleek, II. p. 284. Compare the trifling of Orig. *in Matt.* XVI. 12. Healing by contact in Matthew; by command, "Look up!" in Luke; by words of comfort, "Go, thy faith," &c., in Mark. For the rest, Matthew has, for those that can see, the simplest account; Mark the most picturesque (on the prophetic springing up, see Acts iii. 8); and here, as elsewhere, it must be permitted to Volkmar to find in this poetry the hand of a master. Volkmar's attempt to explain Luke out of Mark is quite impossible, since he is obliged to dissect the spiritually blind man of Mark first into one physically blind, and then into one who is essentially a heathen (Zacchæus). In point of fact, the heathen is not to be unearthed. Hitzig, *Zur Kritik Paulin-Briefe*, 1870, p. 9, well explains the name Timai and Bartimæus from the Syriac and Arabic (to be blind); but Buxtorf, p. 1494 (comp. Lightfoot, p. 450), gives from the Targum, *same, samia, i.e.* cæcus; thence Greek Timæos; on the other hand, Volkmar (p. 503) is inclined to think of *t(h)ame, t(h)ima* (but see Buxt. p. 882, *timmaja, impuri*)=impure (!), therefore heathen, and to read Bartimeas (according to the It. against the Codd.). Origen, *l. c.*, thinks of the Israelitish nobility (τίμιον) of the blind man; Strauss, indeed, thinks of ἐπετίμων, *New Life of Jesus*, Eng. trans., II. p. 154.

[1] Comp. Matt. xi. 5, xv. 14, xxiii. 16 sqq.; Isaiah xxxv. 5; 2 Kings vi. 15 sqq. Orig. *in Matt.* XVI. 10. Volkmar, *Rel.* p. 250 (Jews); *Ev.* p. 503 (Heathens)!

altogether unattested elsewhere.[1] But just that which is said to have occurred at Jerusalem comes in aid of what is reported at Jericho. The former is only singly, the latter trebly, represented by tradition; the former is colourless, the latter fresh and vivid; the former betrays a tendency, the latter appears to be tendenceless, in so far as the artificial location of the Messianic miracles, the miracles of healing the blind, is more appropriate to Jerusalem, or to the immediate neighbourhood of Jerusalem, than to the city of Jericho, which is a considerable distance from Jerusalem. Finally, such healings—and other credible ones are not related—themselves again explain in a new way the still swelling tide of popular enthusiasm, which lies before us as a fact.[2] So far do the grounds for the historical character of this circumstance preponderate; and notably is it storm-proof against objections in one respect, namely, that here again it becomes distinctly evident how in this enthusiastic elevation of the minds of the people—with which the impression produced by the imperial worker of miracles in Alexandria, Vespasian, cannot be compared—in this swelling and surging of the religious spirit of the nation that believed the incredible but happy time of Israel was come with the Prophet of Galilee, a confidence might be created which, according to the distinct confession of Jesus himself ("Thy faith has saved thee!"), might by its stormy impulse directly increase even the bodily vital and nervous forces, and for a time or for ever restore the diseased or lost power of the eye.[3] At any rate, this healing is by far the best attested among all the accounts of the blind in the Gospels. We have concerning such, on the one hand, only general notices, in Mat-

---

[1] Matt. xxi. 14.   [2] There only remains Matt. xix. 2 to be mentioned.

[3] For the genuineness, Ewald, p. 507; Weisse, I. p. 571, particularly, as already Schleiermacher, relying upon the name Bartimæus! On the other hand, Strauss, 4th ed., II. p. 60; *New Life of Jesus*, Eng. trans., II. p. 149. He finds the caustic eye-water of Venturini ridiculous; with Paulus he explained the miraculous healing by Vespasian (comp. above, III. pp. 195 sq.) by referring it to the deception of priests, but now he refers it to the sycophancy of the Egyptian governor (Tiber. Alex. the Renegade, who *first* recognized Vesp.). For other examples, see Paulus, *Handb.* I. p. 543. Frequency of eye diseases, see Winer, *Blindheit*.

thew during the closing Galilean period and at Jerusalem; in Luke, unhistorically, at the time of the answer of Jesus to the Baptist—"the blind see;" and, on the other hand, three further isolated narratives upon which little reliance is to be placed.[1] One is located by Matthew in Jesus' house at Capernaum, but appears to be almost entirely a dependent counterpart of the Jericho incident; the second is given by Mark in Bethsaida-Julias, shorn of the corroboration of the other sources and furnished with all the indications of a later origin, spittle-manipulations and the progressive healing of an operation, with the twilight of supernatural naturalness; the third and most exaggerated, John, the latest sources, furnishes in the Sabbath healing at Jerusalem of the man born blind, in which it is quite evident that the basis is supplied partly by the Jericho healing, partly by that at Bethsaida, both according to Mark's report, whilst the higher point of view—which as ever dominates this very free moulding of the external, material occurrence—is the spiritual blindness of the people and their leaders, removed and yet not removed by Jesus.[2]

[1] Matt. xv. 30, xxi. 14; Luke vii. 21. For details, comp. Strauss, 4th ed., II. pp. 54 sqq.

[2] (a) Matt. ix. 27 (comp. also xii. 22). (b) Mark viii. 22 sq.; above, III. pp. 156 sqq., 184, IV. p. 251. That Matthew took offence at the spittle, &c., will never be forgiven him by Volkmar. A similar rational healing-mystery also in Philostratus, *Vita Apoll.* 8, 26. (c) John ix. 1, where the man born blind and the spittle (with earth) upon the eyes, corresponds to Mark.

Division II.—THE ENTRY INTO JERUSALEM.

A.—From Jericho to Bethphage.

THE rest of the journey of Jesus, from Jericho to Jerusalem, had a strikingly different character from the preceding pilgrimage of several days. The number and the mood of those who accompanied him, of his old and new adherents, now lent to his progress the character of a festival train, and even the lips of Jesus gave utterance to no more of those announcements of disaster which he had repeated from Galilee to the neighbourhood of Jericho.

This remakable fact is very patent, and yet it also had very early become obscured. Whilst the peculiar turn things took is clearly reflected in the Gospels of Matthew and Mark, it has been by Luke, or more correctly by an earlier source of that Gospel, in a very deliberate way deranged, broken in upon, and thus in a certain measure toned down and weakened, by the introduction of traces of that earlier mood of Jesus, as if of a genuine, persistent, unwavering prediction of the actual fatal destiny. When Jesus started forth from the house of Zacchæus, he took up at once—so hastily indeed that the night's sojourn in Jericho loses all claim to credence—a parable which was to scatter and as it were destroy at the birth the prejudice of those who surrounded him, that the entry into Jerusalem was to be the prelude to the immediate appearance of the kingdom of God. But the entry itself, and afterwards the strangely repeated expectation and its correction just previous to the ascension, show that the object of the parable was far from being gained. Jesus spoke of a nobleman who went into a far country to receive a kingdom for himself. Meanwhile he committed to his ten servants ten silver pounds, ten minæ, a thousand francs, with which to trade.¹ But his fellow-citizens hated him, and sent after him an embassy deprecating his sovereignty, just as the Jews, after the sanguinary Pentecost, B.C. 4, had complained to the emperor of Rome against Archelaus, the lord of the palace at Jericho.² The absent man, however, received the regal throne, came back, reckoned with his servants, and commanded his foes, who objected to his rule, to be slain before his eyes.³ This parable very plainly told that Jesus would not at once assume his Messiahship in Jerusalem, that he would fetch his diploma from heaven, and then at his coming again he would with might, nay with violence, carry out his purpose in the nation. Thus his entry into Jerusalem was but a provisional one, the prediction of his future entry on his second advent. And the ground of this postponement was evidently not so much the necessity of divine dispensation, as the hate of the citizens, which became so strong as to lead them to rebellion against the king and to murder, and which Jesus already foresaw with certainty, and, palliating beforehand—if any are disposed to believe the words to be genuine—meant to describe as an immediate or subsequent protestation, not exactly as a deed of violence.⁴ And this precaution against a false interpretation of his entry into Jerusalem,

---

[1] Luke xix. 11 sqq. Comp. Matt. xxv. 14. The Attic mna (Roman mina) is 100 drachmas (Roman denarii). The Hebrew manäh certainly much greater = 100 shekels = 400 drachmas. At any rate, Luke thought (perhaps differently from his source) of the Greek mnai.

[2] Jos. *Ant.* 17, 10, 1 and 2 (sedition against Archelaus); 17, 11, 1 (fifty envoys sent against him to Rome); 17, 11, 4 (his installation, which nevertheless took place, first as ethnarch, by the emperor Augustus); 17, 13, 2 (complaint of the Jews against Archelaus, and his deposition by Augustus). Comp. above, I. p. 257. Similarly Meyer, Bleek, Holtzmann. Sevin has A.D. 7, instead of B.C. 4. The Archelaus picture is at any rate such, that no one can suppose Jesus himself, living so near to the time, would have selected this very unfavourable parallel. But it is in harmony with the spirit of the Ebionite source; see above, I. p. 100, note. Sevin's (p. 33) introduction of Antipas and his situation in the year 33 is unfortunate.

[3] Of the vengeance of Archelaus against those that were refractory we read nothing that is explicit; yet comp. Augustus' futile injunction to exercise mildness, Jos. *Ant.* 17, 13, 2. Also concerning the detestation of Herod the Great (*Ant.* 15, 1, 1), we are now in part more exactly informed by the *Ascension of Moses* than by Josephus.

[4] Comp. Acts ii. 36, iii. 20 sqq. This was, *after* the catastrophe, the doctrinal point of view.

an entry in itself very striking, was not the only one. This eloquent explanation at the beginning of the journey to Jerusalem was followed, according to Luke, by one yet more eloquent, indeed by an exceedingly touching utterance, in the immediate neighbourhood of Jerusalem, at the descent from the Mount of Olives, where a generation later the tenth Roman legion were to take part, by camp and entrenchment, in the work of beleaguering and destruction.[1] As Jesus beheld the city lying before him, he wept over it, as David and Jeremiah had done, and complained, like Moses of old, that she did not know in the day of her visitation what would contribute to her peace; and in words borrowed from the prophets he foretold to her as her punishment dreadful days of siege and a devastation which would leave no stone upon another.[2] His Messianic entry was therefore a renunciation of the entry; he came, in accord with his earlier prediction and yet more with the harsh fate of the following days, not as one who hoped, but as one who was resigned—nay, as the seer who recognized beforehand the significance of his entry as well as its fruitlessness, and who foresaw with certainty, to the very days and decades, his own fall, as well as the fall of the city that resisted her King.

But this picture is not historical, fine as it is. Its non-historical character is betrayed not only by the too exact description of the future and the strikingly numerous imitations of the Old Testament, but chiefly by the silence and the sayings of the other Gospels. These have no gloomy outlook, but they have an entry amid Messianic songs of jubilee. Luke himself, however, has the songs of jubilee, and he alone has the intimation

---

[1] Luke xix. 41. The tenth legion, Jos. *B. J.* 5, 2, 3. The chain of posts on the Mount of Olives, *ib.* 6, 2, 8. The investment on the Mount of Olives and at Kidron, *ib.* 5, 12, 2.

[2] The tears of David (going up the Mount of Olives), 2 Sam. xv. 30; Jeremiah xiii. 17, xiv. 17; Lament. i. 16. Moses, because Israel did not understand, Deut. xxxii. 29. The words of the prophets on the investment of the city, Isaiah xxix. 3; Micah iii. 12, v. 1; Ez. iv. 2. Visitation, ἐπισκοπή, ἐπισκέπτομαι (comp. *pakad* and *pekuddot* (ἐκδίκησις) *hair*, Ez. ix. 1), Vulg. visitatio, is here the friendly visit which gives a blessing; comp *sod Jahve* (LXX. ἐπ.), Job xxix. 4.

that Jesus expressly sanctioned them.[1] In this remarkable life it is possible to bring together many great antitheses, particularly in this last time the conflict between hope of life and gloomy apprehension of death; but it is not possible to admit that Jesus at one and the same time entered Jerusalem with the pageantry of the Messiah yet utterly dispelled the Messianic dream of his adherents, that at one and the same time he allured Jerusalem to himself, yet thrust it from him as irretrievably lost. It would be an evasion to say that he solemnly set up his Messianic claim, although and just because he knew for certain that he should not then obtain recognition. He could have done that without this entry; but with this entry he would have simply misled both the disciples and the people. Or is it thought that he sought his death in this striking way, because he found his cause was lost upon earth, or because he looked for the salvation of the world in his death? To call the thing by its right name, either of these courses would have been but a circuitous way to self-murder. Nay, this verdict would cover the whole journey from Galilee, undertaken with a certain knowledge of its futility and of death, a knowledge full and certain before any action had been taken, such a knowledge as Luke represents Jesus to have expressed from Jericho to the very gates of Jerusalem; whilst the journey is intelligible, humanly possible, a reasonable course of action, a brave deed, only if, beyond all gloomy presentiments, there stood a veiled future, an uncertainty as to what men would do, and a divine omnipotence. Finally, we are released from all solicitude as to relying upon Luke by the tangible and untrustworthy lateness of his reports. The parable above mentioned notably is at once seen to be not only a very unfortunate parallel between Jesus and the detested and abominable Archelaus, but also a later, according to other indications a systematic and violently artificial, construction on the basis of an earlier speech by Jesus; and the prophecy concerning Jerusalem too plainly betrays the late author who transferred his own detailed know-

---

[1] Luke xix. 37 sqq.

ledge of the fall of Jerusalem to Jesus, in the exact description of the palisade works of the Romans, the circle of investment, the ruins in which both city and people found a grave.[1]

But, if Luke be given up, how are we to explain the change in the mood of Jesus, and particularly his approach and entry at the head of masses of the people? Was it not the Baptist who corporeally in the person of Jesus had re-appeared in the plain of Jericho with the restless multitudes that were ready for anything and *now* were actually on the march?[2] In this last particular, we shall not miss the truth if we determinedly assume that Jesus did not intentionally collect the people, and that he did not place his reliance or make his Messianism dependent upon either the moral influence or the physical force of the multitudes.[3] Though it is correct that he, at his entry into Jerusalem, changed his system, that he was unreservedly candid in his confession and his actions, that he resolutely took the name of the Baptist upon his lips and unconditionally recognized him as his forerunner, the idea is nevertheless not warranted that he had thereby declined from himself, and, in impatience, passion, or indeed despondency—as Renan finds it possible—or, somewhat more mildly expressed, in compliance with the pressure of old and new adherents, had fallen back upon the lines of the Johannine popular movement. His change of system by no means consisted of a transition from a spiritual to a politico-physical movement, but is to be found only in the openness of his Messianic confession, which he had hitherto kept in the background, and in a momentary Messianic activity in purifying the temple. And his quiet departure from Galilee, as well as his quiet teaching-ministry at Jerusalem afterwards, must prove that he remained true to himself in his cardinal point, and that he did not attempt to gain his end by placing himself at the head of a large body of the people.[4] And though

---

[1] Archelaus, see above, p. 66, note 2. Destruction of Jerusalem, see on Matt. xxiv. On the relation of Luke to Matt. xxv. 14 sq., see the concluding utterances at Bethany.

[2] Above, II. p. 258.   [3] Matt. xix. 2, 21, xx. 34?

[4] Comp. Renan. Weizs. (p. 545) spoke of a yielding to the disciples and the people at the entry into Jerusalem; comp. my *Gesch. Chr.* p. 93. Equally strong is the assertion that Jesus went to Jerusalem at the Feast of Tabernacles without apostles

he nevertheless entered the city, not quietly, but at the head of a multitude of the people, it must first of all be remembered that even in Galilee he did not drive away from him the people who wished to accompany him, however modest an estimate he might put upon the fickle favour of the crowd and their ephemeral attachment to him. Now, however, he was the less disposed to drive the people away, because he was joyfully surprised by the unexpected popular sympathy, which he took to be a gift from God, and was thereby inwardly strengthened in the midst of his difficult and anxious undertaking amongst strangers. Another reason is to be found in the fact that the public character which he intentionally gave to his ministry at Jerusalem, was powerfully supported by the following of adherents who believed him to be the Messiah, though he did not think of making this following an army and rampart for himself.[1] It is evident that change in the temper of Jesus is to be spoken of only in the sense that his dominant gloomy presentiment was at times relieved by freer breathings, when he, who referred everything to God, felt his soul lit up as by a sunbeam, by the possibility that it might yet be the will of his Father, who with a strong hand and a gracious hint gave him the people, to bring over to him the whole nation, and, without the cup of sorrow, mightily and gloriously to set up the longed-for kingdom of heaven as a celestial wedding gift.

Thus on the morning of the 8th of April, on the arrival-day of the guests of the Jewish Easter festival—a day elsewhere named and in the fourth Gospel confirmed—Jesus with his accompanying crowds set out from Jericho and came to the glittering sun-lit wall of hills which bounded Jericho in the direction of Jerusalem.[2] These bald and broken heights on the

and quite alone preaching the word; that not until the journey to Bethany (Lazarus) did the disciples again join him, and then indeed in order to impel him onwards against his will (Weizs. pp. 517, 527).

[1] We may here recall the mode of representation of the fourth Gospel: All that the Father *gives* me, *comes* to me, vi. 37, &c.

[2] Jos. *B. J.* 6, 5, 3: $\dot{a}\theta\rho o\iota\zeta o\mu.$ τ. λαοῦ πρὸς τ. τ. ἀζύμων ἑορτὴν, ὀγδόη δ᾽ ἦν Ξανθικοῦ μηνός. 8th Nisan and 8th April coincided in the year A.D. 35. Comp. John xii. 1.

west were the refuge of the Jerichotes in war; and they still separated Jesus from his theatre of war, but he scaled them with the courage of the conqueror who sought the stronghold of the foe and of the people of God.[1] The journey of about seven leagues to Jerusalem was a toilsome one, and if the saying of the Greek geographer Strabo, that the bare rocky region round Jerusalem was not "worth coveting," and was therefore left in the hands of the Jews without a struggle, held good anywhere, it was here in particular.[2] The slightly rising road at first followed the moderately easy course which the Wady Kelt cut through the midst of the abrupt fortress-crowned hills of Jericho. A short league takes one from the smiling plain to the inhospitable hills; the road then leaves the Wady Kelt and its western sources to force access to Jerusalem in a south-westerly direction over the side and partly over the summit of the hilly range. The way leads on in the midst of a wild and dreadful solitude, growing steeper and narrower, a veritable rocky pass, with rocky walls right and left and rough stones scattered confusedly under foot.[3] This was the district where the wanderer between Jerusalem and Jericho was most helplessly exposed to the attacks of robbers and murderers; and if the priest and the Levite of the Gospel parable here passed by the bleeding victim upon whom the Samaritan was the first to have mercy, verily it was the extreme of hardheartedness which could come upon a neighbour without condescending to touch him with a friendly and skilful hand.[4] After about two leagues, the worst would be got over. At nearly half-way, one might rest at the inn of the parable, to which the Samaritan brought his charge; and at present there stand right and left of the road in this district the remains of former inns, Khan Chadhur.[5] The way then struck

[1] Comp. Jos. *Ant.* 14, 15, 3; *B. J.* 4, 8, 2: ὀρεινὴ ἀντικρὺς Ἱερ. Jerusalem 3000 feet higher than the Jordan valley. Furrer, *Jericho* in *Bibel-Lexikon*.
[2] The distance, see above, II. p. 234. Strabo, 16, 2.
[3] Jos. *B. J.* 4, 8, 3 (above, II. p. 235, note 2). Furrer, *Wand.* pp. 145 sqq.
[4] Luke x. 30.
[5] Khan Hadhur (Furrer, Chadhrur), according to Kiepert and Van de Velde, to the right of the road; a khan immediately upon the road, left, a little further on.

again among the highlands, for the most part in the narrow valley of Wady-el-Hodh, shut in by high desert hills covered with loose stones and thorn-bushes. Finally, after going two or three more toilsome leagues up and down, it reaches the villages of Bethany and Bethphage, charmingly hidden among mountains and hills, trees and corn-fields, not far from the melancholy, rugged, lava-like wilderness. Thence, after a short and pleasant journey of three quarters of a league, the traveller is in Jerusalem.[1]

B.—THE JOHANNINE CHRIST AT BETHANY.

At Bethany the career of the Johannine Christ at last joins the common course of the Gospels, to which Luke on his part has already at Jericho returned. This career of the Johannine Christ certainly lies infinitely wide of the well-beaten path of this life so well known to us; and the impression of this difference of character, of this strangeness, of this reversed world, remains even after the ways seem to coincide at Bethany. At this point of junction we must not fail to take at least a slight retrospect of the Johannine path. We cannot, in fact, do more than this, if we would avoid retarding the course of the actual history of Jesus at this moment of highest and intensest interest, and coming again into contact with questions the solution of which has been already attempted in the Introduction, and the detailed examination of which later will belong, not to the life of Jesus, but simply to the illustration of this book.

That, according to this Gospel, Jesus was thrice in Galilee and thrice at Jerusalem, is as well known as is the decisive preponderance which the mission in Jerusalem and Judæa—in truth, according to this source, the first and last task of the life of Jesus —constantly usurps.[2] When we review this Judæan activity,

---

[1] Matt. xxi. 1, and parallel passages. Furrer, *l.c.* Plitt, *Skizzen aus einer Reise in's h. Land*, p. 56. More in detail below.

[2] Above, I. pp. 157, 168, 177, III. p. 134. *Gesch. Chr.* p. 19.

we find that, if we will and can strictly and accurately reckon, the first year of Jesus, after the appearance of John in the wilderness, and after the brief Galilean Cana-excursion at Easter, is devoted to Jerusalem and the country of Judæa until December or January.[1] The new visit to Samaria and Galilee is followed first by the briefer ministry at the Purim festival, four weeks before Easter; next, after a forced last sojourn of six months in Galilee, comes the ministry of three months at Jerusalem, from the Feast of Tabernacles to that of the Dedication of the Temple, from harvest until winter.[2] It is simply the Judæan persecution which compels Jesus to seek asylum. He goes in mid-winter, in December, over the Jordan to Peræa, the old baptizing place of John; and on account of the fresh offence which he gives in

[1] Easter, John ii. 13, 23; December, January, iv. 35. Comp. above on the Samaritan journey.

[2] Samaria, Galilee, in winter, John iv. 1, 35. Purim festival, xiv. xv. Adar (Esther ix. 21) exactly four weeks before Easter, v. 1. Expositors, from the Church Fathers downward, strongly support the assumption of an Easter festival here, while a minority also speak of the Feast of Tabernacles or the Feast of Atonement (Caspari, p. 112), or indeed of the Dedication of the Temple. The chronologists, in particular Kepler, Anger, Wies., but also Hug, Meyer, Mai, and others, uphold Purim, which is the most appropriate if we can only rely upon the author giving a connected representation and preserving a chronological exactness, so far as winter appears in iv. 35, Easter in vi. 4, while v. 1 lies between the two. We can, however, place no great reliance upon this, because the author does not attach much importance to externals, for he does not give a detailed description of the feast in v. 1; because, further, iv. 1, 2, 6, 7, do not harmonize with winter, the passage, iv. 35, on which the chronological argument is based, was not written with any chronological motive; and finally because in vi. 1 (4) the Galilean activity just before Easter is so abruptly joined on to the activity at Jerusalem, that the loss of a section has already been surmised. The six months' Galilean activity, vi. 1, 4, to vii. 2. New activity at Jerusalem, vii. 2, to x. 22, 39 sq. The Dedication of the Temple from 25th Kislev [Chisleu] (middle of December), in commemoration of the purifying after the desecration by the Syrians. Jesus' activity at Jerusalem gives us occasion to take exception to Weizsäcker's twofold representation, (1) that Jesus was alone from the Feast of Tabernacles until the death of Lazarus (contrary to John ix. 1, &c.), (2) that he was at Jerusalem only at intervals (*e.g.* afresh at the Festival of the Dedication) (pp. 512, 515), while John represents him as abiding at Jerusalem. The point of these subjective representations, however, is the assertion that, on account of the resultlessness of Jesus' activity at Jerusalem, and on account of its broken character, there was constructed in the Synoptical Gospels the schematism which made Jesus work in *Galilee* and end in Jerusalem, without distinguishing the different periods of his stay in the latter place (p. 513). A restoration of Gabler's favourite Galilee hypothesis (Strauss, 4th ed. II. p. 157), after the manner of Neander (p. 487), Ewald (p. 522), and others.

Bethany before Easter by the resurrection of Lazarus, he flees out of the neighbourhood of Jerusalem three or four leagues northward to the hill town Ephraim, and there remains until six days before Easter, when he re-appears in Bethany preparatory to making a public visit to the festival at Jerusalem.[1] Of the more than two years of his total ministrations, he thus devotes at least one whole year to Jerusalem and Judæa, scarcely more than half a year, and that on compulsion, to his native Galilee.[2]

Jesus' ministry at Jerusalem was certainly, on the whole, in every way unfruitful. If we credit this account, Jesus did not to any extent stoop to the poor people, as the earlier Gospels would lead us to suppose. He violently lifted them to himself in order by that means totally and completely to cast them from him. Hence at the very beginning the putting to shame of Nicodemus, the best among the people; hence the endless, colourless, notional addresses; hence the animosities and the scornings directed against the prevalent belief, tolerated only as prophetic of a better one; hence the rejection of the people and of the men "from beneath," and, on the other hand, the exclusive, wearisome, and defiant self-glorification, from the first Easter to the famous utterance at the Feast of the Dedication: "I and the Father are one."[3] No wonder that, under such circumstances, the ministry of Jesus, despite the divine Sonship, ended in utter failure. His first Easter at Jerusalem is still the richest in hope; many come to the faith although he himself gives his faith to no one, and his baptizing place in Judæa, which he thereupon opens, is so numerously visited, that disciples of John and Pharisees become jealous, and Jesus goes to Galilee to get out of the way of the Pharisees.[4] Then the Feast before the second Easter, according to all appearance the Purim Feast, lays the perma-

---

[1] John x. 40, xi. 1, 6 sq., 17, 54 sq., xii. 1.

[2] The compulsion, particularly in iv. 1 sqq. But also compare vi. 1 with v. 16, vii. 19—25.

[3] John iii. 1 sqq. Animosity against the belief, v. 37, 39, 45, viii. 17, x. 7, &c. Rejection, ii. 23, vi. 26 sqq., viii. 19, 23, 37 sqq. Oneness with the Father, x. 30.

[4] John ii. 23 sq., iv. 1—3.

THE JOHANNINE CHRIST AT BETHANY. 75

nent foundation of enmity and of plotting to compass his death, because on the Sabbath he heals the sick man at the pool of Bethzatha, and declares himself to be the active Son of the incessantly active Father.[1] On account of those plots he remains from Easter till the Feast of Tabernacles in Galilee. At the latter Feast, the people expect him with longing in the Holy City; at last he comes, delivers his longest addresses, but—just as previously in Galilee—he now, by the reproach of terrestrial, nay of diabolical, sonship, and by claiming to be older than Abraham, forces even the willing and thoughtful hearers, even those who had begun to believe, including servants of the Pharisees, into unbelief, indeed to repeated and furious attempts to slay him, from which he escapes, either because the influence of his presence, and God who appoints the times, keep back their hands, or because he conceals himself in some mysterious manner.[2] Three months later, the Feast of the Dedication brings the last resolve. His situation has grown worse, for immediately after the Feast of Tabernacles the excommunication of the believers in the Messiah had been determined upon; even this menace does not prevent the Jews from wishing him to make a direct confession of his Messiahship.[3] He makes that confession: "I and the Father are one." Then they take up stones afresh, seek to lay hold of him, but he, escaping from them, withdraws into Peræa.[4] There is now wanting nothing but the formal and

[1] John v. 1 sqq., 16, 18 (above, III. pp. 215 sq.); comp. vii. 19—25, viii. 40.

[2] Expectation, John vii. 11—13. Belief, vii. 31, 40, 45 sqq., viii. 31. Reproaches, particularly viii. 23, 37 sqq. Older than Abraham, viii. 58. Attacks, vii. 30, 32, 44 sqq., viii. 20, 59.

[3] John ix. 22 (xii. 42), x. 24. This representation is presupposed by Celsus, Origen, *Con. C.* 2, 9. The ban (Heb. cherem, Rabb. niddui, Greek ἀφορισμὸς, ἀνάθεμα, comp. Ezra x. 8; 1 Cor. v. 5, 11, xvi. 22; Rom. ix. 3; Matt. xviii. 17; John xvi. 2; also Buxt., Lightfoot, &c.) is believed by Weisse, I. p. 435, Ewald, p. 452, though the Synoptics show no trace of it, and the public appearance of Jesus in Galilee and at Jerusalem, even in John, refutes the assumption. A poor support of the reality of the ban is the Jewish source, according to which Joshua ben Perachiah, the teacher of Jesus, excommunicated him in the midst of the blowing of 400 rams' horns; comp. above, I. p. 22. Delitzsch, *Hillel*, p. 14.

[4] John x. 24, 31, 39.

solemn determination to put him to death. Jesus brings this on by his arrival at Bethany and by his raising of Lazarus, which he does at the entreaty of the sisters Mary and Martha. The Pharisees are at once informed of the matter, a meeting of the Sanhedrim is held, and in harmony with the advice of the high-priest Caiaphas it is resolved to put him to death. It is also made the duty of every one to denounce him; and soon after, when Jesus, who in the mean time had fled to Ephraim, comes again to Bethany, and the sensation caused by the miracle is revived, the death of Lazarus also is determined upon.[1]

It will be thought cruel and violent when we determinedly reject the whole of this extensive enrichment of the life of Jesus by the Johannine account. This enrichment is no history, but the destruction of history. These journeys, these deeds and miracles, these addresses, these murderous attacks, are unhistorical. We ask for no accumulation of evidence if a clear conviction can be arrived at by a few indications. These eternal wanderings about the country distort the carefully-planned ministry of Jesus into the superficiality—the reader must pardon the expression—of an adventurous and restless spirit. To take one example: in December Jesus is in Judæa, in January in Galilee, in March at Jerusalem, in April in Galilee. This systematic interchange between Judæa, Samaria, and Galilee, is simply the work of the author; and even Peræa and Ephraim, at the close, do not rest upon any better tradition. If Jerusalem was lost, an asylum must be found; Matthew and Mark had recourse to that Peræa through which lay the route of Jesus' actual festival journey; Luke appeared to open the route from Samaria to Jerusalem, in the midst of which—certainly rather too near to Jerusalem—the little town of Ephraim was to be discovered.[2] We have learnt to regard the deeds and miracles as arbitrary transformations of the Galilean miracles; and the purification of the temple at the

[1] John xi. 47 sqq., 57, xii. 10. Thus also Ewald, p. 512. On the calling together of the Sanhedrim by Caiaphas, more in detail further on.

[2] Since this Ephraim could afford no protection on account of its proximity, Caspari (p. 158) places it in the north.

first Easter is rendered ridiculous by the synoptic report which exhibits it at the last Easter. The addresses of Jesus are impossibilities, even when rich in intellectual vigour. It is only the author, not Jesus, who can aim at destroying his own work by contempt of men, of the law, and by inflexible arrogant dogmatism, and at compelling the belief, which must in a comfortless manner again and again reveal itself as a gross belief in miracle or as a cowardly servile faith of fear, to resolve itself into unbelief. That the murderous attacks are monstrosities will appear when it is remembered that they are said to have been continued more than a year without any result, that Jesus escaped most mysteriously half-a-dozen times and more, and that he always re-appeared upon the scene as boldly as if nothing had happened.[1] If in the winter of the first year he passed completely out of the sight of the Pharisees, how could he in March be again at the feast at Jerusalem? If, after this Purim festival, he again withdrew to Galilee under the conviction that his opponents restlessly cherished murderous plans against him, how could he at the next Feast of Tabernacles be working more publicly than ever at Jerusalem? If, at the Feast of Tabernacles, attempts to apprehend him were made again and again, how could he maintain his position for a whole quarter of a year, from the Feast of Tabernacles until that of the Dedication of the Temple? If he was condemned at the Feast of the Dedication, how was it possible for him to come again first from Peræa and then from Ephraim, and at last, in spite of the sentences of death against him and Lazarus, to make a pompous entry into Jerusalem from Bethany? After all, this last entry might be the most intelligible, since, according to the Johannine report, Jesus was resolved to go to meet his death, as indeed in Luke he went to

---

[1] His escapes, (*a*) John vii. 30, (*b*) vii. 44, (*c*) viii. 20, (*d*) viii. 59, (*e*) x. 31, (*f*) x. 39. Comp. also v. 16, 18, vii. 45, xi. 54, 57, xii. 36. The best explanation of these incomprehensible escapes is given, in spite of the Johannine Antignosis, by the Gnosis, particularly by Basilidianism : transfiguratum quemadmodum vellet sic ascendisse ad eum, qui miserat eum, deridentem eos, quum teneri non posset et invisibilis esset omnibus. Irenæus, 1, 24, 4.

his death with the clearest consciousness of what awaited him.¹ But we have already found, against Luke, that such an entry was impossible. In John the impossibility is doubled, trebled. Here, Jesus goes in not merely in expectation of death, but with an exact knowledge of the state of things, of the accumulated sentences of the authorities against himself, against Lazarus, against his adherents, he nevertheless persists in entering, though it was unnecessary for him to bear fresh testimony. Truly, after the conclusion of the preaching at Jerusalem and after the preceding journeys of flight, this direct and conscious seeking his own fall is quite unintelligible on the part of Jesus, who could neither seek death nor—as the most reliable evidence shows—could connect with it the salvation of the world; but it is perfectly intelligible on the part of the author, who did not shrink from the idea that Jesus with deliberate intention prepared a sacrifice which actually appeared to the times that followed as the single fruit of this Messianic journey.²

Moreover, how could he, as John says, have made a pompous entry into Jerusalem, even if we put out of sight the definitive resolves of his opponents, as well as the completion of his testimony, which is characteristically mirrored in the fact that Jesus here, after his entry—in striking distinction from the account of the Synoptics—no longer in effect works among the people from whom he at once hides himself again, but preferably among the Hellenes to whom he explains the fruit of his death, in the main, however, only in the intimate circle of his disciples, —how could he have made a pompous entry, when, after the frequent private earlier entries, a pompous one at this time, particularly after his breach with the people, had been in no wise indicated?³ The author has brought a new event to the

---

¹ John xi. 8, 16, xii. 24. On the Synoptics generally, see above, IV. pp. 272 sqq.

² See above, p. 67. Schleiermacher (p. 387) says that Jesus could not take steps to procure his death. Schenkel (p. 223) says that the character of Jesus is injured by the Johannine representation.

³ Ministry of Jesus, John xii. 20—36, so that Jesus immediately after his entry *hid himself* (verse 36), wherefore the additional short address (verses 44—50) is an

relief of this difficulty.[1] The resurrection of Lazarus must give renewed life to a history that in truth has in all its parts reached its end; it must at the same time explain the fresh resolves of Jesus' opponents to put him to death, as well as the fresh sympathy of the people and the extraordinary ovation they accorded to him at his entry into the city. While Jesus tarried in his first asylum, the Peræan Bethany, there came a messenger from the friendly house of Lazarus in the Judæan Bethany near Jerusalem, a messenger sent by the sisters Martha and Mary to announce the illness of their brother, the friend of Jesus.[2] Jesus delayed going, not from indifference, but with the view of using the illness, nay the death, of Lazarus as a means to a higher end. "This illness," he said, "is not unto death, but for the glory of God, in order that the Son of Man may thereby be glori-

impossibility, in truth only the reflection of the Evangelist continued in a pretended utterance of Jesus. The principal speech is addressed to the Hellenes (verse 23). Then come merely addresses to the disciples, xiii.—xvii. Bunsen is correct in *L. J.* p. 396. Gess is sophistical (retreat merely for *this* day), p. 125.

[1] Comp. Baur, *Kanon. Ev.* pp. 190, 283 sqq. Strauss, *New Life of Jesus*, Eng. trans., I. p. 344.

[2] John x. 40, xi. 1. The name of the place, Bethany of Peræa, is not repeated, but it is the same locality as in i. 28. On this Peræan Bethany (Origen upon John, ed. Lomm. I. p. 238 : Bethabara; hence also Chrys., Epiph.), see above, II. p. 232. Caspari (p. 79) has foolishly placed it in the Gaulonitis, north-east of Capernaum at et-Tell (Bethsaida-Julias, in Seetzen Tellanijeh), and has taken this to be identical with Betanijeh. From this he would explain how Jesus could reach Cana in one day (ii. 1), and would indeed explain the journey also in xi. 1 sqq.! I am totally unable, consistently with what I have said in Vol. II. p. 232, as well on the ground of the fact that John led men out of the towns and villages, to believe in the—already doubted by Baur—historical character of the sojourn of John and Jesus in the village of Bethany in Peræa. According to Origen, *l. c.*, this village has never existed, on which account, as is plain from Origen, Bethabara (in the fourth century, Eus., Jerome, *Onom.* 109, and perhaps as early as Origen's time, a renowned baptizing place) was substituted for it. It is quite possible that the fourth Evangelist found in the word Bethany (see below, p. 90) the certainly incorrect meaning, *house of mourning* (anijah, Greek ἀνία, domus afflictionis, Jerome), and thought this appropriate for the place of repentance, and also for the place of Lazarus' death,—whence, moreover, the striking transition from the one Bethany to the other. Also Wichelhaus, *Leidensgeschichte*, p. 69, and Furrer's article, *Bethanien* : house of poverty. The Peræan Bethany cannot well be derived from onijah = ship house (Bethabara = ford house), thus Possin, Winer, Lange, Furrer. Then it would be called Bethony, and we should have—with Furrer—to find a fresh derivation for the Judæan Bethany. Origen, *l. c.*, makes Bethab. = οἶκ. κατασκευῆς (Joh.), Bethany = ο. ὑπακοῆς. On the name Lazarus, see below, p. 86.

fied." He therefore remained quietly at the same place for two days. Not until the third day did he announce to his disciples that he was going to Judæa.[1] They reminded him anxiously of the attempt to stone him; he reminded them of the twelve hours of the day, and of the privilege of him who walks by day over him who walks by night, viz., that he neither stumbles nor falls. Then he spoke openly, "Lazarus, our friend, has fallen asleep, but I go that I may awake him,"—an utterance which his disciples as usual childishly and more than childishly misunderstood, until he spoke out literally, when Thomas, the melancholy realist, appealed to the others and said, "Then will we also go and die with him!"

When they reached Bethany, Lazarus had already been in the grave four days.[2] Apparently the narrator has fixed the date of death on the day when the report of the illness was sent, and has reckoned two days for the delay of Jesus, and two days for his journey; otherwise we must suppose death to have occurred on the day of Jesus' mention of it and of the commencement of the journey, and reckon four—far too long a time—for the journey itself.[3] However that may be, before Jesus reached Bethany, the "House of Mourning," Martha, who had, we know not how, been informed of his approach, came to meet him, complained, exhibited first only a half belief and then unbelief, until finally she learned to have faith in the Son of God who called himself the Resurrection and the Life. She then hastened, in the name of Jesus, but in reality at the prompting of her own heart, to call Mary, who appeared before Jesus with a whole company of condoling visitors from Jerusalem, and fell at his feet, complaining, weeping, without faith and without hope:

[1] John xi. 4—7.   [2] John xi. 8—17.
[3] The former assumption also in De Wette, Neander, Tholuck, Ebr., Lange, Licht., Luther. The other in Bengel, Paulus, Ewald, Meyer; comp. above, II. p. 232. Starting from the district of Jericho, from Bethany to Jericho would be from two to three leagues; from Jericho to the Judæan Bethany, six leagues. Van de Velde, *Reise*, II. p. 245, also fixes the distance at about ten leagues. That could be travelled in from one to two days. The objections of Meyer—who on his part reduces the four at least to three days—to the above explanation have no force.

THE JOHANNINE CHRIST AT BETHANY.

"Lord, if thou hadst been here, my brother had not died!" Every one wept; Jesus was staggered by the doubt and by the facts, and was moved to anger.[1] "Where have ye laid him?" Jesus was conducted to the grave, outside of the village, near the place where Martha had met him.[2] He then wept himself. Among the Jews the emotion caused by his tears was tempered with dissatisfaction because he was not there before Lazarus died. Afresh provoked, Jesus went to the stone-closed sepulchre. "Move away the stone!" Martha said to him: "Lord, he stinks already, for he has been dead four days." This fact, which was discouraging in quite a different way from the Job's message from the house of Jairus, would change the most firmly established belief into unbelief.[3] "Did I not say unto thee," replied Jesus, "that if thou believest, thou shalt behold the glory of God?" Then the stone was taken away. Jesus, looking up to heaven, thanked the Father that he heard him. He was always certain, he said, that the Father heard him, but because of the people he thanked and appealed to the Father, in order that they might believe in his own divine mission. Thereupon he cried with a loud voice, "Lazarus, come forth!" and the dead man came forth, bound, hands and feet and head, with graveclothes.[4] Jesus caused him to be unbound, and sent him home.

---

[1] ἐμβριμ. (xi. 33, 38), out of Mark i. 43, xiv. 5 (Matt. ix. 30). The angry feeling (not groaning, Tholuck; sighing, Ewald) is occasioned, partly by the unbelief (see verses 33, 37), partly by the mournful fact (verse 35). Hilgenfeld, *Ev. Joh.* p. 259, and *Ev.* p. 296, is quite incorrect in saying that Jesus is angry with himself on account of his human emotion.

[2] *Gloss. Kidd.* 80, 2: cœmet. non erant prope urbem. *Massech. Semac.* 8: prodeunt ad sepulcra atque invisunt mortuos tribus diebus (with reference to an apparent death). Lightfoot, pp. 514, 649.

[3] Critics are so much addicted to rationalism, that not only Paulus (*L. J.* I. ii. p. 60), the upholder of an apparent death, speaks of the absence of smell; but also Flatt, Olsh., Hase, Krabbe, Meyer, Strauss, speak of a mere conclusion of Martha's; and Steinmeyer (p. 201), with Schleier. (p. 233), of a mere preconceived notion.

[4] Schleier. (p. 233) remarks, in connection with the prayer here mentioned, that Jesus was not concerned in the miracle, since not he, but God, was acting, and Jesus only asked with firm conviction; whereby Schleier. naturally wishes to establish an accommodated view, preferably an apparent death. Neander (p. 462) rejects this help. On the binding, Irenæus, 5, 13, 1: symbolum hominis illigati in peccatis.

The astonishment was immense, and faith returned. The next results were the determination arrived at by the Pharisees to put Jesus to death, and the streaming forth of the people of Jerusalem to Bethany, as soon as the wonder-worker returned once more from his temporary retreat at Ephraim, and for the last time entered Bethany and reclined at table with Lazarus the dead-living.[1]

This narrative is impressive and fine, particularly to those who can believe not merely the letter of it, but the essential nucleus, Christ the prince of life for the living and the dead. The miracle wrought upon Lazarus is without doubt the most effective among all Jesus' miracles, and the greatest of all his recorded raisings from the dead.[2] At the very first glance it is seen that the work is a mightier one at the sepulchre than in the chamber of death or at the bier, on the fourth day than on the first; and the advances made upon the earlier instances are tangible. Looked at more closely, we find there is here not only a bringing back of the scarcely extinct life, but the subjugation of death which had already been at work with all the horrors of decay, the subjugation indeed, one might say, of Paradise into which the soul had already entered as a guest.[3] This masterpiece of miracle, therefore, at which Paulus and Venturini tried their hands poorly with trance and life-balsam, and Renan with juggling arts; in the face of which even Pliny the Elder was compelled to withdraw his bitter taunt of the impotence of the

---

[1] John xi. 19—53, xii. 9—11. According to Epiph. 66, 34, Lazarus was thirty years old and lived thirty more, Hofm. *L. J.* p. 357. According to Bunsen (p. 390), he died soon.

[2] Steinmeyer writes zealously (p. 204) against the climax, the superlative character of the miracle (Baur, *Theol. Jahr.* 1844, p. 408, and Strauss, 4th ed. p. 143). But Irenæus, 5, 13, 1, already has the same progressive order, (1) Jair, (2) Nain, (3) Lazarus.

[3] This last objection (comp. Luke xvi. 22, xxiii. 43) has already troubled many. It is true that, according to the popular belief even of the Jews, anima per triduum circumvolat animo revertendi; post hæc conspiciens immutatum vultum, avolat. *Hier. Moed. Kat.* 82, 2; in Lightfoot, pp. 43, 649. Krabbe (p. 344), following Schubert and Fichte, assumes something similar, a gradual setting free of the soul, bringing in for Lazarus the kingdom of God. Fancies of the ancients about the delivery of Lazarus from Hades, Hofm. p. 444 (comp. Rev. xx. 13; Gospel of Nicodemus, ii.).

gods, or with Pilate (in the pretended report to the emperor Tiberius) to recognize the weakness of the heathen gods against the God of the Christians; in the presence of which, finally, Spinoza was willing—in the event of finding proof—to throw up his system and to become a convert to the ordinary Christian faith, —this miracle is in every point admirably calculated to form a brilliant close to the career of Jesus.[1] To sober exposition it is, however, altogether untenable. The earlier Gospels, the faithful narrators of the life of Jesus, the exclusively faithful and copious narrators of his festival journey, know—notwithstanding the vigorous assurances of Meyer—not a syllable about this miracle and the decisive movement which it called forth. Not only do they not know of it, they disprove it, for they write of the festive meal at Bethany without giving the slightest thought to the man of the miracle, Lazarus. To them the crisis of Jesus' destiny is brought about by very different and much more convincing occurrences.[2] These Evangelists know nothing of a

[1] Paulus, II. p. 60; Venturini, III. pp. 310 sqq.; Ammon, II. p. 112; Renan, 15th ed. pp. 372 sqq. According to Paulus, Jesus took the condition of Lazarus to be merely that of trance (as in the Jairus case). A transition to the jugglery of Renan— who represents Jesus as descending from his position of moral purity when the situation led him to despair, and Lazarus, who was perhaps irrecoverably ill, as helping Jesus to a public spectacle (justly disapproved by Hase, Steinmeyer, less severely by Strauss)—is afforded by Paulus and Venturini, in so far as the former represents Jesus as seeing, at the first glance, the movements of the man who it is pretended is dead, and the latter introduces balsam and salve by which the colour is brought again to Lazarus' cheeks; then prayer and the cry to awake! The hypothesis of apparent death—the admissibility of which (comp. above, IV. pp. 169 sqq.) even Krabbe (p. 338) does not absolutely deny, holding the view of a merely deadly illness with subsequent glorification—in one way or another supported by Schleierm. p. 233; Schweizer, p. 156; Hase, p. 204; Ewald, p. 483; Weizs. p. 528; Bunsen, p. 390. Criticism on these views (referred to by Steinm. p. 198), in Strauss, 4th ed. II. pp. 132 sqq., *New Life of Jesus*, Eng. trans., II. pp. 231 sqq. Pliny, *H. Nat.* 2, 5; Pilat. ad Tib., *Anaph.* A. 1. Spinoza, see Bayle, *Spinoze;* comp. Krabbe, p. 333.

[2] In order to explain the silence of the Synoptics—whom Schneck. *Urspr. d.* 1. *Ev.* p. 10, disparages as not being apostles—it has sometimes been assumed that they passed over the fact out of regard for the safety or the feelings of the family at Bethany (thus, after Epiph., Grot., Wetst., Herder, also Lange, III. p. 1132; comp. Press. p. 536), and on that account spoke (Lange) of Mary herself as only "a woman" (Matthew xxvi. 7), as if men writing in A. D. 70—100 and later would still be influenced by such considerations. Sometimes, again, it has been assumed that the writers were influenced by the Galilean standpoint (Gabler, Neander, Krabbe, Ewald, Press.),

sojourn of Jesus in Peræa, or of his dwelling at Bethany in the house of Lazarus and his sisters; on the other hand, they locate him in the house of Simon the leper, out of whom it was reserved for Ewald to create the deceased father of the brother and sisters. Nor do they know that the woman whom Jesus anointed in that house was the mistress of the house, an intimate, and no other than Mary herself.[1] If this objection afforded by the old Evangelists does not suffice, nor the significant trifling with two Bethanies, which recalls so many other artifices of this book, then let us, without taking alarm at the miraculous, examine this Johannine miracle. There can be no one who does not feel very unpleasantly astonished at a whole series of features in this narrative. Can Jesus have sought in such a way an opportunity of working a great miracle, viz., by intentionally waiting, without one serious hindrance—to which it is customary to make such a precarious appeal—until Lazarus was dead, and until he had reached the required stage of stinking?[2] Can he have so restrained his natural sympathy or so neglected the duty of friendship as coldly to sacrifice the interest of his friends to his

or they had defective knowledge of the true pragmatism in the fall of Jesus (Schleierm., Lücke, Hase), to which also the early death of Lazarus contributed (Bunsen, p. 390). Sometimes, still more unfortunately, it has been assumed that, notwithstanding their doubtless increasing knowledge of the miracle, they imposed upon themselves the limitation to narrate nothing beyond their *schema*, the passion week (Meyer). It is much better, with Brückner, to speak simply of an inexplicability, unless one prefers, with Steinm. p. 203, to see in this miracle nothing special. Many apologists, moreover, think that without this incident the key of the history would be lost (Gess, p. 120), everything would be inexplicable—the enthusiasm, the hatred, and the resolve to put Jesus to death (Press. p. 537; comp. Schleierm. and Lücke), and even the ecstatic anointing, together with the remnant of ointment which had been saved from Lazarus (Lange)!

[1] Matt. xxvi. 6; Mark xiv. 3. Ewald, pp. 481, 510. Similarly already, Nic., Theophyl., in Wichelh. p. 69. According to Paulus, Martha was the widow of Simon!

[2] Hindered by successful ministry in Peræa, Neander, Lücke, Tholuck, and others. On the other hand, Meyer thinks well to talk of a knowledge of a divine appointment that it should happen just so and not otherwise; Steinmeyer, of obedience to God. Ewald speaks of suspicion of treachery. Relatively best is Olshausen's explanation that Jesus wished to give those at Bethany an opportunity of exercising faith. Objection to this delay by all the representatives of criticism, Bretschn., Gfrör., Strauss, Baur, Weisse, Hilg., and others.

own? Can he have regarded the death-need of his friend, the sorrow of the sisters, as a means of glorifying the Son of Man, with the view of *afterwards* dedicating to the misfortune which he had helped to bring about, his unnatural tears and his anger? Can he have declared to God that he could have dispensed with thanks for being heard, because he was always certain of it, and that he had made use of the words of prayer to God merely as a means to a very different end, only in order to convince the people of his own divine mission?[1] In fact, an over-wrought stilted narrative and a Christology that is unnaturally distorted and that visibly confounds man with God in the miraculous prescience and knowledge at a distance, not, it is true, of the illness but—and this is the more perplexing—of the increase of the illness and of the death of Lazarus,—all this lies before us here in such baldness, such disregard of delicacy, of truth, nay, of religion, that *not a doubt* can remain of the spuriousness of the whole story.[2]

Fortunately we may say that it was the aim of the author—who has not arranged this scene with so much skill as he has done many others—here as elsewhere, and here still more than elsewhere, rather to show a general characteristic of Jesus and at the same time to lessen the difficulties of his narrative, than to

[1] John xi. 41 sq. Strauss, Weisse, and Baur have spoken here of sham prayer, and unjustly in so far as Jesus did not regard the prayer and the thanks as in themselves unnecessary with reference to God (he prays thus also in xvii.), but justly in so far as the words of the thanks were chosen rather for the men to hear than for God, which is a breach of the religious adoration that man owes to God. Unsatisfactory rectification by the supposition of silent prayers, among others by Neander, Ebr., Krabbe, Lange, Steinmeyer. Certainly in John (an evidence of the overstrained dogmatics) such scenes as the above occur repeatedly, and God takes part in them, xii. 28 sqq. Defective moral decorum also, iv. 7, 16, vi. 5; comp. xi. 28.

[2] Schenkel and Wittichen (besides Strauss, Baur, Weisse, Hilg.) do not doubt the spuriousness, and Schleierm. (p. 233) seeks some means of escape; and Ewald, Hase, Weizs., and others, admitting the glorification, come to the same conclusion. Jesus' knowledge is explained sometimes humanly, by means of a second message (Paulus, and in part even Neander), or by presentiment (Ewald, Hase) and confidence (Hase, Schweizer), strengthened by psychological motives (need, Schweizer; contradiction, Ewald); and sometimes as derived from divine revelation (Neander, Pressensé), divine knowledge and purpose (Krabbe, Lange, &c.).

compel faith in the incident itself.[1] Tradition was strikingly defective in great miracles for the closing period of Jesus' career; therefore the Evangelist wished to concentrate all the divinity, all the life-glory of Jesus, his full power to awaken the nation, his believers, himself out of death spiritual and physical, into one great final picture which should crown the guilt of the nation that rejected him, and should perfect the joyful assurance of the Christians that in the supulchre, in the stone before the grave, and in the death-clothes of Lazarus, they possessed a prototype of the impending resurrection of the Lord and also of their own. That he made use of this narrative for such a purpose is shown by the original elements out of which it is constructed. They lay in the earlier Gospels, chiefly in Luke. There Jesus had introduced, in a parable, a poor sick Eleazar or Lazarus, a "God-help"—the symbol of the Jewish people ill-treated by the powers of the earth, by the Herods and the Romans—who, after his death, was borne by angelic hands to the bosom of Abraham; and also a man clothed in purple, who in the fire of hell begged that Lazarus might be sent to the earth in order to warn his royal brethren of the terrors of the future. "If one go to them from the dead, they will repent." But Abraham had answered: "If they hear not Moses and the prophets, neither will they be convinced though one rise from the dead."[2] This

---

[1] Comp. Weizs. p. 528, and in his manner, Ewald, p. 483. Above all Herder, and Baur, who gives to xi. 25 the emphasis of a central point; even Irenæus, 5, 12, 6; 5, 13, 1. On the other hand, Meyer: nowhere so distinctly the opposite of fiction as here!

[2] Luke xvi. 19 sqq. See above, I. pp. 99, 164, IV. p. 82, note 2. Already Paulus, *Hbb.* II. p. 381, and Schleierm. (comp. Bleek, II. p. 235) were on the right road when they took the rich man for Antipas. More detailed references, above, IV. p. 82. The series is (1) Herod the Great, (2) Archelaus, (3) Philip, (4) Antipas, (5 and 6) the two Agrippas. Sons and grandsons are spoken of as brothers, pares. The wearers of purple (Jos. *Ant.* 14, 9, 4; 18, 6, 6), the men who wore garments of byssus (*B. J.* 2, 1, 1), the carousers (*Ant.* 18, 6, 2) and the rare sympathizers (above, I. pp. 242 sq., 247), the despisers of the Law (above, I. pp. 251, 252), were the Herods. Herod the Great took the road to hell, above, I. p. 253. And did not Archelaus, Antipas, Agrippa I., also? With them the half-heathen Jerusalem went hand in hand (Rev. xi. 8; Matt. ii. 3). In contrast to the rulers of the world, the poor pious people—their representative finally the Messiah, Jesus (*i.e.* Jehovah is succour, above, II. p. 97)—

Lazarus of the parable, already in Luke's Gospel a prototype of Jesus even to the very name, John, conscious of the figurative character of his language and sure that the intelligent among the congregation would understand, represents as rising from the dead. He intended thus to show that the stiff-necked, worldly-minded Moses-nation, which he found depicted in the rich brethren, had, in fact exactly according to the prediction of Abraham, refused to believe "though Jesus did such great signs." He intended also to show that the glory of Jesus had achieved that for his Christians, by his word and his work and his resurrection, which father Abraham himself, almost like one of little faith, had found impossible.[1] The remaining features of the picture are also supplied by the earlier Gospels. The house of Simon the leper is transformed into a house of Lazarus, who also in Luke was covered with ulcers. The brotherless pair of sisters, Martha and Mary, in the unnamed village of Luke become, as to name and character, the sisters of the miracle-man of Bethany. The correct conception of the details becomes simple and complete as soon as we see their natural origin.[2]

at first succumb (Rev. xii. 4; comp. Matt. ii. 3), at last come to honour (Luke i. 52), although the worldly part of the Jews do not so believe (comp. Rev. xi. 13). Another parallel might be found in the six parties of the Jews (counting the Samaritans as one), Heges. ap. Eus. 4, 22; but there would be here no wearers of purple. The original word for Lazarus is Elas(z)ar, from which the Rabbis get the contracted Lasar (as Mattai, at least according to Ewald and Hitzig, from Amittai, hine from ahine [see below, p. 90, n. 4], saron from jesharon), Lightfoot, p. 646. Greek Λάζαρος, Jos. *B. J.* 5, 13, 7. Germanized into Lassner.

[1] Comp. John xii. 37 (Ex. iv. 8 sqq.). Τοσαῦτα is sometimes translated "so great" (De Wette, Lücke), sometimes "so many" (Meyer). For the latter or quantitative conception, we may appeal to the use of language in John vi. 9, xiv. 9, and factually to vii. 31, xi. 47; on the other hand, for the qualitative conception, not only to ταῦτα, iii. 2, μείζονα, xiv. 12 (comp. xv. 24), but also to the spirit of the whole Gospel, which admits only the *élite* of the great miracles, and specially to the—according to Luke xvi.—so decisively great and yet merely pretended miracle of Lazarus.

[2] Thus first Zeller, *Theol. Jahrb.* 1843, p. 89, and Baur, *Ev.* p. 249; Strauss, *New Life of Jesus*, Eng. trans., II. p. 231. Also Schenkel, *Bib.-Lex.* III. p. 292. Even Steinm., p. 205, cannot deny the possibility. With the three passages—(1) Luke xvi. 19 (the poor man Lazarus), comp. also John v. 46; (2) Matt. xxvi. 6, Mark xiv. 3 (Bethany meal); (3) Luke x. 38 (Martha and Mary)—is in John interwoven in an interesting manner (4) Luke vii. 36 (the woman who was a sinner at Simon's house). Comp. below, the anointing at Bethany. Ewald, *l. c.* pp. 481, 510, found in John

C.—THE JUBILANT RECOGNITION OF THE MESSIAH.

Whilst the fourth Gospel represents Jesus as spending a night at Bethany, and thus postpones the entry into Jerusalem until the next day, the early sources are at one in making him pass close by the village. This must at once be admitted to be the more likely, since Jerusalem, and not Bethany, was the goal which had been often announced, and which was now, especially by the disciples and adherents, longed for almost with impatience. Moreover, everything tends to show that the preparation of the Sabbath was about to begin, and if that did not make the completion of the journey legally obligatory before three o'clock in the afternoon, yet the popular custom would make its completion at that time very desirable.[1] The different account given by John is sufficiently explained by the facts that the resurrection of Lazarus converted Bethany into an important station, and that the joyous going forth of the festival guests from Jerusalem to meet Jesus, which this Gospel introduces, becomes possible only when the news of Jesus' arrival and sojourn at Bethany had reached the metropolis, for which some time was

rather the correct emendation of the early tradition, whereby he still finds that the sequence of age in the family was: Mary, Martha, Lazarus (Meyer also upholds this last finding). In fact, we learn nothing about the age of Lazarus, and Martha—*i.e.* the mistress, Jerome, sermone syro domine (mar, mare, not maron, Volk. p. 560; still less = mirjam, Wichelh. p. 70; fem. mareta, marat beta, expression of the Babyl. Jews, instead of baalah, Bux. p. 1247), the woman of the house (notwithstanding xi. 1, 45) —stands first (as in Luke x. 38) in John xi. 5, 19 sq., xii. 2. In so far was Paulus, *L. J.* I. 2nd part, p. 55, nearer to the truth when he called Martha the widow of Simon the leper. In character also she harmonizes with the Martha of Luke; she serves, hastens to meet Jesus, has sanguine hope, and then again as a realist falls back into natural unbelief. Mary is more profound, remains at home, falls at Jesus' feet, weeps, is the special subject of the consolation of the Jews, is perfectly resigned, leaves everything to Jesus, renders at last (xii. 2) the ideal homage. In opposition to the critical explanation, Gfrörer (*Urchrist.* III. p. 313) has found in this event the mythical transformation of the story of Nain (out of which Bethany has grown); comp. Krabbe, p. 342; but Weisse (II. p. 259) recognizes the consolatory utterances about resurrection as original.

[1] The preparation of the Sabbath began at the ninth hour on Friday, *i.e.* three o'clock in the afternoon. Comp. Jos. *Ant.* 16, 6, 2. Bleek, *Beitr.* p. 116.

necessary.[1] But to suppose there were two or more pompous entries, one from Jericho with the festival caravan, a second from Bethany with the disciples, one unprepared for, the other prepared for—a distinction which Paulus makes—gives us too much of a good thing, is in truth only the wretchedly unnatural makeshift of such as wish to adjust differences.[2]

Indeed, the account of Matthew goes so far as to make it appear that Jesus did not at this time enter Bethany at all, and only just touched upon Bethphage. Having come by Bethphage to the Mount of Olives, he sent to the village that lay on the road opposite to him for an animal to ride upon. By this village we are to understand Bethphage, and by no means Bethany, which according to all probability lay further back and had been already passed on the journey; although since Origen it has been customary to make the word refer to Bethany, and in this way it has been thought possible to harmonize Matthew, Mark who mentions only Bethany, and Luke who, without obvious reasons, places Bethphage and Bethany together.[3] Certainly there prevails great confusion upon the question of the superiority of the several Gospel reports as well as upon that of the localities themselves; hence it is not altogether inconvenient

---

[1] John xii. 12. Nevertheless, the Johannine representation has been accepted not only by Krabbe (p. 433), but also by Ewald (p. 519), even by Schenkel (*Bibel-Lex.* III. p. 295), and partially by Weisse (p. 437).

[2] Paulus, *Handb.* III. pp. 22 sqq. Schleier. *Luk.* p. 244; *L. J.* p. 406 ("perhaps in a less degree daily"). Neander, pp. 479, 481. Bunsen, p. 395.

[3] Matt. xxi. 1 should be read, ἦλθον εἰς Βηθφ. εἰς τὸ ὄρος τ. ἐλ. Bethany had been copied from Luke (Mark). πρὸς τὸ ὀρ. is much better attested than εἰς, even in Origen and Jerome (ad). But B C, It., Orig. upon Matt. t. XVI. 10 (more frequently, certainly, πρὸς = πλησίον, *ib.* 14, 17; ed. Knapp. 10; Orig. on John, t. X. 15) have εἰς, and πρὸς is forced in from Luke, Mark. But the first εἰς (εἰς B.) does not necessarily signify an entrance into Bethphage (comp. John iv. 5). If this is admitted (Meyer), then it is not necessary to understand, with most (from Origen to Meyer), Bethany to be the village opposite. It would have been foolish to have named the village whence Jesus sent his messengers, but to have been silent (presumably, again, from prudential motives!) as to the more important village whither he sent. The genuine reading of Mark is ἐγγίζ. εἰς Ἰ. καὶ εἰς Βηθ. Thus, besides It., emphatically Origen (ed. Lomm.), IV. pp. 43, 52 (on the other hand, Orig. on John, *ib.* I. 313 = Luke). In Luke (xix. 29) the same sources establish ἤγγ. εἰς Βηθφ. καὶ Βηθ.

to pass over the former altogether.¹ More closely considered, Matthew is found to possess the advantage of having mentioned the unknown, while the others mention the known; but it was only too easy, as nothing was known of Bethphage, for men to put in its place—with Luke and Mark—that Bethany to which Jesus went back to take up his quarters.² As to the relative position of the two places, the New Testament reports, Matthew's especially, decide that Bethphage was nearer and higher up on the Mount of Olives, Bethany lower and farther off; and with this harmonize not only the communications of the earliest Fathers of the Church—who place Bethphage upon the Mount of Olives and Bethany close to the Mount—and the intimations of later ecclesiastical tradition, but also the declarations of subsequent Jewish literature.³ In that literature there is incidental mention of a Bet-hine, i. e. a date-house, with its dates and unripe figs, a name in which we can find Bethany. But the same literature makes more circumstantial and more exact reference to a Bethphage, or little fig-house, which it describes as a walled, tolerably populous place in the neighbourhood of Jerusalem, with a prospect of the Holy City, and as being, on account of its trifling suburban distance, virtually a part of the city and a sharer in its religious rights.⁴ Two conclusions may be safely

---

¹ Thus Ewald, p. 514; Volkmar, p. 506; and most of the critics.

² Neither can we here decide with Luke-Mark against Matthew; but we cannot prove the priority of Mark to Luke in this doubtful passage. It may be assumed that Luke first substituted the known Bethany for the—to him—unknown Bethphage, and that then Mark erased Bethphage altogether. Bleek also is for Matt., II. p. 297.

³ Matth.: Bethphage, εἰς τὸ ὄρος. Luke-Mark, πρὸς τὸ ὄ. Comp. Luke xxiv. 50. Eus. *On.* 120, Bethphage, πρὸς τῷ ὄ. Jerome, 121 : villula in monte Oliveti. Bethany, Jerome, 111 : in latere montis O. The Christian tradition, see below, pp. 91 sq. Those who would make the two places identical, might appeal to the similarity of the names, and to the fact that, according to the Rabbis, Bet-hine (perhaps Bethany) is also a place of figs (paggim, comp. Bethphage, see next note); but the early notices have clearly distinguished between the two places.

⁴ Bet-hine (ahina, dactylus immaturus, Buxt. p. 38. Lightfoot, p. 202, reads hene), in *Bab. Pesach.* f. 53, 1 : grossi (pagge) bet-hine. Another and more readily suggested derivation of the word Bethany, besides that supported by Lightfoot and others, would be from bet-anja (ena), house of the well (Bronnweiler), after *Targ. Jon.* Ex. xv. 27; Buxt. p. 1633; Wichelh. p. 69. Bet-phage (pag, paggim, Aran. pagin, page, ficus

based upon these notices. In the first place, the present little village El Azirijeh, or village of Lazarus (Lazarium, the Arabic personal name El Azir), which with its twenty or thirty white houses lies hidden in the green of its olive, fig and walnut-trees, and of fields of wheat and barley, on the south-east of the Mount of Olives, at the foot of a spur of the Mount, on the road from Jericho to Jerusalem, and about two-thirds of a league from the latter place, may be regarded as the village of Bethany, not simply on account of its name or of the house and grave of Lazarus shown by pilgrims, or of the stone upon which Jesus is said to have sat and conversed with Martha and Mary, but because the distance and the position strikingly agree with the traditions of John, Origen, Eusebius, and Jerome.[1] But Bethphage, which could not have its place here, because the village of Lazarus is not on the Mount of Olives and does not look upon the walls of Jerusalem, lay—notwithstanding Luke's Gospel, which places it further off—nearer to Jerusalem, either on the road which, skirting the Mount of Olives on the south-west, led through the saddle between that Mount and the Mount of Offence to the Holy City, whose walls here become visible; or, according to the early tradition, midway between the Lazarus village and the top of the Mount of Olives, on the road which,

---

immat.), see Lightfoot, pp. 198, 755. Hug, *Einleitung*, I. pp. 16 sq. Comp. particularly gloss on *Gem. Bab. Sanh.* 1, 3 : Bethphage locus est in conspectu moenium urbis (makom lepanim min chomot hair), quantum ad omnia tamen utebatur jure Hieros. Bethphage is often called chuz lechomot (extra muros), *Pesach.* 63, 2; 91, 1, &c. In some glosses: circuitus exterior urbis, whence then the opinion that *all* the suburbs of Jerusalem were so called. Comp. Buxt. p. 1691; Lightfoot, p. 202; Wetst. p. 459; and as to later critics, below, p. 91, n. 1. The Gospel notice, the earliest we have of Bethphage, serves essentially again to correct the Rabbinical hypotheses. Absurd derivations of the word Bethphage since Origen. According to Origen (upon Matt. t. XVI. 17): οἶκος σιαγόνων, τῶν ἱερέων χωρίον (maxillarum, from Syr. pake). Comp. Paulus, *Handb.* III. i. 114, and the commentators.

[1] Comp. Robinson; Tobler, *Topogr. Jerus.* II. p. 432; also Plitt, Furrer. John xi. 18: Bethany fifteen stadia from Jerusalem. Origen gives the same (following John), ed. Lomm. I. p. 238. Jerome, *l. c.* 111: villa in secundo ab Aelia milliario. Of the memorials of Lazarus there, Eusebius and Jerome speak. The latter says: cujus et monumentum ecclesia nunc ibidem exstructa demonstrat. Eusebius only: τόπος (of Lazarus) δείκνυται. Renan, 15th ed. p. 353: Bethany, au sommet de la colline!

starting in a north-westerly direction from that village, climbed the height of the Mount; or upon the Mount of Olives itself, but by no means on the western descent of the Mount which looks down directly upon Jerusalem, for such a position would contradict everything.[1] We prefer the first position. That still frequented highway was the pleasanter one, and better suited for a pompous entry into the city. Moreover, not a single account speaks of an ascent to the top of the Mount of Olives, and the Talmud nowhere suggests an elevated hilly position for Bethphage.[2] We note here once more the haste with which Jesus presses on towards Jerusalem. He makes no halt in the little, friendly, remote Bethany, nor in the larger Bethphage. It is less a religious punctuality anxious to anticipate the beginning of the day of preparation, than the holy passion of a great cause which drives him restlessly within the walls of the City of God, to his work, to his destiny.

Much more important than this question of places, is that of the kind and manner of the entry of Jesus into Jerusalem. All the Gospels are agreed that he went into the Holy City in an unusual manner, and with accompaniments that unmistakably exhibited his Messianic claims and rights. It is true the Gospels

[1] Luke xix. 29: "as he came near Bethphage and Bethany." Hence (after Robinson) Ewald, p. 514, and Bunsen, p. 395 (on the contrary, Wichelh. p. 70), take Bethphage to be the more remote from Jerusalem! More correctly, Epiph., in Paulus, III. i. p. 167. That Jerusalem was not seen from Bethany is generally acknowledged (comp. Furrer, Caspari); according to Volkmar, p. 509, however, one would catch sight of the Holy City on going out of Bethany. The tradition of the monks, according to Rauwolf, Pococke, and others, in Arnold, *Bethphage*. Recent writers have very bunglingly looked for Bethphage in the village Abu Dis, south-east of Bethany, lying remote among the hills (Arnold, *Oelberg* in *Herz.* X. p. 551). Lightfoot (p. 199) having misunderstood the Talmudic notices of Bethphage so far as to suppose that by that name was designated the lowest part of the Mount of Olives towards the city and a part of the city itself (house of figs), whence the place would appear as a part of the mænia Jerus., Renan (15th ed. p. 386) and Caspari (p. 162) have followed him. Renan understands by Bethphage the eastern pomærium of the city; Caspari, the district of the Mount of Olives as far as Bethany, a supplement of the city, called by the Rabbis Bethphage. But Hug (pp. 16 sq.) and Paulus (*Ev.* III. i. 114) have already shown Lightfoot's error; and it was reserved for Caspari (p. 163) to point to the Chanujot (see Wieseler, *Beitr.* pp. 209 sqq.) in Jerusalem as Bet-hania = Bethany.

[2] Similarly Furrer, *Bethphage* in *Bibel-Lex.*; comp. Sepp, *Jerus.* I. p. 579.

THE JUBILANT RECOGNITION OF THE MESSIAH. 93

present significant differences. It is instructive that the character of the situation largely depends upon whether the demonstrations—which cannot be denied, though they may be toned down—were instigated by Jesus himself, or originated with his disciples and adherents, or finally with the festival guests at Jerusalem.[1] This last is essentially the representation of the fourth Gospel, and is still advocated by modern writers.[2] On the very first day of Jesus' arrival at Bethany, multitudes of the people flocked out to the wonder-worker, though only with the result of provoking inimical resolutions on the part of the high-priests even against Lazarus. But on the next day, when it was known that Jesus was coming to Jerusalem, the multitudes of festival pilgrims met him with palm branches and Messiah shouts, upon which Jesus, either yielding to the instigation or encouragement of the disciples, or perhaps merely with the view of avoiding the thronging of the crowd, mounted a young ass which accidentally stood at his disposal.[3] But the earlier Gospels give the first representation; the disciples and adherents of Jesus form the jubilant festival train, and Jesus himself is not only pleased with all this, but himself takes the initiative by sending, before there was any movement at all, two disciples in a striking manner to

[1] Attempts to tone down are common from Paulus onwards. Not merely is Jesus exonerated from instigating the demonstrations, but they are even converted into something usual during the period of his teaching. According to Schleiermacher (pp. 407 sqq.), the entry was nothing aimed at; indeed, Jesus was accustomed to enter the city early in the morning for quiet's sake; but day after day the people brought him with more or less of display. He made no formal entry, but he submitted to being escorted. According to Renan (15th ed. p. 197), Jesus in his journeys frequently rode upon a mule (with large beautiful eyes and eyebrows), and the disciples indulged in a rustic pomp, laying their garments on the road, marks of honour to which he was very sensitive, and which were again paid to him on his last entry into Jerusalem (ib. p. 387).

[2] John xii. 12 sqq. Similarly Paulus (L. J. I. ii. pp. 82, 91 sq.) and Schleiermacher (p. 407), both of whom assume a double entry, a Synoptical one and a Johannine one, Bleek (II. p. 299), Neander (pp. 478 sqq.), Renan (l. c.), who represents the Galileans as going out of Jerusalem to meet Jesus (comp. also Langen, p. 12). Schenkel, p. 224; Hausrath, p. 435; Bunsen, p. 393.

[3] John xii. 14 should be interpreted by xii. 16.

fetch him an animal for riding from the opposite village of Bethphage.[1]

Which report is the more in harmony with history can soon be discovered. In the first place, it is easier to conceive that a Messianic entry, marked by materially Jewish forms and ending in the cross, was compiled or condensed from a previous writing, than that it was invented. Supposing the idea of a Jewish Messiah to be really antipathetic to the fourth Evangelist, whilst the earlier account favoured the conception that Jesus of set purpose entered Jerusalem as the Messiah of the Jews, the correction would be at once made if the Messianic demonstrations were transferred from Jesus and his adherents to the festival guests at Jerusalem. Certainly this was not historical, and for this reason: as we long since saw, the Messianic movement necessarily and actually began to show itself in the circle of Jesus, and not thus in a sudden agitation—however great might have been the miracle that is supposed to have occasioned it— among festival guests who for the most part had never seen him, and had heard nothing of his Messiahship, which may be said even of those Galileans at Jerusalem to whom Renan has thought well to ascribe the triumphant reception of Jesus.[2] Moreover, the Lazarus miracle altogether vanishes, together with the sojourn of Jesus at Bethany and the flocking of Jerusalem-

[1] Matt. xxi. 1, and parallel passages. As the place, Matthew mentions Bethphage (see above), upon which Justin (*Trypho*, 53), Paulus, Neander, Ewald (p. 514, with otherwise incorrect explanation), by accident agree. Hausrath (p. 435) and others, Bethany.

[2] Renan, 15th ed. p. 387. Schenkel had already, in his *Charakterbild*, p. 224, made the people of Jerusalem share in the proceedings at the entry; he has done this still more in *Bibel-Lex.* III. p. 295, after having found that Jesus, during his sojourn of several months in Judæa, *repeatedly* taught in Jerusalem *before his entry*—a ministry which Schenkel previously denied (*Char.* p. 179). Moreover, he now finds that the festival train—after the preceding marks of homage at Bethany (anointing)—had been *arranged* with the leaders of it. Weisse (pp. 435 sq.) has most correctly upheld the Synoptical account, saying that everything proceeded from Jesus and his Galileans, and *only* according to the Synoptics was the entry, as result of the foregoing actions of Jesus, of worth.

ites to Bethany. And the enthusiasm of the Jerusalemites as well as that of the festival guests never existed at all, according to the earlier Gospels, which describe the astonishment of the Jerusalemites as contrasting violently with the jubilation of those who accompanied Jesus.[1] Finally, not only are the other Gospels the older and the more correct, but John involuntarily establishes the essential correctness of their account. John not merely admits that Jesus himself, though as a second thought, had recourse to an animal for riding, and this unmistakably—as the introduction of the passage from the prophets shows —with a Messianic meaning, if also with a higher one, but he also points to the co-operation of the Twelve and of the "accompanying" people; and the intimation—so often appealed to as an evidence that this author was an eye-witness—that it was not until after Jesus was glorified that the disciples understood the prophetic meaning of the riding in and of what they themselves unconsciously did to him, is a most certain proof that the narrator knew of that essential co-operation of the disciples at the entry which is related by the others, but the main fact of which he passes over in silence, allowing no more to appear than an unconscious proceeding.[2]

But though it may now be assumed as established that the festival escort of Jesus, the disciples most prominently, co-operated with full consciousness in a Messianic entry, there remains, on the other hand, the question whether Jesus himself acted with them or gave the first impulse. This question is a difficult one, although the early Gospels leave no doubt in the matter, and even the fourth is not able altogether to deny his participation. All the historical testimonies we had hitherto examined have shown us simply the Messianic excitement of the disciples and others who accompanied him, and have not given a trace of a

[1] Thus Matt. xxi. 10 sq.

[2] John xii. 14—17. Praise of John in Neander, p. 481. Bleek, II. pp. 299 sq. It is correct that the disciples did not think of the Old Testament, incorrect that they did not think of the Messiah.

Messianic demeanour, agitation, or demonstration, on the part of Jesus. On the contrary, he stood preponderantly under the influence of his dark presentiment, and was constantly guided by that serious and sober spirit which more than once sought to restrain the fanciful hopes of his adherents. And when we look towards Jerusalem and observe the actual labours of Jesus there, he certainly stands in harmony with himself. We see no animal for riding, no royal chariot, but the teacher and prophet of the people who comes from Bethany afoot, walks about in Jerusalem and in the temple, and—the act of purifying the temple excepted—simply demonstrates with the sword of his word, fights, and falls. The supposition readily suggests itself, that the Messianic enthusiasm, now as hitherto, did not proceed from Jesus, but only from those who accompanied him; that Jesus bestrode no animal of his own free will, but either was constrained to do so by his companions, to whom, according to Paulus, he "showed himself complaisant," or that he, not permitting himself to be constrained or commanded, altogether refrained from riding, and that therefore the later Christian narrative made him the author of what really never happened. This last might very easily have occurred, because the Christians wished to see the accepted actual Messiah as Messiah and with the pretensions of Messiahship. In this pompous entry they would eagerly hail and realize a fulfilment of old prophecies, and a prophecy of his future Messianic entry at his coming again from heaven.[1]

The decision of this question apparently depends chiefly upon the historical or non-historical character of the single incident of the introduction into the procession of the animal for riding. In the earlier Gospels this is introduced in a very mysterious

[1] Paulus, *L. J.* II. p. 92. That Jesus yielded to those with him is thought by De Wette (he willingly gave way to the excitement of the disciples, and was willing to let the people decide, comp. Theile, p. 59), Neander (p. 480), Ewald (p. 514), Grätz (p. 236), Weizs. (p. 545). Renan (p. 387) says, Some one brought a she-ass. Neander vacillates lamentably between not bringing and bringing. He also urges that Jesus immediately retreated again.

THE JUBILANT RECOGNITION OF THE MESSIAH. 97

manner, whilst the fourth Gospel apparently much more naturally but in point of fact by no means more credibly, being in truth dependent upon the earlier report, satisfies itself with the assertion that Jesus, after the ovation had begun, found a young ass and sat upon it.[1] But in the earlier accounts, Jesus, after his arrival at Bethphage, expressly sent two messengers chosen from among the disciples to the village in front of him: they would there at once find an ass tied, they were to loose him and bring him back. If any objection were made, they were to say, "The Master has need of him," and he would then be given up without further ceremony.[2] This simplest ground-form of the narrative is nowhere absolutely retained. In Matthew, Jesus asks for a she-ass and an ass's foal, and it is expected of Strauss and ourselves to believe that both animals were brought, covered with garments, and ridden by Jesus.[3] In Luke and Mark, Jesus asks for only one animal, though certainly also a foal upon which no man has sat, not definitely an ass—a species which these authors, in view of occidental ridicule, seem to have veiled—presumably therefore a horse's foal. In Mark, Jesus indicates exactly the place where it was to be found and where it actually stood, just at the entrance of the village, before the door on the highway. In both Luke and Mark, the answer to objections which he gives is not superfluous, for the messengers are questioned in the very words which he anticipates; but, as he also anticipates, they are despatched in peace.[4] These narrations are

---

[1] John xii. 14.   [2] Matt. xxi. 1, and parallel passages.

[3] Comp. Strauss, 4th ed. II. pp. 273 sqq. Even Meyer makes ἐπάνω αὐτῶν (αὐτὸν, then αὐτοῦ, primitive correction, yet made use of by Paulus, *Hdb.* III. i. p. 143), after Theoph., Euth., Fritzsche, refer to the garments, but the principal object is the two animals, and Matthew attaches importance to both. Expositors sometimes imagine, certainly not exactly that a connection between the two animals was made by the caparison of garments, but that both were alternately ridden (Theophyl., Thom. Aq., Nik. Syr., even Fritzsche); sometimes that the author has spoken inexactly (Olsh., Winer), or obscurely (Winer, De Wette), or subjectively (Krabbe, p. 435), and that Jesus really rode only upon the humble foal (!), Justin, *Ap.* 1, 32, 35; thus also Paulus, Ewald, Meyer, Krabbe, Langen.

[4] Luke xix. 29; Mark xi. 1. According to Bunsen (p. 395), Mark enjoyed the advantage of Petrine tradition. The derision of the West (comp. Terence, *Eun.*

to be regarded with distrust. Had Jesus acquaintances in Bethphage or, if that be preferred, in Bethany? Had he ordered of them an ass? Or if not, had he, through higher knowledge, known of the ass and of its whereabouts? Did he ride an ass's foal on which no one had ridden, as if it were a kind of sacred animal dedicated to God and to His service? Did he, indeed—which seemed so important to Paulus and gave so much trouble to Strauss—attach any the least importance to an unbroken animal?[1] Finally, did he ask for both the she-ass and her foal, and did he ride them both? But the chief objection is yet to come. Ass and foal were mentioned in the Old Testament Messianic prediction. "Exult greatly, O daughter of Zion!"—Zechariah had sung—"shout, O daughter of Jerusalem; behold, thy king comes to thee, the just and the conqueror; he is meek and rides upon an ass, and upon a colt, the foal of the ass." What the prophet expressed in picture—the pacific character and humility of the coming king of Israel—was taken by the Jews literally, materially, naturally. At least the Talmudic writings, certainly independent of Christianity though much later witnesses, say a great deal of such an entry of the future king. Sometimes they assume that the ass of the Messiah will be much

---

3, 5, 50: asinus tantus! Cicero, *Att.* 4, 5: as. germanus! and the rôle which the ass plays in Jewish history among the Greeks and Romans, Jos. *Con. Ap.* 2, 9; Diod. 34; Ph. 1; Tac. *H.* 5, 3, 4; Min. F., *Oct.* 9; Tert., *Nat.* 1, 11 sqq., *Ap.* 16; comp. Hitzig, p. 381) was already avoided by the LXX., since they translated it, instead of ὄνος, ὑποζύγιον (comp. Zech. ix. 9), or πῶλος (foal, as in Luke-Mark). Josephus also has, instead of ass, κτῆνος, or indeed ἵππος. The late Jews admitted: ne gentes causam cavillandi arriperent. Yet Celsus does not deride the entry upon an ass. Nor does the heathen scorn of the asinarii cultores, *i. e.* the Christians (Tert. *l. c.*), spring from this. The reason for the general term foal (comp. Justin, *Ap.* 1, 54) instead of ass, in Luke and Mark, had already been seen by Wetstein (p. 608) and Paulus (*Handb.* III. i. p. 151), though it has been entirely overlooked by most. Recently Weisse has seriously attempted to base upon this foundation the quite inoffensive assumption of a horse's foal (p. 573). Comp. also Rev. xix. 11 sqq.

[1] Comp. in the Old Test. Numbers xix. 2; Deut. xxi. 3; 1 Sam. vi. 7. Ovid, *Met.* 3, 12: nullum passa jugum. Horace, *Epod.* 9, 22: intactæ boves. See Wetst. p. 608; Paulus, III. i. p. 147. Justin makes this feature refer to heathenism, the she-ass is Judaism, *Trypho*, 53. The unbroken animal, Paulus, *Handb.* III. i. p. 115; Strauss, 4th ed. II. p. 276. According to Paulus, the animal would be made more tractable by the company of its mother.

THE JUBILANT RECOGNITION OF THE MESSIAH. 99

more beautiful than the most beautiful fleet steed of the Persian king Sapor, who will derisively place at his disposal a noble horse instead of the ass. Sometimes they find that the Messiah will come with the clouds of heaven, according to Daniel, if Israel be good, but in the other case with the ass of Zechariah.[1] This passage in Zechariah—and hardly a passage in Jacob's song of benediction as well—the Evangelists have evidently before their eyes, Matthew and John avowedly, Luke and Mark without naming it.[2] But they have in many ways done violence not only to the spirit of the passage, but also to its letter. Whilst in Zechariah the mention first of an ass and then of a young ass is merely a variation of the expression, in Luke and Mark the emphasis is placed upon the young ass, and in Matthew—more correctly in the emendation of Matthew—the emphasis is placed upon son and dam, although the latter is not mentioned by the prophet as being actually present and running with her son.[3] Is there, now, a probability that Jesus, elsewhere never pedantic in his use of the Old Testament, laid emphasis to this extent, in one way or another, on the letter of the Old Testament, or concerned himself so anxiously and so mysteriously about the

---

[1] Zech. ix. 9. *Bab. Sanh.* f. 98, 1: si boni sunt Israelitæ, tunc veniet in nubibus cœli; si vero non boni, tunc inequitans asino. Lightfoot, p. 349. On Sapor, see below, p. 105, n. 1. Numerous passages from later writers given by Wetstein, p. 460; Wünsche, pp. 51, 60 sq., 67, 70.

[2] Matt. xxi. 5; John xii. 15 (freer). In the main, Matt. gives the text of the LXX., only changing in the beginning the really not fulfilled χαῖρε σφόδρα θυγ. Σ. (John, μὴ φοβοῦ) into an εἴπατε; but at the close he evidently follows the Hebrew (Anger, *Ratio qua loci V. T. in Ev. M.* &c., I. p. 35) with greater exactness (LXX.: ὑποζύγιον κ. πῶλον νέον), a sign of the second hand. See above, I. pp. 79 sqq. The passage giving Jacob's benediction, Gen. xlix. 11 (where Judah binds the young ass, the foal of the she-ass, to the vine), is suggested by the "tied" ass of the Gospels. Had this passage occurred to the Evangelists (Strauss, Volkm.), we should have been told, not of a previously bound animal, but of one that was to be bound by Jesus or by his disciples, and also of the vine. This reference was later detected. Justin represents the animal as bound to the vine at the entrance to the place, *Ap.* I. 32, 54; *Trypho*, 53. Yet he at the same time gives prominence to Zechariah. Comp. Bleek, II. p. 300; Wünsche, p. 70.

[3] In Zechariah ix. 9 it merely says, "and upon the young ass, the foal of an ass" (air ben atonot). Comp. the old translation in Origen, *In Matt.* t. XVI. 16. Hitzig, *Kl. Proph.* 3rd ed. 1863, p. 362. Even Bleek sacrifices Matt., II. p. 299.

ass? Is it on the whole probable that he appeared in Jerusalem with a public and material display of Messiahship?

Relying upon these grounds, we may question the entry upon the ass; but the main fact—namely, the resolve of Jesus to enter as the Messiah—we may nevertheless hold fast.[1] It may have been only the disciples, only those who accompanied Jesus, that brought about the Messianic ovation; but since Jesus yielded and was "complaisant" before the eyes of Jerusalem, he must have thought it right, even though he did not utter the words of approval which Luke puts into his mouth.[2] Moreover, afterwards he spontaneously protracted this Messianism, at least upon one point, when, immediately after his entry, he violently, or with a right derived solely from God and his Messianic dignity, purified the temple. It must therefore be admitted that by his entry he certainly took a bold step forwards. His first step had been to announce himself to his disciples as the Messiah at the close of his Galilean ministry. His second step was by turns to damp and to give play to the Messianic excitement of the disciples and the people. His third step was to cease preventing others from recognizing his divine rights, and even himself to lay claim to those rights. These progressive steps we can understand. Even if it had certainly been his wish to bring the kingdom of heaven near in Jerusalem quietly and gradually, and with a healthy mental progress, as in Galilee—which in Strauss' opinion he really thought of doing—yet all indirect and slow action was now forbidden, not by the impatience of his adherents, but by his clear recognition of the critical condition of affairs.[3] In the face

---

[1] The animal is half admitted by Strauss (*New Life of Jesus*, Eng. trans., II. pp. 290 sq.), who is misled by Zechariah (no longer, as previously, chiefly by Gen. xlix.) as to the whole of the festival entry; and by Volkmar (p. 507), who can admit the acclamations of the people in the presence of the beloved Master who is to bring in the kingdom of God, but who cannot guarantee the ass in view of (1) Zechariah, (2) Gen. xlix., (3) the Revelation, the king's horse in which (xix. 11) has been converted by the Evangelist into an ass.

[2] Luke xix. 40.

[3] Strauss, *New Life*, Eng. trans., I. pp. 384 sq. Yielding to enthusiasm (see above, p. 69), Neander, De Wette, Weizs.

of the irritability of his opponents, in the face of the powerful
means at their disposal of crushing him with the speed of wind
and the force of storm, there remained to him but one chance,
but one dreadful weapon,—reckless publicity, the conquest of
the partially prepared nation by means, not of force, but of idea,
by the bold and complete unfurling of the clearly and loudly
and—to the popular mind—eloquently speaking banner of that
Messiahship the secret of which he had so long hidden within
himself, and of which he had held possession with growing certainty of victory, notwithstanding all he had suffered.[1] That he
was treading a dangerous path he knew, although he never
wished to become a political Messiah, a rebel, as Reimarus
exclaimed. He knew the misunderstandings he should awaken,
the false enthusiasm he should conjure up, the sanguinary reac-
tion he should call forth. Therefore he came staking his life
upon the venture, but also believing that God must finish his
work through life or death, through misunderstanding and recognition.[2] But here we must once more emphatically assert that
there is—notwithstanding the fourth Gospel—as little proof of a
certain foreknowledge of his fate, therefore of a rushing to his
death—which Schleiermacher so earnestly deprecates—as there

[1] Comp. Ewald, p. 512. Weizs. (p. 547) groundlessly rejects the idea of the conquest of the nation.

[2] Comp. Reimarus, *Zweck Jesu*, pp. 144 sqq.: it was ventured upon, he sat himself upon the ass. Does not this mean to incite the people against the authorities:
Overthrow the high council! According to Venturini (pp. 412 sqq.), Jesus carried
out the public entry against the dissuasions of Joseph of Arimathea and Nicodemus,
who promised a peaceful conquest. There was a necessity for a striking and decisive
fact, and that the people should know that he was the Messiah in the better sense of
the word. The entry itself was to show that there was no question of rebellion against
the Romans. Then Nicodemus supplied the required humble beast in one of his ass's
foals from his seat at Bethphage. According to Paulus, *L. J.* II. p. 82, Jesus rode
only in order that he might be visible above the crowd (similarly Neander, p. 481);
he wished moreover to show that he did not fear the hierarchy. Theile, *Zur Biog. J.*,
p. 59: he wished to show the power, but not the will, to set up an earthly kingdom.
Recent writers speak freely of the impossibility of a misunderstanding of his intention; thus Ewald, p. 513; Pressensé, pp. 553 sq. At any rate, he could easily remove
it (Ewald), nay, did at once remove it by his immediate retreat (Neander, Krabbe,
Weizs., Bunsen), and by his death (Pressensé). Mainly he thought only of dying,
Längin, p. 54. Even Schenkel (p. 224) says that it happened in a way opposed to
the theocratical expectations. Quite opposite?

THE ENTRY INTO JERUSALEM.

is of definitive resolves on the part of his foes to put him to death, supposed to have been made one after another, yet before his entry.[1]

Making his entry in such a spirit, he could not entirely forego all external signs of his Messiahship. Not only had he to make himself intelligible to the people by accommodating himself to their material modes of conception, but the Messiahship which he seriously and without accommodation purposed to establish had to be made visible and recognizable in forms and signs which were worthy of him, and which did not contradict his higher conception of this position.[2] The shouts of joy and the songs of praise by which he was met called for no censure. But it was necessary that he should do more than passively receive; he must himself also confess and act. It would indeed have been unworthy of his independence, of his leading and controlling position, if he had simply left it to others to decide whether he should now postpone or not the public utterance—approved or non-approved—of his will, his design. We thus come necessarily to the assumption of an initiative on the part of Jesus, such as that described in the Gospels only in the definite form of the bespeaking the animal for riding and of the riding into the city, an incident which—and this is the best evidence of its genuineness—has been in every way so artificially utilized by Luke and John. And this form itself, when carefully weighed, appears far more characteristic of Jesus than strange and unnatural. If he really chose this form, he most probably did it in imitation of the prophecy of Zechariah.[3] Nevertheless, it cannot on this

---

[1] John xi. 47 sqq., 54, xii. 10, 12 sqq. See above, pp. 75 sqq. Schleiermacher, p. 387 (certainly not Johannine).

[2] Even Schenkel regards the Messiahship as only an accommodation. To Volkmar it does not exist, and the people do homage chiefly only to "the beloved Master." Yet something is said "treacherously" about the Messiahship (comp. above, IV. p. 262, note 1); and plainly already the "Son of David" is historical, even the "Son of God" (Volk. pp. 507, 588). Hitzig also (*Gesch. Isr.* p. 502) has given prominence to the Messianic idea already existing before Christ.

[3] This is held also by Hase, p. 220; Weisse, p. 435; Weizs. p. 546; Schenkel, pp. 223 sqq.; Hausr. p. 436; Ewald, p. 512; partially even by Neander, p. 480; Krabbe, p. 437; Pressensé, p. 553.

account be shown that he here paid a different respect to the letter than he did on other occasions, that he believed the prophecy was to be verbally understood and verbally fulfilled, or that he felt compelled—as to which Paulus wanders very seriously astray—to complete the kingdom of peace of the great Asmonæan, John Hyrcanus, in the sense of the prophets of those days.[1] But since he found himself, nay, recognized a full prediction of himself, in this picture of the meek king; since by means of this very picture he could, as briefly and comprehensively as strikingly and unmistakably to all men of understanding, illustrate and explain his true character as man of peace and peace-bringer; since, finally, in this picture, which had not hitherto been generally incorporated into the Messianic belief of the people, he could at one and the same time veil and reveal himself, very much as he had previously done in the name of Son of Man;—on all these accounts, he appropriated the picture with its details, he adopted the humble riding animal because it characterized himself, and because, to the popular mind, more particularly to his Galilean friends, who were the natural connecting link between him and the nation, it was an easily unriddled token of his dignity and of his claim.[2]

But the detailed portraiture of the finding and of the nature of the animal belongs evidently to the myth, which seeks its

[1] *Hdb.* III. i. pp. 119—142: Hyrcanus was anti-Phar., like Jesus! Later criticism has rather recognized the higher antiquity of the predictions of Zechariah ix. sqq. Hitzig, *Kl. Proph.* 3rd ed. 1863, p. 354, places the oracle ix.—xi. in the time of Uzziah—Jerob. II. (about 800).

[2] Matt. xxi. 10 shows that the people of Jerusalem did not at once know what the entry signified, although "to ride" and "to rule" were inseparable according to Paulus, *Handb.* III. i. p. 116. In point of fact, riding upon an animal was very customary (Shunammite woman, 2 Kings iv. 24); and particularly the prophets—Balaam, Numbers xxii. 21; the prophet out of Judah, 1 Kings xiii. 13—practised it. The above sentence disposes of the common opinion that Jesus declared himself Messiah by means of this entry (Justin, *Trypho*, 53: φανερὸν χρ. ἐποίει, and thus also Ewald, p. 512), as well as the often unjustly lauded communication purposely made by the fourth Gospel that the disciples did not recognize the Messianic significance of this entry until later (comp. below, p. 106). Weisse (p. 435) cautiously, but with justice, says it was a sign of his purpose to visit the metropolis either expressly with the dignity of Messiah and king, or at least with that of a powerful and recognized prophet.

justification in the letter of the prophecies, and partly also in the miraculous greatness of Jesus in knowledge and holiness. Jesus did not exactly know, through higher knowledge, as did Samuel in the Old Testament, where asses and she-asses were standing; and he required, for the letter's sake and his holiness' sake, neither a she-ass nor an ass's foal upon which no man had ridden.[1] At most, according to Eastern custom, he would have preferred the she-ass as an animal of travel, and, again according to custom, he would not have refused to allow any foal it might have to accompany the mother.[2] But either he sent his disciples out at haphazard, since this much-used animal was easily to be met with, and there was no cause to doubt that the loan of one might be obtained for the space of an hour for "the Lord," the Prophet of Galilee; or he made application to an acquaintance at Bethphage, one who dwelt at the entrance to this village, perhaps in the first house, and who he might be sure possessed such an animal, or of whom he might during the last days have ordered one. Indeed, Venturini speaks in detail of a preceding instruction given to his steward at Bethphage by Nicodemus.[3] Such a previous acquaintance with a household at Bethphage, formed in Galilee or during the journey from the Jordan, is as conceivable as friendships in the neighbouring Bethany, which are pretty well attested, for Jesus the same evening claims the hospitality of friendship in Bethany. The bespeaking of the animal in this house would, however, have taken place in exactly the same manner as did afterwards, according to the miracle-less report of Matthew, the bespeaking of the room for the supper at the house of a citizen of Jerusalem unknown to us, but well known to Jesus.[4] And just as he did not in the latter case previously

---

[1] The lost and found asses of Saul, 1 Sam. ix. 3, 6, 9, 20, x. 2.

[2] Numb. xxii. 21 ; 2 Kings iv. 24 ; Job i. 3 (500 she-asses). Renan, 15th ed. p. 387: ânesse, suivie, selon l'usage, de son petit. Comp. Bleek, II. p. 299.

[3] Matt. xxvi. 18. Following the Gospels, particularly Mark, Justin, *Ap.* 1, 32, *Trypho*, 53, gives prominence to the entrance of the place.

[4] Neander (p. 481) also denies the miracle. Hilgenfeld (p. 35) makes Jesus, even in Matthew, know of the ass by prophetic penetration, *i.e.* miracle. A loan from

bespeak the room, but merely assumed the assignment of such to his use by the man with whom he was familiar, so in the other case we have less reason to think of a preceding bespeaking of the animal than of a simple requisition sent to the well-to-do acquaintance or stranger in Bethphage. This appears the more dignified course, as being free from triviality; and the answer put into the disciples' mouths against objections, itself points rather to an unknown man.

After this circumstantial preparation, it is time to pass on to the actual entry and to Jerusalem. The two disciples—probably Peter and one of the sons of Zebedee—brought back the animal of peace, which was and still is very differently esteemed in the East than in the West. It is true that in the East it has quite another character; it is statelier, more active, swifter, vying with the horse in every point, of a brown-red colour, and particularly valued when white marks stripe the dark colour.[1] As an animal for riding, as a beast of burden, in agriculture, in the mill, it was equally prized, ridden, and driven, by women and men; and in contrast with the Egyptian war-horse, which had been naturalized in Israel since the time of Solomon, it was the eloquent national symbol of peace—nay, the divine symbol.[2] The

---

acquaintances or from strangers (who needed only to hear the name of Jesus) is thought of by Paulus, *Handb.* III. i. 18, *L. J.* I. ii. 83. The offer of Nicodemus, who instructed his steward in Bethphage, Vent. p. 415. Higher knowledge, Krabbe, p. 436. Magical clairvoyance, Weisse, I. p. 573.

[1] The name of the ass is honourable, instead of being a term of abuse, Gen. xlix. 14. See, on the other hand, Terence, quoted above, p. 97, n. 4. Yet Homer, Il. XI. 558 sqq., compares Ajax to a strong ass. Comp. Paulus, *Ev.* III. i. p. 118; Ewald, p. 516; Winer, article *Esel*. Abdull. *Denkw. Eg*, c. 3, in Paulus: asini in Aeg. valdi agiles; cursu cum equis certant. Price, *e.g.* in Persia, 100 thalers [£15]. Comp. Pliny, 8, 68. The stripes, Judges v. 10. Lightfoot, p. 349 (answer to Sapor): non est tibi equus centimaculus, qualis est Messiæ asinus.

[2] As. molarius, Matt. xviii. 6. Colum. 7, 2. Beast of burden, Jos. *Vita*, 24, 26. Ridden by women, 1 Sam. xxv. 23; 2 Kings iv. 24. Comp. the holy tradition, above, II. p. 91. Passages in the Prophets, see above, p. 103, n. 2. Horse of Egypt, Exodus xv. 1. Asses and mules in the time of the judges, Judges v. 10, and also of Saul and David, 1 Sam. viii. 16, ix. 3; 2 Sam. xiii. 29, xvi. 2, xvii. 23, xviii. 9; 1 Kings i. 33, 44. On the other hand, horses after Solomon's time, 1 Kings iv. 26 (from Egypt, iii. 1); then under Ahab, Jehoshaphat, 1 Kings xviii. 5, xx. 21, xxii. 4.

book of Revelation—which does not appeal to the tradition of the Gospels—has not made the most fortunate hit by representing Jesus as returning from heaven to earth upon a horse; though certainly the John of the Revelation wrote for Greeks, and his Jesus came not to bless, but to judge and slay his foes.[1] The disciples said nothing to the owner about the use the Master intended to make of the animal; therefore it came without the cover or the cushion necessary for riding. But they themselves quickly understood its purpose; though they hardly thought at once of the words of the prophet—wherein John is correct—yet they knew that Jesus and no one else was to sit upon the ass, and it harmonized with their exalted mood that their Messiah should enter the streets of Jerusalem with honour and distinction.[2] They therefore quickly supplied the deficiency by throwing off their upper garments and piling them upon the animal, whilst they led it to Jesus, assisted him, unaccustomed to riding, to mount it, and then started it on its way.[3] And now it happened as it usually happens when enthusiasm has begun to ferment, and the key-note is struck according to which it can shape and embody itself, without any pre-arrangement, in an harmonious outburst of common emotion. The act of the two disciples, the unusual pomp exhibited by the spectacle of Jesus on the animal which his disciples were guiding, the Mount of Olives, sacred from of old, waiting since Zechariah's time for the revelation of God, together with the proximity of the holy city, set free all the enthusiasm which had been with difficulty restrained, and urged it to utterance, to jubilant participation, to

---

[1] Rev. xix. 11 (after Volkmar, *Quelle der Ev.*).

[2] Saddles not used in the East, but the ass (chamor chabush) was bridled and furnished with a covering (sellis instrati, Abdull.; 1 Kings xiii. 13). On John, see above, p. 95, n. 2.

[3] Throwing down garments at the election of Jehu as king, 2 Kings ix. 13. Luke xix. 35 has ἐπεβίβασαν, but also in Matt. xxi. 7, Sin. and Ital., Vulg., Copt., we read ἐπεκάθισαν, sedere facerunt. Just so Sin. and It. Ver. in Mark xi. 7. By the side of or behind the animal generally ran a boy or servant (naar), Rabb. ass-driver (chammar, Buxt. p. 789); comp. 2 Kings iv. 24. This task was undertaken by the disciples.

devoted co-operation.¹ The two disciples had given up their garments to caparison the animal. But not one of the Twelve, of the adherents, of the majority of the accompanying crowd, was willing to be outdone. They threw off their garments and spread them upon the road; others cut off the young green branches of palms, myrtles, citrons, and willows, bound them in bunches, flourished them right and left and up and down, and strewed them upon the way. There seemed to come to pass a spontaneous fulfilment of the Psalm which the tempter had once in a diabolical spirit commended to Jesus. The festive custom itself belonged originally to the rejoicing at the Feast of Tabernacles; but it had long been extended to ceremonial processions and pompous escorts of all kinds; and even the Roman Agrippa had, a generation earlier, been favoured with this distinction when he returned from Jerusalem to the sea.²

¹ Mount of Olives, Zechariah xiv. 4; Ezekiel xi. 23; 2 Sam. xv. 32; 1 Kings xi. 7 (place of worship and revelation). Expectation of miracle on the Mount of Olives about A.D. 58, Jos. *Ant.* 20, 8, 6. Comp. below, p. 111, n. 2.

² The garments were thrown into a heap, upon which, *e.g.*, the new king Jehu was placed, 2 Kings ix. 13. Similarly *Jalk. Shim.* in Schöttg. p. 170. At the Feast of Tabernacles they were hung out as tokens of joy, Maim. *Succ.* 5, 17: expandit ob decorem atque ornamentum. Lightfoot, p. 349. Oriental custom of throwing myrtle-boughs and garments in the way, *Targ. Esth.* 10, 15: cum exiret Mardochai porta regis, plateæ erant myrtis stratæ (thus also Xerxes before crossing the Hellespont, Herodotus, 7, 54) et atria purpura. *Ketub.* f. 66, 2: de Nacdimon filio Gorion narrant, quod quotiesc. in scholam ibat, vestes laneas ipsi substraverint, pauperes vero venerint eosque a tergo ejus colvolverint. Perhaps that happened ex ambitione. Comp. Ibn-Arabshâh, *Fâk.* p. 26, 19, in Ewald, p. 516. The missionary Zeller found the custom still practised at Nazara, Furrer, *Wand.* p. 66. Bunches (εἰρεσιώνη) of myrtle, willow and palm (σὺν κράδῃ φοίνικος), at the daily procession to the altar during the Feast of Tabernacles, Jos. *Ant.* 3, 10, 4. Thyrsus staves of palm and citron leaves, *Ant.* 13, 13, 5. Palm branches, myrtles and willows, on the authority of Maim., *l.c.* The tender palm branches were called lulabin or lablebin = surculi; comp. Buxt. p. 1117; Lightfoot, p. 349. From the Feast of Tabernacles—the specific feast of rejoicings—the custom was extended (2 Macc. x. 6) also to the Feast of the Dedication of the Temple of the Asmonæans (x. 7), and to every feast day, 1 Macc. xiii. 51 (palm leaves); compare the crowds that greeted Agrippa, above, I. p. 242, and Rev. vii. 9. Matthew has only branches from trees generally; Mark, straw (στιβάδες), perhaps grass, green stalks from the fields, not exactly for smoothing the road (Paulus); John xii. 13, definitely palm branches. Swinging the branches at the altar, *Bab. Succ.* 27: agitatio vel quassatio fasciculorum fuit dextrorsum sinistrorsum, sursum deorsum. Lightfoot, p. 350. Comp. also Delitzsch, *Luth. Zeitschr.* 1855, pp. 653 sqq.; and then Riggenbach's commendation of the fourth Gospel, above, I. p. 184, note. Langen,

To these external signs there must have been added words; and Luke is perhaps not quite correct when he makes these words to be first heard at the descent from the Mount of Olives into the city. Words must have accompanied the deeds, for hearts must speak and minds must give expression to the reverent homage which they feel. This homage, though elsewhere offered only to the greatest or to God, pointed to the approaching kingdom of heaven, and had for its object the bringer-in of the kingdom, the anointed of Israel, who publicly confessed himself by making a conspicuous entry into the city of God in the midst of the people. Even these words which were to be uttered found their precedent in the Feast of Tabernacles. At that Feast the so-called Great Hallelujah, i.e. Psalms cxiii.—cxviii., was sung, as well as, every day at the solemn procession to the altar, with the flourishing of the bunches of leaves, the words from Psalm cxviii.: "O Lord, help, O Lord! Give prosperity!"[1] Many of these words and songs, however, would have become the medium of expressing the festive emotions of the pilgrims to all the feasts, when they drew near to the walls of the holy city. Those very words in particular, and the immediately following, "Blessed be he that comes in the name of the Lord! We bless you, ye who are from the house of the Lord!" would often have accompanied those entries.[2] These verses were now taken up by those who accompanied Jesus; but they were freely and with new meaning altered and broadened, because it was not merely a question of blessing the festival pilgrims, but of naming and blessing the Great, the Unique Person who entered in their midst. That some of these words, that the words, "Blessed be he that comes in the name of

---

Letzte Lebenstage Jesu, 1864, p. 11. The majority (not the mass) of the people (thus also Paulus, Bleek, Meyer), Matt. xxi. 8. The Psalm, xci. 12; Matt. iv. 6.

[1] The shouts for Saul, Absalom, Jehu, 1 Sam. x. 24; 2 Sam. xvi. 16; 1 Kings i. 39; 2 Kings ix. 13. The present shout after Psalm cxviii. 25 sq. It was disputed whether the branches should be flourished at "Lord, help!" (Hillel) or at "Give prosperity!" (Shammai). R. Akiba claims to have seen R. Gamaliel and R. Joshua swing only at the first word, after Hillel, in distinction from the people. Lightfoot, p. 350.

[2] On the original meaning of these words, comp. Hitzig, *Ps.* II. pp. 345 sq.

THE JUBILANT RECOGNITION OF THE MESSIAH. 109

the Lord!" had already, before the time of Jesus, been applied in a higher sense to the coming Messiah, is very possible, but cannot now be established with certainty. For if Jesus himself henceforth used these words in a Messianic sense, and the Christian "Primitive Hymn" was afterwards re-echoed in the congregation, the question arises whether all this is not simply the reverberation—converted into a Christian watchword—of the memorable Messianic entry which the adherents of Jesus prepared for him.[1]

> Hosanna (Help!) to the Son of David!
> Blessed is he that comes in the name of the Lord!
> Hosanna in the (heavenly) heights!

Thus did the crowds that preceded and followed cry aloud, half speaking, half singing, according to Eastern custom, with brief rhythmic repetitions—correctly preserved by Matthew—as of old Saul and Absalom had been followed with the shout, "Let the

---

[1] Matt. xxi. 9, xxiii. 39; Acts i. 11. Comp. the Maranatha of 1 Cor. xvi. 22. The note on ἐρχόμ., above, IV. p. 29, note 3. Of Hallel, *Vajikr. Rabb.* 30, says: dixit R. Abin: in Hallel est aliquid, quod respicit tempus præt., est quod respicit futurum, est quod respicit generationes has, est quod respicit dies Messiæ (Ps. cxviii.), Wetst. p. 461. The Christian Primitive Hymn, Ewald, p. 516.

[2] The three-membered cry in Matthew most readily and most simply connects itself with Psalm cxviii. 25 sq. (*a*) From verse 25 is taken simply the supplicatory word Hoshianna, enlarged by the decisively important reference to the Son of David (hosh. with dative, against Meyer). (*b*) Then follows the first member of verse 26, coming in the name, in fellowship with, not exactly commissioned by. (*c*) Finally, the song returns with fervour to the first supplicatory cry with a glance (and lifting of the branches) back to heaven (bammarom, bammeromim). Mark xi. 9, with its four members, has evidently introduced the third member with its greater particularity. John xii. 13, with its two members, has the second enlarged and expounded by the addition, "and the king of Israel." The paraphrase of Luke xix. 38, in three members, strongly suggests Luke ii. 14. In Matt. and Mark it is not Hoshia-nna, but (as also by the Rabbis) Hosha-nna (Hosanna). Comp. Gospel of the Hebrews in Jerome, *Ep.* 20, *ad Damasum*: osanna bar(r)ama. A. Merx, and after him Hilgenfeld, *N. T.* IV. p. 26, also *Zeitschrift*, 1868, p. 36, explain this from the Aram. oshana, serva nos. Similarly, Volkmar, p. 507. De Wette, Meyer, and Grimm, pass it over. But the former agrees neither with the Psalm nor with the following dative. And Dagesh? Therefore an Aramaic abbreviation of the Hebrew word in the Psalm (comp. 1 Sam. xxv. 26, hoshea) must be assumed, comp. Buxt. p. 992. Buxt. makes the interesting remark that the Feast of Tabernacles and the Lulab were eventually called by the name Hoshana which stood in connection with the former. The cry, see above, p. 108, n. 1.

king live!"[2] Luke ascribes the shout to the disciples, the others to the people. Luke is correct, inasmuch as the shout was commenced by the disciples, perhaps by Peter or the sons of Zebedee, who were the most certain of their Messiah and of their Son of David. But as at the Feast of Tabernacles the words of the precentor were crowned by a "Hallelujah" of the multitude and by a repetition of the closing strophe, so the multitude would take up and repeat the shout of the disciples.[1] At the same time the people would busily relate one to another all those deeds of the Master in Israel—with exception of the Lazarus miracle—which justified his public appearance and the shout of praise itself with which these hundreds, perhaps thousands, were now greeting him.[2]

Thus they drew near to Jerusalem. If it may with some probability be assumed that the road then followed the same course as at present, the last part of the way led in a westerly direction round the Mount of Olives, and then turned at a right-angle to the north.[3] They crossed the last high ground outside of Jerusalem. In the saddle between the middle and the southern Mount of Olives, whose summit, according to Tobler, lies like a head between two shoulders—that is, between the Mount of Olives proper, the Har Ha-Setim, still known as Dshebel Saitûn, and the so-called Mount of Offence—they left behind the meagre vegetation of the eastern Mount of Olives, and reached the cheerful plantations of the western Mount of Olives, as well as obtained a broader view of Jerusalem. How grandly it lay there before them, the stronghold of God towering high among the hills! What a bold foreground was made by the white glistening temple, with its ascending courts, its doors, its porches, the steep rocks crowned with walls, and the strong towers! But the temple itself scarcely surpassed the royal palaces with their magnificent green parks. And inseparably connected with all the visible details—so many of which were reminders only of He-

---

[1] Lightfoot, p. 349.   [2] Luke xix. 37; John xii. 17.
[3] According to Epiph. on Luke xix. 29 (against Marc., *Hær*. 42), the old road ran through Bethany, Bethphage, and Mount of Olives. Paulus, III. i. p. 167.

THE JUBILANT RECOGNITION OF THE MESSIAH. 111

rodian and Roman domination—were the history of a thousand years with its glories and its sighs, a present which groaned for redemption, and a throned God who now or never was to break His silence and to give the solution of His enigma.[1] We can understand that at sight of the holy city and of the temple, the wonder of the world, which in its marble splendour appeared in the distance to the astonished eye, now like a celestial palace, now like a snow-capped hill, and now, especially under the morning beams of the sun, like a sea of fire,—we can understand that at such a sight the voices of the extolling multitude would —as Luke intimates—swell louder, because the people not only looked upon the city and the temple, but were bringing, by the sacred road of the Mount of Olives, the Messiah to the city and to themselves.[2] The mood of Jesus himself cannot be described; it has not been handed down with certainty, and who can sound its depths? But it was not quite the same—clear and untroubled or indeed joyous—as that of the disciples and of the people. He felt satisfaction, and yet was anxious; he yearned towards Jerusalem, and yet had the feeling of strangeness, of antagonism, the choleric excitement of the hero who with the most adventurous daring breaks into the great full camp of his foes.[3] Was there floating before his mind's eye the picture of David when he left the city barefoot and weeping, fleeing from treachery and revolt, with his faithful adherents, over the Mount of Olives to the

---

[1] On Jerusalem, comp. Strabo, 16, 2: a stronghold built upon rocks and well protected. On the temple and the impression it produced, comp. especially Jos. *B. J.* 5, 5, 6; 6, 4, 6 and 8; *Ant.* 15, 11, 3. It was held to be the wonder of the world (comp., besides Jos., Tacitus, *Hist.* 5, 8, 12): "he who has not seen the building of Herod, has seen nothing splendid," qui non vidit templum, cum adhuc exstaret, non vidit aliquid splendidum. Schöttgen, p. 327.

[2] Luke xix. 37. The Mount of Olives road sacred, see above, p. 107, n. 1. Targum on Ez. xi. 23 expressly mentions the Mount of Olives; and the Rabbis lay stress on the Ezekiel passage. *Echa R. præf.:* profecta est maj. div. ab urbe in m. oliveti. Dixit R. Jonath., eam sedisse tres ann. cum dimidio super m. o. et cogitasse, Isr. pœnit. facturum, sed non fecisse. *Schev. f.* 16, 1: superioris fosseo m. o. sanctitas non erat perfecta (sed inferioris), Wetst. p. 459.

[3] Reimarus has coarsely expressed this thus (among well-known assumptions): in this undertaking he may not have been in the best of spirits (p. 144).

Jordan?[1] The words of Jesus given by the later Gospels, in which this mood of Jesus seems to find expression, are untenable, as notably the tearful utterances in Luke upon the obduracy and upon the Roman destruction of the peaceless "city of peace."[2] But the preceding rejoinder to the Pharisees' censure of the songs of praise is also unhistorical. "Teacher!"—thus they appealed to him, apart from the people—"forbid thy disciples!" He is said to have answered, "I say unto you, that if these should be silent, the stones would cry out!"[3] This utterance, borrowed from the prophet Habakkuk, seems full of force and genuine; there seems condensed into it the whole Messianic self-consciousness of Jesus, but also the whole of his bitterness consequent upon his non-recognition among the ruling circles of the Jews.[4] Therefore he expressly approves, justifies, his adherents' songs of praise: if men would not exclaim, the stones, the rocks by the way, dead nature, would be compelled to cry out in the name of God, as it did eventually, according to the Gospel tradition. Without doubt there is consistency between Luke's two notices of Jesus' emotion, the winged answer and the tears, for the pang produced by non-recognition might well overflow in tears. But it evidently follows therefrom that with the tearful utterance the prompt answer falls also. If Jesus, at his entry into the city, was by no means so certain of either success or failure, as Luke in his utterly unhistorical tearful speech now represents, he needed not so bitterly and with such strong emotion—in truth in a mood that was impossible in the midst of these accumulated, exaggerated honours, a mood which might well be described as an overflowing of his self-consciousness—have appealed to the stones by the way against Jerusalem, which had simply not yet expressed itself at all, and had so far had no

---

[1] 2 Sam. xv. 30. Jos. *Ant.* 7, 9, 2.

[2] See above, p. 67. It may be added that Paulus, III. i. p. 150, thought the genuineness to be proved by the non-fulfilment of individual predictions.

[3] Luke xix. 39 sq.

[4] Hab. ii. 11; comp. Jer. v. 3, and after Hab. *Taan. f.* 11, 1. Parallels in the classics, Wetst. p. 788. Paulus, III. i. p. 148.

occasion to express itself concerning a Messiahship beginning with the still unfinished day and not at all seriously affected by the subsequent silence of the metropolis.[1] The stony witnesses therefore plainly do not belong to the Messianic journey of Jesus, but to the reflection of a later time when it could be said the stones would have cried out and would have wept if Jerusalem had been thus silent to its Messiah, and had honoured him in the way in which it did.

D.—THE LORD OF THE TEMPLE.

Leaving behind the last spurs of the Mount of Olives, they came to the bridge over the narrow ravine of the Kidron at the foot of Mount Moriah, or the hill of the temple. This rose up bold and rocky over against the Mount of Olives, 150 feet above the valley bottom. At present the road from the Mount of Olives to the northern part of the city passes, a few hundred feet from the site of the temple, over a bridge that spans the brook-bed at a height of seventeen feet, and then leads to the lion-bedecked Stephen's Gate, so called after the well-known first Martyr of the Church. Formerly, perhaps, it ran a little more to the south over the bridge leading to the now walled-up Golden Gate with its pair of round arches and its Corinthian capitals, belonging to the Roman time, probably to the reign of Adrian.[2] Ascending the hill, they entered Jerusalem and went

---

[1] Plainly it is not to be thought that the prompt answer referred only to the disciples and not also to the people, as if Jesus would say, "If these witnesses of my deeds did not thus (extravagantly !) honour me, the stones must do it." Plainly also it is not to be thought it was spoken in Jerusalem itself in view of the dumbness of the city and in censure of that dumbness. Thus Schenkel, p. 227. Not only does Luke make the saying, xix. 39, precede the coming nigh to the city (verse 41); even against the silent Jerusalem, which did not know the Galilean prophet, Jesus could not, though deeply affected, pronounce such a sentence.

[2] Comp. Furrer, *Wand.* p. 60. Arnold, articles *Kidron* and *Zion*, in Herzog, VII. p. 548, XVIII. p. 603.

directly southwards, according to custom, towards the temple.¹ Jerusalem, the whole city—certainly an exaggeration—is reported by Matthew to have been set in motion. The people were astonished at the strange procession, at the peaceable rider in the midst of the crowd, at the excited behaviour and the songs and the acclamations. Surprised at a movement hitherto unknown, and uncertain about the man who was seen there for the first time, the inhabitants raised the question, "Who is this?" And with joy and pride, with the assurance that the name would express everything, the answer was given: "This is Jesus, the Prophet of Nazara of Galilee!"² Then, as if in confirmation of the answer, there sounded forth afresh the songs of praise which ascribed the most exalted greatness to the Prophet of Galilee, announcing him as the found Messiah. It is not reported that the Jerusalemites and the festival guests already in the city were led by what they saw to think of the Messiah, of the prophet, or that they took any part in the rejoicing. Of course, notwithstanding all the excitability of the Oriental character and all the fame which had preceded Jesus, and which the Galileans evidently took for granted, the people at Jerusalem were still strange to the Galilean movement. They were imperfectly informed about it, and but feebly influenced by it; they were inquisitive but sober-minded, or indeed, as on other occasions, they were surfeited with the excitements of a metropolis, if they were not Pharisaically prejudiced against the poor provincials; hence Matthew himself does not venture to tell of hosanna cries in the courts of the temple from adults, but only from children.³ The interest of the metropolis had yet to be excited: the first disillu-

---

¹ It was expressly forbidden to go to the temple with staff and bag and dusty shoes from a journey, *Misch. Berach.* 9, 5; Lightfoot, p. 314. Comp. the purification of the temple, below, p. 112, n. 2.

² Matt. xxi. 10 sq.

³ According to Jos. *B. J.* 2, 13, 5 (differently *Ant.* 20, 8, 6), the population of Jerusalem supported Felix against the Egyptian-Jewish Messiah who threatened the city from the Mount of Olives. Contempt for Galileans, see above, II. p. 5. Only children cry, Matt. xxi. 15.

sion for Jesus, who in taking his farewell of the people a few days after, spoke sorrowfully of the lacking Messianic cry; and certainly it was still more a disillusion for his adherents, who had cherished an exalted anticipation of the immediate homage of the city, with the heads of the spiritual and temporal authorities.[1] The fourth Gospel goes too far when—following in the track of Luke, who tells of objections by the Pharisees outside of the city—it represents the Pharisees as despairing when they witness the entry. "You see," they said among themselves in their confusion, "that you can effect nothing! Behold, the world is gone after him!"[2] They might shake their heads at the hosts of Jesus, at the popular excitement; but so long as Jerusalem with its festival guests—who did not even go to meet him—looked on in silence, and so long as they themselves gave no token of assent, there was nothing lost.[3]

It was afternoon, perhaps an hour before the commencement of the preparation day of the Sabbath, when Jesus appeared at the gate of the temple court, of the "Mountain of the House."[4] He probably dismounted at the eastern principal gate of the "outer holy place," at the so-called gate of Susa [Shushan], said to be a votive offering of the Jews of Susa.[5] According to the strict theory of the Jews, no one should be permitted upon the temple hill with shoes on, with dusty feet, or with a stick, and it was the business of the temple police to watch the place; but at the time of the Passover festival, with its immense concourse of people, and just now with this stream of men pouring in, such

---

[1] Comp. Matt. xxiii. 37 sq.

[2] John xii. 19. Perhaps, in the meaning of the author, this is to point out that without the will of Jesus (x. 18, xviii. 6) his vanquishment was impossible. But he is fond of the effect of caprice.

[3] Naturally John xii. 19 is connected with xii. 12. Jesus himself missed the sign of the Scribes for the people, Matt. xxiii. 13.

[4] Day of preparation, ninth hour = 3 p.m. The temple site — har ha-bait, after Is. ii. 2.

[5] According to Paulus, III. i. p. 155, Jesus alighted at the foot of the Mount of Olives and went on foot to the temple.

rules could scarcely be punctually observed.[1] He entered the outermost and lowest court, which Christian archæologists speak of as the Court of the Gentiles, because others than Jews might walk here. This court extended to the stone balustrade with the warning pillars which, in Greek and Latin words, bade the intruder into the higher "Holy Place" to halt, and threatened him with death.[2] This court was splendid to look upon, even though it was necessarily wanting in painting and sculpture.[3] On three sides ran a double, and on the fourth a triple, colonnade of brilliantly white monolithal marble columns, twenty-five cubits high, with ornate cedar roofs, while variously coloured stone slabs covered the broad level floor. Here, in these spaces, was the temple market; here were the *Chanujot*, the taverns or booths with the tables of the money-changers, the benches of the traders in objects for sacrifice, of whom the sacrificial cattle and offerings, wine and oil, corn and salt and incense, were bought. Nay, the provisions themselves, particularly the animals for slaughter, the oxen, the lambs, and the doves—the poor man's sacrifice—were here exhibited; and it contributed to the splendour of the festival that, *e.g.*, the lambs were to be counted by thousands.[4] There was a noise and a crying of beasts and men, of sellers and buyers, and a rolling and clinking of money; and even in these sacred spaces men could not keep pure from the hankering after speculation and profitable bargaining. The very sellers of doves screwed up their price to a gold denarius. The brokers, who exchanged the moneys of the festival guests from three quarters of the globe, current Greek, Roman, or old Jewish coins, for the half-shekel, the indispensable temple tribute of two francs, were legally entitled to the *agio* of the twelfth of a franc

---

[1] See below, p. 118, n. 2. Jos. *B. J.* 5, 5. Winer, article *Tempel*. Comp. also H. Merz. in Herzog, XV.

[2] Jos. *B. J.* 5, 5, 2.

[3] See Vol. I. pp. 251, 305 sqq.

[4] Otherwise was it desolata domus, *Hier. Jom.* t. 61, 3, in Lightfoot, p. 350. On the Chanujot (from chanah), Buxt. p. 793. Wieseler, *Beitr.* pp. 209 sqq. There were places for sale of things also outside, *e.g.* on the Mount of Olives, Lightfoot, p. 410.

for every half-shekel they exchanged, even when they gave two half-shekels for one shekel. The priests who had oversight of the temple were themselves not quite innocent of this trading.[1] This chaffering in the holy place at once roused the indignation of Jesus, though the obtuser feelings of the Pharisees were as little scandalized by it as are those priests of Christian churches who allow their cathedrals and their mass altars to be surrounded by fair booths. It seemed to be no hindrance, but rather an aid, to the pure, blameless, meritorious service of God. The secret indignation, which Jesus had probably felt on former visits to the temple, was now supplemented by the impulse at once to assert his Messianic rights and duties, solemnly and without any consideration for the dilatory people or his watchful enemies, but in the sight of God, who had given over to him the temple along with his office. A different temple inspector from the Roman Herodian of the lofty couch of the palace! In a spirit of zeal, in a spirit of stormy excitement such as we never saw him exhibit on any other occasion, and which reminds the fourth Evangelist of a prophecy of Psalm lxix., he began to drive out from the court buyers and sellers, he overturned the tables of the brokers and the benches of the dealers, and cried, " It stands written, My house shall be called a house of prayer, but ye make it a den of thieves!"[2] In his happy extemporizing manner he had here brought together two brief and apposite passages from Isaiah and Jeremiah; and with a mental reference to Hosea, his favourite prophet, he had in one strong utterance distinguished between and defined true and false religion, the religion of the heart and of prayer, and the

---

[1] Lightfoot, pp. 350 sq.; Wetst. pp. 462 sq. It is certain that the temple money was paid in the older Jewish coin, which was still current from the time of the Asmonæans (comp. also the expression shekel ha-kodesh), not in the Gentile double drachmæ or denarii. Comp. Paulus, III. i. p. 162; also Lightfoot, Wetst., Winer. On the κόλλυβος, properly "a small coin," and the temple tribute generally, see above, IV. p. 326, n. 3. On the participation of the priests, see below, p. 118, n. 1.

[2] Matt. xxi. 12 sq. and parallel passages; John ii. 14, 17. The latter verse after Ps. lxix. 9 (kinat betecha achalatni). Luke and Mark: "ye have made," from the standpoint of the destruction of this cult. The temple administrator of the Romans (ἐπιμελητὴς ἱεροῦ, Ant. 20, 9, 7), Agrippa, II. Ant. 20, 8, 11; Bibel-Lex. III. p. 59.

religion of the market.[1] According to John, he prepared a scourge of rushes, and drove out not only the men but also the cattle, and poured the small coin of the money-changers upon the ground; whilst Mark is content with adding that he would not allow any one to carry vessels, baskets, and provisions through the temple, a practice which, though forbidden, was indulged in for the sake of shortening the distance from one part of the city to another.[2] It may here be remarked that it is not the most fully developed naturalistic treatment which best accords with the character of Jesus. In this so striking transaction it must have been necessary for Jesus, for the Messiah, to preserve a certain degree of dignity, and he could not descend to a display of uncurbed anger and to such a clearing out and guardianship of the temple courts as would have become a policeman.[3]

The extraordinary sensation which this first appearance of Jesus must have made, even though it were limited to the acts reported by Matthew and Luke, is at once seen in the stupefied and unresisting retreat of the sellers and money-changers; but as much also in the reverent quietness of the people, and in the speech-

[1] The passage is compounded from Is. lvi. 7 and Jer. vii. 11. Mark adds, after Isaiah, "for all nations" (xi. 17), in a universalist sense, of which Jesus at this time was not thinking at all. According to Volkmar (pp. 512 sq.), the prosaic Evangelists have excluded this fine phrase. One is at any rate also reminded of Hosea vi. 9, comp. vi. 6. The milder utterance of Jesus in the fourth Gospel, respecting the sellers of doves, may recall Zech. xiv. 21 (Canaanite=merchant). Paulus (*Hdb.* III. i. p. 161) would explain the strong expression, "den of thieves," from the participation of the priests and Levites in the gains of the sellers. This view can find support in Jerome and Maimonides; see Wetst. p. 463. But one would be less inclined to think, with Paulus (p. 164), of the many robbers in Israel.

[2] *Bab. Jevam.* f. 6, 2 (just like *Berac.* 9, 5, Lightfoot, p. 314): quænam est reverentia templi? Ne quis eat in montem domus cum baculo suo et calceis suis, crumena sua et pulvere in pedibus suis. Non per illam faciat viam suam transitivam nec faciat locum sputationis. Also of the synagogue, *Megill.* f. 27, 2: nunquam feci (says R. Eleazar) syn. viam transitionis. Lightfoot, pp. 450, 500. Comp. also *Josua Ap.* 1, 7: ne vas quidem aliquod portari licet in templum.—Nulla re, quæ ad cibum aut potum attineat, in templum delata. Nothing but ignorance of the facts can explain the exposition that no sacrificial implements in kettles and pans were any further to profane the true spiritual temple (Volkmar, p. 512).

[3] Just here Lücke found in John the true eye-witness, whilst he adversely criticised the quite as highly coloured additions of Mark; comp. Strauss, 4th ed. I. p. 728. On the other hand, Bretschneider, *Probab.* p. 43, vigorously opposes the scourge-swinger.

lessness and inactivity of the priestly temple guard. It must here be remembered that in fact in these courts only the temple guard, with the temple captain at their head, and in the last resort the high-priest himself, had any authority; and that the sellers and money-changers sat here not merely according to ancient usage, but with the sanction of the legal ordinance itself. The sellers supplied the indispensable materials for sacrifice; the money-changers both negociated the payment of the old and legal temple tribute, and were evidently also its receivers. In so far Jesus, according to Jewish sentiment, laid hold not only of what was profane, but of what was sacred; and ancient and modern criticism teaches us that such an encroachment by Jesus was both ethically and physically impossible.[1] And yet the universal popular sentiment, notwithstanding all conventionalism and Pharisiac superstition, perceived that he had given expression to his zeal only against the profane in the holy place, in the name of the Holy One. On that account, neither hand nor tongue moved against him; and it is to be assumed that during the immediately following days, out of respect to the man of Galilee, the market remained wholly outside the temple spaces, since the continuance of the market inside would only afresh have exasperated Jesus, who went daily to the temple, or, if he subsequently winked at the abuse, would have completely discredited him in the eyes of the people.[2] Thus was this scene in Jerusalem the correct com-

---

[1] Already Origen on John, t. X. 16, points out how difficult it is to conceive of such a course of conduct, extending the use of the scourge (Weisse also would abstract something even from the Synoptics) on the part of the carpenter's son. On that account he is inclined to a symbolic interpretation; he thinks that belief in the letter of the account can be retained only if we think of Jesus' $\theta\varepsilon\tilde{\iota}\alpha$ $\delta\acute{v}\nu\alpha\mu\iota\varsigma$ banning the enemies, which in fine, as later Jerome and even Mosheim confirm (Paulus, III. i. p. 156), would be the greatest of the miracles, greater than that at Cana. See, recently, Strauss, 4th ed. I. pp. 729, 731; more recently, Volkmar, p. 514.

[2] Paulus speaks of support received by Jesus from other earnest men, wherein Strauss finds the most questionable sedition. On the psychological explanation by Olsh. and Lücke, comp. Strauss, 4th ed. I. p. 731 sq. Strauss speaks also against such an explanation, thinking, with Paulus, that an attempt to make a moral impression upon such "animal-men" would miscarry. But that objections of this kind have little weight, is seen in the victory of the ancient prophets over people and kings.

plement of the Messianic entry, a novelty in dignity, power, and action, so that the Galilean Prophet, who in very deed testified and acted like an ancient prophet even to staking his life against abuse, was no longer ridiculed by any individual in Jerusalem. It was, to all external appearance, the most brilliant day of his life; he the strong servant of God, the people half enthusiastic, half respectful, the enemies paralyzed and scattered,—one would think that on this day after the first success in the temple, it would have been easiest for him to succeed in the urging forward his bloodless victory even to the possession of the sanctuary and to the homage of the masses.[1]

When looked at more closely, this victory is seen to be only the precursor of a lost battle. The purger of the temple, the disperser of the temple market, was not the complete, the true Jesus. That this mode of acting looks so strikingly similar to that of the ancient prophets, particularly of Elijah, is in itself an evidence that Jesus in the most decisive point of his new career represented only the Jew, the zealot like that Judas Maccabæus who purged the temple of the heathen abomination of Antiochus, or like Mattathias, Judas Sariphæus, Matthias ben Margalot, and Judas Galilæus. At most he represented the epigone of the prophets, not the man of the new religion.[2] The fundamental ground of objection here is not the interest exhibited in that external temple cult which the conversation with the Samaritan woman in particular seems to deride, an interest apparently so retrogade, so old-Jewish, so foreign to Jesus' teaching concerning the worship of the heart; for we can nevertheless understand this, since Jesus had not yet thought of an abolition of the material places of worship, and even if he had, he might have been indignant at the flagrant connection between the profane and the symbolically holy. But the ground of objection is found chiefly in the coarse-

[1] The Fragmentist (p. 149) thinks of an "overthrow" of the Sanhedrim by the people, and a setting up of Jesus with his seventy disciples.

[2] Comp. the temple purifying of the Asmonæans (basis of the Feast of Dedication, of the Chanukkah, Greek ἐγκαίνια, John x. 22), 1 Macc. iv. 42 sqq. See also above, I. pp. 251, 261.

THE LORD OF THE TEMPLE. 121

ness and harshness of a scene in which the Son of Man of Galilee is so much missed.[1] The impression produced is severe, gloomy, alarming; the religion of the soul's joy in God the Father, the Galilean religion of love to our neighbours, nay, the personality full of the sorrow and the ardour of love,—these find no expression here. It is another than himself; and we cannot suppose that in such a way he won the success which so spontaneously greeted the proclaimer of the children of God, the consoler of the poor people, the healing benefactor of the sick. In fact, we see that in Jerusalem he has become far more respected and feared than loved, and that very strikingly he has performed no recorded miracle of healing.[2]

The cause of this was not merely that in Jerusalem he stood upon new ground, where there was not the Galilean sympathetic atmosphere from which the miracles of faith took their rise; the cause was in himself, since he was above all the fighting zealot, and it was in the people who were unable to forge a bond of love.

---

[1] Doubts against the literal historical truth already in Origen upon John, t. X. 16. Woolston, in Strauss, 4th ed. I. p. 732, the latter of whom, however, finds even the Old-Testament prototypes (as Mal. iii. 1 sq.) insufficient, and supposes as the basis of the account an actual opposition of Jesus to the abuse. Weisse also (p. 437) is not inclined to admit a zeal for the temple, as Jesus would thus be the most zealous supporter of the ceremonial law. He therefore seeks, like Origen ($διάλυσις\ νόμου$), a symbolical meaning: it was a token of the power lent for the purification of the sanctuary in a higher sense. Schenkel also (p. 229) supposed that Jesus intended to show the temporary character of the whole temple service, and to inaugurate the new temple of all nations. But all this does not agree with the positive, conservative sense of the passage in Matt. xxi. 13, while it harmonizes with unhistorical views of Jesus' attitude to the Old Testament. Moreover, such a conception leads ultimately to the annihilation of the fact itself, for, according to Volkmar (pp. 511—514), Jesus was the reformer of the temple system only in his historical influence and initially ($ἤρξατο$! as Mark vi. 7, but also xiv. 33, &c., often), and the getting rid of the moral and physical contradiction is the veritable purification of the life of Jesus. Every one sees that the above was not the aim of the transaction, not even in Mark, and that this exposition leaves the real life of Jesus empty, and leaves it impossible to understand why the entry—standing upon a kindred basis—is not to be denied, and why Jesus was put to death at all as an insurgent (pp. 588, 590).

[2] Ewald certainly speaks (p. 518) of his having, according to Matt. xxi. 14, again healed all kinds of sick! The Wolfenbuttel Fragmentist had already more correctly given prominence to the absence of miracles, pp. 149 sqq., 216, 249 sq. Instead of healing, he had only scolded.

But why was he here other than he had been in Galilee? In the first place, because he came as a stranger and because he came inspired with the consciousness—increased by the eloquent silence of the Jerusalemites—of antagonism to that gross worship and its masters, and of a struggle for life and death; and in the next place, because he came as the openly declared and manifest Messiah. As the unproclaimed Messiah in Galilee he could obey the promptings of his own innermost nature, and bless with the charms of his loving words, with the fullness of his heart's sympathy. As the avowed Messiah at Jerusalem he was compelled publicly to concern himself with the general condition of the people, with the prevailing circumstances as a whole, the corruption of which he could at first do no other than oppose, attack with bitterness, and destroy with energy. This modification of the character of his ministry was for him an historical tragical necessity, because he was the Messiah, and because he could not at Jerusalem preface this Messiahship by his Galilean preparation or indeed re-mould it into higher spiritual forms. But it not only indirectly prejudiced the revelation of his innermost character, of the religion most peculiar to himself, it also directly clouded and destroyed his success.[1] He stood forth with outward acts, with catastrophes, with reformations, with organizations; but his nature, his gifts, his strength, his inclination, did not lie in this sphere. Hence there lacked also consistency and tact; he himself broke off when he had only begun. Instead of dethroning the reigning spiritual powers and pressing forwards to a reconstitution of the theocracy and its organs, and of the worship of God—things which he touched only in their outworks—he at once reverted to the Galilean system, to his own proper nature, to teaching and discussing, although both space and time for this were here evidently wanting. He left everything beyond to God, and factually ceased to be the Messiah who had been

---

[1] The Fragmentist (pp. 144 sqq., comp. above, p. 101, n. 2) says, in his usual manner, that Jesus lays his mildness by, and becomes violent and restless as one who is already measuring his strength with the temporal power.

yesterday proclaimed and who he yesterday really was. By this inconsistency—which was his consistency—he made his fall doubly certain. He undeceived the people whom he had enticed into a recognition of his Messiahship, but who afterwards—very imperfectly understanding his doctrinal addresses themselves—could see the Messiah neither in such theocratic deeds of power as the purging of the temple, nor in such divine signs and miracles as were looked for from the Messiah, nor in miracles of healing; and he irritated and encouraged the hierarchy who, when listening to the more innocent doctrinal addresses and disputations, never forgot the Messiah of the entry, and the temple purifier with his passion for rule and revolution, but were no longer much afraid of the Rabbi who had become quieter, and who was again declining in the estimation of even the people.[1]

What the popular opinion, based upon so many hints of the Old Testament, expected of the Messiah, is to be found expressed in a series of Messianic experiments, and principally in a striking parallel of the sixth decade. About the year A.D. 58, an Egyptian Jew, called by his believers Prophet, by those in power Deceiver, led nearly 30,000 adherents from the Jordan deserts to the Mount of Olives. He promised miracles and signs from the hand of Divine Providence; the first and weightiest "sign of freedom, of salvation," was to be the falling down of the walls of Jerusalem at his word of command; and this was to be followed up by the overpowering of the Roman garrison by his armed body-guard, and the domination of the people.[2] But when the procurator Felix treated the matter seriously, and stormed the Mount of Olives with cavalry and foot, not only did the 30,000 flee with such haste that only 400 were killed and 200 taken prisoners, but the people of Jerusalem turned away from the ideal dream to co-operate with the real power, and exhibited as much zeal in persecuting the Messiah as if they had never asked and longed for him. It would be an odious injustice to

---

[1] Ewald (p. 530) also says the movement did not grow.
[2] Jos. B. J. 2, 13, 4 sq., comp. 6, 5, 2; Ant. 20, 8, 6.

do as the Roman tribune Claudius Lysias did in the case of Paul at Pentecost, A.D. 59, viz. to compare Jesus with the Egyptian who defended his cause with phantasies and with arms, for Jesus—and in truth Paul also—fell using as his weapon the most genuine religion; but we may compare the popular expectations and the popular disappointment.[1] Whoever lifted up the standard of Messiahship, excited hopes of deeds, decisions, miracles, redemptions, liberties; whoever failed to satisfy those hopes, or retreated from the cause once begun, was trodden under foot not only by the armed opponents, but by the people themselves.

The prelude of this tragedy came on the same evening. Matthew and Mark are agreed in reporting that the high-priests and scribes met together to consult against him immediately after the purifying of the temple.[2] But Matthew inserts here a narrative which is wanting to the other sources. After the temple purifying, blind and lame—according to Volkmar again, they were heathens —went to him and were healed.[3] Children and youths cried in the outer court, "Hosanna to the Son of David!" Astonished at his miracles and vexed at the exclamations, Jesus' opponents went to him: "Dost thou hear what these say?" But the disavowal which they wished for, he did not utter. "Yes," answered he to their question; "did ye never read, Out of the mouth of babes and sucklings thou hast ordained praise?"[4] These narrations are unusually characteristic; the circumstances are soberly told, the plaudits of the more ardent youths are characteristic, whilst older men are silent; Jesus' answer has the spirit and colour of his answers, and is particularly apposite when we see the point of the Psalm from which he quoted: an ascription of praise, a

---

[1] Comp. Acts xxi. 38, also v. 36. [2] Matt. xxi. 15; Mark xi. 18.

[3] Matt. xxi. 14. Volkmar (pp. 142, 513) says that Matthew has thus in a new way introduced the *temple of all peoples* (Mark). He might also only have thought of 2 Sam. v. 6, 8.

[4] Matt. xxi. 15 sq. Hosanna, as above, p. 109. So the received text; Osanna, Tisch.; Hos'anna, Reg. Petr., and others. Jesus referred to Ps. viii. 2, from which Psalm he may also have drawn his title of Son of Man; see above, III. p. 81. That the passage refers primarily to God (Strauss, 4th ed. II. p. 282) is no ground for objection.

defence against thine adversaries ! Moreover, the harshness and the negation-character of his appearance in the temple would be admirably moderated and complemented by the deeds of compassion, by the exclamations of the children, signs that even in his storm at Jerusalem he did not repudiate his innate sympathy with misery and his Galilean friendship for children.[1] But a decisive evidence against the miracles is afforded by the silence of the other sources, by the indefiniteness of the so thoroughly picturesque signs, and finally by the fact that the sick would have been scared away by the harsh severity of his appearance in the temple, a severity which could be toned down only by placing the healings at an earlier stage in the entry.[2] Similar reasons may puzzle us as to the children. Jubilation and confiding familiarity must have been prevented by such intimidating occurrences; and why did the opponents seize upon the shouts of the children, if Jesus at this moment had committed his capital crime of lordship over the temple ? Moreover, we understand the author's fondness for Messianic quotation. If, however, any one objects to renounce this scene—and there is room for objection because it stands in no intimate connection with the colourless narrative of the healed, and it shows not only colour, but also the genuine, spirited, fully-equipped Jesus in the use of his favourite passage—he must do what the author himself does not really hinder him from doing, viz. he must place the scene before the temple purifying, and transfer it to the moment of the entry into the temple, when the Jerusalemite youths sympathize more quickly than their elders with the Galilean jubilant train, and have recourse to the palm-branches that would in any case have been swung, and to the Messianic shouts, whose contagious

---

[1] Comp. Stolz in Paulus, *Handb.* III. i. p. 165, who says, "I always thought it very fine that Jesus could pass so easily from an exhibition of fiery zeal to the performance of deeds of humane helpfulness." Hence also Ewald's (p. 518) belief in these miracles. The children are unconditionally admitted by Neander, p. 482; Ewald, p. 517; Hausrath, p. 437.

[2] Comp. Matt. xi. 5; 2 Sam. v. 6, 8. This Davidic incident might have been present in the writer's mind.

influence would be suspected by the hierarchy even in this harmless form.[1] In their perplexity and excitement, the opponents open the struggle by seizing upon the second best, upon what came first, upon the Messiah cries of the Galileans and the children, and not upon the temple purifying, the inquiry into which they reserved. From all these grounds Jesus escaped his opponents, whose astonishment, vexation, and suspicious alertness, particularly described by Mark, he must have seen. "They sought how they might destroy him."[2] The attempt against him was not yet, however, arranged. The people were still in a state of astonished admiration, and the opponents were afraid of the people; under their protection, thinks Mark, who dreams of doctrinal addresses, Jesus remained until the evening.[3] But he went away earlier, according to Matthew's more probable account.[4] He retired for the first time from the attack which he saw coming, and which he was not willing to crush in its first stages by a still more decisive assault with the aid of the people. Under the consciousness that the struggle for life and death had begun, and with the feeling, which he showed as early as the next day, that he with his non-material weapons must succumb, he departed out of the city,—itself a proof that he knew he was not safe and had exposed himself to danger. The exit was different from the entry. He separated himself from the masses of the people, and, accompanied only by his adherents, went out

---

[1] Comp. *Succ.* c. 3: parvulus, quam primum agitare fasciculum novit, tenetur ad gestandum fasciculum. Lightfoot, p. 351. Above assumption also in Langen's Last Days of Jesus (p. 14): at the entry into the temple; comp. Hausrath, p. 437. According to Ewald (p. 517), the boys continued to sing the challenging song through the streets. Those who derive everything from Old-Testament parallels can refer to—besides Ps. viii.—Joel ii. 16; Susanna 45; Jos. *Ant.* 4, 8, 48 (weeping of the children at the death of Moses). Comp. *Hier. Sot.* f. 2, 3: ad mare rubrum etiam infantes cantarunt (Luke i. 41) in utero matrum (Lightfoot, p. 493). *Bav. Bathr.* f. 12, 2: sapientia ablata est a prophetis et data est stultis et pueris; comp. *Syn. Soh.* and *Soh. Ex.*, in Schöttgen, p. 115.

[2] Mark xi. 18.

[3] Mark xi. 18 sq. Weisse, I. p. 436, defends Mark. The other Gospels, he says, have abbreviated, I. p. 574.

[4] Matt. xxi. 17.

THE LORD OF THE TEMPLE. 127

of the gate, doubtless by the footway leading to the Mount of Olives, over whose summit he went to the quiet Bethany. According to Matthew and Mark, he here took up his quarters for the next few days, while Luke seems to think of his spending the night in the open air upon the Mount of Olives, as he did in the last Gethsemane night.[1] The house into which he entered was probably that of Simon the leper, into which we are led by the events of one of the last evenings.[2]

We must not omit to mention expressly that two Gospels do not fix this act of purifying the temple on the day of Jesus' entry into Jerusalem. It is true that these Gospels themselves differ much one from the other. According to Mark, the temple purifying was on the second day; according to John, instead of being at the close, it was at the beginning of the ministry of Jesus, at the first Passover feast.[3] The divergence of Mark is in itself unimportant, but it says very little for the fidelity of this author.[4] It is best explained by the author's wish to exhibit a series of tangible daily works at Jerusalem and two judgments in one day, and particularly to create room for Jesus to pass twice by the celebrated unfruitful fig-tree between Bethany and Jerusalem,

---

[1] Matt. xxi. 17; Mark xi. 11 sq.; Luke xxi. 37. Strauss (*New Life of Jesus*, Eng. trans., I. pp. 385 sq.) makes a good harmony of the accounts by saying that Jesus spent the night sometimes at Bethany and sometimes in a lodge on the Mount of Olives. For the rest, even Luke would confirm the assumption of the spending the night in a house, since αὐλίζ. means this also (comp. Matt. *l.c.*), if it were not for Luke ii. 8, and if the village Bethany were mentioned as well as the "Mount of Olives." Wetst. (p. 464) and others thought—quite apart from Luke—of a spending the night in the open air, as it was the custom to do at the Feast (in tents and booths) on account of the overcrowding of the city. Renan thinks not only of Bethany, but also of the farms on the Mount of Olives, where Jesus had many friends. According to Venturini, Gethsemane belonged to Lazarus, and an estate in Bethphage to Nicodemus! Bethany is regarded by Grätz (III. p. 240, comp. also Furrer), though without any ground beyond that of the very questionable etymology, "House of Poverty" (Furrer, art. *Bethanien* in *Bibel-Lex.*), as a place of lepers; by Dixon, as a place of poor people; and therefore also by Hausrath (p. 436) as the resort of the less wealthy guests.

[2] Matt. xxvi. 6.

[3] Mark xi. 11 sq., 15; John ii. 13 sq.

[4] Bleek is here also correct, II. p. 307, against the defenders of Mark. Weizs., p. 91, is sceptical.

which on the second day was distinctly seen to be withered.[1] Against Mark stands the double testimony of Mark and Luke; and there is no doubt that the Messianic act is much more appropriate to the entry day, with its exaltation of feeling and its popular expectations, than to the second day, which would naturally inaugurate rest, sobriety, and the ebb of excitement. Moreover, nothing exceeds the tameness of the close of the first and even of the second day in Mark, except that barren place after the choice of the disciples, where Mark arbitrarily omits the Sermon on the Mount, which gives pith and force to that choice. Jesus, going to the sanctuary, "looked upon" everything, and, as it was evening, immediately went back to Bethany. Could the Messiah, entering the city with honour and pomp, escorted by the people, have confined himself, like a tourist or a private person on his travels, to an inspection of what was interesting and antique? Could he have calmly witnessed the disorder and deliberately postponed until the morrow the exhibition of a passionate zeal? Could he have left the city to go to Bethany when he had but just come to the city, and when he was driven out by no such animosity as that which he, in a marvellous way, is said to have braved the next day until evening?[2] Much more daring is the divergence of the fourth Gospel. Lukewarm criticism has, indeed, been able down to the present day to find it possible that Jesus should have twice—at the beginning and at the end—undertaken that Augean work which was needed to be done twice on account of the persistent repetition of the abuse. But this criticism is disarmed by the facts that circumstances could not have repeated themselves with scarcely the difference

---

[1] The two judgments: the fig-tree and the temple purifying, xi. 12—15. With respect to Jesus' visits to Jerusalem, Mark, in order to procure two days for the fig-tree, inserts a third day, dividing the first (with entry and temple purifying) into two days: (1) Entry day; (2) cursing and purifying; (3) withering and disputation. Comp. below, p. 145.

[2] With barrenness and the impossible the second day also closes, xi. 15, 18 sq. The $\pi\epsilon\rho\iota\beta\lambda\epsilon\psi$, xi. 11, is a mere mannerism, iii. 5, 34, v. 32, ix. 8, x. 23. According to Hausrath (p. 436), already on the first day the clamour makes a bad impression upon Jesus; hence the purifying on the second day!

THE LORD OF THE TEMPLE. 129

of a hair—the money-changers, the oxen, the doves, the reprimand of Jesus, which however is toned down, and the opponents' demand for his authority; that the transaction was great only once, the second time it would have been a merely mechanical repetition; and that the sources themselves are discreet enough to narrate it only once and not twice.[1] But if it be one and the same incident, then the question forces itself upon us, which of the Gospels has related it correctly and at the right place?[2] In the face of the fixed tradition of the older Gospels, the younger source is at once discredited; and the point of the great objection, that Jesus opened his ministry in the world without any tact at all, is taken away only by representing that the violence of this transaction excited the Jews to a very moderate degree. But as this detail is itself unhistorical, so are also the other details. The zealotism of Jesus is exaggerated, his censure toned down, the objection of the Jews is transferred to the same, i.e. the false, day, the answer of Jesus converted into a morbid mystery the basis of which, moreover, could and did belong only to the last days of Jesus.[3] Finally, it is clearly to be discerned how com-

[1] Luthardt, following Hofm., subtly argues out a distinction: in the Synoptics, Prophet; in John, Son of God, &c. Meyer would show the difference in John ii. 19! In favour of two similar transactions, Chrys. and others, particularly many moderns, including Paulus and Venturini, Tholuk and Meyer, Lange and Langen, Caspari, Hengstenb., Rigg., not to forget the latest defender, Gess. Sieffert was inclined to find possible an assimilation of two original more dissimilar accounts. For one transaction, Origen and his contemporaries (upon John, t. X. p. 15), Luther and the entire recent criticism. Weisse (I. p. 438) justly reckons the repetition as sheer pedantry.

[2] For John, Wetst., Ammon, Sieffert, Neander, Lücke, De Wette, Brückner, Krabbe, Bleek, Bunsen, Ewald, Renan, Weizsäcker. For the Synoptics, Luther ("it seems to me that John here hops over the first three years"), Ziegl., Theile, Strauss, Weisse, Baur, Hilg., Schenkel, and others. In Neander (p. 211), the famous explanation of the Synoptical mode of narration is still commended to the adherents of John: since to the Synoptics there existed only one festival journey to Jerusalem, and the question, Matt. xxi. 23, appeared to point to a severe conflict, the purifying of the temple has been introduced at the end.

[3] The exaggeration, John ii. 15; the toning down, verse 16; the premature objection, verse 18; the reference to the destruction of the temple, verse 19, according to the Synoptics (Matt. xxvi. 61), an item of evidence in the trial at Jerusalem, in John ii. 21, moreover, unhistorically interpreted, and if historically interpreted belonging at any rate to the period immediately preceding his death. See below. In an article upon three Christian chronologists, in the *Protest. Kirchenzeitung*, 1869, pp. 49, 51,

pletely this deed of purification is of one spirit and mould with that public avowal of Messianism which Jesus made only at the close; and this history ceases to be intelligible when we find reticence in the finish at Jerusalem and open avowal in the beginning.[1] In truth, it is therefore only the author who found it necessary that *his* Gospel should leave no doubt about the decisive breach of Jesus with the dominant Judaism at the very beginning, and at the same time to disencumber by this transposition the end of Jesus from any the slightest reproach of a self-earned fall through a material Messianism.[2]

But while John violently tore the incident of the temple purifying—which he made use of much too soon—from the last ministry of Jesus in Jerusalem, he was compelled to crown the last entry of Jesus with unhistorical, though intellectually remarkable, novelties, just as he had introduced it with such.[3] Here we see the significant approach of Hellenes, as previously the procession of Jewish festival guests,—an edifying fulfilment of conscious and unconscious, of his own and of Jewish maliciously spoken, prediction, a fulfilment greeted by Jesus in wise self-restraint as an earnest of the apostolic time which must grow out of his death, must spring from the decay of the re-germinating seed. And next we see an elsewhere quite unknown divine sign from heaven, which changes the mood of

I have afresh explained the forty-six years' duration of the building of the temple (comp. above, II. pp. 379 sq.). See also Gutsehmid (who explains it from Luke iii. 1) in Wieseler's review, *Lit. Centralblatt*, autumn, 1869. Sevin, p. 3. English expositors have already shown Jesus' want of tact in John: Lücke, I. pp. 435 sq.; Strauss, 4th ed. I. p. 730.

[1] Weizs. p. 325 (similarly Neander, p. 211) says the transaction does not harmonize *at all* with the generally circumspect and *reserved* (!) behaviour of Jesus in those days, but it has the character of an appearance for the first time, of a bold act opening a new course; and moreover, in the Synoptics, the event stands isolated, no corresponding effect follows it. As if the question in Matt. xxi. 23 could better refer to anything else, and as if John ii. 18, 23, would be a more appropriate and more powerful result! Ewald (p. 520) recognizes, much more correctly than W., that the temple purifying would have had a much more significant sense at the end than at the beginning,— but John had good grounds, and it is in place even there!

[2] The first is illustrated by John iv. 21, the second by xii. 12, xviii. 20, 36.

[3] See John xii. 20 sqq.

THE LORD OF THE TEMPLE. 131

Jesus, depressed by the sudden thought of death, into one of triumph, glorifies and transfigures him, and gives him a certainty of overcoming the princes of the world.[1] That these are pure fictions is so much the more readily seen because the transfiguration, with the voice from heaven, as well as the sadness of Jesus, belong, according to the older Gospels, to quite different periods in his career, and especially because the historically so well-attested scene of lamentation in Gethsemane—which actually occurred immediately before the apprehension of Jesus, therefore in the course of the following days—is here transferred to the entry, certainly in a most diluted and weakened form; in the form, indeed, of a momentary cloud, out of which there broke victoriously the heavenly voice and Jesus' most exalted self-consciousness.[2] In a few words of reminder and of warning, hurried in every respect, the last testimony of Jesus was uttered before the people, from whom Jesus hid himself by withdrawing entirely into the narrow circle of his twelve disciples. In the older Gospels, however, the great—in John long since exhausted—teaching ministry of Jesus in Jerusalem now first begins.[3]

---

[1] John xii. 12, 20. Prediction of Jesus, iv. 23, x. 16. Scorn of the Jews, vii. 35. It is disputed whether the Hellenes were Hellenistic Jews or pure heathens or Gentile-Jewish proselytes. Comp. Acts viii. 27. According to the context, the last. Thus Neander, p. 509; Weizs. p. 546. According to Goldhorn's curious opinion, the proposal of the Hellenes to come to Jesus brought on his conflict.

[2] Certain Hellenes as unhistorical as the multitude of Jewish festival guests, xii. 12. Transfiguration and voice from heaven, Matt. xvii. 1. Hour of sadness, Matt. xxvi. 36. How arbitrarily it is arranged is seen from the introduction of the words of Matt. xvi. 25, x. 24, in John xii. 25 sqq. Comp. particularly Baur, *Kanon. Ev.* pp. 197 sqq. Even Ewald is able to speak only of a glorification of the earlier account (p. 528). Neander (p. 512) sees here difficulties which cannot be altogether solved, but holds fast to the account. Bleek is more certain, *Beitr.* p. 272. Gess perfectly, pp. 125 sqq. Comp. also Weizs. p. 546.

[3] See above, p. 78. The last utterance of Jesus, John xii. 44, quite isolated, and introduced without locality, without one new idea, is a cross to all expositors. Most —Ewald included (p. 530)—take refuge in the explanation, which contradicts the text, that Jesus had spoken this earlier, and the Evangelist subjectively brings everything together at once.

Division III.—THE DECISIVE STRUGGLE.

THE struggle for supremacy which was occasioned by the entry of Jesus and his public act in the temple, was, during the following days, not only continued, but brought to a decisive issue. While Jesus, on his side, retreated from acts to words, not out of fear, nor through indecision, but in obedience to the spirit of his ministry, the opponents on their side were not inclined to long disputations after Jesus' first acts had revealed his views; and even the words of the Galilean gave the impression that they must be dangerous to the hitherto so well-tested spirit of subjection which characterized the people. Every power which, while indulging in a stubborn belief in its monopoly of authority and its unlimited supremacy, is disagreeably surprised by a sudden popular movement, is only too ready to have recourse to a sudden and harsh exercise of force. In this case, Oriental passion, religious conceit, hierarchical pride, and—perhaps the most justifiable motive—the recollection of the unhappy political and religious popular commotions of thirty or forty years before, led to prompt resolves.[1] But much in this struggle remains obscure. The Gospels are fond of bringing upon the stage from the very beginning the whole Sanhedrim, high-priests, scribes, and elders, or at least the representatives of that supreme spiritual Council which afterwards condemned Jesus. And then they give the encounters in such a close array as to make it appear that all these conflicts developed themselves in unwearied succession in the course of one day. With reference to the first point, however, it can be seen to be tolerably certain that the earlier attacks proceeded almost entirely from the old foes of Jesus, from the Pharisees, the leaders of the modern popular

[1] See above, I. pp. 254 sqq., 261.

piety; and that then the struggle was continued by the hierarchs of office, the high-priests with the harsh party of the Sadducees, to be finally taken up by the Sanhedrim. And with reference to the second point, there are several significant interruptions of the struggle perceptible, which, as the chronology of the death-year of Jesus must show more in detail, make possible the restoration of a terminus of these conflicts lasting at least three days.[1]

A.—THE ASSAILANTS.

Like a dauntless hero, Jesus was already on the way from Bethany to Jerusalem early on the morning of the 9th of April.[2] This day was probably a Sabbath, and we might suppose, since Jesus went a distance of fifteen, and not merely six, Greek stadia, that he broke the Jewish Sabbatic law, the law of the "Sabbath day's journey."[3] But we nowhere find this charge made against him; and since it was impossible for the holy city to contain the thousands or indeed millions of the Passover guests, and since it was necessary for many to find their night-quarters in the villages

[1] Schenkel having recently introduced a ministration of Jesus at Jerusalem before the entry, there happen to him after the entry *immediately* betrayal, the Last Supper, and Gethsemane. *Bibel-Lex.* III. p. 295. Again, Weizs. (p. 532) found "several days" too few for the conflicts that followed; but these fell earlier, since, according to John's more correct account, Jesus hid himself! Where, again, are the sometimes lauded and sometimes despised Synoptics?

[2] Matt. xxi. 18. Here at the commencement Strauss's words (4th ed. I. p. 646) may be recalled: the controversies, after the entry, are certainly *in a superior degree genuine*, because they are carried on so entirely in the spirit and tone of the Rabbinic dialectics (only this?) of the time. On the other hand, the hyper-criticism of Volkmar has recently unceremoniously explained away *everything*.

[3] The Sabbath-day's journey, Talm. techum ha-shabbat (on the ground of Exodus xvi. 29), is the longest distance which the Jew should go, on account of the rest of the day. According to the Rabbis, 2000 cubits; according to Epiph. *Hær.* 66, 82, six stadia, about a Roman mile. Comp. also Acts i. 12, and Jos. *B. J.* 5, 2, 3, according to which authorities the Mount of Olives was a Sabbath-day's journey (Acts), or six stadia (Jos.), from Jerusalem. On the other hand, Bethany was fifteen stadia, John xi. 18.

of the neighbourhood or in the open air, it is intelligible that approach to the temple must have been made easier, and that this was effected partly by a relaxation of the Sabbatic limitations, and partly by artificial theories of the distances and of the relations of different places.[1] A surprising light is thrown upon this by the Talmudic intimation that Bethphage, the neighbour of Bethany, was regarded as undivided from Jerusalem, insomuch that the Passover lamb could be eaten at Bethphage as at Jerusalem.[2]

Like Jesus, the people—and they for Jesus' sake—were early present in the outer courts of the temple.[3] But the foes also made their appearance betimes, in order to suppress or at least to moderate the popular agitation. As Jesus, according to Matthew and Luke, was teaching the people, or, according to Mark, was walking about in the holy courts, there came to him priests, elders of the people, and Pharisaic scribes, but not—as the Gospels exaggerate—the whole Sanhedrim, with the great question which was left unsolved on the previous evening: "By what authority doest thou these things, and who gave thee this authority?"[4] What things they meant they did not say. Their brevity was not that of bashfulness, but of displeasure at unheard-of, unspeakable things, things which one would not like to mention and could not even briefly recapitulate; for they certainly meant everything together—the entry, the purifying, and the teaching

---

[1] Comp. Geiger, *Sadd. und Phar.* 1863, p. 18: artificial ideal connection of localities (erubin, mixturæ, Bux. p. 1657, comp. Herzog, XV. p. 624). But not only was the conservatio vitæ dispensatory, but also the urgens necessitas (Wetst. p. 499).

[2] See above, p. 90.   [3] Luke xxi. 38.

[4] Matt. xxi. 23; Luke xx. 1; Mark xi. 27; comp. John ii. 18. Luke says indefinitely "one day" ($\dot{\epsilon}\nu$ $\mu\iota\tilde{\alpha}$). The three Gospels represent more or less the whole Council, the Sanhedrim, as going to him; Matt. the high-priests and elders (generally $\pi\rho\epsilon\sigma\beta$., Luke xix. 47, $\pi\rho\tilde{\omega}\tau o\iota$ $\lambda\alpha o\tilde{\upsilon}$); Luke and Mark the scribes also, evidently the whole Sanhedrim. Luke and Mark introduce the scribes because Matt. xxi. 45 assumes their presence. Of the action here of the whole Sanhedrim, it is plain that we must not think, as all that follows shows. There are, therefore, as the limitation in Matthew at the beginning and the hint at the close best indicate, several hierarchs, certainly not yet the Sadducean high-priest Caiaphas, but individual high-priests, elders of the people, and scribes of the Pharisaic party.

in the temple.¹ They now asked—not, as some have said, in the character of a judicial commission of inquiry, but yet as members of the hierarchy—with magisterial emphasis, for his legitimation, for a complete statement of the authority itself and for the giver of that authority.² They might think that he could not escape, that he would be compelled either to show the authority of the high-priests and of the Sanhedrim, or to give himself into custody as a human self-willed author of disturbance and promoter of sedition. For these dead guardians of dead ordinances had hardly thought of a third resource, of the Divine authority. But they found their match: if the zealot of yesterday was no longer before them to drive out of the sanctuary the audacious and unclean questioners, as unworthy as the money-changers and the dealers, the dreaded, ready-tongued, acute disputant of Galilee was there, scorning the fetters with which little men would bind him. And bolder, more determined than ever were his words. But while those words were open, their meaning was hidden; and though they were an answer, they rather challenged from his opponents an answer, from the embarrassment of which they were fain to escape. Here we have a most splendid encounter of the great and the self-conscious with the puny ones who dared to challenge him. He disdained to canvass at once their right to put the question; perhaps they had the right, perhaps there were among them official persons, priests in charge of the temple, and heads of the school whose teaching was influ-

---

[1] Similarly Bleek, Ewald, Weizs.; Meyer is inclined to think only of the temple purifying and the healings (!). Ewald (pp. 520 sq.) naturally omits the temple purifying—which is nevertheless the most important—since he does not accept it; and Neander (p. 211) has the fanciful notion that this question in the Synoptical narrative first called forth the temple purifying. On the other hand, Weisse (I. p. 438) much more correctly recognizes how appropriately the attack follows the temple purifying. Neander (p. 487), in his Johannine prejudice, has fallen into scepticism regarding the whole of this incident. There is a noteworthy similarity between this proceeding and that in Acts iv. 7; comp. also iv. 11 with Matt. xxi. 42, iv. 16 with Matt. xxi. 25 sq. If a dependence can possibly exist here, it must be on the side of the later Acts.

[2] The commission, in Schenkel, *Bib.-Lex.* III. p. 293. An embassy from the Sanhedrim, Neander, p. 487.

ential even in the Sanhedrim. He proposed to them a higher counter-question, which cut to the very core of the subject: "So will I also ask you a question; if ye answer me, then I will also tell you by what authority I do this. The baptism of John, whence was it? From heaven or of men?"[1] Here was a whole world in a word. More openly than ever before did Jesus here appeal to John. He named, or indicated as his predecessor and his legitimation, the terror of the Pharisees and of the hierarchy, but also their victim, the man of the people, the popular agitator. His baptism, the rejected, proscribed Jordan baptism, the sign of conspirators, he spoke of as sent from heaven, as a gift of God; and in the same sense and spirit, in one and the same connection, he would derive from heaven his entry, his temple purifying, his preaching of the kingdom of heaven, his Messianic preaching, as John did his baptism.[2] He might have said this at once; but his terrible weapon was to compel *them* to say it, to compel them to confess or deny it in the face of the clear truth which had dawned upon every unprejudiced man in Israel with exception of the Pharisees, and in the presence of the multitudes of people who, according to both the Gospels and Josephus, would not permit any attack to be made upon the great dead.[3] The Gospels reveal the consultations of the perplexed hierarchs, who are quite correctly represented, even though not a word that could be written down came out of their mouths. "If we say, From heaven, he will say to us, Then why did ye not believe in him? But if we say, Of men, we fear the people, for all hold John as a prophet." The answer, therefore, was that of children, of women: "We do not know." Jesus also has now done with the matter;

---

[1] From heaven = from God, usual mode of expression, Schöttgen, p. 172. Wetst. p. 465. Comp. above, III. p. 44, n. 1.

[2] Volkmar, p. 521: it is *possible* that Jesus had already attached a value to the precedence of the Baptist! Thus can only he speak who no longer believes in anything historical.

[3] Matt. xxi. 26; Luke xx. 6; Mark xi. 32. Comp. above, II. pp. 339 sq., IV. p. 224.

THE ASSAILANTS. 137

with the proud calm of a victor who has repulsed an arrogant and vigorous onset, he retorts, "Neither do I say to you by what authority I do this."¹

But if he had done with his answer, he had not done with his attack. The sins of the hierarchy were his theme. The severity of his criticism was moderated by the parabolical form to which he had recourse, and which he used with admirable mental calmness and with the most perfect art of his best Galilean times, as well as by the subtle intention of extorting from his taciturn opponents themselves a voluntary or reluctant but just confession. In a first parable, handed down by Matthew alone and unquestionably genuine, he exposed the sins of the last time. Following up what he had just said, he placed in contrast the attitude of the Pharisees and of the people respectively towards John, and compelled the former to utter a "No" against themselves, and a "Yes" for John and the people.² "What think ye? A man had two sons. Going to the first he said, Son, go work to-day in the vineyard. I will not, said the son; but afterwards he repented and went. The man went to the second son with the same command. Yes, sir, said the second, but did not go. Which of the two did the will of his father?" The opponents answered at once, "The first."³ Here he had them. "Verily I say unto

¹ In Luke xx. 6: all the people will stone us! Comp. Donatus on Terence, *Eun.* V. 5, 11 (Wetst. p. 466): perturbatur; nec negare potuit nec consentire volebat, et ideo quasi defensionis loco dixit: *nescio*.

² Matt. xxi. 28. Weisse's partiality for Mark (II. p. 109) leads him to regard the story of the two sons as inappropriately introduced. Volkmar's criticism (pp. 164, 520) finds that Matt. here gives a mutilated version of Luke's parable of the Prodigal Son, which parable has in fact grown out of Matthew; and that all these parables, especially in Luke, are only variations upon Mark ii. 17.

³ Comp. Rabb.: impii promittunt multa et servant pauca. Schöttgen, p. 173. The reading here varies. Particularly, according to B in verse 29, the elder son at first promises, while in verse 30 the younger at first refuses, wherefore the Scribes in verse 31 praise the second (ὕστερος, δεύτ., noviss.). But the preponderance of authority is for the above reading (Tisch.), and the variation is sufficiently explained (Meyer) from the usual relation of two to Judaism and heathenism among the Fathers, a relation which was specially supported by the kindred but evidently later parable of the Prodigal Son (Luke xv.), but a relation which is unhistorically introduced into Matthew, and even in Luke is not the original sense of the parable.

you, that the publicans and the harlots go into the kingdom of God before you. For John came to you in the way of righteousness, and ye believed him not. But the publicans and harlots believed him. And ye, when ye saw it, repented not afterwards so as to believe him."[1] He here very finely depicted the positive and negative attitude of the people and of the Pharisees towards God. The people as a whole are the elder son. They had imperfectly fulfilled their call to work in the service of God; they had roundly refused, and yet at last they, even to the very grossest of them, to those who had gone the furthest in the direction of moral ruin, learnt to repent and to long for the kingdom of God under the preaching of John. The Pharisees and Scribes—the younger son, who was to compensate for the degeneracy of the elder one, the representative of all piety, of all holiness—had amid much show of respect honoured his "Sir," had promised everything that was good, every good and righteous work, and yet had not performed what was promised, had least of all performed it in the decisive days of the preacher of righteousness, and even had learnt no shame, no penitence, no faith, from the penitence and reformation of the most depraved.[2]

While Jesus placed in the foreground the divine call of the most recent past, the divine mission of John and its diverse results, he also, implicitly at least, threw a light upon the whole past of the people and of the Pharisees, as well as upon the present in which he was the continuer of the work and of the experiences of the Baptist. Now, however, in a second and detailed parable, communicated by all three Gospels, he displays upon the foundation of the first a still grander *tableau* of the

---

[1] "In the way of righteousness" does not mean, "as an upright man" (Meyer), but as "teacher of uprightness" (Bleek); comp. above, II. pp. 238 sq.

[2] An apparent incongruity between the parable and its interpretation is caused by the fact that the first assenting—or refusing—answer does not belong to the ministry of the Baptist (against Schenkel, p. 234), but precedes it; the second answer, the correction, belongs to this ministry. Yet there is nothing in the way of the assumption that the bringing in of John was intended to illustrate *only* the second, and not the first, answer, which rather lay in the whole previous national history.

general history of divine revelation of the kingdom and of hierarchical sin. He enumerates the whole series of ill-treated servants of God from the first to the last. The last is now no longer John, but the Greater than John, namely, the one now first openly called Son of God, who was in Jerusalem, who was speaking, and who in truth himself was already awaiting the fate of the messengers of God.[1] "A man, a householder," he said, taking up a well-known parable of Isaiah's, "planted a vineyard, put a hedge about it, dug a wine-trough in it, and built a tower. He then let the vineyard to husbandmen and went into a far country.[2] When the time of fruit drew near, he sent his servants to levy from the husbandmen the tax in kind."[3] But he sent them in vain. According to one account, there were three servants, who one after another were maltreated worse and worse, even to wounding and death. According to the other and evidently more appropriate form of the parable, there were two groups of servants, the second stronger than the first, each maltreated by blows, the husbandmen proceeding even to the length of murdering and stoning them.[4] Finally, the lord resolved to send his son, as the third or the fourth. "They will be awed by

---

[1] Matt. xxi. 33; Luke xx. 9; Mark xii. 1. Luke erroneously says Jesus addressed himself to the people, contrary to what he himself tells us in xx. 19.

[2] Isaiah v. 1 sqq., comp. iii. 14, ix. 10. Similarly the Rabbis, Schöttgen, p. 173. Hedge or wall against beasts; wine-trough, into which through a latticed opening the must flows; tower = watch-tower, Isaiah i. 8, Song of Sol. i. 6. Rabbis, in Schöttgen, p. 173: ædificavit turrem in medio in eaque custodem constituit. Comp. Winer, *Kelter* and *Wein*.

[3] Matt.: his fruits. Luke and Mark, more exactly: of the fruits. This refers to the Old-Testament tenth, not to the Syrian or Roman land-tax (1 Macc. x. 30; Jos. *Ant.* 14, 10, 6) of one-third or one-fourth.

[4] Matt. has two groups, Luke and Mark three single servants. A further difference is, that in Luke the first is beaten, the second is beaten and also shamefully treated, the third is wounded as well; in Mark the second is wounded in the head (ἐκεφαλίωσαν ἀ. λ.), the third slain. Mark also, to tally with Matthew, adds that a number of others sent were beaten or slain. We can here but choose between Matthew and Luke; and the duality in Matt., with the Messiah making the triplet, is simpler and better conceived; the groups of servants (comp. Jer. xxv. 4) justly diminishes the authority of the individuals in proportion as it shows the determined urgency of the lord.

my son!¹ But the husbandmen, when they saw him, spoke among themselves, This is the heir; come, let us kill him and seize on his inheritance.² They said it, seized him, cast him out of the vineyard, and slew him. Now, when the lord of the vineyard comes, what will he do to those husbandmen? Miserable men, he will miserably destroy them, and give the vineyard to others.³ Have ye not read in the Scriptures"—and here he referred to those verses of Psalm cxviii. which immediately precede the words sung when he made his entry into the city—"The stone which the builders rejected, that is become the corner-stone; this has been done by the Lord, and it is marvellous in our eyes! And he who falls upon this stone"—he added, in holy passion, quoting Isaiah and Daniel—"will be bruised and broken; but he upon whom it falls, it will crush him to pieces."⁴

He had intelligibly and solemnly spoken from the judgment-seat of higher history concerning the history of Israel and of the rulers of Israel. The whole of this long history, with all its complicated paths and windings, presented itself before his keen eye as one connected process of divine gifts and challenges, and of human refusals to do what was right. This plantation of God, separated from the wilderness of heathenism, adorned with the

---

¹ Luke xx. 13: my beloved Son. Mark xii. 6: only beloved Son,—assumed by Gess (p. 124) to be important, although this is only dogmatic development.

² Heir, with a reference to Messiah, after Ps. ii. 8; Gen. xv. 2 sqq.; Gal. iii. 29, iv. 1. Hebraic joresh and ben meshek.

³ According to Luke and Mark. The play upon the word in Matt. xxi. 41. On Matthew's text, see below, p. 143, n. 2.

⁴ Ps. cxviii. 22 sq. Comp. Isaiah xxviii. 16. According to the Greek αὕτη, the translation must be "this (corner-stone)" (Meyer). But possibly the LXX. translated only slavishly; in the Hebrew stands sot (Gr. αὕτη), but it signifies "this" (neuter), Ps. vii. 3. Comp. Bleek, II. p. 322; Hilgenfeld, 1868, p. 39. The word of the Psalm has reference to the despised nation lifted up again by God. Hitzig, II. p. 345, Asmonæan Jonathan. Messianic application by the Rabbis. Schöttgen, p. 174. The second passage in Matt. xxi. 44 and Luke xx. 18 (see Isaiah viii. 14; Jer. vi. 21; Dan. ii. 34, 44, sq.; comp. also above, I. p. 324, upon Messianic stone that broke to pieces the kingdoms of the earth) is not quite established in Matt. Tischendorf has struck out the passage on the authority of Origen, Eus., D., It., but—as Hilgenfeld also mentions (p. 39)—against the strongest attestation, Sin., Vat., Ephr., It., Syr., Chrys., Aug.

noble vine of the divine ordinances in human nationality, protected by the tower of the sacred citadel, the temple of God, was Israel. The husbandmen were the successors of Moses, the priests, Scribes and Pharisees, the representatives of the God who had withdrawn himself after the Sinaitic revelation, and, with a reservation of ownership and of fruits, had handed over to them the cultivation and use of his property. The servants were the prophets early and late to the time of the exile and of John, the unsuccessful, scorned, beaten, slain tithe-collectors of God.[1] Only one can succeed them, the last and highest representative of God, commanding respect even from the rebellious, the Son, the Messiah; and his mission was not directly the prosperity of the nation, but the genuinely Johannine restoration of the down-trodden rights of God, the collection of the fruits which had been refused to God, and which God cannot allow to be refused to Him throughout the centuries.[2] But the Messiah himself foresees his own destiny; he has long anticipated it, since yesterday he has seen it with his own eyes; the rightful heir of the vineyard is, like Joseph by his brethren, received by the husbandmen with looks of jealousy and murderous intent. The rebellion, which he is to quell, is already complete: it has passed from the refusal of the fruits to the repudiation of vassalage, to the audacious, cold, definite choice of self-government instead of the government of God and of the king, to the deposition of God in the deposition of his messenger cast out of Israel with insult.[3] Having reached this height, Jesus, in the excitement of the moment, is no longer able to preserve the calm of the parable; he not only changes the figures and casts the crushing stone at the lords of the temple, but he passes from factual representation to personal application,

---

[1] The tower = temple, comp. Book of Enoch, 89 sq. Also many of the Fathers since Chrys. explain tower = temple (hedge = land, winepress = altar). The husbandmen are not, as is generally assumed, the people, but the custodes (see above, p. 139, n. 2); comp. also Matt. xxiii. 2, 13.

[2] Comp. Matt. iii. 8.

[3] Aristocracy of the priesthood had been introduced in the place of kings, Jos. *Ant.* 20, 10. See above, I. p. 257.

from exposition to plain, direct, severe condemnation. The vengeance of God cannot tarry: struck by divine wrath, the rebels must fall, the vineyard must pass into other and fresh hands. "The others" who receive the vineyard are *the* other one; it can only be the Messiah, the heir; it can only be himself, with his disciples and adherents. The stone, rejected by the builders, chosen by God as the corner-stone, as the support and middle point of his terrestrial edifice, every one would understand to be that person who then, within the walls of the temple, ran the risk of being shamefully cast out and slain by the keepers of the temple.[1]

Agreed as the Gospels are in general concerning this grand self-revelation of Jesus—in which destructive criticism again miserably fails to see anything but an invention of the dogmatic artist—yet they exhibit many differences in detail, of some of which mention has already been made.[2] Two important points, however, remain to be considered. In a very interesting way, Matthew makes the Scribes themselves give the verdict upon the husbandmen. Jesus imposes it upon them to be—as in the former parable—their own impartial judges, to utter their own crushing condemnation, which he needs afterwards only to certify, only to illustrate.[3] But this account is contradicted by Luke and Mark, who do not represent the verdict as being repeated, but put it in the mouth of Jesus alone. Moreover, Matthew's account does not harmonize with the fact that the opponents immediately afterwards, madly falling upon the parable-speaker who depicted *them*, very clearly pointed out the author of the words, while they themselves must have been too shrewd to pronounce such an emphatic condemnation of the husbandmen,

---

[1] The direct application in Matt. xxi. 43 was not made (according to Luke and Mark, and also Matt. xxi. 45).

[2] Volkmar (p. 521) simply says that as the temple purifying did not take place, there was no occasion given to a conflict. Weizs. (p. 126) thinks of a construction of the parable, which at any rate shows a diversity of elements, out of Jewish apocalyptical books. On the similarity between Matt. xxi. 42 and Acts iv. 11, see above, p. 131, n. 1.

[3] Matt. xxi. 41, 43. This repetition of xxi. 31 at once speaks against verse 41.

THE ASSAILANTS. 143

particularly after the preceding example.¹ More important still is another point. The "others" who receive the vineyard are, according to Matthew, such as will render up the fruits in their season; nay, according to the subsequent explanation of Jesus, which was probably introduced by the Gentile-favouring editor, quite a different people, to whom the kingdom of God, taken away from the hierarchs and the Jews, is to be given with the prospect of a fruit-rendering in the sense of the kingdom of God.² Evidently there is here an allusion to the transference of the kingdom of God from the Jews to the Gentiles; and thus also has Luke understood it, who, without speaking of "another nation," makes the assembled Jewish people cry, "God forbid!" Most of the expositors have also thus understood it.³ But this passage of Matthew and this exposition of Matthew and Luke must be regarded as interpolations, however much we might wish to retain one of the few passages which would establish the decisively important turning of Jesus' gaze from the Jews to the Gentiles. Here the silence of Mark, and even of Luke, speaks loudly enough, especially as their advanced standpoint would at once have welcomed and adopted such an utterance of Jesus had it been a reliable tradition. But even Jesus' words themselves

¹ An argument against Matthew is afforded by the very unskilful interpolation of verse 43 between 42 and 44, assuming the genuineness of these; and, finally, by the close, verse 45, which points to the party, and not to the whole nation. It may be surmised that verse 43 belongs to the editor, as well as the variation in verse 41.

² Matt. xxi. 41, 43, opp. Luke xx. 15 sq., Mark xii. 9. Meyer sides with Matthew; Bleek, more correctly, takes the other side. The hand of the editor in Matthew is suggested by the repetition and exegesis of verse 41 in verse 43, and by the application —out of harmony even with Matthew—in this verse; see previous note. And why have not Luke and Mark repeated out of Matthew the welcome $\xi\theta\nu o\varsigma$? Comp. Köstlin, p. 44.

³ As early as the Fathers (Eus., *Theophan.*, *Nova Patrum Bib.* IV. p. 124, in Hilg. 1868, p. 39), the Gentiles were here thought of. Thus Neander still, p. 504. Of recent writers, Fritzsche and Hilgenfeld (*l. c.*) make even the corner-stone refer to the Gentiles. Of the critical school, Baur, Hilg., Volkmar, assume the former reference to be self-evident, Volkmar even in the form of Mark, who, however, correctly speaks only of "others." Schenkel (pp. 234 sq.) also makes the vineyard mean the nation, "the others" the Japhetites. More cautiously Meyer and Bleek, Jews and Gentiles. Against the reference to the Gentiles, Pfleiderer, *Jahrb. deutsch. Theol.* 1868, p. 149. Isaiah v. 1 sqq. was seductive; but Jesus' parable is different.

speak to the contrary. The husbandmen from whom the vineyard is to be taken are not the Jews who render no fruits, but only the keepers, the builders, the spiritual heads of the Jews, who refuse the tribute of fruits to the lord. If the vineyard were taken from them, it would evidently neither be taken from the people, who in truth were themselves the vineyard of God, nor be given to the Gentiles. And if it were taken away, certainly the Gentiles could not step into possession of the rights of the hierarchs. Moreover, the context plainly shows that by the "others," who were to receive the vineyard, Jesus understood, not the Jews, not the Gentiles, but the Messiah, or the adherents of the Messiah. If any one still fosters a doubt respecting these Gentile utterances, that doubt must be dispelled by the consideration that Jesus was in conflict simply with the hierarchs and not at all with the people, and that he would therefore have shown little fairness and little wisdom had he rejected the people along with the hierarchs, and, by announcing the transference of their sacred rights to the heathen, had fundamentally exasperated the people whose decision he must still await, whose belief in John he had only just been applauding, and whose zealous thronging round him was his own special protection against the hierarchs. The parable, therefore, would be understood in such a sense as it is shown to have been by the close. That close reveals, in Matthew as well as in Luke, no popular exasperation on account of the parable, but simply the rage of the hierarchs, who noted that everything had been pointed at them, and at them exclusively.[1]

Upon this misunderstanding of Matthew's depends yet another. In the order of events on this day, in Matthew, in a somewhat different way in Mark, the cursing of the unfruitful fig-tree is placed first.[2] This opening of the day is, however, intelligible only when we see its close. On the morning-return from Bethany to Jerusalem, Jesus felt hungry. He saw by the way, probably

---

[1] How obscure and perverted is here again the address of Luke xx. 9, 16, 19!
[2] Matt. xxi. 18; Mark xi. 12; on Mark, see below, pp. 145, 150.

THE ASSAILANTS. 145

on the fruitful western side of the Mount of Olives and in sight of Jerusalem, a fig-tree. He went up to it, but was disappointed, finding on it nothing but leaves. Then he cursed the tree: "Let no fruit grow on thee henceforth for ever!"[1] And immediately the fig-tree dried up. But according to Mark, who depicts the commencement and progress of the miracle rationally and with profundity and dignity, the effect of the curse was not apparent until the following morning, when it was visible to the very roots.[2] It has long been understood that the deeper meaning of this transaction was a spiritual symbolism in the manner of the ancient prophets, namely, the material representation of judgment upon Israel, who had been unfruitful towards their God, a representation more forcible than very many prophetic symbols, because the miraculous destruction of an organic life by a word, in truth a divine word, guaranteed in an alarmingly convincing manner the certain and mighty advent of the judgment of the nation.[3] Without any assistance from Matthew and Mark, expositors have been compelled to seek beneath the external miracle—which it has been attempted to retain—this deeper sense, because the punishment of an unfruitful tree at the prompting of temporary hunger must necessarily appear to be a

---

[1] Return, Matthew. On the other hand, Mark speaks very vaguely,—it happened after leaving Bethany. In the neighbourhood of Bethany, Jerusalem could not be seen (notwithstanding Volkmar, p. 509), though the sense of the narrative points to the visibility of the city (see below). Tree by the road: it was a maḳom muphkar, loc. communis, not privatus (Lightfoot, p. 351). Figs, moreover, flourish ubi multus pulvis, max. frequenti via apposita. Pliny, 15, 21. Fruit-gathering not forbidden, Deut. xxiii. 25; Matt. xii. 1. Jesus came upon it; he had not to go up to it (Fritzsche).

[2] Mark xi. 20. According to Strauss (4th ed. II. p. 230), no more words are to be wasted as to the preference. Sieffert, Neander, Meyer: Mark more exact and more original! But Steinmeyer (p. 249) will retain Matt. and Mark; he does not admit that the result was not instantaneous, only the perception of it by the disciples (described in Mark) followed afterwards.

[3] The Fathers, and Neander, Bleek, Krabbe, Gess, Meyer, and Steinmeyer, although these all retain the miracle. The more recent criticism completely repudiates (Strauss, De Wette, Hase, Weisse, Schenkel, and others) the external miracle. Also Ewald, p. 523, and Weizs., p. 548, are among the number. Prophetic symbolics, *e.g.* 1 Sam. xv. 27; 1 Kings xi. 30, xxii. 11; Jer. xiii. 1, xviii. 2, xix. 1, 10, xxvii. 2. But Matt. and Mark make no allusion to symbolic meaning; see next page.

VOL. V. L

blind and sensual deed of anger and revenge against an innocent tree and an unfree nature, therefore—really in the sense of the temptation narrative—an abuse of miraculous power.[1]

Whilst this conception is doubtless correct, there is much light to be gathered from the relation in which this miraculous sign stands to the events of the same day. The incident of the fig-tree is only an illustration of the parable of the husbandmen in the vineyard, a conversion of word into fact. Hence it is at once plain that only Matthew, and not Mark, gives it in the right place.[2] The fig-tree is the representative of the vineyard. In point of fact, the fig was planted in vineyards. Next to the vine, it was the noblest, most productive plant in the vineyard; and in antithesis to the slender, tender vine-stock, it best represented the strength and elevation of a nationality,—it was the symbol of Israel.[3] The fruit of the fig-tree corresponded to the fruit of the vineyard: in the parable, the tribute of fruit was not given; here the fruit did not grow. But the husbandmen who cultivated the vineyard, the fig-tree, have disappeared, because the Evangelist had already, in the parable, confounded them with the vineyard itself, with the people of Israel, and their fruit-tribute with the fruit-bearing of the popular life. Thus it is not the husbandmen who perish; but the vine itself, the fig-tree, the nation of Israel withers, and "others" come instead. It is

---

[1] Comp. Matt. iv. 3 sq. The innocence of the tree mentioned by Augustine, *De verb. dom. in Joh.* 44: quid arbor fecerat? quæ culpa arboris? Ἀναίτιον ὄν, Euth. The expositors seek help in the supposition that the tree was previously rotten, therefore not so innocent (Paulus, even Neander and Bleek).

[2] In Matthew, on the same day are the fig-tree and the parable of the vineyard; in Mark, the fig-tree and the temple purifying, which latter contains no rejection of the Jews at all, but rather a reformation (against Volkmar). Those who would follow the faintest traces might appeal to Mark xi. 17, or (with Steinm.) might compare the looking round in xi. 11 and in verse 13. Here is seen afresh that Mark arbitrarily re-arranged the events, and brought the fig-tree primarily into connection with the temple purifying instead of with the vineyard parable. Would Jesus have purified the temple on the Sabbath?

[3] In the Old Testament, the vine and the fig quite commonly stand together, the fig-tree in the vineyard. Comp. the parable in Luke xiii. 6, here doubly important. Israel compared to fig-tree and figs, *e.g.* Hosea ix. 10; Micah vii. 1; Jer. viii. 13, xxiv. 1.

THE ASSAILANTS. 147

therefore evident that the early incident of this day precedes the morning conversation in the temple only as being both prediction and fulfilment, the words in the temple being, symbolically at least, by anticipation realized in fact. But it is also evident that the early incident was either not historical at all, or at least did not fall upon this day, because it was simply only the misunderstanding of the Evangelist that found in the parable a rejection of the Jews, a calling of the Gentiles in the place of Jews; whilst the sense of the parable had nothing whatever to do with a rejection of the Jews. This misunderstanding belonged primarily, however, to another than our Evangelist, since the latter apparently came into possession of it only by inheritance. For this Evangelist, like Mark, has certainly no suspicion of the symbolical significance of the withered fig-tree. Both perceive simply a punitive miracle of the most restricted character: the tree, deceiving the eye and disappointing hunger, is condemned as such without any reference to Israel. Hence the miracle is followed by no word of earnest admonition, but merely by an *excursus* upon miraculous power in the well-known sentences of Jesus. Briefly, the material single miracle is itself its own end, and not the means to a higher one.[1] This already obscure representation must necessarily have been preceded by another, in which the higher meaning of the miracle was more conspicuously shown. If, however—as we must infer—in this earlier source the symbolic miracle of the fig-tree was ascribed to the day of

---

[1] Matt. xxi. 20 sqq.; Mark xi. 20. Here Volkmar's opinion that Mark voluntarily and consciously produced this symbolism fundamentally contradicts itself. His daring exposition of Mark's Mosaic passage about forgiveness must also be quoted (p. 515): Christ can curse, but the Christian—must forgive. Better still in Paulus, III. i. p. 159: Trust, but no fanatical enthusiasm! The poor plight of the Mark-hypothesis upon this point has been already mentioned by Krabbe (p. 443) against Weisse (*Petrin. Tradit. des Markus*). In the form given it by Volkmar, that hypothesis is in a still worse plight. Let the reader also refer to the monstrous expositions of Lange and Steinmeyer, according to which the words in Matt. xxi. 21 and Mark xi. 23 stand in the closest connection with the punitive miracle. According to Lange (II. p. 323), the mountain that falls into the sea is Zion, Israel scattered among the Gentiles. But according to Steinm. (p. 253), Jesus says rather: "Ye shall not only actually execute the judgment upon Israel, but ye shall also overthrow the mountain of heathenism."

the sentence against the husbandmen of the vineyard, then this earlier source, as Matthew afterwards, must have made that sentence apply to the people of Israel. Therefore the error as to the parable belonged to the earlier source, the error as to the symbolic punishment to the later one.

But if Jesus certainly did not inflict the symbolic punishment upon the fig-tree on this day, did he perhaps inflict it on another day?[1] This assumption is at once rendered questionable by the fact that on none of the following days did Jesus absolutely reject Israel. And if he did not reject, or indeed curse, Israel, then he did not curse the tree, which as a mere tree he could not curse. Here also comes in the silence of Luke concerning this miracle. There may be very different opinions as to the possibility of the miracle itself; but without falling back upon the desperate resource of rationalism—according to which Jesus, with the connoisseur's eye of the tree cultivator, detected the diseased condition of the tree, prognostically foresaw its speedy catastrophe, and then the disciples attached too much meaning to his words—doubt of this miracle of severest style is at once aroused by the fact that human finiteness and divine omnipotence do not easily co-exist so naively as here in Jesus' limited knowledge of the fruitfulness of the tree and his unlimited power over the tree.[2] Moreover, it has been abundantly shown that the

---

[1] Bleek offers the new hypothesis that the incident took place about the time of the Feast of Tabernacles (John vii.); his chief reason is the difficulty about the figs, which remains to be considered.

[2] Paulus, *L. J.* I. ii. p. 98: Jesus had noticed the decay of the tree (naturally a tender plant, Pliny, 15, 19 sqq., 16, 46, &c.); its weakness increased with the heat. Then follows the verification of the death of the tree, according to Mark. Venturini (II. i. p. 429) brings in the simoom. Neander (p. 484) makes Jesus only hasten the crisis of the tree! Bleek, on his part, for the purpose of giving, not a physical, but a moral explanation of the miracle, postulates a diseased tree to which there happened only what was right. Hase thought of natural magic (p. 221), though without adhering to that view. According to Lange (p. 322), God, combining his æonian ministry with that of his Son, caused the tree to wither as a prognostic for Israel. The words of Christ killed the tree, since they, called forth by the operation of God, appealed to the operation of God, and thus, together with that operation, they pierced through the nature-sphere of the tree with annihilating effect. A mountain of phrases that of itself topples over into the sea!

mission and work of this Messiah was not malediction, and especially malediction that took effect, whether upon trees or men or nations, or even his own nation, the nation which Jesus loved to the end, and which on its own part had not hitherto challenged the final judgment of Jesus, more correctly of God. But the mission and work of this Messiah was blessing instead of cursing, and only apocryphal Gospels have taken delight in the punitive miracles of Jesus. How naive, even to excess, is the painstaking of recent authors to prove a fault of the tree, whilst they were rather compelled to establish the consummated guilt of the nation and the justice of the severest punishment![1] Neither can we see any purpose in this great spectacular miracle, which, had it happened, must have taken place, not in the narrow circle of the disciples, but before the people whom it concerned, or at least must have been explained to the disciples themselves,— nothing of which, but the opposite, occurred.[2] Again, the miracle dissolves in our hands when we examine its details. A hungering Jesus, a serious search after figs, cannot be thought if the aim of the miracle was altogether different, if it was comprehensive, universal, spiritual, in contrast to the temporary sensuous prompting and wrath of hunger.[3] There could have been no expectation of finding ripe figs in the beginning of spring, for the early figs—as Jesus himself knew and indeed said shortly after

[1] Blessing, not curse, Strauss, 4th ed. II. p. 225; Hase, p. 221; Neander, p. 484; Bleek, II. p. 313 (the last two make Jesus give the tree the last blow). Against the questioning of Jesus' right over the tree and its possessor, Lange (II. p. 320) has spoken of the "field-keeper demeanour" of criticism.

[2] Paulus, III. i. p. 170; Hase, p. 221; Strauss, 4th ed. II. p. 232. According to Sieffert (pp. 115 sqq.) Jesus had previously explained the matter to the disciples; according to Meyer, all the succeeding utterances allow of no doubt; according to Krabbe (p. 442), sagacious Orientals easily understood the reference of Jesus. Therefore only the Gospels did not! On the other hand, others, on account of the one-sided utilitarian application of Jesus, have had recourse to the gross conception that Jesus simply wished to give a proof of Messianic miraculous power, Euthym., Ullm., Fritzsche; comp. Strauss, 4th ed. II. p. 233.

[3] Paulus (p. 97): because nothing could be prepared on the Sabbath, Jesus went to Bethany without his breakfast. It could still better be said : on the Sabbath nothing was eaten until the close of the synagogue. See above, III. pp. 202 sq.

in an address at Jerusalem—passed through a slow process of delicate development of fruit buds and of modest unfolding of leaves, until they ripened for the June harvest; the summer figs ripened yet later, while the trees on which the late autumn figs remained hanging until some time in the spring would then be without leaves.[1] Therefore there was no foliage, there were no figs, to be sought or found either here or there, as Mark says quite correctly but very unskilfully in his narration of the punitive miracle: "For it was not the time of figs."[2] If it was not the season for figs, how was it he looked for them?[3] And if it was an abnormal spurt of nature—a miracle upon a miracle— that a single fig-tree stood prematurely full of leaves, why should he curse the tree, since what he wished for could be produced only by the same unnatural growth which forced forth the leaves—nay, which quite consistently corrected itself by

[1] Winer, *Feigenbaum*. Paulus, *Handb*. III. i. p. 168. Tobler, *Denkbl. aus Jesus*, pp. 101—103. Ewald, p. 523. Bleek, p. 312. The summer figs do not ripen until August; the late, dark-coloured, violet figs, which ripen in the autumn, and often remain hanging through the winter, hang upon leafless trees. And though they often remain when the tree in the spring is putting forth fresh leaves (Pliny, 16, 27; Colum. *De arb*. 21, in Paulus, p. 169), the foliage—in contradistinction to the text—is still weak. We should do best to think of quickly-grown early figs (Paulus), and such Jesus might have met with in Gennesar, where figs ripened (Jos. *B. J.* 3, 10, 8) through ten months in the year (that is, with exception of Jan. and Feb.). But, on the other hand, Matt. xxiv. 32 shows that Jesus still looked forward to the fig harvest.

[2] Matt. xi. 13. Paulus (p. 98): it had not been a good season for figs! Also Cler., Olsh., Lange, Steinm. (assenting). Other instances of wrong treatment of the text in Strauss, 4th ed. II. pp. 227 sqq., and Meyer. The awkwardness of Mark's remark is (in fact, since Origen on Matt. t. XVI. 29) almost universally admitted, even by Neander and Bleek. Holtzmann and Scholten consider it, as did the ancients, to be a later addition. Volkmar (p. 510) knows what to say even here: at Easter there were no figs; just when the fulfilment of all the promises came, Israel had *no time* to bring forth the Messianic faith, for mere worldly care and thought. What a play of contradictory notions! And the explanation of Steinm. (pp. 249 sq.; see Lightfoot, next note), which does not wander so far from the text, is a failure: it was at this season of the year quite unusual; but as the fruit usually came before the leaves, Jesus might expect fruit. In point of fact, the Gospel says the contrary.

[3] Woolston, *Disc.* 4: what would be said if a husbandman in the spring looked for fruit on a tree and hewed it down as a punishment? Lightfoot (p. 353) says that just because it was not the proper season Jesus sought fruit, and went—according to the Mark addition, xi. 13—to the tree that was seen afar off, which nevertheless promised fruit. But the Evangelist does not make his pragmatic remark to explain the action of Jesus, but to explain the barrenness of the tree.

producing no fruit?[1] It may therefore be certainly concluded that the incident is not historical, and that for the sake of the idea there was introduced into Jesus' last Easter time a myth which did not wholly harmonize with the reality, with the Easter time as it actually was.

It still remains credible that what Jesus did not do in deed, he at least spoke in words, and that what he said was through misunderstanding or with a shrewd intention clothed in the garment of fact. And this assumption is correct, when correctly placed. By no means did Jesus utter such words at Jerusalem, words which would in every way contradict his attitude towards the people; and by no means did he ever say that Israel must wither or be suddenly dried up under the hands of God.[2] If he spoke in a parable of Israel as a fig-tree that bore fruit to its divine gardener, he could at any rate have mentioned a withering or a being dug up only by way of warning. Now, we have such words of his, and we have them in the same Luke that knows nothing of the incident of cursing the fig-tree.[3] In Galilee, Jesus —as we saw—spoke of the fig-tree in the vineyard, upon which the owner sought fruit and found none. He commanded the overseer of the vineyard to dig up the tree, but the overseer

---

[1] To the above interpretation—punishment of the deceptive sport of nature in the tree—Meyer and Steinmeyer have taken a fancy, following Neander and Bleek. Tholuk (*Glaubwürd.* p. 426) refers to the miracle of Mohamed, who called a tree to him because it was too much trouble to go to the tree. Similarly he compares the feeding of the 5000 with the few dates for a hungry army.

[2] Yet Weisse (I. p. 576), on the strength of the Petrine tradition of Mark, finds it probable that the words of Jesus (without miracle) were spoken at that time in Jerusalem and concerning the same. Weizs. (p. 548) also believes in an actual malediction which was afterwards converted into a myth.

[3] Luke xiii. 6; see above, IV. p. 121; comp. Matt. iii. 10, vii. 19; John xv. 6; Micah vii. 1; Isaiah xxxiv. 4. Thus the whole of the recent criticism. Only in Volkmar (p. 510) is to be found the self-condemning assumption that the original picture is in Mark, but Luke has correctly understood it and transformed it into parable! The ancients (Ambrose on Luke), as Neander and Steinmeyer still, prefer to assume that Jesus himself executed at last the threat then given. Volkmar thus expounds Mark: Israel has (thus, essentially, the early writers, down to Neander) the show of external honour (leaves), but not faith (fruit). When the fulfilment of all promises came, when Jesus came to the fig-tree, Israel had no time. Hence malediction: Let no one henceforth find fruit, that is, no Messiah come again (p. 509).

interceded and obtained for it a respite. Out of this parable the mythical incident of the fig-tree on the Mount of Olives has been ingeniously developed. As Jesus failed, even at the end, even at Jerusalem, to call forth the fruit of the repentance of Israel, the gracious respite which he himself had granted seemed to have come to an end. Since he himself felled, nay, without hand or handicraft annihilated, the fig-tree by a mighty divine word, he satisfied the Old Testament prophecy, the Divine majesty, and his own dignity.[1] He was the conqueror and the judge of Israel whilst Israel judged him; and his judgment, executed by symbol on the tree, looked into the future, seeing Israel wither and die under the visible anger of God and of the despised Messiah. So thought an after age, while he thought differently. For he is correctly drawn, drawn as Christian, and not as Jewish, when he is represented as being to the end what he was at the beginning, viz., in view of the severity of God, what he called himself—not the destroying but the interceding overseer of the vineyard.

The first attempt at apprehending him crowned the events of this day. The hierarchs noticed more and more distinctly that the parables pointed only at them, menaced only them; and that the man who menaced them had the audacity to call himself the corner-stone of the future. Furiously enraged, they therefore prepared to throw themselves upon him. "They sought to take him"—say the Gospels—"but they feared the multitudes of the people, who looked upon Jesus as a prophet." Therefore either by their behaviour, by the signs and words that passed from one to the other, their plot was betrayed and then again given up because of the multitude, or Jesus was actually taken hold of and then let loose again, because the threatening multitude, by eye and hand and voice, forbad his apprehension. Thus the result of the day was a divided one. In the popular opinion, Jesus had won. It is true the Messiahship had declined to the office of Prophet; but even his adherents had not, at the entry,

---

[1] Predictions of an exactly similar kind, Jer. viii. 13; Ez. xvii. 9, 24.

sharply distinguished between Messiah and Prophet. And now it was not merely the adherents, but the whole Jewish people as then represented in the temple, that had recognized his right to the honoured name of Prophet, and were earnestly resolved not to expose him to the vengeance of the hierarchs.[1] And as things were going, what name *now* fitted better than that of Prophet, the repetition of the title which the people of Galilee, obeying their presentiment, had already found for him? The exhibition of Messiahship was at a standstill; on the contrary, the temple purifying showed first, and next the controversy of this day still more, the zealous, judicial Prophet; and the public recognition of the prophet of Jericho and Machærus showed the genuine, bold successor of that prophet. But on the *other* side, the violent attempt of the Scribes showed a resisting body quite as resolute, smaller in number but stronger in position and unitedness; and the daring to take a step against Jesus sufficiently evinced the self-reliance, the determination, and the growing determination, of that corporation. For the moment, the one stream might keep the other in check and compel it to make a quiet retreat. But under the same popular protection, the forerunner had nevertheless finally fallen. Moreover, the successor did not stand in the wilderness, but in the midst of the city of priests, face to face with the energetic leaders and with their willing accomplices; and the prophetic character, which was believed in, did not sufficiently cover the Messianic one, the confession of which belonged also to that day and yet was not accepted,—a wonderful point in this representation, a point which, while it shows a public inquiry into the previously questioned Messiahship, also fatally drags the unquestioned prophetic character into the pit.

The violent attack repelled by the people could naturally issue only in a retreat of Jesus to Bethany from the controversies and the temple, as on the entry day; whilst on the other side the opposing party necessarily betook themselves to considering in

---

[1] Matt. xxi. 45 sq. (prophet); Luke xx. 19; Mark xii. 12.

what new way the *fiasco* of the authorities could be repaired and the action against the rebels introduced. Thus in the three Gospels there is an admirable connection established between the cessation of the opponents and their new onset, between the renunciation of violence and the attempt at stratagem, the result of a Pharisaic consultation.[1] But the Matthew Gospel has violently disarranged this order of things by placing an impossibility in the midst, namely, a new parable of Jesus to his disciples, and which Jesus is said to have spoken immediately after the attempt to take him was thwarted.[2] In a certain sense, this resumption by Jesus would have been grand. Jesus would have looked like a hero, a victor, a lofty-souled man of peace, if after the attempt he could have gone on as though nothing had happened, without resentment, without aversion. Whilst in the fourth Gospel he so unseasonably and with such wearying frequency condemns the murderous attack, here he is made to remain in his full parable-calm, in his striving and his patience, endeavouring to convince and to win over by his spiritual utterances.[3] But we have already shown, in the introduction to the Gospels, how unhappily this interpolation— apparently belonging to the editor—interrupts the continuity of the narrative, and that the other Gospels exhibit no trace of it, although its subject-matter would attract them.[4] Moreover, we now readily note that while the fresh parable slightly resembles in idea and form the previous parables, looked at more closely it ignores the whole situation, harshly attacking, not the hierarchs, but the people, the protectors of Jesus just before. We note also that it describes, too far-seeing, the future non-success of the Apostles among the people, instead of the non-success of Jesus,

---

[1] Matt. xxii. 15; Luke xx. 20; Mark xii. 13.

[2] Matt. xxii. 1—14, just in the midst between the two contiguous natural extremities of the historical thread.

[3] In John, Jesus, without any provocation, before other men, and at a much later time, recalls, to condemn it, the attempt in v. 16, 18; see vii. 19 sqq., viii. 37, 40.

[4] See above, I. pp. 83, 84, note. Weak objections of Gess, p. 122. It may be that the people compelled the hierarchs to "stifle" their anger: could Jesus calmly withdraw?

who, however, at that anxious moment could alone be thought of. Finally, this parable of the marriage feast of the Son of God is not original; it is of late origin, artificially constructed out of two parables spoken by Jesus in an altogether different manner, one in Galilee, the other perhaps at Jerusalem.[1] From the parable of the feast, to which Jesus, the servant of God, vainly invited the people of Galilee, and from the second parable of the testing garment at the feast, is derived Matthew's marriage feast of the Messiah, whose Apostles, from A.D. 35—70, were rejected, despised, slain, like the old servants of the lord of the vineyard, till God burnt Jerusalem, and, from A.D 70—100, assigned the kingdom to the Gentiles, yet only to the bridal-clothed peoples that respected the legal-moral ordinances.[2]

B.—The Tempters.

Jesus' third day at Jerusalem, a Sunday, the 10th of April, had apparently a less threatening character than the two previous

[1] The compilation begins in xxii. 11. But already in the first part Luke is more original; see above, IV. pp. 118 sq. Strauss, 4th ed. p. 637; *New Life of Jesus*, Eng. trans., II. p. 352. Weizs. p. 178. Volkmar, p. 170. Comp. Pfleiderer, *Jahrb. d. Theol.* 1868, p. 149; on the other hand, however, Weisse, II. pp. 110 sqq. Neander, p. 503. Gess, p. 122; and others. With xxii. 11 begins not only a new point of view, but also one that directly contradicts the former, the unconditional calling in of the people from the highways, of the first that can be found. And how severe is the punishment in verse 13 (on account of the garment) in comparison with that in verse 7 (for murder), although Jesus never said a word about the punishment of the burning of Jerusalem and the slaughter of her children. *Post-apostolic horizon* (Barn. 16), an impossibility and an absurdity for the time and situation of Jesus. The glance at Luke xiv. 16 confirms this observation. This intermixing is recognized by Strauss, 4th ed. I. p. 639 (comp. Schneck.), Gfrörer, De Wette, Ewald; denied by Neander, p. 503; Weisse, II. pp. 110 sqq.; Holtzmann, p. 199; Weiffenb. p. 72; Hilgenfeld, 1868, p. 41. Weisse and Holtzmann think of a simplification of the parable by Luke.

[2] More in detail, above, IV. pp. 118 sq. (comp. with Luke, Jos. *Ant.* 18, 2, 3), as well as below, Division III., A., upon the sermon to the people. The messengers in Matthew evidently not prophets, as in xxi., but apostles; the wedding garment = moral or legal righteousness (Hilg., Meyer). The $διέξοδοι$ are understood to be the heathen, as early as Clem. *Hom.* 8, 22, and the garment to be baptism. Neither Jesus, nor even Paul or the Revelation, has connected the destruction of Jerusalem with the calling of the Gentiles.

days. We find no brutal attack by the Pharisees; we witness farcical proceedings on the part of the Sadducees; we discover evidence of an absence of united action by the two great parties, and particularly evidence of the keeping aloof of the dominant Sadducean hierarchy; finally, we have vigorous and yet pacific answers of Jesus without any stormy results—nay, followed only by the admiration of the opponents and by the astonishment of the people. Nevertheless, the decision, the fate of Jesus, drew nearer. The Pharisees, as well as he himself, were again upon the spot. Yesterday's defeat before the people had not discouraged them. Their purpose was not changed, only their strategy. A party meeting of the Pharisees—mentioned, as plainly as correctly, by Matthew alone—had resolved upon a fresh plan of battle. Naked brutal force, which excited the people, was to be relinquished, and guile was to be employed, so that by question and answer they might, in a pacific and argumentative way, arrive at the employment of force, which now meant legal apprehension, indictment, and condemnation. With the Pharisees, however, there was grouped another party, not the most influential, but nevertheless a powerful one, the Herodians, who here for the first time, indeed by name for the only time, appear upon the stage of Gospel history or of history at all.[1] According to all

---

[1] Matt. xxii. 15 sq.; Luke xx. 20; Mark xii. 13, comp. iii. 6. See above, IV. p. 230, note. More in detail in my article *Herodianer*, in *Bib.-Lex.* III. p. 65. The expression in Matt., συμβ. ἔλαβον, does not mean, "they consulted together," comp. Matt. xxvi. 4 (Wilke-Grimm), but, corresponding to the Latin consilium capere, "they formed the resolve" (a rendering applicable to all the passages, xii. 14, xxvii. 1, 7, xxviii. 12; Mark has for it, ποιεῖν, iii. 6, xv. 1). What it is resolved to do can be introduced by ὅπως, or as elsewhere (xxvii. 1) by ὥστε. Luke, in distinction from Matt., speaks (1) of the Sanhedrim as the sender out, xx. 1, 19 sq., (2) of spies generally as emissaries (just as he is prone elsewhere vaguely to generalize the historical and the geographical). Mark gives (1) with Luke, the Sanhedrim as the sender out, xi. 27, xii. 13, (2) with Matt., the Pharisees and Herodians as the emissaries. Volkmar's criticism maintained (p. 522) that Mark gave the original, since Luke and Matthew, each in his own way, found the sending out of Pharisees and Herodians by the Sanhedrim, the natural enemy of the Herodians, of the *protegés* of Rome, to be improbable. As if the Herodians were the *protegés* of Rome; as if the parties could not have made a compromise; as if, finally, an initiative on the part of the Sanhedrim (even in Hase, p. 223) were now already to be thought of (see above, pp. 133 sq.).

THE TEMPTERS. 157

evidences, this was not so much a religious as a political party.¹ The name indicates this, as does also the controversial question which was submitted to Jesus. It is, moreover, to be inferred from the entire absence of any mention or of any probability of the rise of a religious party connected with the name of Herod, and particularly from the impossibility of identifying the Boëthosians, the semi-Sadducees after the time of king Herod, with the Herodians, or of making them partizans of the Pharisees.² They were, therefore, most likely the Jerusalemite adherents of the Herodian house, perhaps of Antipas, probably of the Herodian dynasty generally. Even in the last case, the sympathies of the party would find their centre in Antipas, who at that time, after the violent clearance made by the Romans, remained the only still reigning son of Herod, and was fond of appearing as Herod on his coins.³ They were not exactly servants or commissioners of Antipas, Jesus' territorial ruler, for in the former case the expression used would have been different, and in the latter a

¹ They were held to be a religious party as early as by Tert. *Præscr.* 45: qui Christum Herodem esse dixerunt. Then Epiph., Philastr. Recently Ewald in particular, IV. p. 534, V. pp. 97 sqq. (people like the Essene Menahem, the courtier of Herod, see above, I. p. 367, of whom Lightfoot thought), and Renan, 15th ed. p. 226 (Boëthosians). Recently, Hitzig, *Gesch. Isr.* p. 559, who falls back upon a sect in the sense of Tertullian.

² The Boëthosians of Renan would be more tangible than the party of Ewald. But they passed as semi-Sadducees (see above, I. pp. 261, 355) and as political diplomatists, who sided sometimes with the Herodians, sometimes with the Romans; Jos. *Ant.* 17, 13, 1; 18, 1, 1; 20, 1, 3; *B.J.* 5, 13, 1. A political party (thus already Wetst. p. 473; Schl. p. 395; Neander, p. 488) is suggested by the name; comp. Cæsariani, Pompejani, Vitelliani. "Adherents of Herod," *Ant.* 14, 13, 1; 14, 15, 10; 16, 9, 3. "Royal," *Ant.* 17, 10, 3; *B.J.* 2, 17, 6 sq.

³ Both the conception of "Herodian" and the period forbid us to think of partizans of Rome (De Wette, Neander, Baumg.-Crus., Winer, Wies., Ewald, Hitzig, Volkmar), as the interests of Rome and of the Herods, since the death of the great king, and especially since the incorporation of Judæa after the deposition of Archelaus, had been widely separate, and the attack upon Jesus would else have been much too inconsiderate and abrupt. Thus already Wetst. p. 473: Her. neque Cæsaris. dominationi neque Judæorum libertati favebat. The interests of the Herodians lay in the direction of a restoration of the kingdom of Herod the Great in the place of provincial dependence upon Rome, and this was for a short time achieved, not by Antipas, but by his fortunate rival Agrippa I., at the moment when the inheritance of Archelaus, Philip, and Antipas, seemed swallowed up by the Romans. Neander, it is true, already makes (p. 488) Antipas to be king.

serious co-operation of Antipas in the trial of Jesus would have been apparent. But with the party ideal of a restoration of the kingdom of Herod the Great, perhaps in the person of Antipas, mistrust of a popular agitation in favour of a democratic Messiah was as intimately bound up as was repugnance to the direct Roman domination.[1] The coalition of this party with the Pharisees was a suspicious indication that the opposing forces were beginning to draw together. These two previously so antagonistic parties were bound together by no stronger interest than simply that of a common enmity to a third, to the suddenly formidable pretender, the Messiah. Their coalition was facilitated by the diminution of the favour with which the Pharisees regarded the Roman domination, which a few years afterwards was so readily exchanged for Herod's nephew, Agrippa I., and his banquets.[2] But when the Pharisees and Herodians went to Jesus together, how long would it be before the frigid and now scoffing Sadducees, the real masters of the temple, would become associates in the unnatural convention, the third party in the confederation whose first foundations had been laid by the fiery zeal of the pious, and whose connecting bonds had swallowed up the policy of the pious? On other occasions also the Sadducees combined with their deadly foes, the Pharisees, if it was to their interest to do so, or if they could not withstand a popular Pharisaic movement. Here at first, indeed, they come forward harmlessly, bringing before Jesus merely a scholastic controversy

---

[1] Servants of Herod (thus, however, Luther, Fr.) would have been differently expressed (comp. Matt. xiv. 2; Luke xxiii. 11; and Josephus, who always speaks only of friends, officials, slaves, freedmen, *Ant.* 17, 8, 4; 17, 9, 3; 18, 6, 3 sqq.; 19, 7, 1; *B. J.* 2, 15, 1, &c.). Add the reasons given above. The account in Luke xxiii. 7 is not historical (see below), and would itself show that Antipas had not previously interfered, even though he (Luke xiii. 31) had conspired against Jesus in Galilee. If Antipas and his people had seriously acted in Jerusalem against Jesus, the proceedings against Jesus would have taken a different form. A specific political party, distinguished from the Roman, distinguished from one of mere allegiance to Antipas, was thought of not only by Wetst., but also by Schleierm., Bleek, and Meyer.

[2] See above, I. p. 275; *Bib.-Lex.* III. p. 52. A fraction had already under Herod made a covenant with royalty, Jos. *Ant.* 17, 2, 4; *Bib.-Lex.* III. p. 34. Covenant with Antipas, *ib.* p. 44. See also above, I. p. 307, IV. p. 344.

which could only embroil them with the Pharisees, whilst they at the same time, with their scorn of the resurrection, drew no compromising speech from Jesus, and won no applause from the people. But having once put in an appearance, they became active organs of the opposition; and the vigorous repulse by Jesus, as well as the growing unrest of Jerusalem, compelled them to take up energetically a front position which at first they may not have sought. The vanquished parties feel disgraced before the people, they note the threatening character of the situation, and they calculate the consequences of the Messiahship, which rise as clearly before their eyes as the Messiahship itself. With the instinct of self-preservation, they combine to form one line of attack, and the decision is hastened. This is the significance of that day—it means reconciliation, the coming together of the old parties in the face of the new one, of the Messiahship; and one Gospel points out that the Sadducees were regarded as confederates of the Pharisees from the moment when they appeared in the field against Jesus, and that the spirit of conspiracy, the passion of the solidarity of interests, more than counterbalanced the Pharisees' hatred of the tenets of the Sadducees and their joy at the overthrow of the latter by Jesus.[1]

Thus Pharisees and Herodians appeared together before Jesus. Not only the latter, but the former also, were to Jesus fresh personages, as it were still unsoiled, not already disposed of or rendered obnoxious or suspected by previous controversy, personages therefore whose inquiries after truth he could unsuspectingly listen to and candidly answer, whose flattering address he in his surprise and joy could be gratified with and could reciprocate and reward with prompt trustfulness. For the Pharisees put forward several of their disciples, obscure men whom Jesus did not know, men that were also young zealots in the cause of God, and whom the Galilean zealot, under the impression produced by honest looks and intentions, would readily trust.[2] "Teacher,"

---

[1] Matt. xxii. 34. Combined action of the Pharisees and Sadducees, above, I. p. 364.

[2] Matt. xxii. 15; Luke xx. 20; Mark xii. 13. According to Matt., the Pharisees are the active party; according to Luke, xx. 1, 19, the Sanhedrim, who, after secret

began the messengers, "we know, we are fully convinced, that thou art truthful, and teachest the way of the Lord in truth— that is, purely—and that thou carest for no one, for thou dost not look upon the face of men. Tell us, what thinkest thou? Is it lawful to give *census* (tribute) to Cæsar or not?" How beautiful was all this,—this respectful title of Rabbi, which the Pharisees of the previous day had never used—this final recognition, even by the pious and the respectable, of the brave, upright, fearlessly candid man of God—this secure confidence in asking so weighty and ticklish a question, which might cost even the questioners their lives.[1] Candour demanded candour, the appeal to bravery challenged bravery. Jesus knew necessarily that such ideas were continually fermenting among the Pharisaic youth, and that the Herodians, instead of being favourable to Rome, ardently wished for a reversal of political relations. Therefore why should he mistrust the new allies? The Pharisees had calculated with consummate shrewdness; but this shrewdness had culminated in the secure conviction that Jesus would give a negative reply, and that he would be compelled to atone to the Romans with his life. In supposing he would reject the tribute, his opponents measured him entirely by his *début* and his confession. His first appearance before the public was looked upon as the beginning of a religious-political insurrection; and the last great insurrection had been the work of the Pharisaic fellow-countryman of Jesus, Judas the Galilean, who, a generation before, at the time of the valuation, had charged the people to obey God rather than men, and to pay to the Roman no valuation, no *census*.[2] It is said also that Gamaliel, the head of the Pharisees, classed Jesus with Judas and Theudas, men of revo-

observation (Luke vi. 7; Mark iii. 2), send out watchers, ἐγκαθέτους, subornatos insidiatores, yet evidently Pharisees (righteous, comp. Luke xviii. 9). Volkmar's laudation of Mark is indefensible, even though the sending of Pharisees and Herodians by the Sanhedrim is in itself possible (see above, p. 158, n. 1). Matthew is superior to Mark also in the details of the narrative (Mark xii. 14!).

[1] Comp. the Roman severity towards Judas Gal. and his sons, Jos. *Ant.* 18, 1, 1; 20, 5, 2; above, I. p. 262.

[2] Above, I. p. 261.

lution.[1] Jesus' public confession, however, was at one time John the Baptist, at another the Messiahship; and the one as well as the other prompted him to revolution and to the driving away of the Romans, and therefore to tread afresh in the footsteps of Judas the Galilean. But with a negative answer he would not only publicly give himself forth to be what he was, he would at the same time irretrievably commit himself to his ruin. Repudiation of the tribute was repudiation of the legality of the Roman rule, high treason against emperor and empire, the first principle of revolution. And in proportion to the terribleness of the blow which the rebellion, under the leadership of Judas, had dealt to the early rule of Rome at Jerusalem, in proportion to the sanguinary character of the revenge taken with sword and crucifixion by Rome, finally, in proportion to the anxiety with which the continuous fermenting of the dreams of freedom originated by Judas was observed and watched, would be the unquestionable certainty that the Roman procurator would without delay punish the new Galilean upon the cross. In fact, Luke has most distinctly referred to this as the aim of the opponents.[2] A speedier issue than this, and, what was still more important, a better one, could not have been discovered. The hatefulness of the trial and execution of Jesus in the eyes of the people would thus lie entirely on the side of the Romans, and not of the Pharisees; whilst a religious trial was full of risk on all sides, since it would expose the party to the popular hatred, and presented no certain prospect of the good-will and the indispensable co-operation of the Roman procurator. All these sources of anxiety—the hatred, perhaps the rebellion, of the people, the non-compliance of the governor, and then a ludicrous issue to all their efforts—were happily removed by the *census*-question plan of

---

[1] Acts v. 36 sq. We say nothing here of the unhistorical character of this passage in its details. Gamaliel must have spoken the words after A.D. 44—46 instead of in A.D. 36. It is interesting to notice that Jos. *Ant.* 20, 5, 1, makes the revolution of Theudas precede that of the sons of Judas, which perhaps explains the error of Luke, even though he was not acquainted with the Jewish historian.

[2] Luke xx. 20.

attack, a plan conceived and prepared in a masterly way, and one to which Jesus and Pilate and the people must accommodate themselves with the necessity of the pieces upon a chess-board.

But He was himself, and he was different from what they thought he must necessarily be. Above all was he different inasmuch as he saw through their cards, and moreover—independently of this—was not in his principles what they took him to be. "Why tempt ye me, ye hypocrites?" he replied, noting the Jewish malice in the question itself as well as in the faces of the questioners, and taught by the position of affairs to suspect villany. Hence he assumed the old, customary tone towards the new friends, the old foes, and by talking of temptation showed that he saw, in the precipitation to which they would compel him, a snare that might not only be his ruin but might lead him into sin. "Show me," he continued, "the coin of the *census*," the money in which it was customary to pay it. They brought him a *denarius*, a piece of ten, the common Roman coin which represented the popularly hated though moderate capitation-tax, the symbol of slavery to the Gentiles. This coin bore the image and the legend of the name of the reigning emperor, Tiberius. By accident, or more probably as the result of cunning calculation, the coin was one which bore the full expression of the Roman domination. The emperors, down to the Flavii, caused special coins to be struck for Judæa, without an image, in deference to the Jewish faith, and with merely the name of the emperor and the customary Jewish symbols.[1] But naturally, especially at the festivals, the very numerous image-impressed coins flowed into

---

[1] Comp. Eckhel, Cavedoni, Saulcy, in my description of the Herods, *Bibel.-Lex.* III. Ewald, p. 82. Wies. *Beitr.* p. 84. The census-coin itself (Matt., Mark, κῆνσος; Luke, φόρος) represented the capitation-tax, the tax which was most palpable to the people as a whole (tributum capitis, ἡ καθ' ἑκάστην κεφαλὴν εἰσφορά), as distinguished from the land-tax which affected the well-to-do, and was paid in kind (Jos. *Ant.* 14, 10, 6) and silver (also larger money); hence also in Mark, in codex D, ἐπικεφάλαιον, It. Bobb. capitularium; and this capitation-tax itself amounted to a *denarius*. Jos. *B. J.* 2, 16, 4; comp. Wieseler, *Beitr.* pp. 109 sqq., 118, only that Wieseler, on behalf of his erroneous exposition of Matt. xvii. 24, is disposed to assume that the Jews on their part were compelled, by a special severity, to pay two *denarii*, the *didrachmon*.

the money-market at Jerusalem. It was such a genuinely and distinctively Gentile coin which was shown to Jesus, and it was secretly hoped that his anti-Roman indignation would at last burst forth against the signs of double abomination, the sign of servitude on one side and that of idolatry on the other. But quite the contrary. Jesus, different from the Jews, did not take offence at the heathen image; it was not the outside that was unclean to him, but the inside.[1] Nay, the image supplied to him the argument, or completed the argument, which the inscription introduced. "Whose is this image and this superscription?" asked Jesus, examining the coin without any exhibition of abhorrence. "Cæsar's," they answered. "Then give," he now said solemnly, "the things of Cæsar to Cæsar, and the things of God to God!"[2] This was an utterance worthy of Solomon, and more than that. For this argument of Jesus was no merely apparent argument, and his answer was no principle-less wary evasion. The current coin was to the Jews a symbol and representative of the recognized ruling power; and the factual ruling power was, to the faith in Divine Providence professed both by Jesus and the Pharisees, the ruling power ordained of God.[3] When he, like the Pharisees, in this sense acquiesced in the Roman domination as in a dispensation of God, he by no means asserted that this dispensation of popular oppression—as he had previously designated the Gentile kingdoms, the Roman empire—should

[1] *Avod. Sar.* f. 6: a heretic sends a denarius Cæsaris to Rabbi Judas. Quid faciam? Accipiam eum? Dixit ei Resh Lakish: accipe et projice coram eo in puteum. Wetst. p. 474. The scruples of the Essenes concerning coins is mentioned by Hippol. *Philos.* 9, 26 (above, I. p. 372).

[2] Chrys.: τὰ τῷ Θεῷ παρ' ἡμῖν ὀφειλόμενα. Justin, *Ap.* 1, 17: ὅθεν Θεὸν μὲν μόνον προσκυνοῦμεν. Matt. xvi. 23. Above, IV. p. 269. Ancients and moderns have quite mistakenly thought of the temple tribute of God, or indeed (Tert., *Marc.* 4, 38, even Erasmus, Neander, Lange, Hofmann in Meyer) of the human soul, the image of God.

[3] *Hier. Sanh.* f. 20, 2: Abigail asks David: tu rex es? He answers: Samuel anointed me. She: atqui moneta domini nostri Saulis adhuc obtinet. *Maim. in Gezel.* c. 5: ubic. numisma alic. regis obtinet, illic incolae regem istum pro domino agnoscunt. As well as the coins, the seal of the king passed current, Lightfoot, p. 330. Comp. 1 Macc. xv. 6. Lightfoot, p. 355, and Wetst. p. 474. Wieseler, *Beitr.* p. 84. Determinism of Jesus, *Gesch. Chr.* p. 20; and above, II. p. 180.

necessarily remain for ever; and still less did he assert that this terrestrial dispensation could obscure or supersede the fundamental divine dispensation of the people, the legal subjection to God. To this last he gave emphatic expression, not only to prevent any misunderstanding that he was a partizan of Rome either from principle or sycophancy, but in order to remain true to himself; for to him the divine dispensation naturally stood high above the Roman; to him, the former was first and unconditioned, the latter second, conditioned, organized, and therefore capable of being again decomposed; and he spoke of the latter first only because the question had concerned it. Upon the temporary character of the Roman empire he was silent, again not out of fear or craftiness, but because the counsels of God were hidden from him, because he left it to God, even though he might hope for and indeed expect a change from God.[1] It would therefore be quite as incorrect to find in Jesus' answer merely a subtle Jewish evasion and withholding of his real opinion, as to find in it an unconditional recognition of the Roman domination, or an unconditional renunciation of terrestrial redemption of the people and of terrestrial rule of the Messiah.[2] The first has been already sufficiently refuted; the incorrectness of the second is proved by all that the fundamental principles of the kingdom of heaven and of the Messiah idea have long since shown both in the popular opinion and in the views of Jesus. The rejection of the historical character of the whole, by the most recent criticism, has no ground to rest upon.[3] His foes must have felt disap-

[1] Even a Josephus (*B. J.* 5, 9, 3; *Ant.* 10, 11, 7; 10, 10, 4) looked beyond the Romans (above, I. p. 324); how much rather Jesus (Matt. xx. 25).

[2] A mere evasion and refusal of the external command (comp. Luke xii. 13), thought of by Wetstein, De Wette, Volkmar, who assumes an indefinite mean. Hase, p. 224: a casting back of the question upon those who recognized Rome. Schenkel, pp. 239 sq.: separation of Church and State, tax not from the religious but the legal point of view. Wittichen, *Idee d. Menschen*, 1868, p. 196: passive obedience, as to the emperor, so to God, *i.e.* the temple! Even Meyer thinks (as already Justin, *Ap.* 1, 17: Χαίροντες ὑπηρετοῦμεν) of a representation of the principle of a conscientious duty towards the authorities (whence Rom. xiii. 1).

[3] Volkmar (p. 521) thinks that the doctrine-shaping Mark intended to draw within narrower limits the extravagant, *marvellous*, and—to the Jews (Acts xiii. 11 sqq.)—

pointed above measure, completely overthrown, for they had achieved nothing. They had neither, as they had wished and expected, unmasked him as a rebel and an enemy to Rome, nor even, as they might have afterwards wished, as a traitor to God, to the people, to their liberty, to their future, to their longing for Messianic salvation. On the contrary, he would be advantaged in his relation to the Romans by his friendly utterance, and among the people by his law-honouring confession, his theocratic "But" to his Roman "Yes." Thus we can understand it when the Gospels themselves tell us that his tempters went away astonished at his answer, and speechless.

The sagacious conjecture of Hitzig has placed close to this first cunning attempt to disconcert Jesus, the well-known incident of the charge against the woman taken in adultery, an incident which, with all its effectiveness and its undeniable real grandeur, has in eighteen hundred years won a settled resting-place, a home, in not one of our Gospels. In point of fact, this incident stands—though its right here is very much controverted —in the fourth Gospel, in connection with a Feast of Tabernacles six months earlier; and several MSS. of no authority give it in Luke at the close of the last struggle of Jesus, immediately before the beginning of the Eastertide.[1] But though John and

highly offensive vindication of the rights of the temporal authorities of Rome by Paul, Rom. xiii. 1 sqq., to set aside the subjection theory of his there marvellous master. Religion and politics are not to coincide—each in its place! Such a poet, with such words at such an eminently suitable place, would be no mere inferior disciple of Paul; he would be more than the master. Who would, indeed, have looked for a correction of Paul here, and who can find it to-day? Are not the deeper ordinances of God reserved even in Rom. xiii. 1, 5, 8 ?

[1] John vii. 53—viii. 11. Several late codices place the incident at the end of the Gospel; other late ones after Luke xxi. 38. The question of the textual criticism must be regarded as solved (comp. Lachm., Tisch., Meyer, Scholten). Though more than 100 codices have it (in John, the important Bez. at their head), the determining codices are without it, Sin., Vat., Al., Ephr., Reg. Most of the Fathers and most of the ancient translations are without it (Ital. divided). In the middle ages, Euth. Zig. knew that it was wanting παρὰ τοῖς ἀκριβέσιν ἀντιγράφοις, or was furnished with obeli (or asterisks). The most important vouchers, besides It., are Jerome and Augustine, as well as *Constit. Apost.* 2, 24, 4. Since the reformation, the external genuineness has been denied by most critics, even by Lücke, Neander, Tholuck, Olsh., Bleek, Luther, Brückn, Ewald, Guer., Krabbe, Hengst. It has been defended recently by Hug, Maier, Ebr., Lange, Hilg.!

Luke have opened their doors only murmuringly and with signs of reluctance, how courteous and friendly Mark again stood forth, offering, according to Hitzig's divination, to the vagabond passage a chamber so quiet, so habitable, and—more than all that—no mere inn-room, but the actual old home itself!¹ Among three temptations of Jesus by the Pharisees, this was plainly the middle one! After the political complot of the Pharisees and the Herodians, the religious one of the Pharisees and the Scribes! And before the foolish question of the Sadducees concerning the condition of the seven wives in the resurrection, the faithlessness of the wife on earth!² We leave, therefore, the vagabond passage in this asylum. Whilst Jesus, having come in early from the Mount of Olives, was teaching in the temple, Scribes and Pharisees brought to him a woman, a Jewish representative of the woman of Samaria, who had been taken in the act of adultery. Placing her in the midst, they said: "Teacher, Moses commanded stoning; what sayest thou?"³ They sought grounds for an accusation. Then Jesus bowed down and wrote with his finger upon the earth,—this was, according to Jeremiah, the symbol of forgetting, of forgiveness.⁴ But his opponents did not understand him and his delay, they stood waiting and excited. "Let him that is sinless among you be the first to cast the stone at her!" said he, lifting himself up, and then he stooped down again and

---

¹ On the internal evidences in John, see next page. In Luke xxi. 38, however, the history of the controversial sayings is already ended; it would be an extraordinary appendix. Hitzig's exceedingly sagacious vindication of Mark, in his *Joh. Markus*, pp. 205 sqq. Then also Holtzm. p. 92, who claims the incident for the source of the Synoptics.

² Partly Hitzig's, partly my own, exposition.

³ Levit. xx. 10; Deut. xxii. 24. Hitzig (p. 209) and Ewald (p. 480) have removed empty objections against the stoning based on this passage and the Rabbis. Stoning was the customary punishment under the law; and strangling, mentioned by the Rabbis, is not in the Old Testament. According to *Sotah*, 1, 5 (in Casp. p. 146), the trial of such women (to whom therefore the exclusion of the unclean, Jos. *B. J.* 5, 5, 6, did not fully apply) took place at the Nicanor gate, the eastern gate, which led from the court of the Gentiles to that of the women.

⁴ Jer. xvii. 13. Others (as early as Euth. Zig.) think of a desire to ignore the circumstance, on the part of Jesus. Comp. the Rabbis, in Schöttgen, p. 366, where, however, the case is not exactly the same. The first is more significative.

THE TEMPTERS. 167

continued to write.[1] Now there was a change; struck by the arrow of conviction, one after another slunk away, the old masters first and their disciples more tardily. "Woman," asked Jesus, lifting himself up again, "where are those thine accusers? Has no one condemned thee?" "No one, Sir," said she. "Neither do I condemn thee; go, and sin no more!"[2]

This incident is among the most affecting in the Gospels, even in John's. In its unpretentious sentences there is a wealth of conception, of invisibly visible intellectual movement; in its concise treatment there is rapid variety, to which the law of contrast, introduced in a masterly manner, lends its tragic force. Danger beyond deliverance, and yet deliverance; evident, foul, freshly contracted guilt, and yet an ideal; massive conceit and secret pangs of sin, perfect righteousness and unmitigated harshness, honourable publicity and intriguing strategy, over and above all, an abyss of saving love and yet holiness, overflowing religion and yet wisdom, hottest battle for life and death and yet moral weapons and victory of conscience. But even this incident is not strictly historical. In the first place, it is rejected not only by the older Gospels, even by Mark, but also by John, whose language and context it disturbs.[3] It disturbs Mark, and

---

[1] The witnesses threw the first stones. Deut. xvii. 7; Acts vii. 58.

[2] Recalls the sick man in John v. 14.

[3] The non-Johannine in expression, in scenery (the Mount of Olives from the Synoptics), in the construction of a controversy upon the Law, has been sufficiently shown by expositors; the linguistic side particularly by Credner, *Einleitung*, p. 231. Since Baur's analysis of the Gospels, every one knows that the controversies in John vii. viii. are fatally interrupted. Particularly, as to the person of Jesus, vii. 16, 28 sqq., is in conflict with viii. 13; vii. 24 with viii. 15; vii. 30 with viii. 20; vii. 33 with viii. 21. The passage between tears the rest in two without one contribution to the context. Only viii. 15 (yet see vii. 24) *seems* to point to our passage; but why does not vii. 51 receive its due in the interpolation? The resolute vindicator of the genuineness of the passage (Hilg.'s article, John's Gospel not interpolated, in *Zeitschr.* 1868, pp. 451 sqq.) continually makes unimportant objections. Only our section would explain how Jesus came to be in the temple, viii. 20. But in vii. he is continually in the temple. Next he thinks John viii. 12 sqq. could not take place on the last day of the Feast of Tabernacles (vii. 37); there must be therefore (on account of the interpolation itself, viii. 2) a fresh day referred to, namely, on the ground of ix. 14, the Sabbath following the Feast of Tabernacles. But, in point of fact, everything to viii. 20, more correctly to viii. 59, must belong to the last day of the Feast of Taber-

it disturbs the fundamental conception of the Synoptics, that Jesus, particularly at Jerusalem, solemnly recognized, and did not annul, the Law.[1] Neither is it quite free from artificial features, apart from the conduct of Jesus, who mysteriously— scarcely possible in Mark and John—stooped and stooped again and wrote upon the earth. In reality it is only a very transparent clothing of an idea. Men of the Law, with Moses in their hand and with their ceremonial righteousness, were never so much affected; Jesus never went so far in forbearance as to make it possible for men to suppose him capable of patronizing adultery and of coming into contact with fresh foul sin without a shudder, without indignation, of at once excusing, palliating, wiping out either coarse or refined sins, an idea which gave offence to the early Church.[2] Finally, the decisive proof is found in the character of exaggeration which marks the narrative as of later construction than the simpler, earlier accounts. The oldest Gospels know of a Jesus who received publicans and sinners.[3] A later source, in Luke, has already constructed there-

nacles and to no fresh day, after which ix. 1 introduces a fresh day, a Sabbath (verse 14). But would they have stoned upon a Sabbath?

[1] The arguments for Mark, though without the support of a single codex, have been developed by Hitzig, Holtzmann, Volkmar; and Mark's fondness for the mysterious may also be adduced. But Holtzmann has pointed out what is like Luke, and Volkmar what is unlike Mark; and I would further ask how could Jesus' indifference to, his breach of, the Law be followed by the then certainly extremely naive question as to the greatest commandment (Mark xii. 28)? Thus the incident must be put later, at least as late as Mark xii. 34, as a fresh and last unmasking question. But could such a question still be thought of when Jesus had expressed himself so definitely for the *whole* Law, as is stated in Mark and still more in Matthew, and when no one henceforward ventured to ask any question, Mark xii. 34! Must we then still introduce this silence by the putting to shame that resulted from the conflict about adultery?

[2] Already Augustine, *De Conjug. adult.* 2, 7, says: hoc infidelium sensus exhorret, ita ut nonnulli modicæ fidei vel pot. inimici veræ fidei, credo metuentes *peccati impunitatem dari* mulieribus suis, illud quod de adulteræ indulgentia dominus fecit, auferrent de codd. suis. Similarly, in the tenth century, the patriarch Nikon (Cotelerius, *Patr. Ap.* I. p. 236: the Armenians rejected the passage, βλαβερὰν εἶναι τὴν τοιαύτην ἀκρόασιν τοῖς πολλοῖς. If this were a sufficient reason—and it has appeared plausible to many, including Hitzig (p. 223) and Holtzmann (p. 74)—to explain the rejection, ι there should have been a campaign opened in the Gospels against publicans, sinand harlots, paralytics and thieves.

[3] Matt. ix. 9 sqq., xi. 19, xxi. 31.

THE TEMPTERS. 169

from the picture of a woman who on account of her sins is decried by the Pharisee Simon and his associates, but who, by the loving service of her anointing, gains the Lord as a defender; whilst real history knows indeed of an anointing by the hand of a woman, but not of a sinful woman.[1] The Gospel of the Hebrews, in its earliest form in the second century, had a similar narrative, which was more highly coloured than Luke's, inasmuch as the woman was accused to the Lord of *many* sins.[2] The latest exaggeration is presented by the interpolation in Luke and John. The many sins are condensed into one most heinous and fully proved sin, the charge becomes an actual legal accusation, death stares the accused in the face, Jesus forgives, and death flees as well as the accuser, who has become speechless and is put to shame far beyond the measure to which Simon was put to shame. Thus our narrative will have been formed upon the basis of Luke and the Gospel of the Hebrews. Its author was none of the older Evangelists, nor Mark, nor a disciple of Mark, although a user of the ancient tradition. But he was a friend of the fourth Gospel, one who not without success imitated the forms, the colours, the surprises, the dramatic style of that book, especially the Christ elevated above all that was trivial and shortsighted, the Lord who was without sin in contrast to the Samaritan woman, to the Pharisees, to all, the Son of God with serenity of soul mastering the Law. And he carried his contribution with a delicate subtlety to that place in the Gospel, to those controversies of Jesus with his opponents, where it found in all respects the most suitable lodgment, and yet did not altogether escape question.[3]

---

[1] Luke vii. 36 sqq.; comp. Matt. xxvi. 6; Mark xiv. 3.

[2] Papias, ap. Eus. 3, 39: ἐκτέθειται δὲ καὶ ἄλλην ἱστορ. περὶ γυν. ἐπὶ πολλ. ἁμ. διαβληθείσης ἐπὶ τ. κυρίου, ἥν τὸ καθ' Ἐβρ. εὐ. περιέχει. Hilg. (1868, p. 24) finds it possible that the Gospel of the Hebrews introduced Matt. xix. 3 with this illustration. Very commonly is this incident identified either with that of Luke, or with that of John (Rufinus, Lücke, Bleek), against which Meyer rightly declares himself. Hitzig thought (p. 224) that the Ebionites changed the offensive adultery into the indefinite sins of Papias.

[3] It is very usual to speak of the Synoptical ancient tradition (comp. Hitzig, Holtzmann), of the primitive relics of evangelical history from the apostolic time (Meyer,

We turn, then, from the spurious interpolation back to the anciently attested sources and their description of the last struggles of Jesus. On the same day, but without concert with the defeated Pharisees and Herodians, Sadducees approached Jesus.[1] Their commencement of the struggle is very different from that of the Pharisees. The latter fought at once for life and death, because they were zealous for the ordinances of the Law, because Jesus had opposed them from the beginning, and because he had robbed them of the people. The Sadducees, the calm, proud, socially respectable party of the men of official dignities and of high-priestly robes, at first took a merely contemptuous notice of the Galilean movement. There had been many similar movements, and in none of them had the uncultured, miserable people undermined the foundations of their—the Sadducees'—power. Hence the latter had never, or hardly ever, publicly met Jesus even in Galilee.[2] Neither were they as yet alarmed by the movement at Jerusalem. As they had but little to do with the Galilean Messiah, they were anxious neither to make a public accusation, nor to withdraw the people from Jesus; they wished simply, with their wisdom and self-conscious skill in disputation, to make him and his adherents, and particularly the whole of that foolish nation with their dreams of the future, ridiculous. Therefore they chose as their theme the doctrine of the resurrection, which it was well known they denied.[3] They were aware that Jesus believed in and taught a resurrection, and that on account

Krabbe, p. 413; Neander, p. 418). But the accommodations and the Johannine type are to be detected. Ewald (p. 480) speaks of "a later stock."

[1] Matt. xxii. 23; Luke xx. 27; Mark xii. 18. Sadducees, without article (or several of the Sadducees, Luke). On the other hand, the reading in Matt. should be οἱ λεγ. —and not merely λέγοντες, notwithstanding Sin., Vat., Bez.—as in the majority of MSS. (also Sin., corrector) and translations, particularly It. The falling away of the article is explicable from verse 24. The same day, expressly in Matt. Paulus (*L. J.* I. ii. p. 199) makes the Pharisees and Sadducees allied parties after the resurrection of Lazarus. Schenkel (*Bib.-Lex.* III. p. 293) quite correctly makes the Sadducees approach Jesus only as scoffers.

[2] Matt. xvi. 1. Above, IV. p. 230, note; also I. pp. 353 sqq.

[3] Above, I. pp. 360, 363. *Sanh.* f. 90, 1 : hi sunt, qui partem non habent in sec. fut.: qui dicunt, legem non esse de cœlo et resurr. non probari posse ex lege. Schöttgen, p. 176. Comp. Lightfoot, p. 355.

of the close connection between the day of the Messiah and the day of eternity, his Messiahship itself involved the claim to introduce and bring about sooner or later the judgment of God and the resurrection.[1] They knew him to be in this respect altogether on the side of the popular belief and the Pharisees. They regarded and fought with him as an offshoot of Pharisaism, though they noted the difference that while he connected judgment and resurrection more or less closely with his own person, Pharisaism connected them with the omnipotence of God or with the Messiah who was yet to come. They began, therefore, with derision, only afterwards to end with force more resolutely than the Pharisees; they began in opposition to Pharisaism, only at last to make alliance with it. They had previously, however, as carefully considered their derisive attack as had the Pharisees their tempting question; with genuinely Jewish casuistry, they had prepared a special case which was to demonstrate in a striking manner the utterly fantastical character of the human dreams of the future, and to demonstrate therefore both the right and the duty of modest restriction to the sphere of the present time.

Their special case is emphatically an extravagantly elaborate fancy. "Teacher," said the aristocrats to Jesus, with carefully measured courtesy, "Moses said, if a man die having no children, his brother shall as brother-in-law marry his wife, and raise up seed unto his brother.[2] Now there were with us seven brothers,

---

[1] On this connection, see above, IV. pp. 292 sqq.

[2] Matt. xxii. 24 (the simplest and most original of the three accounts). According to Deut. xxv. 5, supplemented—on the basis of the LXX.—from Gen. xxxviii. 8. For the expression ἐπιγ. καὶ ἀναστήσει σπ. is from Genesis. The bridge, however, from the one to the other passage is formed by the Hebrew jibbem, not expressed (συνοικήσει, LXX.) by the LXX. in the first passage. From this it follows (1) that the author understood Hebrew; (2) but he used mainly the Greek translation; (3) he is the forerunner of Luke and Mark, who bring the passages together without that exact knowledge which, however, was requisite for the connection of the two. See Anger, Rat. I. p. 20. See above, I. pp. 79 sqq. Hilgenfeld, 1868, p. 41, note 3, is incorrect. The marriage here spoken of is the Old Testament leviratical marriage (levir), or brother-in-law marriage. The Sadducees had been previously engaged in controversy about this with the Pharisees. Hilg. l. c. Yet this has no reference here.

and the first married and died, and as he had no seed he left his wife to his brother; likewise the second also, the third, to the last of the seven.¹ Last of all, the wife died. Now, in the resurrection whose wife will she be of the seven? For they all had her!" Unquestionably, modern unbelief never brought into the field a better instance against the things of the future than did these ancient Sadducees. But one thing has always been overlooked, namely, that sarcasm and gainsaying reckon with impossible figures by taking as proved what has to be proved, by superficially and pompously transferring the present, which alone they believe in, to the future which they do not, but others do, believe in, and by then loudly exclaiming about contradictions, monstrosities, impossibilities. The refutation was made once for all by the Master who repelled the carefully planned onset of the Sadducees with two words, in his marvellously quick presence of mind, yet very differently from the way in which Pharisaism denounced this folly.² "Ye err, not understanding the Scriptures, or the power of God." He demonstrated both to them. First, the power of God. "In the resurrection they neither marry nor are given in marriage, but they are as the angels in heaven."³ In faith in the omnipotence and wisdom of his God, which had already come before him in the various stages of the terrestrial

---

[1] The number is a round figure, and has nothing to do with the seven so-called sects of the Jews (Heges. ap. Eus. 2, 23; 4, 22). "With us" (Matt.) shows the concrete character of the case that occurred, or, more correctly, was invented.

[2] Comp. in an exactly similar controversy the answer of R. Johanan ben Sakkai to the Baithosians: shothim, minnain lachem? stulti, unde hoc vobis? *Gloss. in Taan.* f. 17, 1. Lightfoot, p. 924; Buxt. pp. 1220, 2347.

[3] Paraphrases in Luke xx. 34—36. Comp. Clem. *Hom.* 3, 50. Likeness to angels, *Book of Enoch*, 104: ye shall become companions of the heavenly hosts. Similar, 39; comp. 41: it shall come to pass in those days, that the elect and holy children will descend from the high heavens, and their seed will be united with the children of men. According to R. Nathan (*Pirke Abot*, 36), man has already three things in common with the angels, and three with the beasts. According to *Soh. chad.* 20, 1, animæ justorum sunt in cœlo septimo et fiunt angeli ministratorii Deumque celebrant. Schöttgen, p. 178. With Jesus (comp. *Book of Enoch*, 39) the condition descends to the earth. According to Hegesippus (Eus. 3, 20), the successors of Jesus before Domitian had spoken about a $\beta\alpha\sigma\iota\lambda$. $\dot{\epsilon}\pi o \nu \rho$. $\kappa\alpha\grave{\iota}$ $\dot{\alpha}\gamma\gamma\epsilon\lambda\iota\kappa\dot{\eta}$. This is indeed the view of the later writings in the New Testament. Above, IV. p. 284, notes.

creature, he here announced, contrary to the grosser Jewish and even Pharisaic view—the view readily presupposed by the Sadducees, and yet one which had already been broken away from by thoughtful men—that faith in the glorification of human nature, even to its corporeal part, which Paul later more copiously developed; and, going beyond Paul, he announced a belief in a human dignity which was ultimately to rise to an equality with angels.[1] Then he expounded to them the Scriptures, and indeed *those* Scriptures which they estimated most highly, and on the authority of which especially they sought to resolve the future of the resurrection into a long life upon earth—namely, the books of Moses. "But concerning the resurrection of the dead, have ye not read what is spoken *to you* by God when he says: I am the God of Abraham and the God of Isaac and the God of Jacob? God is not a God of dead men, but of living!"[2] Resemblances to this forcible argument—which in profundity certainly goes beyond and does violence to the letter—are to be found in the later Jewish literature, although there absurdity is never far off.[3] So much the more on this account should we guard ourselves

---

[1] Grosser views in *Soh. Gen.* f. 24: mulier, quæ duobus nupsit in hoc mundo, priori restituitur. Schöttgen, p. 176. Comp. Maimon. in Wetst. p. 476. More refined views, *Bab. Berach.* f. 17, 1: Rab illa frequenter in ore habuit: in mundo fut. non edent neque bibent, non generabunt liberos, non exercebunt commercia; non est ibi invidia neque odium neque rixa, sed justi sedebunt coronis cincti et delectabunt se splendore majest. div. Similar examples in Schöttgen, pp. 176 sq. Fine sentence in *Bab. Sanh.* f. 92: sicut Sanctus (Deus) vivit in æternum, ita et illi vivent in æt. (Luke xx. 38). Lightfoot, p. 363.

[2] Exodus iii. 6, 13, 15 sq. In Matt.: God says to you; in Luke, only: even Moses; Mark: in the book of Moses, how God said to him. Both: at the bush. In Luke (xx. 38) it is finely continued: unto him all live (after Paul, Gal. ii. 19; Rom. vi. 10: to live to God, to Christ).

[3] Very similarly (but late and dependent upon our passage), R. Menasse ben Isr. *De resurr. Mort.* 1, 10, 6: Deus dixisse legitur Mosi: ego sum D. patrum tuorum, Abrah., &c. Atqui D. non est D. mortuorum, quia mortui non sunt, sed vivorum, quia vivi existunt (resp. animæ). Schöttgen, p. 180. But there are not wanting foolish arguments based on such passages, wherefore Strauss unjustly appeals to the great similarity (comp. Neander, p. 490). *Gem. Hier. Berach.* f. 5, 4: justi in morte dicuntur vivi. Unde probatur? Because it is said (Exodus iii. 16): that is the land which I have sworn to Abraham, &c., lemor. . . . . Quid sibi vult vox lemor? Abi et dic patribus, quodc. promisi vobis, præstiti filiis. *Taan.* f. 5, 2: Jacobus, Jer. xxx. 10, conjungitur c. semine suo. Jam vero posteri vivunt, ergo et Jac. vivit.

against talking of the subtle Rabbinism of Jesus, or of a later base interpolation in the case of an argument that sprang from the pure gold and out of the full heart of a penetratingly searching religious presentiment. Jesus' firm belief in the resurrection of the dead came to him long before his Messianic consciousness and before his Messianic hopes. From the beginning, it came to him as a consequence of his conviction of the dignity of man and of the love of God towards His highest creature. We learn from our present passage how Jesus sought to find for this belief a firm foundation in the Scriptures, and how, neither with painstaking nor with art, but with the holy instinct of a soul searching the profoundest depth and recovering there its inner presentiment and certainty, he above all learnt to regard as weighty the title that was frequently in the mouth of God, and was in particular ever recurring in the calling of Moses: "I am the God of Abraham, of Isaac, of Jacob." He could not think that God would be continually appealing to dead men, would connect with dead names His holy declarations, nay, His vows of faithfulness to the descendants of those men. He was compelled to think that the men who lived in the heart, in the memory, in the conscience of

Schöttgen, p. 182. R. Tanchum thought the very reverse: God had connected his name only with the dead (fathers), and the exception, Gen. xxviii. 13, is explicable quia pulverem Isaci respexit. Meyer justly avoids the error of Strauss, who, endorsing the Fragmentist and ridiculing Olshausen's boasting and the shifts of the theologians (4th ed. I. p. 647, *New Life of Jesus*, Eng. trans., I. p. 356), speaks of the Rabbinical dialectics of Jesus. What is here called Rabbinism, is a profound appreciation of the eternal validity of such a divine covenant with men, the A B C of Christianity, miserably trodden under foot by modern Pantheism. This "grandeur of view" and this world-historical insight into the value of personality for God has been finely emphasized by Weisse, I. p. 583; as has been by Weizs., p. 359, the "noble application" of the words of Scripture—as free from trivial adherence to the letter as from allegorical licence—in the light of higher faith. Similarly Neander, p. 490, and De Wette, to whom the dry, apathetic logic of Strauss (*l.c.*) holds up the paltry analogy: he who does good to the children of a friend for their father's sake, thereby expresses no opinion whatever concerning the continued existence of that friend. Volkmar (p. 525) finds indeed the proof to have no force; it is rather jesting and irony of Mark against the faith in the dead letter! In fact, the Pauline writer concocted the whole, for at the time of Jesus the resurrection was certainly not so much talked about. This is knowledge and understanding! The old heathen Tacitus (*Hist.* 5, 5) knew better.

THE TEMPTERS. 175

God, also actually lived as great ones, as friends and *protegés* of God. And to him the lot of the great ones would also be shared by the little ones, by all men to whom now in a widened sense the saying applied : not a God of the dead, but of the living ; no ruler of generations that had ceased to exist, but of living, loved beings in His own image. A worthy conclusion from his doctrine of divine sonship, even though that doctrine still lacked *the* conclusion which Christianity has carried beyond Judaism : a God of the living not merely in the future, at the resurrection, as if God renounced His living creatures for thousands of years, but in *that* life which, thanks to the love of God and to the divine kinship of the human spirit, is the quick answer, the immediate loosening, of death. It is not told what the victorious antagonists of superstition, the Sadducees, answered Jesus. But though the Gospels give no answers, there is as little evidence of mutilation in the Gospels here when Jesus is at Jerusalem as previously when he was in Galilee. In the face of such forcible utterances, the artificers in words, the pickers of phrases, the concocters of stories, could remain silent. But the people, as Matthew relates, were much astonished at such doctrine. It was, indeed, the belief of the people themselves that he had vindicated ; it was the province of solemn and sweet mystery that he, like one who knew and was an eye-witness, had entered upon and opened ; and the vigour and clearness and convincing power with which he did this, produced an indescribable impression. More illustrious than ever, the hero from Galilee stood there, his foes his footstool, and the people newly enchained, roused afresh for the Prophet, the God. Nay, even many of the neutral Scribes saw the antagonism, the enmity, again bridged over, if we can credit Luke. The victory over the daring denial of the Sadducees was at the same time their victory. " Teacher, thou hast well spoken."[1]

[1] Matt. xxii. 33 ; Luke xx. 39. This expression in Luke would be in itself, psychologically, very conceivable, taken in connection with the high estimate in which the Scribes held this doctrine, a doctrine common to Jesus and themselves (Acts xxiii. 6 sqq.), and with the standing rivalry between themselves and the Sadducees, which

The distinctive party of the Pharisees, however, by no means allowed themselves to rest. The splendid victory over the Sadducees, instead of leading to conciliation, led to renewed exertions, as if, in the overthrow of the Sadducees, they had to mourn over and avenge their own.[1] This is, in fact, the form the matter assumes in the decidedly most original and unusually vivid account by Matthew; whilst Luke has omitted the fresh conflict, transferring its counterpart to Samaria, and Mark has introduced a marvellously sweet-sour narration, partly an attempt at making advances to Jesus and partly an ambush—an unhappy compromise between Matthew and Luke.[2] At the same time, Matthew's account is in favour of fixing the fresh disputations upon the next day; while in Mark the conversation flows on with the less interruption because the isolated Scribe—whose siding with Jesus is there shown—at once, in his individual independence of party, and with a disposition favourable to the victor of Sadducean unbelief, listens to the prompting of his heart.[3]

would have been sure to break up the unnatural temporary alliance. This sentence of approval is, nevertheless, unhistorical, (1) because of the already too far advanced hostility towards Jesus, which in Luke xx. 40 (immediately afterwards) is itself confessed; (2) because of the evident free editing of the older material by Luke, who in xx. 39 sq. passes over the controversy concerning the highest good—which in Matt. and Mark follows the above, but which Luke connects with the story of the Good Samaritan, x. 25 sqq.—and at once closes the controversy in a plausible manner, in such a manner, however, that the closing formula in Luke xx. 40, taken from Matt. xxii. 46, directly contradicts the pragmatism in verse 39.

[1] Strauss, 4th ed. I. p. 650 (ignorantly, see above, I. p. 364), follows Schneck. (*Urspr.* pp. 45 sqq.) in censuring this artificial juxtaposition by the writer who unites antagonistic parties on the authority of traditional reminiscences. He says that even Mark has here the better grouping, though he had only a subjective reason for that grouping.

[2] The temptation is established by Matt. xxii. 35; Luke x. 25; Mark xii. 34. Even Schenkel and Volkmar admit it. Paulus thinks of a tempter "in a good sense." Luke xx. 39 sq., but comp. in x. 25 the secondary formation of the Good Samaritan (comp. Strauss, 4th ed. I. p. 650); yet this is assimilated to Matt. xix. 16. Mark xii. 28 has combined Luke xx. 39 sq., and also Luke x. 25 (the independent mention of the two principal commands by the lawyer), with Matt. xxii. 34 sqq., and has naturally brought out the excellent point that the Scribe came with sympathy (Mark xii. 28), and nevertheless—as the close gives it (xii. 34)—as opponent and tempter. Volkmar takes no objection to this, though he thinks he has a right, on account of the ἀ. λ. of Matt., νομικὸς, to hand that over to Luke (p. 529).

[3] Matt. xxii. 34; Mark xii. 28.

THE TEMPTERS.

According to Matthew, the Pharisees have heard of the overthrow of the Sadducees, and, after Jesus' fatal double victory over both parties, have again consulted. The result of their consultation is another tempting question, which, however, according to all these indications, would not be put until the next morning, Monday, April 11.

The new temptation of that day showed a certain abatement, a paralysis, an exhaustion of resisting force and of self-confidence. For the question of the Law, which was now proposed to Jesus, could not compare with the former questions in incisiveness, significance, and determinative force. But as the question of authority was used up, and the political accusation had miscarried, a definite indictable religious crime must be sought and found. Naturally the Messiahship could have been marked as such, as also Jesus' Galilean nonconformity to the Law. But the former could not be laid hold of since the entry, and the latter was imperfectly attested and far to fetch. Hence some new evidence was necessary; and the opponents therefore hunted and groped busily, and at the same time vaguely, after fresh grounds for accusation. If it were sought to discover a defect concerning the Law in Jesus, the question which was proposed to him was not altogether inappropiate. He was asked as to the weightiest commandment, whilst the Law itself, externally considered, was distributed into a number of independent commandments made almost equally weighty in their inculcation and sanctions. Among dogmatists and systematists there had certainly shown itself a tendency to distinguish between great and small commands, light and heavy, weighty and unimportant. Hillelites and Shammaites engaged in lively controversies thereupon; and in contrast to the Shammaites, with their adherence to the letter, the great Hillel at least, a preparer of the way for Jesus, penetrated to the essence of the Law, to what was ultimate and essential, to the love or indeed to the fear of God, and to the love of our neighbours.[1] So far it might appear that there had been brought to

[1] *Edaj.* 4 : hæ res ad præcepta leviora pertinent ex sent. Shammæanorum, ad gravia ex mente Hillelianorum. The people were advised to follow both! Schöttgen,

Jesus rather a much discussed controversy of the day, or a nice point disputed among the schools, or an enticing proposal to attach himself to Hillel, than a tempting question. But when we look closer, we see the tempter there. The Jews as a whole, Hillel included, were led by the ceremonial spirit which dominated them to look for the greatness of the Law chiefly in little things, or, as Jesus had long since so bitterly and reproachfully said, in the ordinances, not in the roots of religion and morality, though these were spoken of by name. It very commonly happened that those commandments of Moses were called great with which the Lawgiver had associated the threat of extirpation from among the people; but such were for the least part the higher rules, they were the ordinances of the Sabbath, of circumcision, of purification, of sacrifice.[1] And when, as was very customary, the people were exhorted to keep the little as well as the great commandments, the hidden motive was not the encouragement of a higher degree of conscientiousness, but a miserable patronage of trivial services.[2] And when the famous Hillel

p. 186. Hillel's rule about one's neighbour, above, I. p. 337, note 4. The rule concerning God, *Shebu.* f. 39, 1: scito, totum mundum contremuisse, quo temp. Deus præceptum illud promulgavit: non assumes nomen Domini Dei tui in vanum. Reliqua omnia levia excepto illo de non profanando nomine Dei. Schöttgen, p. 184. Wetst. p. 486. Comp. *Pirke Abot*, 5, 17; above, I. p. 350, note 3. Small and great commands mentioned in the Talmud, kal (easy), vachomer (great measure), hence mizvot kallot (rekot) and chamurot (rabbot). Bux. p. 789; above, III. p. 301.

[1] Very usual (*Shebu.* f. 39, 1), præc. gravia, quibus pœna excisionis et mors a Synedrio decreta imponitur. Schöttgen, pp. 184, 189. Now this death was the punishment not only of idolatry and the like (Lev. xx. 2, 6, 27), the cursing of parents (xx. 9), incest (xx. 17), but also of Sabbath-breaking (Ex. xxxi. 14), uncircumcision (Gen. xvii. 14), breaches of the laws of sacrifice (Lev. vii. 20, 25), ceremonial uncleanness (Numb. xix. 20), the eating of forbidden food at feasts (Ex. xii. 15, 19) and on other occasions (Lev. xvii. 14). Independently of this *norma*, the prohibitions relating to dishonouring God and slaying man, the commands relating to the Sabbath, circumcision, and honouring parents, were called great; the commands relating to the erection of tabernacles, the letting parent birds escape from the nest (Deut. xxii. 6 sq.), and the washing of hands, were called little.

[2] *Tanch.* f. 78, 4: observa præcepta levia eodem modo quo gravia. *Debar. rabb.* f. 258, 1: non libratis præc. legis. Called levia only because men are parum solliciti about them. The commandments to honour parents, to let the mother bird fly away, not to kill, and to wash the hands, are equally great, and have the sanction of equal rewards. Schöttgen, pp. 185 sqq. Wetst. pp. 296, 486.

commandment about washing of hands at certain times was changed from a little command into a great one, and when the haughty words were spoken of the traditions of the dealers in trivialities, that "in distinction from the great and the little in the Law, the commandments of the lawyers were all great and weighty," then, in fact, the question as to which was the greatest commandment became an apposite strategic question for the men of the Law to put to the repudiator of *their* Law.[1] If they had in view the letter and external works, and were suspicious that Jesus depreciated or rejected just what was weightiest in the Law, the external ordinances of ceremonial cleanness and of the divine service, of the Sabbath and of the sacrifices, it was not an improbable calculation that his answer to the question as to the greatest commandment would present to them, as welcome matter for accusation, a curtailment of the ordinances, or perhaps a vigorous sally against the whole system of ordinances.[2] And the better to throw him off his guard, they this time made no show of a formal deputation; they sent, not several, but an individual lawyer, so that Jesus might suspect nothing and unreservedly reveal his whole heart.[3]

"Teacher," the tempting lawyer said to him courteously, "which commandment is great in the Law?"[4] But no one could ever take him by surprise, and least of all in this province, in his favourite province, which not long before at Jericho he had fully discussed with the rich young man, and which long before

---

[1] *Tanch.* f. 73, 2: si quis manus p. cibum non lavat, est ac si hom. occideret. Schöttgen, p. 185. Then the rule in Buxt. *Syn.* p. 315: manus pedesque mundissime habeto, nam certe hoc præc. parvum non est. *Ib.* p. 164: magnum est præc. de zizit, of the fringes! Wetst. p. 295. *Hier. Berac.* f. 3, 2: amabilia sunt verba scribarum præ verbis legis; nam v. legis sunt gravia et levia, at v. scribarum sunt omnia gravia. Lightfoot, p. 330.

[2] Schenkel (p. 243) incorrectly: they wished to see whether he would not (as Messiah) put himself in the place of God. Against this, Gess (p. 127), with justice.

[3] Comp. the subsequent assembling of the opponents, Matt. xxii. 41. Luke also (x. 25) isolates this lawyer.

[4] Mark, not μεγάλη, but πρώτη πάντων; brought in from Matt. xxii. 38 (Mark xii. 31). A second commandment could not properly follow the question in Mark, but it could that in Matthew.

he had pondered over while making his own mental analysis of the relation between Moses and the ordinances. But with a full consciousness of the seriousness of his position, Jesus this time gave the fullest, the most comprehensive, the most unmistakable, and the most unassailable answer. To the young man he had mentioned only the one principal rule of love of one's neighbour; to the lawyer he presented as great two principal commandments, of which he refused to make either less than, or subordinate to, the other; and then to the two commandments he added all others, the host of commandments, which he did not reject, but which he simply saw as rooted in the two great ones that gave the key-note, and as deriving from them force and value and light and purpose. With a sure hand he laid hold of the fifth and of the third books of Moses, and from the great starry heaven which was to lighten and direct the ways of Israel, he extracted the dominant sun-stars: " Thou shalt love the Lord thy God with thy whole heart and with thy whole soul and with thy whole mind. This is the great and first commandment.[1] A second is like to it: Thou shalt love thy neighbour as thyself.[2] Upon these two commandments hang the whole law and the prophets."[3] It is the old Master, separating the kernel from the shell, discovering the kernel in the divine-human vibrations of man's spirit, in religion and yet also in morality,

[1] To be thus read according to the earliest MSS. Syr. Cur. (harmonizing with Mark), magnum et primum.

[2] Deut. vi. 5; Lev. xix. 18. In the first passage the Hebr. has: in or with thy (whole) heart, soul, might (meod). The LXX. has $\dot{\epsilon}\xi\ \dot{o}.\ \delta\iota\alpha\nu o\acute{\iota}\alpha\varsigma,\ \psi\upsilon\chi\tilde{\eta}\varsigma,\ \delta\upsilon\nu\acute{\alpha}\mu.$ (Al. also $\kappa\alpha\rho\delta.,\ \dot{\iota}\sigma\chi.,\ \delta\iota\alpha\nu.$). Matthew, with $\dot{\epsilon}\nu$ and $\kappa\alpha\rho\delta.$, adheres to the Hebrew, but adopts the $\delta\iota\alpha\nu.$ from the LXX. instead of $\delta\upsilon\nu.$ Luke and Mark, following partly Matt. and partly the LXX., add the $\dot{\iota}\sigma\chi\dot{\upsilon}\varsigma$ (LXX. $\delta\upsilon\nu.$) to the three moments of Matt., Luke making the $\delta\iota\alpha\nu.$ of Matt. the fourth, Mark the $\dot{\iota}\sigma\chi\dot{\upsilon}\varsigma$. Their quartet contradicts the text and itself points to Matt. Comp. Anger, *Ratio*, I. p. 36. Interesting explanation in *Berach.* f. 61, 2, why three designations, Schöttgen, p. 189.

[3] *Beresh. R.* 24 on Lev. xix. 18: dixit R. Akiba (equal to Hillel): haseh kelal gadol, hæc est complexio, summa regula legis. Often among the Rabbis, caput, stomachus, res, a qua totum pendet. Greek: $\dot{\epsilon}\xi\ o\tilde{\upsilon}\ \tau\grave{\alpha}\ \pi\acute{\alpha}\nu\tau\alpha\ \H{\eta}\rho\tau\eta\tau\alpha\iota,\ \dot{\epsilon}\xi\ \check{\omega}\nu\ \kappa\rho\epsilon\mu\alpha\mu\acute{\epsilon}\nu\eta\ \pi\tilde{\alpha}\sigma\alpha\ \psi\upsilon\chi\grave{\eta}$; $\dot{\epsilon}\xi\alpha\phi\theta\acute{\epsilon}\nu\tau\epsilon\varsigma\ \dot{\alpha}\pi\grave{o}$, *Trypho*, 42. Comp. Rom. xiii. 9. Latin: suspensum est, pendet, cardo rei est (ubi litium cardo vertitur, Quint. *Inst.* 12, 8, 2; comp. 5, 12, 3. Virgil, *Æn.* i. 672). Comp. Wetst. p. 478.

in the duality which is unity because it is love to God and to the children of God. It is the old Master, who knows how to honour the shell as well as the kernel; for, seeing with his penetrating glance not only through the Law, but through all the documents of the Old Testament, he knows that every commandment of Moses, every injunction of the Prophets far and near, is supported, dominated, therefore glorified and eternalized, by the great fundamental rule. Nothing could ever be advanced against this noble and truly conservative exposition of the Law. That Jesus had mentioned the greatest, no one could deny, even though this great commandment might be forgotten both in theory and practice; and as to what was little, but esteemed great by the teachers, Jesus had let fall no syllable of depreciation, for—as with those teachers and yet differently—with him the great made it great, the eternal made it eternal.[1]

It has been mentioned that Mark has treated this conversation not as possessing a distinctively tempting character, but rather as a friendly and—if the expression be permitted—a fraternizing conversation. Delighted with the successful repulse of the Sadducees, one of the lawyers on his own account proposes the question concerning the first commandment of all. He greets the answer of Jesus—who names not only the first but also the second commandment—with the loudest and most solemn assent to the duty of loving God, or, more correctly, since the lofty ethics of Jesus are transformed into formal dogmatics, to Jesus' belief in God, and to the two fundamental rules the observing of which is better than all sacrifice and burnt-offering. Wherefore Jesus—in a manner which reminds us of Mark's young man whom Jesus loved at once—closes with the conciliatory, nay, encouraging, words, " Thou art not far from the kingdom of God !" But gratifying as such a change to peace after perpetual strife, edifying as such a real spiritual success, a success resulting not solely in the silencing of embittered vanquished foes, might be, it is nevertheless not historical. Though it may remain an open

---

[1] See footnotes on pp. 177 sq.

182   THE DECISIVE STRUGGLE.

question whether it is probable that a Scribe, accustomed to discipline, would have broken away from his party and acquired through Jesus his independence, and adopted a watchword which no one but Jesus had strongly emphasized, there is tangibly a contradiction when this account is compared not only with Matthew but also with Luke, although the latter gives the incident at another place. It is equally tangible that the whole account is a development out of Matthew and Luke, which culminates in the Evangelist's endeavour to exhibit to his later age the golden rule of Jesus, monotheism and humanity as the uniting symbol of Jews and of Jewish and Gentile Christians. As tangibly have we here a violent interpolation, for the closing remark, "No one after that durst question Jesus at all," on the one hand completely overthrows the conciliatory character of this conversation, and on the other hand betrays the artificial connection of this account with the brief text-form of Luke.[1]

Matthew, however, shows that the Pharisees were no longer disposed to engage with the invincible disputator, though a great number of them had approached, curious—and speedily disappointed—to hear the result of the question by the individual who had been put forward.[2] They stood dumb round about, with

---

[1] Mark xii. 29, 32 adds to Deut. vi. 5 (Matt. xxii. 37) the introduction, Deut. vi. 4, not only, as elsewhere, for the sake of completing the details, but, as in xi. 17, for dogmatic reasons. He wishes to exhibit the monotheism of the Jews—of which Jesus could *not* here be thinking, since it would be necessarily implied—as an ecclesiastical *symbolum* (in which sense also John xvii. 3 is to be understood) which was binding also upon the Gentile Christians. We are hereby reminded that this was the Alpha and Omega of Judaism (after Mark, Clem. *Hom.* 3, 57), and the Shemâ and the Echâd, the daily prayer, of the Jews. Wetst. p. 480. Wichelh. p. 285. The watchword of the Scribe, with reference to sacrifice (in Mark), is for the rest that of Jesus, only in another form, Matt. ix. 13, xii. 7, of which this passage of Mark has, however, no trace. Mark is indebted not only to Matthew, but also to Luke, with respect to the sympathy of the Scribe, which in Luke xx. 39 is unhistorical (comp. on the other hand Luke x. 25), and also with respect to the Scribe's independent knowledge of the summa legis (Luke x. 27). Whilst Neander (p. 491), Weisse (I. p. 585), and even Gess (p. 127), have found Mark's account plausible, De Wette and Bleek have acknowledged his contradictions. Volkmar has thought the words οὐ μακρὰν εἶ too liberal for the Jewish-Christian Matthew; only by faith in the Son of God could a man become blessed, according to him! Does that stand anywhere in the narrative of the rich young man, &c.?

[2] Matt. xxii. 41.

threatening looks, and yet completely helpless. Then the rôles were exchanged, as on the previous day. The assaulted became the assailant. What he said was certainly in the spirit of his previous conversation, in which he manifested such an extreme moderation as might have been expected to compel a mutual understanding and reconciliation, whence the misconception of the second Gospel may be in part explained. But the attacking speech belonged to a new and most important field of battle,— it was a mild, instructive attempt to convince the opponents of their prejudices. The theme appeared to sweep completely away from the former one, and yet it was directly derived from that. From his attitude towards the Law and the Prophets, authorities which he was charged with repudiating, but which he so solemnly upheld, the direct sequence of ideas led him to his Messiahship, which was looked upon with equal distrust, indeed as a breach of the Law and the Prophets, while in his own conviction it was the very end and aim of Moses and the Prophets.[1] Thus he took up again that most important and most decisive controversial point from which he on the second day, and from which his opponents since the third day, had kept aloof. Certainly he did not so take it up again as to call himself Messiah, but he took it up in such a way as to expose the erroneous ideas of the Pharisees concerning the Messiah, and thus to refute their thoughtless denial of *his* Messiahship. A last faint hope may have inspired the unyielding gatherer together of Israel. The conviction and persuasion of the cultured, the learned, the guides of the people, concerning the higher spiritual sense of his Messiahship, might yet bring about the recognition of his Messiahship; and this example of the leaders of the nation might yet be followed by the adhesion of the dependent, uncultured people who were withholding their sympathy. Or, even though he hoped for nothing, he may have wished on his own part to do the utmost

---

[1] According to Hase (p. 224), Jesus only intended to discourage his opponents from continuing the wordy strife. According to Schenkel (p. 245), the hierarchs had assiduously caused the report to be everywhere circulated that Jesus had fraudulently claimed to be the Messiah though he lacked the necessary descent.

to explain his position and to bring about a distinct understanding.[1] He turned sharply to those who were assembled near him, not to the multitudes of the people, as Mark says, but to the Pharisees: "What think ye concerning the Messiah? Whose son is he?"[2] "David's," answered they, in accordance with the universal belief of the people, and also with the words of the Old Testament; but a prudent reticence and a timid anxiety combined to prevent them from adding a word of amplification or of polemic against *his* Messiahship. Then *he* spoke further, proposing a troublesome question in which there lay a wealth both of provocation and of instruction: "But why does David in spirit call him a Lord, when he says: The Lord spoke to my Lord, Sit thou at my right hand, until I shall have laid thy foes under thy feet? If David calls him Lord, how is he his son?"[3]

When we seek for the meaning which Jesus connected with this question and protest, we must not suppose that he intended distinctively to deny the Davidic sonship of the Messiah, whether with the view of establishing a higher view of the Messiah, or, as is now often said, with the view of explaining a personal defect in his Messiahship—that he was not descended from David.[4]

[1] Comp. Matt. xii. 30, xxi. 31, xxiii. 13, and Schleiermacher's assertion (p. 373) that Jesus held his recognition to be compatible with the continuance of the existing theocratic authorities.

[2] Matt. xxii. 41; Luke xx. 41; Mark xii. 35. According to Matt. he asks the Pharisees, and they answer. According to Luke, he speaks to the antagonistic Scribes, without waiting for or receiving an answer. But according to Mark's unfortunate exegesis of Luke, he is teaching the crowds of people in the temple, and asks them: "How say the Scribes that Christ is David's son" (Luke: how say they)? As if Jesus, after the manner of the fourth Gospel, would have thought of holding theological conversations with the people. And how abrupt this antagonism towards the Scribes after the scene of conciliation! The offensiveness of this procedure of Jesus is recognized—*against Mark*—by Weisse, I. p. 586; Hausrath, p. 438. On the other hand, Neander (p. 493) very remarkably prefers Mark, and finds the offensiveness unworthy of Jesus.

[3] Ps. cx. 1. "In the spirit" means by inspiration of God. Thus also the Rabbis, in spiritu, Schöttgen, p. 190. Wetst. p. 479. In comparison with prophecy, "the spirit" ranks as of secondary degree. Schöttgen, p. 191.

[4] The latter, Strauss, *New Life of Jesus*, Eng. trans., I. p. 304 (4th ed. I. p. 649, undetermined), Weisse, Schenkel, Holtzmann, Hausrath, Reville, Weiff. Volkmar (pp. 530 sq.) thinks that Mark would here *retract* Paul's admission (Rom. i. 3) that Jesus was of the lineage of David, and that the whole narrative is the work of the Pauline poet

As the popular opinion of the Son of David was very definitely based on the Old Testament itself, as Jesus himself, up to his entry into Jerusalem, readily accepted the Messianic title of "Son of David" from the mouths of his most intimate adherents, as his own counter-question by no means denied to himself the sonship of David, but simply inquired into the compatibility of this sonship with lordship, the supposition of an attack upon the Davidic sonship has no support.[1] There is quite as little support for the supposition of an apology with respect to a Messianic qualification in which he himself was wanting. For it is as certain, from the testimony of the Apostle Paul and from that of the disciples at the entry, that Jesus passed as a descendant of David, as it is from this incident itself that Jesus without any hesitation directed the controversy to a subject which, according to all traces, was never referred to by his opponents, and which nevertheless, according to the above supposition, taken in connection with his opponents' unalterably materialistic and literal mode of conception, would have been his most vulnerable point.

and didactic author. Jesus might have thus answered, but at that time, and even until the time of Paul, this question had not been much discussed. Upon this sonship in general, see above, II. pp. 25 sqq. Granting that the Nazarenes knew simply nothing of this high lineage of the child of their city (Matt. xiii. 55), and that the formation among the Apostles of an actual belief in such a descent, based upon the official title, is quite (?) conceivable, there remains, on the other hand, the firm testimony of Paul—who was not careless in his assertions, and like all Jews attached importance to lineage, as he did to his own (Phil. iii. 5)—while the silence of the Nazarenes about the nobility of a decayed family proves nothing. On the duration of the Davidic line, and on the continued discussion of the question, comp. also Hitzig, *Gesch. Isr.* p. 361, although H. himself doubts, and thinks that Jesus has been regarded as a descendant of David, *without careful investigation*. The ideal of an Israelite and descendant of David to become Messiah, in Schöttgen, and Hase (p. 86).

[1] In the expression lies no support of the negatory view, although even Gess (p. 129) finds this in itself possible from πῶς. The expression in Matt. and Luke (πῶς ἐστι) rather favours (1 Cor. xv. 35) the actual descent from David, the denial of which would lie only in ἄν εἴη (Acts viii. 31) or ᾖ (Matt. xxiii. 33), or ἔσται (Luke i. 34; 1 Cor. xiv. 7), or δύναται (Matt. xii. 29 ; Mark iii. 23). But the expression in Mark (πόθεν ἐστί, comp. vi. 2, viii. 4) means: qui fit ut (Luke i. 43); at most: qui fieri potest ut. Whilst Schenkel (article *Jesus* in *Bib.-Lex.*) believes the scale to turn in favour of the negatory view, the affirmatory view is firmly upheld by Neander (p. 495), Weizs. (p. 540), Hase (p. 61), Beyschlag (p. 62), Press. (p. 340), Gess (p. 128), Godet (*Divinité de I. Chr.*, 1869, p. 20), Weisse (*N. T. Theol.* p. 58).

Whence it rather follows that the Davidic sonship could not be wanting to the man who introduced it as a topic of conversation, whilst no one mentioned it against him. On the other hand, the purpose of his question about the Messiah was this; he wished to show his opponents to how small an extent the meaning of Messiahship was exhausted by the Davidic sonship, by the derivation from the great earthly sovereign, and indeed by the popular opinion of a restoration of material empire which accompanied this derivation.[1] "How"—that is, "in what sense"—"is he then David's son?" By putting the question thus, he at the same time gave the plain answer: according to human birth he is to be a descendant of David, but not according to his vocation and his dignity, as if he were nothing more than a repeater of the Davidic royalty. The Messiah may and will descend from the house of David, but this descent will be the smallest part of his greatness. As certainly as David called the Messiah a greater than himself, so certainly he, at the distance of a thousand years, through which he was carried forward by his presentiment, bowed and cast himself in the dust before this his *Lord*.[2] This lordship, then, receives its intrinsic character and expression in the announced elevation of the Messiah to be the throne-associate of God, which, according to the passage and to the whole Psalm, comprehends three things,—viz., his divine sonship instead of a mere Davidic sonship; his being misunderstood and rejected by his foes, the rulers of the Jewish people; and finally also, after a temporary elevation to heaven, his glorious restitution upon earth

---

[1] Similarly De Wette, Neander, B. Crus., Bleek, Meyer. Beyschlag and Gess, soaring higher, think of a superior, supernatural origin, Beyschlag even of pre-existence; but Neander and Weisse only of higher dignity. Critical doubt even against the testimony of Paul has recently become so strong, that Volkmar has called that testimony very unreliable in general, and even in the notice of the Lord's Supper. What will men now build upon? Referring to this passage, Volkmar (p. 534) has boldly said that not only did Jesus possess nothing materially Davidic, but if the conception of a Messiah as son of David had then been already in existence, there would have been no Christianity.

[2] According to Weizs. (p. 541), Jesus, although son of David, had expressed himself against the designation *which he had approved at the entry.*

THE TEMPTERS.

and upon the ruins of his foes, by the omnipotence of God his Father. And in this Psalm, how remarkably do the words sound in verses 2 and 3, words generally altogether overlooked, and not expressly quoted by Jesus himself, but silently kept in view: "Rule in the midst of thy foes! Thy people come voluntarily in the day of thy military might!"[1] By this reference he made sufficiently clear what he understood to be the higher dignity of the Messiah, and that under this higher, now mistaken but soon recognized dignity of the Messiah, he himself understood his own personal dignity. Since his foes mistake concerning him, they do not know the true character of the Messiah and of Jesus; they seek merely the son of David, and do not find even that, because he foregoes the temporal glory of the son of David. In the mean time, he is now already more than the son of David, he is the Son of God, the spiritual representative of God, the spiritual giver of blessing to men, though in the lowly form of the Son of Man; and soon he will be still more, when God shall place the misunderstood of men first upon the heavenly and next upon the earthly throne, although his throne even then will not be so much the throne of the powerful ruler as, according to the words of the Psalm itself, that of the blessing priest.[2]

It may be questioned whether Jesus himself spoke such words, whether it is not more likely that the later community put these words, these very significant closing utterances against his foes, into the mouth of him who, according to their belief,

---

[1] The foes are really contained in the first verse, which was quoted by Jesus, still more plainly in the second, and the people in the third. It is to be noted here that Jesus, taking account of the contents of Old Testament passages, suggests still more than he quotes, just as Matt. xxi. 16 in relation to Ps. viii. 2 (see above, p. 124).

[2] Ps. cx. 4: priest (according to the oath of God) for ever, after the order of Melchisedec. Beyschlag (*l.c.*) has forced too strong a meaning out of the Psalm, by finding indicated there a pre-existence—if only an ideal one—of the Messiah. On the other hand, Strauss (*New Life of Jesus*, Eng. trans., I. p. 304), has got rid of a higher exposition by saying that the Gospels have nowhere propounded the view that Jesus, according to the spirit, is a higher nature, proceeding immediately from God. This is correct against Beyschlag; but a higher spiritual dignity, without any claim to having come immediately from heaven, is abundantly claimed by him, Matt. xi. 27, xii. 28, xiii. 17. Our passage supplies nothing fresh thereupon.

had been lifted to heaven.¹ Support for this conclusion may be sought partly in the popularity of this Psalm among Jews and Christians as a Psalm of Messianic proof, partly in the still traceable abruptness, subtlety, and resultlessness of Jesus' question, and partly, perhaps chiefly, in the factual inutility of the passage from the Psalm for the here attempted production of Messianic proof, a circumstance which encouraged Dr. Paulus in the hypothesis that Jesus gave expression to a doubt of the Davidic composition of the Psalm.² This last objection would indeed be the weakest, for the results of recent criticism of the Psalm—according to which it was certainly not composed by David, but was addressed by an unknown writer to David, "his lord," perhaps however to a much later prince, Uzziah, or one of the Maccabees—decide nothing whatever as to the conception of Jesus and his time.³ If the time of Jesus believed in the composition of Psalm cx. by king David—a belief which is indicated by the later superscription of the Psalm—then Jesus, since he was no scholar, doubted or objected to this assumption as little as he questioned the genuineness of the book of Daniel; and thus, with correct and irresistible logic, he would have insisted upon the fact that David, *if* he was the author, pointed beyond himself to a Lord, and in truth to a Messiah, to whom was to be ascribed a lordship very different from his own. The other grounds of suspicion of the genuineness of the words of Jesus have no force. The passage is consistent with itself; it is less profound than acute, but it is not exactly subtle; and even if it

---

[1] Comp. Hitzig, *Ps.* II. p. 321; *Gesch. Isr.* p. 361.

[2] *Midr. Teh.* on Ps. cx. 1 : temporibus N. T. Deus Messiam sedere jubebit ad dextram et Abrah. ad sin. suam. *Beresh. Rabb*, f. 83, 4 : intellig. rex Mess., quemadm. de eo dicitur ψ. 110, 3. Comp. *Soh. Num.* Schöttgen, p. 192. Wetst. p. 479. Even in the LXX. the Psalm is mysteriously interpreted, cx. 3 : ἐκ γαστρὸς πρὸ ἑωσφόρου ἐγέννησά σε (Logos). Langen, p. 396. Christian use, by Paul, 1 Cor. xv. 25, 27; Acts ii. 34; Heb. i. 13. The hypothesis of Paulus, *L. J.* I. ii. p. 115; comp. Strauss, 4th ed. I. p. 648.

[3] Comp. Ewald and Hitzig. One might also translate le-David : to David (Ewald). Hitzig (to David from the dedicator) thinks of the royal priest Hyrcanus. Neander (pp. 495 sq.) quite correctly : should the Psalm not be Messianic, Jesus did not engage in such an investigation.

THE TEMPTERS.

be, it is genuinely Jewish, genuinely Scribe-like, in the spirit of those Pharisees with whom Jesus was then engaged in controversy. Moreover, it fully expresses the real, undeniable conviction of Jesus. And who would be able to decide whether it was the Christian Church, and not Jesus the searcher of the Scriptures, the Scripture-taught announcer of his own fate, that took hold of this passage, a passage so remarkably characteristic of Jesus' situation at the time? Finally, all the early Gospels agree here; and the resultlessness of the question itself, the absence of all and any answer on the side of the questioned and indeed even of Jesus, is rather an evidence of genuineness because of simplicity, than a sign of spuriousness and intrusive interpolation.

"No one was able to answer him a word." With this remark Matthew closes at the right place this last conversation with the Pharisees; "neither durst any one from that day forth"—he thus adds—"address to him any further question."[1] This silence upon the most difficult question, a question to which a solution could the less be found the lowlier, the more Davidic, the more terrestrial the Messianic expectation, was just as natural as the disinclination for, nay the fear of, further disputation, after the most hopeful attempts had so completely miscarried. Men were ashamed before Jesus, and they were ashamed before the people, who, as inconvenient witnesses, listening gladly to Jesus—as Mark inserts—still remained standing by even up to the proposal of the question about David.[2] But the issue of the fear was not surrender, the issue of the victory was not a change of side; for from the beginning the opponents had not sought instruction

---

[1] Matt. xxii. 46. In Luke xx. 40 this passage (only: durst no more ask) stands after the conversation with the Sadducee, with whom, according to Luke, the disputations come to an end; in Mark xii. 34 it stands after the question of the Scribe. In both cases, therefore, earlier. But Luke has there arbitrarily abridged, and has thought it pragmatically more appropriate to insert the terminating remark at the point where the attacks are checked, and before Jesus' attack upon the silent opponents, although Luke has done this incorrectly, since the remark is not in its right place until the opponents have been completely reduced to silence even when challenged by Jesus. In Mark, who is half inclined to follow Luke, the sentence stands very awkwardly at the conciliatory close of the conversation with the Scribe.

[2] Mark xii. 37. In the non-reply, Hase (p. 224) sees only the Christian verdict.

and certainly had received none, at least in the obscure and yet, as they thought, sun-clear Messiah question. In so far had the last shimmer of hope disappeared. The fruit of the futile intellectual campaign was the return of the foes to the beginning, to the straightforward campaign of force.

C.—The Last Disclosures and Announcement of Woe upon the System.

During Jesus' conflicts with the hierarchs, in the Gospels his sayings to the people fall entirely into the background. They are referred to only very generally. But while it is to be assumed that the disputations with the opponents, to which the people also listened, absorbed a good part of the time and strength and attention of Jesus, there can, nevertheless, be no doubt that Jesus directed a series of addresses more or less lengthy to the people. This is rendered certain by the facts that he was moving about the temple from morning till evening, and that his chief end and his chief support were the people.[1] An intimation upon this point is to be found not only in Jesus' words of farewell to Jerusalem, and in the subsequent accusation that he had spoken of the destruction of the temple, but also in the tempting questions of his opponents; for the attack of the Pharisees concerning the greatest commandment may have been suggested by Jesus' doctrines concerning law and custom uttered in the hearing of the people, and the Sadducees' scorn of the resurrection may have been called forth by his public announcement of the judgment and the last things. These popular addresses of Jesus, unfolding his doctrine of the kingdom of heaven, his insistance upon repentance, his threats of the judgment, as they had been

---

[1] Activity in Jerusalem, Matt. xxi. 18; Luke xix. 47, xxi. 37; Mark xi. 19 sq. Teaching, Matt. xxi. 23, 26; Luke xx. 1, 6, 9, 45, xxi. 37 sq.; Mark xi. 18, 32, xii. 35, 37 sq. Popular favour, Matt. xxi. 26, 46, xxii. 33; Luke xix. 48, xx. 26; Mark xi. 32, xii. 12, 37.

formerly unfolded in Galilee, as they must have been brought to bear upon the popular conscience afresh, more urgently and more forcibly on this his last and most decisive mission field,—these popular addresses have been passed over by the Gospels, it may be chiefly because the Evangelists were hastening to the crisis and would not repeat the Galilean copious exhibition of the sayings of Jesus, which may have been in part actually repeated. Moreover, it may in some cases have happened that sayings uttered at Jerusalem were transferred to Galilee. Luke has very visibly and to a considerable degree obliterated all distinction of place in the speeches he has reported; while Matthew has, at least possibly, transferred the sayings of Jesus about sacrifice in the temple and swearing by Jerusalem, the City of the Great King, to the Galilean Sermon on the Mount.[1] Again, it may be granted that at least the parable of the man who had not on the wedding garment—which Matthew places at Jerusalem, together with that of the marriage feast—might belong as well to Jerusalem as to Galilee, as a word of warning to the careless, unprepared guests of the approaching kingdom of heaven.[2] As the locality for this preaching to the people, which has become to us almost invisible, we have the outer temple courts to think of. Besides the outermost court, the great inner courts of women and of Israelitish men were used for assem-

---

[1] Comp. Luke xi. 37, xiii. 34; Matt. v. 23, 35. But the Johannine *velleités* (even Hase, p. 223) are to be rejected, since the quantity and contents of these speeches are suitable *only* for Galilee.

[2] Matt. xxii. 11. See above, IV. pp. 118 sq. While the parable of the Feast, to which this little parable attaches itself, belongs *only* to Galilee, the close, which does not reject the people, but only admonishes them to make just preparation, may have actually belonged to the last sermon. Weisse (II. p. 112) places the parable at Jerusalem because he understands by the man without the wedding garment (as did also Olsh.) Judas the betrayer. On the closing saying, "Many are called," &c., comp. (Weisse, II. p. 108, and Zeller, in Hilg.'s *Zeitschrift*, 1867, p. 203), besides 1 Cor. ix. 24, the sentence in *Phædon*, 13: ναρθηκοφόροι μὲν πολλοί, βάκχοι δέ τε παῦροι. Hebrew, nikra (mekora, Is. xlviii. 12; Talmud, mitkere, Buxt. p. 2110) and bechir Jahve. A notable distinction from Paul, with whom the pre-temporal election is infallibly fulfilled in the temporal calling, Rom. viii. 28 sqq., xi. 2, 28 sq. With Jesus the two fall apart, and the election itself is made perfect in time, and then in relation to subjective performance. In Matt. xx. 16, the passage is spurious.

blies connected with religious questions.¹ When the temple was destroyed, there were six thousand persons crowded together in one of the outer courts.² Solomon's Porch may have been one of Jesus' favourite halting-places. Later it became a place of resort of the Apostles, and is mentioned by the fourth Gospel—perhaps not merely by prolepsis—as a place in which Jesus was wont to tarry.³ It is distinguishable by its position from the "Royal Porch" of King Herod, on the south side of the temple. Solomon's Porch lay on the east of the outermost court, therefore at the principal entrance into the temple. On account of its position, it was usually called the east porch. It derived its other name from its builder: it was a venerable, antique relic of the long crumbled temple of Solomon.⁴ At the abrupt descent from the temple hill into the Kidron valley, it is said to have rested upon a stone wall 400 cubits high. The porch itself was composed of colossal marble rectangular blocks, every stone six cubits deep and twenty long. When in A.D. 65, just before the destruction of the temple and of the city, and when all building in the temple was ended, the people of Jerusalem desired Agrippa II. to restore this antiquated and partly decayed structure, the king nervously shrank from the work, which would require time and money without end, and preferred to employ the more than 18,000 men who had been at work on the temple in the paltry task of paving Jerusalem with white stones.⁵

A second place of resort of Jesus can be more certainly pointed out, being mentioned not only by John, but also by Luke and Mark. This was the treasury, which Jewish tradition, in close

---

¹ Jos. *B. J.* 2, 17, 3; comp. below, p. 193, n. 1.

² Jos. *B. J.* 6, 5, 2. The whole temple quadrangle was (Jos. *Ant.* 15, 11, 3) four stadia (half a Roman mile) in circumference.

³ Acts iii. 11, v. 12; John x. 23.

⁴ Jos. *Ant.* 15, 11, 5 (Herod); 20, 9, 7 (Solomon). Certainly in the Jewish War (5, 5, 1; comp. *Ant.* 15, 11, 3) Josephus refers to Solomon at first only the lower walls, but then also the porch. Ewald (p. 471) asserts, against all probability, that the porch was so called as the meeting-place of the teachers of wisdom, and that Josephus was here under a mistake.

⁵ Jos. *Ant.* 20, 9, 7.

harmony with the New-Testament accounts, places in the court of the women.[1] The latter was situated at the entry of the inner quadrangle of the sanctuary, fourteen steps higher than the court of the Gentiles, fifteen steps lower than the westerly and more inwardly-placed court of the men, next to which was the court of the priests, and then, twelve steps higher than the court of the men, the temple building itself. Jesus' resort to this place does not show that, at Jerusalem as in Galilee, he found or indeed sought success chiefly among the women. This large space (according to the Talmud, having a length and breadth of 135 cubits) was called the court of the women simply because it formed for them the extreme limit of their allowable approach to the temple; but it was open to all the people, and the torch dances of the Feast of Tabernacles, as well as the assemblies of the people, were held here. Here in particular were the gifts for the temple, that fed the temple treasury with its many millions of sacred money, thrown into the trumpet-shaped money-chests, which, for security's sake, were narrow at the exposed end but broad within, and of which there were thirteen, with separate inscriptions for their different objects.[2] A charming scene is

[1] Luke xxi. 1; Mark xii. 41; John viii. 20. In the Old Testament, lishkah (nishkah) bechazre bet elohim, γαζ. ἐν αὐλῇ οἴκου θεοῦ, Neh. xiii. 7. Aram. korbana, Jos. B. J. 2, 9, 4. Matt. xxvii. 6; Mark vii. 11. Rabbis also, bet gaza. Comp. Jos. Ant. 19, 6, 1 (the treasure chamber, τὸ γαζοφυλ.); B. J. 5, 5, 2; 6, 5, 2 (twice plural, τὰ γ.). Writers have often (on account of Josephus) distinguished between treasure chamber and treasure houses. In point of fact, the actual temple treasure (ὁ θησαυρὸς, οἱ θ—οὶ) lay, according to all traces, in the building of the temple itself, in the τοῖχος ναοῦ, B. J. 6, 8, 3; comp. 1, 7, 6; 1, 8, 8; also 2, 14, 6; 2, 15, 6 (Antonia, by the temple, Ant. 15, 11, 7); further, Ant. 14, 4, 4; 14, 7, 1; comp. 8, 4, 1; on the other hand, B. J. 2, 3, 3, Ant. 17, 10, 2 (pointing to the courts), do not harmonize with the rest. The treasure chambers with utensils and money, of which there were several, and to which τὸ γαζ. in Ant. 19, 6, 1 (in the sight of all), comp. 15, 11, 3, itself also belonged, were, according to Josephus (in the first passages), as according to the Rabbis, in the courts, especially in the court of the women (Lightfoot, after B. J. 5, 5, 2), where Jesus taught. Rabb. (tractate Shekalim) in Lightfoot, pp. 193, 406, 635. Obscure, Meyer, Bleek (II. p. 348), and Wies. (Beitr. p. 211). More in detail below.

[2] Azarat nashim, γυναικωνῖτις, B. J. 5, 5, 2. Tac. Hist. 5, 8 : vigiliis, feminis clausum. Tabernacle feast, Lightfoot, p. 193. An assembly of the people at the eastern brazen gate of the inner sanctuary (Nicanor gate), B. J. 2, 17, 3. On the shopharot, trumpet-shaped money-boxes, see Lightfoot, pp. 405 sq. Out of these thirteen money-

drawn, at least by Luke and Mark, from the court of the women.[1] Jesus, who even at the approach of his end at Jerusalem had not lost his Galilean fondness for observation, watched the people as they threw their money into the temple coffers, money which was not alms for the poor of Israel, for whom sufficient provision was otherwise made, but the payment of dues or free gifts to God and the multiform temple service.[2] Among the givers the rich predominated; and not only heavy copper—of which Mark speaks —but gold and silver was dropped into the sacred coffers by unwearied zeal for the honour of God, and by the highly developed righteousness of works.[3] There Jesus saw a very poor widow carry to the money-chest her two scraps of copper, the smallest existing coins allowed in the temple, together worth scarcely two or three centimes.[4] "Verily, I say unto you," spoke he, touched, to those around him, lauding this pearl of pious poverty even though that poverty might have been mingled with superstition, "I say unto you, that this poor widow has thrown in more than they all; for all these have thrown in gifts out of their superfluity, but this

boxes, three times in the year three general coffers of twenty-seven seahs, *i.e.* above forty Roman modii, had to be recruited and filled. *Jom.* f. 64, 1. *Shekal.* c. 3. The temple treasure, at the time of Pompey and Crassus, amounted to two thousand talents (twelve million francs), besides the value of the gold about the temple, eight thousand talents (forty-eight million francs). Jos. *Ant.* 14, 4, 4; 14, 7, 1.

[1] Luke xxi. 1; Mark xii. 41. Luke has the simple account, Mark throughout a coloured one.

[2] Comp. Maimonides' enumeration of the objects to which the thirteen chests were allotted. *Shekal.* 2. Lightfoot, pp. 405 sq. Therefore Volkmar (p. 535) speaks incorrectly of the support of the poor and the oppressed. In a foot-note to p. 536, he is obliged to correct himself, and yet the "Christian communism" remains. On this occasion, Mark (xii. 41) depicts Jesus' observant sitting over against the treasury. But the conversation is carried on so exclusively with the disciples, that Volkmar's *schema* is quite erroneous: "Ye sacrifice falsely" (as though Jesus was addressing the Pharisees).

[3] Luke mentions first *only* rich givers, Mark at once mentions the people generally.

[4] The λεπτὸν (thinness) is the eighth part of an *as* (one), which is the tenth part of a *denarius*, the last being not quite a franc (the Talmud reckons shene peruthot [scattered], two *prutha* to a farthing). The *as* was already proverbial as a paltry piece of money; see above, III. p. 307, IV. p. 319. A single *prutha* might not be given for sacrifice, Wetst. p. 618.

woman has thrown in out of her want all the living that she had."¹

Nevertheless, the Gospels have not withheld from us the most weighty of all the addresses to the people at Jerusalem; and they could not withhold it, because it contained Jesus' farewell to the people, his last admonitions, as well as his last annihilating criticism against Pharisaism, to which he for the moment was compelled to leave the field, and indeed to commit the people with the interests of their piety. The vigorous denunciation of the Pharisees, delivered in the hearing of the people, which Matthew has preserved to us at the close of the public ministry at Jerusalem, may be spoken of as genuine in the main, and in point of fact it proves its own genuineness by internal evidence.² Evidently it does not belong to the same day as the last controversy with the Pharisees, since after that controversy the narrator himself makes a significant halt, and the general mood of Jesus is a very different, a profoundly solemn and passionately excited, one. We are led, therefore, to think of one of the immediately following days; and as it is improbable that the last days of Jesus should have been vacant and unoccupied or should have been dropped out of the narration, we can fix upon the first of

---

[1] This incident stands only in Luke and Mark, not in Matthew, who, according to Volkmar (p. 537) passed it over because of its defective *communistic sense*. As if he had not given the passage about alms, vi. 1, and that about the rich young man and the poor, xxvi. 9. I decline to endorse the suspicion that this incident, unknown to Matthew, is simply a fabrication of Luke's Ebionite source, though it certainly harmonizes with the spirit of that source (xi. 41, xii. 33, xvi. 1 sqq., xviii. 3, xix. 8); but, in view of its relative simplicity, I accept the incident as genuine. I believe that Matthew passed over the narrative, which was perhaps known to him, because its effect would be lost, nay, it would form a disturbing element in the midst of the tragical conflict and end (comp. Weisse, I. p. 588). On the other hand, Luke and Mark, not regarding the situation, introduced this incident the more willingly because they had immediately before, in the brief anti-Pharisaic address, exposed the false piety of women. According to Mark's impossible account, the scene would have tranquilly *followed* (xii. 41) the struggle with the Pharisees as the close of the ministry at Jerusalem; but Luke, xxi. 1—5, gives it more correctly in the form of an anecdote, careless of the historical connection. The last three addresses in Mark are thus grouped by Volkmar: (1) Ye hope erroneously, (2) Ye go about falsely, (3) Ye sacrifice falsely! Did the Rabbis sacrifice?

[2] Matt. xxiii. 1.

the following days, Thursday the 12th of April.[1] Though this seems to introduce a certain violent change in events and in the attitude of Jesus, making him, in the midst of his standstill, in the midst of the relaxation of hostilities, and directly after the moderation which he himself had exhibited on the previous day, blow the war trumpet loudly and defiantly, whilst he was at the same time keeping fully in view the end of his ministry and his departure,—though it appears, on this very account, that some event or some decisive turning-point must lie between these two situations, but which the sources have in an incomprehensible way hidden and withheld from us, it is nevertheless not so. In truth, the attitude of Jesus, his views in those four days from the 8th of April to the 11th, had become sufficiently decided.[2] One day after the other had witnessed the implacability of his foes, the incubation of dark purposes in the temple cloisters, though one day after the other had had to tell of the futility of binding the new Samson. But the people, the impartial witnesses, had come at least not much nearer to him.[3] Whatever interest might be felt in or respect paid to him, there was no revival of enthusiasm and Messianic faith after the first essay had miscarried. The zealot works and the disputations awoke respect rather than love or even only appreciative recognition, and called forth the application of the test of Prophethood much rather than of that of Messiahship. In point of fact, a Messiah who fought only with words, and who used only words to support his claims against an old faith, was the opposite of that which the letter of the prophets had spoken of and the people expected. Hence it was natural enough that no one should resolutely espouse his cause or resolutely break with the authority of the teachers of the Law; that many, without taking any notice of him, should carry on their temple worship according to ancient custom, as

[1] Matt. xxii. 46 favours the close of a day.

[2] Renan (15th ed. p. 213) thinks that a week would be much too short for the last ministry of Jesus at Jerusalem. See above, p. 113, n. 1.

[3] This is recognized also by Ewald (p. 530): the sympathy was, as his opponents saw, at least not increasing. Reimarus, pp. 149 sqq. Geiger, p. 121.

did those rich persons and that poor woman; and, again, that many should now already have decided to support the existing system, the venerable sages, and the sanctified ordinances, against the reckless, unintelligible modern, whose aims they could not definitely calculate upon[1]. Jesus' very last address to the people which concerns us here, will produce just this impression. For these reasons, however, Jesus could close as violently as in this address we find he did. The close, which his opponents had not yet made and still less the people, he was able to make without violently hastening the catastrophe, since he already, with a penetrating glance that looked through everything, watched the approach of his catastrophe from night to morning and from morning to night.[2]

Yet there lies a complete net of difficulties over these last sayings of Jesus, to which in John, as a far-off parallel, nothing so nearly corresponds as the conflicts with the hierarchs after the healing of the man born blind. But Luke and Mark give, at this closing point, only a few small portions from Jesus' warnings to the people about the Scribes.[3] And even these cannot compare in antiquity, vigour, and fulness of meaning with the introduction to the address in Matthew, and they betray a later origin not without dependence upon Matthew, to whom they point both in their detailed arrangement and in their general character, since the post of forlorn hope allotted to these few sentences is best explained from the necessity of giving at least something like a companion piece to the forcible address in Matthew.[4] This little

[1] *I.e.* a part of the subsequent blood-party, Matt. xxvii. 20, 25.

[2] When Schleiermacher (p. 407) objects to the offensive action of Jesus, Matt. xxiii., he only shows that, in his preference for John, he quite overlooks the actual historical tension of the situation. How much more correct is Weisse, I. p. 441.

[3] Luke xx. 45; Mark xii. 38; according to Luke, addressed to the disciples in the presence of all the people (formerly Tisch. read incorrectly, πρὸς αὐτοὺς, *i.e.* the Pharisaic opponents); according to Mark, addressed to the people. Hase also admits (p. 224) that Luke and Mark offer only a single representative passage, and Luke xi. only fragments. The Johannine far-off parallels, John ix. 40—x. 18.

[4] Matt. xxiii. 5—7 has three members, each again of two parts: (1) phylacteries and fringes; (2) first place, first seat at feasts and in synagogues; (3) greetings at

forlorn hope, however, which so greatly lacks the completeness of what is in Matthew, is explained in a striking manner by Luke's having already used up, at two points in Galilee, the great material of Matthew. In doing this he follows his peculiar sources that were to some degree indifferent to the requirements of date and locality. Similarly Luke transposed to Galilee the conversation at Jerusalem with the Scribe; and the Galilean utterances about the Pharisees harmonize marvellously well with the abbreviated saying at Jerusalem given by the same author.[1] Here there is no doubt that these passages are by Luke quite incorrectly transferred to Galilee, since the vehement woes against Scribes and Pharisees, with the points of attacks upon which they are based, are decidedly more appropriate to Jerusalem than to Galilee; and the lament over Jerusalem, which Jesus had vainly endeavoured to gather to himself, seems an utter impossibility on the soil of Galilee.[2] Notwithstanding this decision in favour of the correctness of Matthew's localities, it would

market and being called Rabbi. On the other hand, Luke and Mark have five simple members: (1) clothing, (2) greetings, (3) synagogues, (4) feasts, (5) (unrepresented in Matthew, since it is not genuine there, the only valuable occurrence of it being in Luke and Mark) creeping into widows' houses. The secondary character of this account in general is shown (1) by the suppression of the antique phylacteries and fringes, for which "state robes" are substituted; (2) the suppression of the being called Rabbi; (3) the suppression of the mental motive for the detailed acts (Matt. xxiii. 5); (4) addition of the widows; (5) re-arrangement of the original Nos. 1 and 3 in Matt. as 1 and 2, No. 2 in Matt. as 3 and 4. Comp. Luke xi. 43. According to Holtzmann, *Ev.* p. 200 (comp. Schenkel, p. 250), Matthew has more completely utilized the sources.

[1] Luke xi. 37, xiii. 34, x. 25. Strauss thought also of Luke xiv. 7 sq., but this parable may be independent. The so-called Galilean utterance, xi. 43, is repeated in Jerusalem, xx. 46. Comp. xi. 50 sq. (Matt. xxiii. 33) and xx. 47; Mark xii. 40. Mark followed Luke the rather because he was glad to dispense with the Jewish sayings.

[2] With respect to the controversial address in Matt. xxiii. (Luke xi.), not only Schleiermacher (p. 407, Jesus was not able to irritate!), but also Weizs. (p. 456), assume that Matt. has placed it too late, and Luke more correctly; Weizs. says it belongs to the context of Matt. xv. On the other hand, Weisse (I. p. 441) recognizes the perfect fitness of time of this enormous boldness of speech, and Schenkel (p. 250, and *Bib.-Lex.* III. p. 293) the more correct position in Matt. How can any one (Weizs.) say that the frightful vehemence of the address in Matt. xxiii. is in harmony with the spirit of Matt. xv., and is in its place anywhere except at the threshold of the catastrophe? That the passage concerning Jerusalem (Luke xiii., Matt. xxiii.) at any rate fits in only at the close of the history of Jesus, is admitted almost without exception (comp. Neander, p. 497).

still be possible to find at least the contents of the Galilean "Woes" of Luke more original than those of the "Woes" placed by Matthew at Jerusalem.[1] But in the main a very different result is here capable of being established. For the formerly often lauded introduction of these "Woes" in Luke by a midday meal in the house of a Pharisee is altogether fictitious, since Jesus could not in honour return hospitality by predicting woes; and he could not requite the censure for not washing his hands by the merely apparently apposite proof of the worthlessness of the Pharisaic cleansing of dishes, since Pharisaic invitations to table could no longer be talked of at Jerusalem.[2] But the division of the seven "Woes" of Matthew into three—in reality four—pronounced against the Pharisees, and three against the lawyers, belongs again to that later inventiveness which similarly struck into two series the "Blesseds" of the Sermon on the Mount, a series of "Blesseds" and a series of "Woes." It is very easy to show that Pharisees and lawyers could not be classified in this manner, notwithstanding the ingenuity of the classification; and that the order of sequence of Luke's "Woes" exhibits a constant reference to Matthew.[3] Finally, it is necessary only to detect the crude

[1] Formerly Schleierm., Schulz, Schneck., Olsh., thus expressed themselves; Neander, Tholuk, Bleek, took a middle position; again, Holtzmann (p. 200) favours Luke; Schenkel (p. 250) finds Matt. too diffuse. According to Volkmar, of course Matt. must be dependent upon Luke, and the latter upon Mark (vii. xii.). Matt. is said to have lent to Jesus the Rabbinic controversies of the second century. On the other hand, Strauss, De Wette, Hase, Meyer, Hilgenfeld, have placed themselves on the side of Matthew. Even Weizs. (p. 460) admits that Luke xi. gives merely an excerpt.

[2] How much has the appropriateness of the occasion in Luke been lauded by Schleier., Neander, Olsh., and others; but how adroit it was of them to represent the no longer "Attic" attacks of Jesus (Strauss) as possibly not taking place in the house! The utter inappropriateness and inexplicability from Matt. xv. 2 of this fictitious interpolation of Luke (climax), have been particularly emphasized by Strauss (4th ed. I. p. 694); and even Weizs. appears to be unwilling to defend this preface (p. 456).

[3] Luke (xi.) gives the following four antitheses, with three "Woes," against the Pharisees: (1) cleanness of vessels (without "Woe"), (2) tithes, (3) vanity, (4) similarity to sepulchres. Then the three "Woes" against the lawyers: (5) vices, (6) sepulchre building, (7) withholding of key of knowledge. Even without glancing at Matthew, the violence used in constructing the two rubrics can be seen, rubrics which Luke himself can never separate, v. 17, 30, x. 25, xx. 39 (comp. Bleek, II. p. 170). Nos. 5—7 have no special application to the lawyers, nor 2, 3, to the Pharisees; and 1, 4, and 6, are mutually inconsistent, while 7 is lame in every respect. Then when we look at

Ebionite principle in the treatment of the question of the purification of dishes—according to which the giving away the contents of the dishes as alms purifies the dishes, nay everything Pharisaic—in order to recognize the later false reconstruction of Matthew's speech of Jesus by the hand of that Ebionite Evangelist whom Luke is fond of following.[1]

At the same time, the long and important address to the people in Matthew, although, according to Hilgenfeld's acknowledgment, containing what is most genuine and most original, and by no means obnoxious to Volkmar's arbitrary charge of consisting of a Jewish disputation of the second century, is not altogether unimpeachable; and here Luke can, in a subordinate degree, help towards the discovery of the truth.[2] This address, according to Matthew directed to the people and to the disciples, really falls into at least three distinct addresses—an address to the people, another to the disciples, and a third to the Pharisees.[3] For

Matthew we find there: (1) a much more organic order of sequence (see below, p. 209); while, on the contrary, Luke, guided by his fictitious motive, has converted the fifth "Woe" into No. 1, has then manipulated the "Woes," 4, 6, 7, and has ended with the first; he has, moreover, most unskilfully dragged in, from an altogether different series of addresses (Luke xx. 46; Matt. xxiii. 4, 6), the "Woes" in xi. 43, 46, which are altogether devoid of antithesis. (2) In Matthew there is much more originality of detail than in Luke xi. 39—41 (vessels), xi. 42 (tithing), xi. 44 (sepulchres), xi. 47 (sepulchre building); see below. The separation of the two classes, Pharisees and men of the Law (in Luke xi.) is derived simply from the Pharisees and Scribes of Matt. xxiii. 2 sqq., comp. xv. 1. In distinction from Matthew and Mark (ii. 16, yet comp. vii. 1), Luke places the more general category (Matt. xxii. 35), Scribes, commonly as here in the second rank, v. 17, 30; Acts v. 34. In Josephus, instead of $\gamma\rho\alpha\mu\mu\alpha\tau\tilde{\epsilon}\iota\varsigma$, generally stands $\dot{\epsilon}\xi\eta\gamma\eta\tau\alpha\dot{\iota}$ $\nu\dot{o}\mu o\upsilon$, Ant. 17, 6, 2; 17, 9, 3; 18, 3, 5; 20, 2, 4. Also $\sigma o\phi\iota\sigma\tau\alpha\dot{\iota}$, 17, 6, 2; B.J. 1, 33, 2; 2, 1, 1 sqq. Juvenal, 6, 544: interpres legum solymarum.

[1] The passage against which the charge lies, Luke xi. 39 sqq., opp. Matt. xxiii. 25 sqq.

[2] Hilg. *Zeitschrift*, 1868, p. 43. Volkmar, p. 535. The tithes, the sepulchres, the temple gold, this pathos, this acuteness, this intellectual vigour, out of the second century! Even the brief anti-Pharisaic sayings in Luke and Mark are to Volkmar only strokes of Mark's pencil. But Matthew, whose artistic disposal of his material even Weizsäcker (p. 459) praises, does not once exhibit to Volkmar a good arrangement.

[3] Matt.: people and disciples; Luke: xx. to the disciples before all the people, xi. to the Pharisees; Mark: to the people. Weiz. (p. 461) is inclined to think only of the disciples, Hilg. (p. 43) of the multitudes that had accompanied Jesus from Galilee. Weisse (II. p. 116) correctly distinguishes two addresses, one to the people and one to the disciples.

instance, Jesus could not possibly have introduced into the midst of an address to the people admonitions to the disciples concerning their one teacher Jesus, nay Christ, concerning their heavenly Father, their brotherhood, their mutual helpfulness,—subjects which he had elsewhere discussed in a narrower circle.[1] Further, in an address to the people, he could not possibly have launched his long-drawn "Woes" at the Pharisees, as if he were speaking to them,—unless indeed we regard him as a rhetorician; he could have stood forth with the "Ye," "Ye blind!" "Ye hypocrites!" only if the Pharisees, and not merely the people, were before him.[2] Neither can the difficulty be explained by supposing that Matthew forgot to mention the Pharisees. For the address to the people assumes that the Pharisees were absent, or at least that their presence was not obvious; while, on the other hand, the address to the Pharisees assumes that their position was not in the background but in the foreground. Moreover, it is altogether impossible that at one and the same moment Jesus should have admonished the people to render some kind of obedience to the occupants of the seat of Moses, to the Pharisees and their teaching and commands, and yet have cast the Pharisees down into the dust by a veritably annihilating hail of accusations against both their living and their teaching; or that he should have given counsel to the people after the manner of a sympathetic, anxious, and in a certain sense trusted friend, and yet should immediately afterwards have taken occasion from the "Woes" pronounced against the Pharisees, to reject Jerusalem, together with the Pharisees, as a contumacious and prophet-murdering city.[3] Thus we here see plainly that Matthew,

[1] Matt. xxiii. 8—12, comp. also only xx. 26—28; further, the Sermon on the Mount and the sending forth of the disciples.

[2] It is remarkable that no offence has been taken at this. Yet Philippi's Commentary on the Epistle to the Romans discovers mere rhetorical figures in Rom. ii. 1, 17.

[3] Weizsäcker (p. 459) lays stress upon the former contradiction of annihilating conflict and tolerant mildness. He holds the mildness to be a later softening qualification introduced in the Jewish-Christian interest and based upon the earlier standpoint of Jesus. Schenkel (p. 251) also finds that Jesus did not utter such sentences as Matt. xxiii. 3, but that the author had inferred them from the closing words of verse 3. On

according to his wont, has brought together under the half-correct heading "for people *and* disciples," things that are related and that nevertheless do not belong to each other; and the easy transition from the delineation of the Rabbins before the people to the mention of the one Rabbi before the disciples, thereby becomes specially instructive.[1] But a trace of this original division of the material is to be found even in Luke, who has in particular distinguished—although by no means sharply—between the address to the people and that to the Pharisees. On the other hand, Luke's separation of the lament over Jerusalem from the "Woes" pronounced against the Pharisees is hardly to be regarded as original, and a better place than this is certainly not to be found for the lament.[2] But the three addresses which are thus to be divided—one to the people, one to the Pharisees, one to the disciples—must be so arranged that the address to the people comes first, the "Woes" addressed to the Pharisees next, though very possibly spoken on the same day, while the admonition to the disciples is to be placed indefinitely in the last days and in the midst of the addresses of farewell.[3] Probably the only spurious part of these addresses is the reference to the fate of the righteous and of the apostles in the "Woes" pronounced against the Pharisees, and the lament over Jerusalem has also

the other hand, Paulus, *Exeget. Handb.* III. i. p. 312, brings in the idea that Jesus only permitted what was actually Mosaic. But before a critic adds to and cuts out, he should be careful to discover whether Jesus could not thus speak, and whether in a certain situation he did not very probably thus speak. Or is it seriously supposed that such utterances can be better explained out of the apostolic age than out of that of Jesus? Comp. Gess, p. 293.

[1] Make a division between Matt. xxiii. 2—7 and 8—12.

[2] Luke xi.: to Pharisees; Luke xx.: to disciples and people. Sharp distinction wanting, comp. Luke xi. 43 and xx. 46, Luke xi. 46 and Matt. xxiii. 4. The lament over Jerusalem, Luke xiii. 34, unskilfully separated from xi. 51, and placed at xiii. 34 in combination with the prediction of Jesus' own death, uttered as a message to Herod, xiii. 31 sqq.

[3] This is also the order in Matt. xxiii. 1 and 13. Moreover, it is psychologically more probable that Jesus should pass from the relative toleration of the Scribes in the address to the people, to the violent attack upon the Pharisees, than that he should take the opposite course. See below. The admonition to the disciples, Matt. xxiii. 8—12, may belong to the last quiet hours with the disciples, comp. Luke xxii. 24.

its doubters, although both utterances possess the testimony of two Evangelists.¹

If we place Jesus' last address to the people quite by itself on the morning of Thursday, April the 12th, it is not then in the strictest sense a farewell address, but one of general instruction concerning the Law, ordinances, and Pharisaism. But though the form of farewell is wanting, the unreserved explanation of the character of Pharisaism, the remarkable summons to obey the prescriptions of the teachers of the Law, the expression of sympathy with the poor people groaning under the loads which their unmerciful teachers had imposed upon them,—all this is such a wonderful mixture of opposition and resignation and sorrowful state of mind, that the discourse of Jesus—rightly pushed forward by the narrator to this closing point—produces the overpowering impression of a last disclosure, of the last and most necessary and most useful hints and rules, of the testament of one who is about to depart, who has loved and cannot cease to love his nation, even though he has been disappointed by it. His instruction given to the people concerning the Pharisees has great similarity to the earlier instructions given to the disciples, and at last to the people, concerning the yoke of the Pharisees, their human commands without number, their neglect of the divine Law in teaching and still more in action, their vanity, their ambition, their hypocritical system. But very remarkable is the difference that he enjoins the people at Jerusalem to obey the teachers of the Law, whose ordinances he in Galilee rejected and committed to the judgment of God. Must we here charge him with a declension from himself, perhaps indeed with pusillanimity in the face of the piety that was so firmly and securely established at Jerusalem, or with an attempt to free himself from the enormous difficulties by which he saw himself encircled? This does not, in truth, require discussing,—a decisive testimony against it is found in the independent openness and reckless daring which now play about his lips. Candour and compliance

¹ See below.

in one—they show a new, deliberate, self-conscious system, a most sagacious connection of principle with the requirements of the situation, with the commandment of the moment. While perceiving that he could not tear from the people their faith in the teachers who were highly esteemed throughout the land, and that it was not given to him, even with the best will of the people, in this span of time, with convincing, enlightening force to establish a distinction between the Law and the ordinances, and the worthlessness, nay the absurdity of the latter, he, like a physician who saves what remains salvable, laid hold of the resource of commending to the people the Law-teaching of the Pharisees, if the Law be only actually *observed* in a pious, self-sacrificing spirit, and not merely confessed in words or with sham deeds.[1] This expedient rested in part upon the fact that the Law and the ordinances were bound together by a hundred links. It also in part rested upon the double perception, first that the unripe nation, in its inability to separate the two, must either lose both, the ordinances together with the holy Law of God, or retain both, with the Law the ordinances; and second, that the observance of the Pharisaic ordinances would do but little harm, if at the same time the Law were also in some sort observed—nay, that here and there the observance of the ordinances might carry with it a religious blessing, just as would the observance of the little things of the Law itself, if those little things were but observed and performed in humility and self-abnegation, and in combination with the great commandments of love to God and love to one's neighbour.[2] In having recourse to this grand expedient, which brought together principles and actual circumstances by stripping the principles of a too rigid obstinacy, Jesus must naturally have put out of view all the abuses, evasions, and morbid exaggerations of the Law by the ordinances, which he had always condemned, to which he could

---

[1] Respect for the Scribes, see above, I. pp. 332 sqq., 344, 364 sq. On this passage, comp. Paulus, quoted above, p. 201, n. 3.

[2] Matt. xxiii. 23, v. 18 sqq., xxii. 36—40.

never ascribe the character of pious actions. But what he in his broad formula sorrowfully relinquished, he expected to make good and to restore by leading on and stimulating the people to a general fidelity to the Law and to a general observance of it. At most he was thinking merely of a transient interim. As certainly as he believed that he would again appear before his nation as the Messiah of God after a brief period of dishonour and rejection, so certainly was he assured that the time was then dawning in which God would destroy not only his foes but also their teaching, the cruel burden of the people, would root out human doctrine, and would afresh establish his pure Law as his own eternal ordinance.[1]

Hence in this light the last doctrinal monitions of Jesus, addressed not to the disciples, whom he would not again deliver over to the Pharisees, but solely to the people, are both intelligible and, on account of their sympathetic tone towards the people— who were shepherdless and, whether disobedient or obedient to their teachers, unfortunate—truly and powerfully affecting. Upon the seat of Moses, he said, the Scribes and the Pharisees had placed themselves.[2] By these opening words he pronounced them to be not called of God, but violent intruders into the office of legislating for, teaching, and guiding the nation. As he proceeded, however, he admitted—quite in the spirit of his Jewish belief in Providence—that they could nevertheless rule and command by the permission and the forbearance of God, as long as it was pleasing to God. "Everything, *therefore,*" thus he continued

[1] Matt. xv. 13, xxi. 33 sqq. Gess (p. 293) correctly: provisional bond.

[2] Matt. xxiii. 2: al-kisse Mosheh jashebu. Seat, judgment-seat, kisse, Talm. also katedra, also masc. katedrin, Buxt. p. 2164. *Seph. Hakkab.* f. 61 : sedit in cathedra ejus (successor fuit). Golden seats of the Jewish council at Alexandria, *Bab. Succ.* f. 51, 2. Authority of the Jerusalem Sanhedrim, *Maim. Mamr.* 1: fundamentum legis traditionalis et columna doctrinæ. Quic. Mosi, magistro no. ejusque legi credit, illis inniti tenetur de rebus legis. Lightfoot, p. 356. Comp. the preference of the teachers to the Law, above, I. p. 335. In ἐκάθισαν, Paulus, Meyer and Bleek (but not De Wette, Hilg.) found violent intrusion expressed ; at least the Greek word, with what follows, implies it; comp. also Matt. xv. 13. Yet see also xxi. 33. Galat. (ap. Lightf. p. 356) thought the aorist pointed to the antiquated character of their position (as Luke xix. 46). The words of Jesus are quoted, Clem. *Hom.* 3, 18.

in this train of thought, "whatsoever they say unto you, do and observe, but do not according to their works, for they say and do not."[1] It is evident that he had pretty much the same views of the rule of the Romans as of that of the Pharisees : both were, as facts showed, divinely permitted, divine dispensations though only dispensations of discipline, divinely commanded though only for a time.[2] "For they bind"—thus did he strengthen his description of their unconscientiousness, they showing themselves to be harsh, heartless tyrants, caring only for their own comfort —"they bind heavy burdens and lay them upon the shoulders of men; but they themselves will not lift a finger to put them in motion."[3] Next comes the disclosure of the real value of their merely apparent, eye-serving piety in the matter of clothing, in attending the synagogues, and in zeal in praying: it is all vanity, ambition, covetous self-seeking. "But they do all their works to be seen of men.[4] They make broad their phylacteries and enlarge the tassels of their garments.[5] They love the first cushions at feasts and the first seats in the synagogues, and greetings in the markets, and to be called by men, Rabbi![6]

[1] *Targ. Hier.* on Numb. xxiii. 19 : hom. dicunt, sed non faciunt. *Chag.* f. 15, 2 : memineris doctrinæ ejus et not memineris operum ejus, Schött. p. 192; Wetst. p. 480.

[2] Matt. xxii. 21. Also xxi. 33 ; see above, p. 141.

[3] Matt. xi. 28; comp. Isaiah xlvi. 1. It is otherwise said by R. Judas, *Berach.* f. 22, 1: etsi aliis levia imponam, mihi gravia impono. Finger, *Abot Nat.* 2: non tetigit me ne quidem digito suo minimo. Also classic, $\mu\eta\delta'$ ἄκρῳ τ. δακτ., digito, extr. digitis. Wetst. p. 480.

[4] Comp. Matt. vi. 1 sqq.; above, III. p. 331. Ἀνθρωπάρεσκοι, *Ps. Sal.* 4, 8, 10.

[5] Here the Hellenizing of the text in Luke and Mark : ἐν στολαῖς. The phylacteries, the tephillin, above, III. p. 343. Jos. *Ant.* 4, 8, 13, favours the literal conception of Ex. xiii. 9, Deut. vi. 8. Phyl. capiti, brachio (left arm) affixa. Great superstition : these phylacteries (=amulets, comp. Bleek, II. p. 343; Hausrath, p. 418) put demons to flight, are substitutes for the study of the Law, have great promises. Observate præc. meum de Teph. ego vero id ita vobis imputabo, ac si dies noctesque in lege mea sudaveritis. Buxt. p. 1743. Lightfoot, pp. 272, 330, 356 sq., 517. Schött. p. 192. Wetst. p. 481. The tassels, zizit, above, III. p. 343. Weighty, Lightfoot, p. 357. See above, p. 179, n. 1.

[6] Sedere loco præcipuo, beresha (rosh), Wetst. p. 481. Comp. Luke xiv. 7. Rabbi : on the mistaken objection of Grätz (IV. pp. 74 sqq.), Volkmar (pp. 86, 457), Strauss (*New Life*, Eng. trans., I. p. 382), see above, III. p. 15. Was it not already said in the Old Testament, abi, abi (2 Kings ii. 12), for which the Targ. rabbi, rabbi (Wichelh.

THE LAST DISCLOSURES. 207

They devour widows' houses, and that under pretence of long prayers. These shall receive greater condemnation!"[1] A remarkable contradiction runs through this address. The address both takes away from and gives to the Pharisees a divine right; more than that, it follows up the admonition to subjection with violent and bitter renunciations, in fact with a series of repudiations and of instigations to repudiate, that in reality overweighs the exhortations to obedience.[2] It was the contradiction in the circumstances, the perception of the inherent wrongness of the system and of the necessity of its maintenance, that gave rise to the contradiction in the address and its sentiments. He wished to uphold, and yet he was obliged to judge and condemn; he was compelled to destroy, almost against his will, and more than he wished. There is no doubt, however, as to the justice of the brief and vigorous description, for we cannot haggle over the matter and say, "They were not all thus." The mass of them were exactly thus; and the system, the spirit of holiness by

p. 229), and in the year A.D. 38, mari, marin (also obscurely, mori from mar, mare, not moreh, Buxt. p. 1246), see *Bib.-Lex.* III. p. 52! Then the old saying of Shemaia: hate the Rabbinate, *Pirke Abot*, I. 10. Schött. p. 197. Customary diplasiasm, rabbi, rabbi, Lightfoot, pp. 357 sq. Wetst. p. 481. Exaggerated estimate of the title: a Rabbi more than a king, Lightfoot, p. 358. Of Johanan ben Sacchai it is reported that in the market he first greeted every one, Wetst. p. 481.

[1] This single passage, the only overflow from Luke and Mark, I accept unconditionally as genuine. Type, Ezekiel xxii. 25. Devout women, Jos. *Ant.* 17, 2, 4; 18, 3, 5; 20, 2, 3; *B.J.* 2, 20, 2. Above, I. p. 344. The wife of Pheroras, brother of Herod the Great, paid all fines for the Pharisees, above, I. p. 252. Comp. also *Ps. Sal.* 4, 4 sqq. Later Christian teachers were charged with seeking specially to influence women, Celsus, 3, 55 sqq. Also the Talmud speaks of manifold plundering of widows. *Sot. Hier.* f. 20, 1 : inter plagas, quæ a Pharisæis proveniunt, etiam hæc est: est qui consultat cum orphanis, ut alimenta viduæ eripiat. Of such a widow it was said: plaga Pharis. tetigit illam. Schöttgen, p. 199. Covetousness of the Pharisees, Luke xvi. 14. The pretensions, Lightfoot, p. 358. Long prayers, comp. Matt. vi. 2. Lightfoot, p. 358. Schöttgen, p. 200. In particular it was advised to protract without end the Dalet in Echad (the one God, in the prayer Shemâ), and for it was promised the seventh heaven. Fortunately the more reasonable did not become extinct, who said: preces justorum breves sint!

[2] The exhortation to obedience, the approbation of the Pharisaic teaching by Jesus appears (see above, p. 201, n. 3) to Schenkel (p. 251) and to Weizs. (p. 459) not genuine, but marked by a Jewish-Christian colouring.

works, led in that direction.¹ On the other hand, again, there can be no doubt that Jesus did not serve the people with this duality of representations. The fundamental thought was good and ingenious and wise; but, by not restraining the strong indignation of which he was the subject in view of all this abnormal piety and of the cruel frustration of his ministry as Saviour, he failed in this way to establish that middle position which he wished to establish; he simply destroyed to some both Law and ordinances, whilst he drove the others over to the side of the opponents against whom he inveighed.

Thus far, certainly, this last address to the people stands very closely related to the last address to the Pharisees; and this supplies an explanation of the fact that Matthew has brought the whole together into one context. We are, however, compelled, for the reasons given above, to make a division. It is also evident that, in the last address to his opponents, Jesus went still further than in his address to the people; without reserve he pronounced a distinct "Woe," and that against the doctrine which he had in the other address forbearingly upheld. Though we have no means of deciding whether Jesus uttered this "Woe" against the Pharisees on the same or on one of the following days, it is credible that, at once letting loose all the anger of his inner opposition and of his indignation against the frustraters of his Messiahship, and perhaps further irritated by the Pharisees' contradiction of his address to the people, he proceeded on the same day to his final deliverance, to his final breach with the Pharisees, the witnesses of which the people themselves must necessarily be.²

The preaching of "Woe" against the Pharisees and Scribes—

---

[1] The idea of painted Pharisees (colorati, fucati) already expressed by king Jannæus, above, I. p. 344. Lightfoot, p. 360. Schöttgen, p. 199. Also *Ps. Sal.* 4, 7: οἱ ἐν ὑποκρίσει ζῶντες. *Assumpt. Moys.* 7, 4: ficti in omnibus. Then comp. the descriptive sentence in *Midr. Esth.* 1, f. 101, 4: decem portiones hypocriseos sunt in mundo: novem Hierosolymis, decima vero in toto terrarum orbe. Schöttgen, p. 198.

[2] Above, pp. 195, 202. Comp. Luke xi. 53 sq. We see the people, Matt. xxiii. 1, 37.

which has as little to do with the curses that close the five books of Moses and at the same time the ministry of Moses, as it has with the "Woes" of the Revelation of John, but evidently refers back to the cries of the ancient prophets, particularly of Isaiah —is a comprehensive summary of the whole of Jesus' opposition to the Pharisees from the Galilean days.[1] It is true it does not by far comprise everything which he had said in Galilee to the disciples, the people, and the Pharisees themselves; but it makes a selection of what is characteristic, it adds fresh points of attack which Jerusalem might offer, summarizes the general attitude of the opponents to the Old Testament and to the kingdom of God, and develops itself in a model order of battle. In the seven "Woes," the first place is given to the judgment against the foes of the kingdom of God, whose proselyting zeal for their lost cause stands in sharp contrast to the hindrances to the progress of the kingdom of heaven. The third and fourth "Woes" denounce their false teaching of the Law; the fifth and sixth, the slovenly efforts after purity by the "pure;" the seventh definitively reverts to the attitude of the Pharisees towards the prophets—the announcers and forerunners of Jesus—whose graves they build, and in doing so prove themselves to be the sons of those that murdered the prophets. The language is poured forth in a foaming torrent, sharp and clear but also excited and passionate, bitter, ironical, at the same time sorrowful and sympathetic. It is a genuine creation of Jesus and is original, notwithstanding its remarkable resemblance in matter to the Psalms of Solomon and the Ascension of Moses. It is certainly not, as some would persuade us, the creation of a Rabbi of the second century; but it

---

[1] The Ebal curses, Deut. xxvii. 13 sqq. (altogether only conditional). The three "Woes" of the Apocalypse, viii. 13 sqq. (of a physico-cosmical kind). On the other hand, see Isaiah v. 8 (in the chapter about the vineyard), the six "Woes;" x. 1 a "Woe" against the Sopherim with their unjust statutes. Also Hab. ii. 6 sqq. has five "Woes." Thirty "Woes" in Book of Enoch 94—100.

[2] How weak and arbitrary are, on the other hand, the six or seven "Woes" in Luke: (1) cleanness of vessels, (2) tithes, (3) vanity, (4) concealed sepulchres, (5) burdens of the people, (6) sepulchre building, (7) key. See above, p. 199, n. 3. The "pure," above, I. p. 341.

is the fruit of the one great moment into which was compressed all the noble—though by Celsus and Reimarus depreciated—anger of the sublime man who felt the presentiment that he should fall a sacrifice to the powers of darkness from which he, with the fulness of superior strength and love, longed to deliver his unhappy people.[1]

"Woe unto you, Scribes and Pharisees"—thus began he with a two-fold "Woe"—"ye hypocrites, because ye shut the kingdom of heaven against men; for ye neither enter in, nor let those that are entering go in!"[2] Woe unto you, Scribes and Pharisees, hypocrites, because ye compass sea and land to make one proselyte, and when he is made, ye make him two-fold more a son of hell than yourselves!"[3] In a crushing manner, this commencement showed the contrast between the icy coldness towards the question of the age and of the day, namely, towards the growth of

---

[1] Comp. *Ps. Sal.* 4, 3 sqq., the remarkable resemblance: ποικιλίαι ἁμαρτιῶν, ἐν ἀκρασίαις, οἱ ὀφθαλμοὶ ἐπὶ πᾶσαν γυναῖκα, ἐν ὑποκρίσει ζῶντες, ἀνθρωπάρεσκοι. *Assumpt. Moys.* 7, 4 sqq.; pestilentiosi et impii, dicentes se esse justos; sibi placentes, ficti in omnibus suis et omni hora diei amantes convivia, devoratores gulæ, [paupe]-rum bonorum comestores, dicentes, se hæc facere propter misericordiam eorum, &c. Hitzig (*Geschichte Isr.* p. 502) has pointed out the similarity of the *Ps. Sal.* The *scolding* of Jesus was censured by Celsus (2, 76) as ungodlike, nay, as humanly irrational: ἀπειλεῖ καὶ λοιδορεῖ κούφως, ὁπόταν λέγῃ, οὐαὶ ὑμῖν, &c. Similarly Reimarus, pp. 144 sqq.

[2] Matt. xxiii. 13. Comp. the keys, xvi. 19. The construction in Luke (seventh "Woe," xi. 52): Ye have taken away the key of knowledge (daat, Hos. iv. 6; patach of the exposition of the Scriptures, and of the key mapteach, Luke xxiv. 32; Lightfoot, p. 531; therefore clavis and accipere clavem a symbol of the teachers of the Law, Schöttgen, pp. 199, 209), is fine: one cannot go into the house of the kingdom, not only because it is violently closed (Matt.), but also because it is hidden from knowledge, kept back, displaced. And that withdrawal of the knowledge was the chief sin of the hierarchy; on the other hand, they had not *violently* forbidden admission. Yet it is easily seen that the withholding action of the Scribes could be spoken of as Matthew speaks; further, that in Luke the artificially introduced νομικοί must be described as men of knowledge in contrast to the drastic Pharisees, and that the aorist of Luke in a suspicious manner (like xix. 46) shows his late date. Comp. Clem. *Hom.* 3, 18, where Matthew and Luke are joined together and the words of Jesus thus given: κρατοῦσι μὲν τὴν κλεῖν, τοῖς δὲ βουλ. εἰσελθεῖν οὐ παρέχουσι. Also xviii. 15 sq.

[3] Proselyting zeal of the Jews, above, I. p. 305; but also arrogance, so that the proselytes were often called the scabies Israelis. Lightfoot, p. 358. Schöttgen, p. 202. Gehennæ filii or hæredes, often by the Rabbis. Wetst. p. 485. With the duæ gehennæ, *Jom.* 72, 2, the expression διπλ. has nothing to do.

the kingdom of heaven, and the feverish zeal to gain proselytes to the dead ordinances: an antithesis the more striking because in the one case thousands of men longing to enter in, nay the whole nation, came under consideration, while in the other only the miserable capture of one Gentile soul, and because in the one case the kingdom of heaven was in prospect, while in the other there was in truth nothing but hell and double hell for the still more ordinance-blinded pupil.[1]

But why has he only hell to offer them? He shows it in the *four* violent attacks upon the *system* itself, upon its legal dicta, upon its requirements as to purification. "Woe unto you, blind guides, who say, Whosoever swears by the temple house, it is nothing; but whosoever swears by the gold of the temple, he is bound."[2] These miserable depreciations and invalidations of oaths—such as Jesus had long before in another way censured—according to which only oaths and vows by what was materially most costly in the temple, by its golden overlay that ran over the marble and glittered like the sun, by the golden vessels, gates, doors, and decorations, or indeed by the millions of the temple treasure, were to be held as binding—these were matters of fact, and afforded a self-speaking monument of the frivolity, the low range of thought, the outspoken mercenary spirit, of these watchmen of Zion.[3] Therefore he went on, compassionating, confuting, enlarging: "Fools and blind, which is greater, the gold or the temple that sanctifies the gold? And again ye say, Whosoever swears by the altar, it is nothing; but whosoever swears by the sacrificial gift that lies upon it, he is

---

[1] Comp. only Tac. *Hist.* 5, 5: pessimus quisque spretis relig. patriis tributa illuc gerebant. Transgressi in mores eorum idem usurpant, nec quidq. prius imbuuntur, quam contemnere Deos, &c. Juvenal, 14, 101. Or comp. the Jewish-Christian proselytes in the Epistle to the Galatians or in that to the Corinthians, who outdid the zeal of the teachers (Rom. ii. 19), Gal. iv. 9, 21; 2 Cor. xi. 20.

[2] Matt. xxiii. 16. Leaders of the blind, xv. 14; Rom. ii. 19. Pedagogues, 1 Cor. iv. 15. Blind, *Tanch.* f. 71, 4: melius esset, impios esse cœcos. Schött. p. 151.

[3] Above, III. pp. 311 sq. On the golden adornments of the temple, Jos. *B. J.* 5, 5, 3—6; 6, 8, 3. Altare sanctificat, vasa sacra sanctificant. Schöttgen, p. 202. Wetst. p. 485. Avarice, Luke xvi. 14, xx. 47.

bound.[1] Ye blind, which is greater, the gift or the altar that sanctifies the gift? Whosoever, therefore"—thus, with sound, faultless, and acute logic, he draws his inference—"whosoever swears by the altar, swears by it and by all that is upon it. And whosoever swears by the temple, swears by it and by Him that dwells therein. And whosoever swears by heaven"— another carelessly permitted form of protestation—"swears by the throne of God and by Him that sits thereon."[2] Thus, in this first question concerning the Law, he censures the frivolous obscuration, weakening, disintegration of the clear language of the Law. In that which now follows, he denounces the rebellious obliteration of what was weightiest in the Law, the unblushing sacrifice of the moral in favour of the material and external, practised with a dilettant extravagance. "*Woe* to you, Scribes and Pharisees, hypocrites, because ye tithe mint and anise and cummin, and have let go the weightier matters of the Law, justice and mercy and fidelity. The latter ought to be done, and the former not left undone. Blind guides, ye strain out the gnat but swallow the camel."[3] In fact, a more contemptible, a more

---

[1] Adjurare per cornua altaris interioris (altar of incense), Wetst. p. 485. Jesus means the altar of burnt sacrifice in the court of the priests. Fools, comp. 1 Cor. xv. 36, and above, p. 172, n. 2.

[2] The meaning of Matt. v. 34 (above, III. p. 311) is here still plainer.

[3] Matt. xxiii. 23 sq.; Luke xi. 42. Here, again, the preference is plainly due to Matthew. Luke gives, (1) in addition to mint, the also sweet-smelling but bitter-tasting rue (also in Varro, *Ling. Lat.* 5, 103, along with menta; Pliny, 19, 37, along with anethum), and (generally) every garden produce; (2) passes over $τὰ\ βαρύτ.\ νόμου$, and comprises that in $κρίσις$ and $ἀγάπη\ θεοῦ$, passes over therefore the— certainly more difficult to understand—$πίστις$, and changes $ἔλεος$ towards men into $ἀγάπη$, nay, distorts it into $ἀ.\ θεοῦ$; (3) leaves out entirely the straining out a gnat. The commands to pay tithes (only in general of the principal produce), Levit. xxvii. 30; Numb. xviii. 21; Deut. xii. 6, xiv. 22. In xiv. 22, $δεκάτη\ παντὸς\ γεννήμ.\ τ.\ σπέρματος$, but verse 23 limits it to corn, must, and oil. Thus still in the restoration period, Neh. x. 39, xiii. 5, 12. Express mention in the Bab. Talmud, *B. Jom.* f. 83, 2: decimatio olerum est a Rabbinis. ʽΗδυοσμ. (sweet-smell) = mentha (Talm. minta); anethum = dill, anise, cuminum, cumin. The trivial rules of the Rabbis (Luke xviii. 12 shows their conceit as to actual observance), particularly concerning anise, cumin, but also all other garden produce, Lightfoot, p. 359; Schöttgen, p. 203. Luke has rue (ruta, according to Pliny, *Hist. Nat.* 19, 45, much planted, particularly among fig-trees), because this very plant was declared free of tax. *M. Sheb.* 9, 1. The weightier matters, see on Matt. v. above, III. pp. 299 sq., and on Matt. xxii. above, p. 177.

THE LAST DISCLOSURES. 213

ludicrous antithesis could not be exhibited than this paltry legal punctiliousness that observed the smallest ceremonial detail, in contrast to the broad lack of conscientiousness in life. Those whom Jesus condemned not only taught—charging the disobedient with deadly sin—but also practised that punctiliousness, even to the tithing of the smallest and most unimportant fruits of the earth (even rue), for the benefit of the temple, whilst the Law itself mentioned only the more important produce, corn, oil, and must or fruits; they, again, in the direction of morals, sinned most grossly against the commands of love, nay even against those of righteousness and truth and faith.[1]

This picture from life, the gnat and the camel, a sign of their fondness for trivialities in general, and at the same time an apposite portrayal of the fastidiousness at table that would be offended at the presence of a gnat,—this picture led Jesus on to refer to their purifications, the renowned climax of that observance of the Law which gained for them the admiration of the people, and which was yet so terribly unrighteous.[2] "Woe unto you, Scribes and Pharisees, hypocrites, that ye make clean the outside of the cup and of the dish, but within ye are full of robbery and excess. Blind Pharisees, cleanse first the inside of the cup, thereby its outside will be clean also." In view of the outward washing of household vessels so persistently carried on with the most passionate and the holiest zeal, he here pointed

Judicium et eleemos. non fecit, Wetst. p. 486. Jesus meant rules of love of one's neighbour (his principle, Matt. ix. 13); Luke, of love of God. Straining out the gnat, here figurative, was seriously practised by the careful Jews. Buxt. p. 516. Figurative also by the Rabbis. *Gitt.* f. 90, 1 : quemadm. varii sunt hom. mores circa ea, quæ deglutiunt, ita etiam circa uxores. Est qui ubi musca in poc. s. inciderit, eam tamen effundit nec ebibit (alius deglutit). Foolish exposition in *Nizzach. vet.* 248 : Jesus here called himself camel. The muscas, *i.e.* the prophets, they accept; camelum deglutilis h. e. necem mihi machinamini. Schöttgen, p. 204.

[1] Comp. *Sanh.* f. 83, 1 : qui comedit non decimata, reus est mortis. Lightfoot, p. 553. See also Schöttgen, p. 26. On the tithing of many articles there was a difference of opinion, *e.g.* in the case of anise, was tithe to be taken of only the flower, or also of the seed and the plant? Wetst. p. 486. Comp. rue, in the previous note. A saying in the *Pirke Abot*, 1, 16, under the name of Gamaliel I., gives the caution : tithe not according to conjecture too much!

[2] Above, I. pp. 304, 341; IV. p. 20.

with telling and unpitying appositeness to the inner spiritual
cleansing of the wine cups and meat dishes filled with trespasses
against justice and truth and love, and with abuse of the pious
fancies of laymen and widows, the cups and dishes emptied
at private and public feasts with greedy eagerness—as the
"Ascension of Moses," as late as the second century, complains
—and the cleanness of which seemed to him restored by righteous
acquisition and spotless intention, without any polishing and
furbishing.[1] And from their dishes he turned, in the sixth
"Woe," to the men themselves, the likenesses of their bright
vessels, but also the copy of a new picture which the Eastertide
just then presented to him. In the month before the Easter
month, at the end of the rainy season, about the 15th of Adar,
the sepulchres at Jerusalem were carefully whitewashed. This
was done not so much—as many of the people and Jesus himself
might have thought—that at Easter Jerusalem might be, even
to the very graves, the adorned daughter, as that the unclean
places, contact with which would render men obnoxious to
ceremonial penalty, might be made warningly conspicuous.[2]
This custom had struck Jesus, and at once his mental eye saw
in the graves which made themselves conspicuous by their white-
ness, his mortal foes, the clean, the Pharisees. "Woe to you"—
thus, therefore, he continued his address—"Scribes and Pharisees,

---

[1] Comp. the variation in Luke xi. 39—41. In particular, verse 40 exhibits a general idea (comp. Matt. xv. 18) which is not at all apposite; while verse 41 gives the
Ebionite opinion, as if with the giving away of the contents of the dishes the uncleanness of the contents would be removed. For the exegesis that makes the inside represent the soul of man (the Fathers, and even Neander) is incorrect. Also Bleek, II.
p. 166, for Matthew. The zeal of the Jews for purifying, Mark vii. 1 sqq.; comp.
the trivial considerations of the Rabbis whether a vessel is wholly or partially unclean
if it is spotted on the outside or the inside. Schöttgen, p. 204. Wetst. p. 488. *Ps.
Salom.* 4, 3: ἐν ποικιλίᾳ ἁμαρτιῶν κ. ἐν ἀκρασίαις. *Ass. Moys.* 7, 4: amantes convivia, &c.

[2] *Shekal.* c. 1, h. 1 : 15. mens. Adar emendant vias et plateas etc. et pingunt sepulcra.
They were washed over their whole superficies (like the stones of the altar of burnt
sacrifice at Easter and the Feast of Tabernacles) with lime and water, after the rain
had washed off the former coating. It is expressly said: ut locus immundus dignos-
ceretur, particularly by the priests! Calce alba instar ossium! Lightfoot, pp. 356,
359 sq. Schöttgen, p. 206. Similar figure in Ezekiel xxii. 28, xiii. 10.

hypocrites, because ye are like whited sepulchres that outwardly appear charming, but within swarm with dead bones and all uncleanness. So ye also outwardly appear righteous unto men, but within ye are full of hypocrisy and iniquity!"[1]

A fine association of ideas led him at last to the seventh, the closing "Woe." Among the sepulchres, which, in consequence of the genuinely Israelitish belief that the dead in death, and still more after the resurrection, continued to dwell upon the earth, were very carefully built, and which even now surround Jerusalem, particularly on the south and east, he saw also the graves of the prophets, at the present day shown to the east of Kidron on the Mount of Olives.[2] Israel and its Scribes built to the prophets stately sepulchral chambers, mausoleums, cenotaphs, pyramids, and columns. They thus proclaimed the exact service they performed, the sepulture of the prophets and of the kingdom of God. "Woe unto you, Scribes and Pharisees, hypocrites, that ye build the graves of the prophets and adorn the monuments of the righteous, and say, Had we been in the days of our fathers, we should not have been partakers with them in the blood of the prophets.[3] Therefore"—thus spoke he, with a startling and bold transition which obliterated the subtle and in reality false self-distinction of the sons from their fathers, and extorted from the exculpation itself, and from the reparation for crime, a guilty confession of fellowship in crime—"therefore ye

[1] Matt. xxiii. 27. More briefly, Luke xi. 44. But the chief idea—that the Pharisees appear adorned—is unskilfully altogether omitted here; one only does not see that there are graves there, but the $\mu\nu$. $\check{\alpha}\delta\eta\lambda\alpha$ do not look strikingly attractive. "Ye appear," that is the colorati, picti, Lightfoot, p. 360. Schöttgen, p. 199. Ficti in omnibus suis, *Ass. Moys.* 7, 4.

[2] Comp. Robinson's *Palestine*. Hausrath (p. 438) remarks that the most southerly monument is now called that of Zechariah. The high-priests, also Scribes, had their venerated sepulchres in Jerusalem, later in Galilee, *e.g.* that of Annas, *B.J.* 5, 12, 2; comp. the grave of David, *Ant.* 7, 15, 3; of Herod, 17, 8, 3; of Helena (pyramids), 20, 4, 3; the splendid grave which Philip the tetrarch had built in his life-time, 18, 4, 6. The pillars which were sometimes set up were descriptively called naphshot, souls. Interesting contradiction, *Gem. Hier. Shek.* (c. 2, h. 5) f. 47, 1: non exstruunt $\mu\nu\eta\mu\epsilon\tilde{\iota}\alpha$ (naphshot) justorum, nam dicta eorum sunt memoria eorum. Lightfoot, p. 360.

[3] R. Akiba: si nos fuissemus in synedrio, non esset unquam quisq. interfectus. *Macc.* c. 1, h. 17; Lightfoot, p. 370.

bear witness to yourselves that ye are the sons of the murderers of the prophets.[1] And ye ! fill ye up the measure of your fathers ! Serpents, brood of vipers, how would ye flee from the condemnation of hell ?"[2] He concluded by a transition from holy anger to the profoundest sadness. In the fate of the prophets he had beheld his own fate, in the sepulchres of the prophets his own sepulchre. "Jerusalem, Jerusalem"—into this solemn prophetic lamentation he compressed his acute pain on account of the futility of his career from Galilee even to the holy city, a futility due to the religious rulers of Jerusalem—"Jerusalem, that kills the prophets and stones them that are sent to it, how often would I have gathered thy children together as a hen gathers her young under her wings, and ye would not. Behold, your house"—according to Isaiah, the unforsaken house—"is forsaken to your loss; for I say unto you, ye shall not see me henceforth until ye shall say, Praised be he that comes in the name of the Lord !"[3]

It has been mentioned that the address in Matthew is some-

[1] Here also Luke xi. 47 (against Matt. xxiii. 29) has leapt over the chief point of the application. The paradox of the identification of the sons as witnesses with their fathers is possible only by virtue of the self-exculpation of the sons (Matthew), not of the mere sequence of murder by the fathers and of grave-building by the sons (Luke). Proverb, Ezekiel xvi. 44 : as the mother, so the daughter.

[2] Only in Matt. xxiii. 32. Implere mensuram and judicium gehennæ also in the Rabbis. Wetst, p. 490. In the Old Testament, jasaph (sapha) chatthat al ch. Is. xxx. 1. 1 Thess. ii. 16.

[3] Matt. xxiii. 37 ; Luke xiii. 34. Ἔρημος (allusion to the destruction)—as was simply assumed by Weizs. p. 548—is to be struck out in Luke ; and even in Matthew, notwithstanding Sin., Ephr., Bez., and Tisch., it is not established. Lachm. rightly left it out on the authority of BL It. Desolation of Jerusalem certainly often threatened in the Prophets. Comp. Hos. ii. 3 ; Micah iii. 12. But Is. lxii. 12 (comp. Deut. xi. 12) comes chiefly into notice; and according to that, the reference is not merely to a "handing over," but to a "forsaking." Complaint of disobedience, Jer. vii. 25, xxv. 4 ; 2 Chron. xxiv. 19. The protecting bird, Isaiah xxxi. 5 ; Deut. xxxii. 11, i. 31 ; Joel iii. 16. Very frequently in the Rabbis. *Vaj. rabb.* s. 25, f. 168, 4 : gallina, quando pulli ejus teneri sunt, congregat eos et ponit sub alis suis, ipsos calefacit et pro ipsis humum pedibus effodit. Further, venire, colligi sub alas Dei, shechinæ. Schöttgen, pp. 207 sqq., particularly also of proselytes. Expressions in the classics, Wetst. p. 492. Belief in a better reception (which was wanting at the entry into Jerusalem, Matt. xxi.), comp. *Hier. Taan.* f. 64, 1 : si resipuerit Isr. vel. uno die, illico adveniet redemptor. *Kimchi* on Isaiah lix. 16 : multi pœnit. acturi sunt, cum signa viderint redemptionis. Hilg. *Zeitschrift*, 1868, p. 49, thinks of Rev. xi. 13.

what more copious than it has been here given. According to Matthew, before the lamentation over Jerusalem, Jesus not only showed the filling up the measure of their fathers by the sons, but also the advent of the righteous judgment of God upon the Pharisees and the whole generation to avenge the death of all the righteous men and prophets from Abel, the son of Adam, to Zechariah, the son of Barachiah, in truth even to his own Apostles.[1] Evidently there is here a certain coherence; but the lack of coherence is still more marked.[2] For how could Jesus leap from the prophets to his Apostles, and indeed speak of the latter under the altogether unusual titles of prophets, wise men, and Scribes, without mentioning what was most important and most decisive, himself and his approaching fate? How could he speak of the persecution of the Apostles, and afterwards only of *his own* rejection and recognition? How could he threaten the living generation with bloody judgment, and in the subsequent lamentation over Jerusalem only with temporary forsaking? We here detect the interpolation.[3] The spuriousness of this passage is, however, definitively proved by the great improbability that Jesus should have predicted the fate of his Apostles, with all the details of their sufferings and the modes of their death, nay, that he should have had time to busy himself so minutely with the future, while to him the present moment

[1] Matt. xxiii. 34; comp. Luke xi. 49.

[2] By no means in the structural connection, as Bleek (II. p. 175) thinks, quite unjustly preferring Luke at διὰ τοῦτο; still more so Volkmar, p. 519. The structural connection in Luke is only smooth, that in Matthew is full of significance, whether we bring δ. τ. into connection backwards with πῶς φύγητε or πληρῶσ. (De Wette), or forwards with ὅπως ἔλθῃ, verse 35 (Meyer). In particular, the transition in Matthew from the renunciation by the Pharisees of the sins of the nation against the prophets to the direct imputation of these sins to the Pharisees, is full of significance.

[3] We are reminded of well-known and in part earlier utterances of Jesus by the words prophets, wise men, and Scribes (= Apostles), Matt. xxiii. 34, and x. 41, xiii. 52. Scourging in synagogues, x. 17. Fleeing from city to city, x. 23. The interpolation can be recognized by noting that in verse 33 mention is made of a punishment of the Pharisees; in verse 36, of a punishment of the people; in verse 38, again, of a pardoning of the people; and that when verses 34—36 are rejected, verse 37 joins on well to verses 32 sq. Jerusalem stands *en rapport* with the murderers of the prophets, but is not identical with them, wherefore the absolute condemnation falls upon the murderers, but only temporary abandonment upon Jerusalem.

was full to overflowing. And here is light at once. A later age that placed in the mouth of Jesus the prediction concerning the Apostles, just as it did in the parable of the marriage, is quite plainly to be detected in the menace of the punishment of the living generation for the murder of the righteous men from Abel to Zechariah, i.e. to the end for old, in truth for new, things.[1] The murder of the prophet Zechariah, the son of Barachiah, more correctly the son of Jehoiada, was committed about the year B.C. 839. It is impossible that Jesus should have quoted this as the latest of the murders of righteous men, as if the hundreds of years, nay the thousand years, since had been without guilt, and as if the living generation of Scribes and Pharisees were at all responsible for that ancient royal murder.[2] On the other hand, everything becomes clear when we think of the murder of the later Zechariah, the son of Baruch, who in the beginning of the Roman war (before Easter, A.D. 68) was murdered within the temple by the zealots, the genuine fruit of Pharisaism, even though the latter wished to deny its fruit. It is true this Zechariah was no prophet, but according to Matthew himself, as well as Josephus, he was a righteous man, like to Abel who opened the series of the mortal sacrifices to wickedness.[3] At

---

[1] See the likewise spurious later passage, Matt. xxii. 6.

[2] The well-known prophet, one of the twelve, is called in the Hebrew the son of Berechiah (Zech. i. 1). In Matt. xxiii. 35, he is confounded with Zechariah, the son of Jehoiada, who, according to 2 Chron. xxiv. 20, was stoned by king Joash (B.C. 878—838) in the court of the temple. The confusion occurred, as it seems to me, because the former (Zech. i. 1) is also called the son of Iddo, and the Rabbis also call the second Zechariah filium Iddo (Lightfoot, p. 362). Futile attempts at reconciliation in Lightfoot (p. 362), Wetst. (p. 491), and later writers. Luke prudently drops the name of the father (xi. 51); but the Gospel of the Hebrews makes the correction, fil. Jojada, which Hilg. would take to be the original (Hilg. *N. T.* IV. p. 17, &c.). Apart from the error, it is striking that a murder about B.C. 839 should appear as the limit downwards. Even the Old Testament mentions, *e.g.*, the later murder of Urijah, Jer. xxvi. 23. And why not John the Baptist? It is said here, without any illustrative force, that the Jews felt the murder in question very deeply, and in the Old Testament canon 2 Chronicles was the last book (thus Meyer, and even Hilgenfeld). Can men read? Matt. xxiii. 35: *ye, ye* have slain!

[3] Jos. *B.J.* 4, 5, 4: τινὰ τῶν ἐπιφανεστάτων ἀποκτεῖναι προθέμενοι Ζαχαρίαν υἱὸν Βαρούχου. He is a righteous man (μισοπόνηρον), who accused the Zealots of all their παρανομίαι, was acquitted even by the Sanhedrim, which though arbitrarily

this date, therefore, near the close of the apostolic period, just before the fall of Jerusalem, originated this prophetic saying of Jesus, in which, for the sake of historical propriety, the name of the son of Baruch was converted into that of the Old Testament son of Barachiah, so as to cover the anachronism; but the circle of the Apostles and Christian teachers was very unhistorically mixed up with Old Testament prophets, wise men, and Scribes.[1] The fact that Luke has also, as well as Matthew, accepted this passage in his "Woes" pronounced against the Pharisees, by no means aids the establishment of its historical character. One might find an important superiority in Luke by supposing that to him a prediction concerning the Apostles—although he alone seems to mention them—did not really exist, but that Jesus derived his utterance about Prophets and Apostles, that is the sent of God generally, from an unknown earlier Old Testament prediction.[2] The whole address, however, in Luke has the appear-

appointed was mindful τοῦ δικαίου, then ἐν μέσῳ ἱερῷ διαφθείρεται. Beginning of the year A.D. 68; comp. *B. J.* 4, 7, 2. After Hammond and Krebs, he was thought of particularly by Hug, Credner, Ammon, Gfrörer. There are not wanting refutations (Theile and others) which are correct only in so far as a prediction by Jesus would be an absurdity, and which are called for only so long as there is no doubt of the genuineness of the whole. The passage rather gives a hint as to the age of Matthew. A second hypothesis was very unfortunate: this Zechariah was the father of John the Baptist, but his father is not designated either as Berechiah or as Baruch, and his death is apocryphal fable (*Ev. Jac.* 23; comp. Hilg. *Zeitschrift*, 1868, p. 47). This hypothesis was upheld from Origen to Hilgenfeld, who however now withdraws it.

[1] Neander (p. 497) finds no difficulty in the prophets, &c., in Matt. xxiii. 34, it is the unity of theocratical development; in xiii. 52 also, the Apostles are called Scribes, and in the Apostolic Church there were prophets (1 Cor. xii. 28). I will add that in Matt. x. 41 prophets are also spoken of; but would Jesus have made a title which he had once given to his disciples for the sake of comparison, their chief title? He did not predict the apostolic period with its details. Therefore the mention of those details rather points to the *later* period.

[2] Not only is the introduction to the passage in Luke xi. 49 not better than in Matthew, but the passage itself, although somewhat shorter, lacks the originality of Matthew (comp. only Matthew's γραμμ. and δίκαιοι), and the designation of Abel as prophet is a blunder. Even in Clem. *Hom.* 2, 16; 19, 9; comp. 3, 26; 17, 4, Abel is only a righteous man, Adam a prophet. The introduction of the utterance as said by the Wisdom of God, has often led critics to regard it as a quotation from a writing by Jews or Christians with some such title as "Wisdom of God" (Paulus, Hengel, Baumg.-Crus., Ewald, Bleek, Weizs.; recently also Strauss, Hilg.'s *Zeitschrift*, 1863, p. 84, *New Life of Jesus*, Eng. trans., II. p. 66). But Neander (p. 467, after Twest.)

ance of being late and untrustworthy; the Apostles and even the suspected Zechariah, although prudently mentioned without his father's name, are in reality here also; while the introduction of the speech looks exactly like a quotation from Matthew, and would, in case of greater originality as compared with Matthew, be a conclusive proof of the unhistorical, apocryphal, and obscure origin of this part of the address, a part that is introduced by a more than mysterious formula.

It would perhaps appear to some to be consistent to give up also the lamentation over Jerusalem, with the spurious section which it closes.[1] It may be thought that the passage is more appropriate to a later age than to Jesus. It may be said that he had not so often gathered Jerusalem together, that he had never ministered at Jerusalem with the full Galilean love, and that he could not exactly accuse Jerusalem—which heard him eagerly, or at least protected him—of unwillingness, of obstinate resistance. Finally, the desolation of Jerusalem and its restoration in case of a Messianic greeting of the returning Messiah, was the faith, the hope, of the apostolic age. In the bird's-eye view taken by a later time, in which all the details were obliterated, men were able to talk about endless futile efforts of Jesus on behalf of Jerusalem, i.e. properly speaking, of Israel. This expedient of pronouncing the passage spurious would naturally be the simplest way of disposing of the objection long ago so forcibly raised against the old Gospels in favour of the late Johannine book, that the one incidental lamentation over the long work at Jerusalem throws light upon the Johannine account

and Meyer thought of an important introduction of a saying of Jesus; Ritschl and Baur of the passage in Matthew; comp. also Hilg. *Zeitschrift*, 1868, p. 46. Since Luke is later than and dependent upon Matthew, it is probable that he either thought, by mistake, of an Old Testament passage (Olsh. suggests 2 Chron. xxiv. 19), or, in forgetfulness as to decorum in his historical representation, thus introduced Jesus as if he were in reflection and devotion, for which not only the Proverbs and the Book of Wisdom—from which Neander quotes vii. 27—(or, according to Volkmar, 4 Esdras xiv. 47), but also sentences in Matt. xi. 19, 27, xii. 42, form precedents.

[1] In fact, Hilg. (p. 49) questions only this very passage, whilst he accepts the previous one as the original text of Matthew. But his reasons are not weighty, and ἔρημος is uncertain.

THE LAST DISCLOSURES. 221

of a long residence at Jerusalem, and justifies that account against the "Galilean" Gospels, which here make an involuntary admission.[1] But the beautiful and evidently thoroughly ancient passage could be given up only with sorrow.[2] Thus felt, thus spoke Jesus, particularly in this lofty moment of retrospect and close. The hen with her chickens—that was *his* picture and that was *he*; and already in Galilee, in the presence of the Pharisees, had he, just as here, spoken of his efforts to gather the people together.[3] But, as everything shows and as Eusebius already saw, by Jerusalem he meant not only the city but all Israel, misled by the builders, by the masters of the tower, by the holders of the key, all Israel lukewarm through foreign guilt and their own foolishness, all Israel persisting in their indifference or in their unbelief.[4] The house which he forsook, without threatening it with destruction, was the whole Israelitish commonwealth that had its centre at Jerusalem. But the Messianic recognition which was ultimately to be brought about, not, it is true, among the builders whom he committed to the judgment of God, but in the nation awakened from its illusions by the signs of God,—this was the hope which, according to all reports, he confessed and undeniably even before the Sanhedrim, in order thus to see the parable of the two sons afresh exemplified in a "No" which should be transformed into a "Yes."[5]

[1] Comp. only Neander, Bleek, Lücke, and all the defenders of John; even Strauss formerly, 4th ed. I. p. 471; and now again Schenkel, *Bib.-Lex.* III. p. 291, who sees a reference to a several months' residence of Jesus at Jerusalem.

[2] Weisse also retains it as genuine, II. p. 120.

[3] Comp. the antique stoning, against Matt. xxiii. 34. And comp. Matt. xii. 30 with xxiii. 37.

[4] Eus. *Theoph.* in *Nov. Patr. Bibl.* IV. p. 127: τέκνα τῆς πόλεως ὀνομάζει τὸ ἰουδαϊκὸν πᾶν γένος. Comp. Micah iii. 10, 12, iv. 8, 13; Zeph. iii. 14; Zech. i. 19, ix. 9, xii. 2 sqq., xiv. 21; 4 Esdras x. 7 (Σιὼν ἡ μήτηρ ἡμῶν); Gal. iv. 25, τέκνα Ιερουσαλήμ. Just so upon this point speaks Hilg. (p. 49). We cannot think this utterance directed merely against the hierarchy, although it immediately follows the announcement of punishment upon them. It is too general, it is too sad, it is also too mild in its verdict. It must be remembered that to Jesus the people were not merely standing before his mind's eye, but they were actually present before him.

[5] Neander (p. 498), with many others, erroneously explains the house as the destroyed temple; the words, "until ye shall say," he expounds, "others than ye, later

According to Matthew, Jesus ended his addresses to the people and his conversations with the Pharisees on this Thursday, the 12th of April. The other Gospels know at least of nothing greater to add. It is true that Luke and Mark, after the address to the Pharisees, give the narrative of the widow and the temple coffers; and Luke, followed in part by John, closes this pre-Easter time with the general formula that Jesus spent the days teaching in the temple, and the nights upon the Mount of Olives; whence it might be concluded that Jesus had persevered in his active ministry at Jerusalem up to the last moment.[1] It may be thought that this manly courage and this witness to the very end best accord with the office and mission of Jesus, and directly provoked the hierarchs' interposition determined upon in the two following last days; whilst a two days' retreat to Bethany—which, otherwise, we should have to accept—would have been a dereliction of duty, and also a signal for the cessation of the violent measures of the foes. Against all this, the actual closing of all addresses in all the Gospels two days before Easter is eloquent enough; and the incident of the widow—which is immediately attached to the address to the Pharisees, and in truth occurred before it—and finally the indefinite formulas of Luke and the others, have no force to the contrary.[2] This representation of the events, adopted by all the Gospels, and carried still further in John by the communication that Jesus hid himself immediately after the entry, from the 9th to the 13th of April, could be invalidated only by the very precarious assumption that they have inaccurately crowded the controversies into too few days.[3] But this representation of the events is supported by two decisive facts. The last address to the Pharisees plainly announced the

men"! And Weisse (II. p. 121) also refuses to understand the return as a material one.

[1] Luke xxi. 1; Mark xii. 41. The general notice by Luke of Jesus' teaching ministry *after* the address about the future, xxi. 37. Comp. also Matt. xxvi. 55; John xviii. 20.

[2] Matt. xxvi. 2; Mark xiv. 1. On the widow, see above, p. 194.

[3] John xii. 36. The above is a very common assertion. Weizs. pp. 273 sqq.

retreat of Jesus; and its well-armed attack upon the system and the men of the system would lead to such a decided rupture, that he could not speak again, or would have to fear that any further speech or action would be followed by immediate apprehension or violence. Hence Matthew correctly reports that Jesus left the temple and retreated to the Mount of Olives immediately after the close of this address.[1] A second fact is the well-established sojourn of Jesus in Bethany, on the occasion of the feast there in the course of the last two days before the Passover, as well as his remaining in Bethany on the morning of the day of eating the Passover lamb, whilst he sent his disciples to the city, and did not go thither himself until he went privately in the evening. From all this it is safe to conclude that Jesus remained away from the city, and spent the time in Bethany and on the Mount of Olives, from midday on the 12th until evening on the 14th of April. This retreat was no flight, and it was no concealment in order to save his life; his remaining in the immediate neighbourhood and his going into the city to celebrate the Passover on the 14th, prove the contrary. This retreat was only a procrastination of the fall which he saw was imminent. He would not throw himself too rashly into the hands of his foes. He wished to take his farewell in quiet, to arrange the affairs of his community, if possible, once more—nay, the first as well as the last time—to eat the Passover with his disciples, in this Easter solemnity instituting for them an eloquent symbol of the death to which he was hastening.[2] For he could not hope that in this pause his foes would reconsider their position, certainly not that a miraculous turn of affairs would be brought about by the arm of God. He would be more likely to hope for the latter when the attempt to seize him was being made, than in this quiet heated pause. But while he himself, in spite of this temporary

---

[1] Matt. xxiv. 1. After the controversy with the Pharisees, Luke (xi. 53) mentions ambushes and questionings by the Pharisees; but how untrustworthy in the whole of this connection!

[2] The Fragmentist (p. 152) charges Jesus with cowardly absence from the temple; already Celsus, flight and hiding, 1, 65 sq.; 2, 8 sqq.; 2, 67, 70.

truce, purposed and was compelled to bring his work to an end, his foes were regarding his cause and the situation in exactly the same way. His retreat was no plea to them for peace. They were aware of the secret glowing passions, the secretly rooting convictions. It behoved them to indulge in no idle procrastination, but to strike a vigorous, decisive blow, so long as he was still before the public and was in the neighbourhood, so long as those festival crowds reverently looked up to him and inquired after him, whilst at the same time the danger from those crowds had as completely disappeared as had that from the Prophet himself who was in hiding.

Division IV.—THE FAREWELL.

The Gospels report a triple leave-taking of his followers by Jesus, one on the Mount of Olives, another at Bethany, another at the last supper at Jerusalem. The leave-taking on the Mount of Olives is marked by teaching and admonition, that at the Bethany meal by the last cordially serious sociality, that at the last supper at Jerusalem, the crown of the farewell, by an intenser form of both these characteristics. At Jerusalem, the feast of friendship became the festival of the new religion, which distributed its gifts, revealed its prospects, and made known its requirements. When we consider everything, we understand why Jesus withdrew; and we readily give up any prejudice in favour of finding a leave-taking only in the farewell addresses in John's Gospel.

A.—On the Mount of Olives.

According to the Gospels, according to Matthew most distinctly, Jesus forsook—as indeed his closing address in which he finally broke with the Pharisees compelled him to do—the temple buildings; and with his band of followers he struck into the road over the Kidron to the Mount of Olives and Bethany.[1] Looking back, they would see opposite to them the lofty hill of the temple standing forth as grandly and overpoweringly as on the first hopeful day of the entry, like the tower of the parable majestically rising from the terraces of the courts to the gold-glittering marble heights of the House of God.[2] This is the situation to which the

---
[1] Matt. xxiv. 1; Mark xiii. 1. That his adherents also accompanied him is shown by Matt. xxiv. 3.
[2] See above, pp. 111, 121. Θαυμασιώτατον ἔργον, Jos. B. J. 6, 4, 8. Comp. Tac. *Hist.* 5, 8: immensæ opulentiæ templum, and the whole description there. Meyer,

great prophetic utterance of Jesus belongs; though Luke misplaces the whole proceeding in the temple and in the hearing of the people, and Mark puts at least the introduction of the speech at the departure from the temple, as if the seriousness of the situation permitted Jesus or his disciples to take yet another quiet and loving glance at the temple, as Mark had already twice represented them as doing.[1] The disciples looked back with an eye to the material temple. He looked backwards upon a closed, past history, upon the futility of his ministry; but he also looked forwards to the condemnation of this futility. They admiringly pointed out to him the gates, the porches, the temple itself, one hundred and fifty feet high and long, with the gigantic stones of five-and-twenty cubits in length, lying one upon another like the stones of a fortress.[2] "See ye not all this?" thus spoke he, with solemn and fearful brevity, in the old words of the prophets. "Verily I say unto you, there shall not be left here one stone upon another which shall not be thrown down."[3]

This utterance of Jesus is more readily doubted than discredited. As well as the following address about the future, it has often been pronounced to be an interpolated prediction.[4] The destruction of the temple, which actually took place thirty-five years afterwards, Jesus could not have foreseen. Moreover, the Reve-

---

after Chrys. and others, very awkwardly makes the words in Matt. xxiii. 38 give the disciples occasion to point to the temple. But there was there no reference whatever to the temple.

[1] Luke xxi. 5; Mark xiii. 1 (ἐκπορ. against Matt. ἐξελθὼν ἐπορ.); comp. Mark xi. 11, 27.

[2] The size of the stones, Jos. Ant. 15, 11, 3, and B. J. 5, 5, 6. Length 25 (according to B. J. single stones 45), height 8 (5), breadth 12 (6) cubits.

[3] Matt. xxiv. 2, and parallel passages. Comp. Micah iii. 12; Jer. xxvi. 18: Sion should become heaps of stones, ijim, the hill of the temple a forest. See also the first destruction, 2 Kings xxv. 9, 13.

[4] Thus in particular the critical school since Baur, *Untersuch.* pp. 604 sqq.; comp. Köstlin, Hilgenfeld, Strauss, Volkmar; but recently Hilg., *Zeitschrift*, 1868, p. 65; also Pfleiderer, *Jahrb. d. Theol.* 1868, pp. 134 sqq. In spite of my having (above, I. pp. 64 sqq.) sufficiently exposed the arbitrary character of this assumption, idle repetitions are continued as though no protest had been made. The genuineness of the prediction is upheld also by Paulus, Fritzsche, Weisse, Schenkel, Hausrath, Holtzmann, Weizsäcker.

lation of John shows that on the very eve of the actual destruction, at Easter, A.D. 69, the fall of the temple was considered impossible in Jewish and Jewish-Christian circles.[1] Yet it has already been shown elsewhere, that this counter-proof is altogether invalid; while for the actuality of the utterance of Jesus —which was not literally fulfilled, and thereby reveals its early date—good evidence can be adduced.[2] In the first place, the expression of Jesus' foes in the Sanhedrim is here of importance : " I can destroy the temple of God and in three days build it up again." Though this may be—as the early Gospels say—a false testimony when put in this form, yet it escapes censure and harmonizes remarkably well with many menaces of Jesus, particularly with words uttered on the Mount of Olives, as soon as it is made to mean that he taught a destruction of the temple by a divine judgment upon the carnal temple servants and despisers of the Messiah, and a material or spiritual rebuilding in the Messianic kingdom of the future.[3] A second proof is given by the accusation of the martyr Stephen, in the beginning of the apostolic period, one or two years after the death of Jesus, an accusation which a conscientious investigation cannot show to be

---

[1] Köstlin, p. 18 (also Pfleiderer) lays stress upon the fact that the Apostle Paul shows in Rom. xi. no presentiment of such a catastrophe. The fact is, that the fate of Jerusalem did not intimately concern him; comp. also 1 Cor. ii. 6, vi. 2, 19 ; 2 Cor. vi. 16; Rom. ii. 1—24; 1 Thess. ii. 15 sq. Volkmar thinks (p. 539) indeed that the catastrophe of Jerusalem was not at all calculable ; the struggle under Barkochba was carried on outside of Jerusalem round the fortress Bether. Date of the Revelation, see above, I. pp. 57, 66, where A.D. 68 is the date given. Recent critics fix it between A.D. 68—70. Having proportionate regard to the imperial and other evidences of date (Tac. *Hist.* 2, 8) as well as to the traces of Easter (i. 7, 10, 18, ii. 7 sq., iii. 20 sq.), I have, in I. p. 223, dated it at Easter, A.D. 69.

[2] Above, I. pp. 66 sq. That the utterance of Jesus was not literally fulfilled is seen in the facts that the temple was really burnt, but was *not* demolished by human hands, and that stones of it remain standing firmly. Καταλύω is essentially the expression for pulling down, Jos. *Ant.* 15, 11, 3 (of the temple). But after the taking of the city, nothing except the walls of the city were pulled down, certainly not the temple, which was reduced to "ashes," *B.J.* 6, 4, 6 sq.; 6, 5, 1; 7, 8, 7. Pulling down of gates and walls, *B.J.* 6, 5, 2; 6, 9, 1; 7, 5, 2, in general: μέγεθος τῶν ἐρρηγμένων κατασκευασμάτων.

[3] Matt. xxvi. 61, and parallel passages. Menaces, comp. Luke xiii. 3, 9 ; Matt. xxi. 41.

a fabrication by the author of the Acts, or a free version by Luke—the historian in both cases—of the words about the temple which Jesus was charged with uttering, but must regard only as an essentially true reminiscence of a primitive Stephen-source. The charge against Stephen ran thus: "We have heard that he said, Jesus the Nazoræan will destroy this place and change the customs which Moses delivered unto us."[1] It might be said that this commission, this future, was first ascribed to the Messiah on his second advent by Stephen; that no such announcement was made by Jesus, who, indeed, never said anything about the abrogation of the Laws of Moses. But who does not see that Stephen could not have spoken thus definitely concerning this peculiar future judgment of the Messiah, if there was an utter lack of tradition upon the subject, and that the actual tradition of Jesus' words concerning the extirpation of the Pharisaic human teaching stood by the side of Stephen's menace of an alteration of the Mosaic customs; again, that the tradition of Stephen essentially harmonizes with the double, triple tradition of the words of Jesus in the Gospels? Thus it happens that we can conceive the words of Jesus to have been uttered, without having recourse to the miracle of prediction.[2] Purely human calculation must already have had a presentiment of the destruction of the temple as the end of the unnatural condition of the people, as the end of the heathen rule and tyranny, and of the spirit of revolt which—justified and unjustified—continued to smoulder. Such a catastrophe had already once been brought about by the Chaldean heathenism; and Rome, in association with the Herods, had since the time of Pompey six times threatened or indeed commenced a similar destruction. This Jewish presentiment can be shown

---

[1] Acts vi. 14 (καταλῦσαι, as in Matt. xxiv. 2, xxvi. 61). The place is, according to verses 11 and 13 and vii. 48, the holy place or temple. The question of the sources of the Acts has been but little elucidated by the critical school (with exception of Zeller); on the other hand, by Schleiermacher, Schwanbeck, Lekebusch.

[2] Comp. Paulus, Fritzsche, Strauss (in the earlier *L. J.* 4th ed. II. pp. 347 sqq.); also Weisse (who, however, again speaks of magical clairvoyance, I. p. 591); recently, in particular, Colani, *Croy. Mess.* p. 209; Schenkel, p. 258.

to have expressly manifested itself more and more strongly from year to year after A.D. 50. It would therefore be ridiculous to consider it impossible in the decade A.D. 30—40, when the preconditions already existed, from the revolt of Judas Galilæus to the provocations of the procurator Pontius Pilate.[1] But Jesus was influenced by another calculation, a solid, certain, though not supernatural calculation based upon the religion that knew God to be the Ruler, that believed in providential dispensations even where the iron hand of Rome seemed to destroy the grounds of faith in such dispensations. Hence now, when the Roman power was already the rod of divine discipline, when by the will of God the blind leaders were leading the people into the pit, when indeed those blind leaders were thrusting the Messiah of God out of the temple of God which they had desecrated and converted into a den of robbers, it was inevitable that he, if he believed in God and in himself, should believe in the corrective judgment and in the eagles of the supreme tribunal whose organs stood ready right and left, and whose victims must be not only the evildoers, but also the temple in which the power of those evil-doers, their insolence, their violence, their works-holiness, their uncleanness, had a home and a centre.[2] We have already seen that he predicted the pit to the blind leaders, judgment to the hypocrites, downfall to the possessors of the stronghold: is it then a great thing that he should make the stronghold—by no means

---

[1] The temple threatened at the conquest by Pompey, above, I. p. 235; by the Romans and Herod, *ib.* p. 237. Easter revolt against Archelaus, *ib.* p. 254. Pentecost revolt against the Romans and Archelaus, and pillage of the temple by Sabinus, *ib.* p. 256. Also by Crassus, *ib.* Pilate's fight in the temple, Luke xiii. 1. On Pilate, see above, I. pp. 266, 305, II. p. 224. Anticipations of the downfall of the temple, Jos. *B. J.* 2, 12, 5; *Ant.* 20, 6, 1; *B. J.* 2, 15, 4; 2, 16, 4; 2, 17, 10; 2, 19, 5, &c. Comp. above, I. p. 67. According to the Rabbis, Simon Justus, in the Syrian period, had already prayed for prevention of its downfall, Herzf. III. p. 245. Josephus finds it in Daniel, *Ant.* 10, 11, 7; and Strauss thinks it possible that Daniel, without any experience of the destruction which Josephus and the Rabbis (placing the birth of the Messiah in the time of the destruction) had before them, had already given this direction to men's thoughts in the days of Jesus, *L. J.* 4th ed. II. p. 349.

[2] The Roman rod of correction, Matt. xx. 25; Luke xiii. 1. Punitive judgment upon Israel, Luke xiii. 3, xvii. 37.

the city, as has been often fabled, but the temple—share the general catastrophe with its possessors ?[1]

But the great speech concerning the future cannot boast a credibility equal to that of the isolated utterance of Jesus. This speech, although on the whole excellently well attested—not, it is true, by the latest, but by the three older Gospels—presents so many difficulties, that one's perplexity is equally great whether it is taken in hand critically or uncritically, whether its genuineness be admitted or denied.[2] Strict believers are perplexed at seeing Jesus calculate the future from such a Jewish standpoint and give to it such a speedy and limited termination; and in order to save him from the reproach of illusion, the letter of his utterances has been maltreated, the periods have been extended, or the forms and the periods, definitely as they are stated, have been—in part not without complaints that the Evangelists have given a gross and coarse version of what was said—volatilized into indefinite ideal pictures and perspectives.[3] The freer view is

---

[1] That in Matt. xxiv. 2, and particularly 15 sqq., the destruction of the city itself is included, is however maintained by most critics, from the Fathers down to Strauss, Baur and his followers, even Weizs., Schenkel, and Holtzmann ; but already Paulus, III. i. p. 141, and Fritzsche, upon the passage, remarked the opposite. Comp. more in detail upon xxiv. 15, above, I. pp. 64 sq., below, p. 238.

[2] The want of harmony between the testimony of the Synoptics and that of John was already seen by Fleck, *De Regn. Div.* p. 483. The whole school of Schleiermacher also consoled themselves with that want of harmony, either renouncing faith in the Synoptics or (in spite of Neander's protest, p. 501) spiritualizing them.

[3] The ways of escape on this side, in Strauss, 4th ed. II. pp. 347 sqq., also in De Wette, Meyer, Bleek. Particularly suspicious is the *close connection of the return*, the closing event, *with the history of the time*, the events that preceded the close. Help has been sought in the following hypotheses: (1) this connection does not exist at all in reality: either everything, including Matt. xxiv. 15, belongs to the close (prophetata de fine, noviss. tempore), Iren. 5, 25, 5, or everything is only what comes before in time (the rationalists; partly down to Olshausen, Weisse, Hase, Bunsen, Schenkel). (2) The connection exists, but it is possible to separate: in particular, Luke keeps the periods more apart (Schleier., Neander, recently Gess, pp. 134 sqq.); but in Matt. also the closing time does not begin until xxv. 31 (Lightfoot, Wetst., Flatt), or at earliest xxv. 1 (Rud. Hofmann), or after xxiv. 22, so however that afterwards long periods between the destruction and the second advent are described (Ebr. 1842); at least Matt. xxiv. 14 (as also much more plainly Luke xxi. 24) indicates a long course of events in time (Kern, *Tüb. Zeitschr.* 1836, pp. 141 sq.). (3) A separation can no longer be made, and Jesus himself did not make a separation; but

ON THE MOUNT OF OLIVES. 231

also exposed to danger. In case these sayings are admitted to be genuine, there is the danger of ascribing to Jesus conceptions of time the most limited and contradicted by the actual result ; but in case the sayings are resolutely denied, there is the danger of robbing this life of its principal features, nay, of completely annihilating the great anticipations and the sacred claims of this life, that thus is made to suffer defeat in the conflict.[1]

Here, however, first of all, it behoves us to obtain, more minutely than in ordinary cases, all the information we can concerning the contents and compass, the age and credibility, of the great speech which in a tolerably uniform shape, and evidently based upon a common, independently used source, appears in all the three Gospels.[2] We find here many important grounds of

help can be derived from the theory of Jesus' so-called perspective mode of viewing the future, after the manner of the prophets, in which the near and the distant flow together (Bengel, Hengstenberg, Olsh., Kern, Beck, Krabbe, Pressensé; on the other hand, already Neander, p. 500). (4) It is no longer possible to make the separation, even though Jesus did it; but the "confusion of the periods" (Pressensé, p. 587) is explained by the fact that the Evangelists, in part already the Apostles, have confounded the invisible with the visible advent of Jesus, comp. Eichh. and Kuinöl; more recently Neander, De Wette, Meyer, Bleek, Hausrath, partly also Weisse, Schenkel, Ewald, Hase, Krabbe, Press., Gess.

[1] The former in Paulus, III. i. pp. 343 sqq.; comp. Strauss, 4th ed. II. p. 347 ; the latter, the critical school. Strauss believes in error on the part of Jesus, II. pp. 341, 356. Speaks with more reserve in *New Life of Jesus*, Eng. trans., I. pp. 327 sq. Very gross opinion of the Fragmentist, that the Apostles invented it all with the aim of recovering their mode of life exempt from care, pp. 184, 201 sqq.

[2] Its limits, Matt. xxiv. 1—44 (or 51) corresp. to Mark xiii. 1—37, Luke xxi. 5—36. Recently the belief in one feeding source has become almost universal : the Gospels are seen to stand mutually independent, yet united by a given something. Notwithstanding the industrious search after the date of origin, by Baur, Köstlin, Hilg. (not to speak of R. Hofm., *Weiderkunft Chr.* 1850, p. 10, and Gess, pp. 131 sqq.), the analysis of the speech about the future has not been sufficiently carried out (Hilg. regards Matt. x. as the original eschatological speech, which should have followed chap. xxiii., chaps. xxiv. xxv. being of later origin); on the other hand, Weizs. and Pfleid. have recently begun to point out other dissimilarities in the speech than merely the antithesis of particulars and universals. Pfleiderer's essay in the *Jahrb. deutscher Theol.* 1868, pp. 134 sqq. (*Composition of the Eschatological Speech in Matt.* xxiv.) treats verses 4, 5, 9—14, 23—28, 32 sqq., as interpolations, disturbing the connection, the progress, intentionally introducing retardation. Here are many things correct in detail; but the other Gospels are too little taken into account; and if only retardation was aimed at, why not such in the centre, ver. 29 ? The literature on the eschatological speech, particularly in Hase, p. 228; Bleek, II. p. 349.

doubt. In the first place, this speech has many counterparts, the matter of which comes more or less into immediate contact with it, as more particularly the address about the future which Luke, in chap. xvii., has placed immediately before Jesus' entrance into Judæa.[1] Here there arises not only the question whether the speech on the Mount of Olives justifiably combines in itself all this important material; but also the wider one, whether it can compete with its rival in originality and naturalness. We shall return to that rival, and shall then find at least that it offers on the whole greater guarantees. But we now confine our attention to the speech on the Mount of Olives. This is presented to us by all the Gospels, even by Luke, in a well-attested manner, in a definite situation, wanting altogether to the other speeches. Yet it is very soon discovered that in its entirety it is by no means to be regarded as an original speech uttered by Jesus. Even when we purge it of the alterations and interpolations which the several Gospels have very evidently to a greater or less degree introduced, there still remain against its primitive form—so far as that can be restored—notwithstanding a full recognition of the grandeur of its plan, the two objections of a lack of unity and a lack of probability.[2]

---

[1] Similar portions in Matt. vii. 15 (comp. xxiv. 5, 24), x. 17—23 (comp. xxiv. 9—13, yet more Luke xxi. 12—19; Mark xiii. 9—13). Luke xii. 11, 12 (comp. xxi. 12—19), xii. 35—46, particularly xvii. 22—37 (comp. Matt. xxiv. 22 sq., 27 sq., 37—41).

[2] The original form may, in brief, have been this: (1) Matt. xxiv. 1—8 (ver. 3 shorter); (2) Mark xiii. 9—13 (with erasure of the inserted verse 10); (3) Matt. xxiv. 15—25 (verses 17 sq. also assumed in Luke xxi. 21, notwithstanding xvii. 31; verses 26 sq., in Luke rightly placed elsewhere xvii. 23 sq.; the point of junction evident from Matt. xxiv. 25, Mark xiii. 23); (4) Matt. xxiv. 29—51 (with exception of verses 37—41, which passage corresponds to Luke xvii. 26 sqq., and of small additions in verse 30, upon which comp. Luke xxi. 27, Mark xiii. 26. The prejudices in favour of Luke (Schleier., Neander), and of Mark, or of Mark and Luke (comp. Holtzm., Schenkel, Bunsen, Volkmar) have already been refuted or lessened by Strauss, De Wette, Meyer, Bleek. Matthew is here not absolutely original (verses 3, 9—14, 26—28, 30 [partly], 37—41); on the other hand, in detail mostly superior and original, xxiv. 1—3, 8, 14 (fin.), 15, 29. The superiority of Luke over Matthew lies principally in xxi. 12—19, and in the absence of the additions, Matt. xxiv. 26—28, 37—41. At the same time, he is to a greater degree than Mark second to Matthew, not only in periphrastic expression, but in the alteration of the oracle, which is plainly made to refer to the speedy destruction of Jerusalem, and whose final close is retarded,

ON THE MOUNT OF OLIVES.   233

There is less lack of formal unity—although breaks and joins are not wanting—than of material unity.[1] For how much of self-destroying contradiction has been crowded into these lines! The speech of Jesus gives excellent practical moral admonitions and consolations for the disciples, and at the same time busies itself with unfruitful heathen and Jewish higher politics, and indeed with an exhibition of heathen-Jewish-Christian signs of the times.[2] The speech addresses itself exclusively to the Apostles, whose future position in Israel appears to be isolated and menaced on all sides. At the same time, however, it addresses itself as a faithful friend to the whole Jewish nation, and urgently counsels migration from Jerusalem.[3] The speech is limited in its whole spirit to the position of the Apostles and of Jesus within the Israelitish nation; and nevertheless it adopts—at least in the form given to it in Matthew and Mark—the perspective of the universal propagation of Christianity, although the hatred of all, or, as Matthew has it, of all nations seems to contradict this.[4] The speech begins with the destruction, with the passing away, of the temple; yet it afterwards announces the most elaborately

comp. xxi. 9, 12 sqq., 20—24, 25—28, 31, 34—36. On the other hand, Gess (p. 135) overflows with praise of the words in Luke xxi. 24, which he holds to be genuine and weighty, and to have been rescued from oblivion by Luke's industrious search, while recent criticism regards them rather as of later date. On the whole, Mark shares in the superiorities of Luke, but at the same time holds himself back somewhat from his neoterisms. He also has (with Matt. xxiv. 22—25) xiii. 20—23, whilst Luke has very intelligibly rejected it. Yet he is secondary in xiii. 1—3, 10, 14, 18, 23 sq., 29, 33—37. Volkmar, on his part, regards Mark as author of the reprisal against the Johannine Apocalypse with its calculations of the future (in which, however, Mark himself is caught), admitting (like Weizs.) the possibility of a preceding apocalyptic pamphlet. According to him (pp. 538 sqq.), Matthew has interpolated from Luke xii. and xvii. Comp. in general, above, I. pp. 64, 95, 114. Details below.

[1] A want of connection, depending upon the working up together of different materials, is evident in Mark xiii. 9 sqq. and parallel passages. The combination of the separate Gospels (previous note) is not here the question.

[2] Comp. only Matt. xxiv. 32 sqq., *and* the series of signs, xxiv. 4—29.

[3] Matt. xxiv. 9 sqq. *and* 16 sqq.

[4] Matt. xxiv. 9 sqq. (x. 17—23) *and* xxiv. 14, but also already xxiv. 9. In Matthew, verse 14—in Mark, xiii. 10—is very evidently interpolated, and in this section most of the corrections have been made here and there in verses 9—14. Comp. against both, Luke xxi. 12 sqq., 24.

detailed desecration by the heathen.¹ Finally comes what is most decisive. The speech contains the most exact serial arrangement of the times, the most definite enumeration of both the great and the insignificant facts of the future, and is therefore in truth a computation of the periods and the days until the second advent. And yet it closes with numerous warnings of the sudden coming of this second advent, and with the remarkable acknowledgment that even he himself does not know the day or the hour,—a warning and a confession which at one blow overthrow the whole of this sharply outlined cloudland of the future, the whole of this edifice of artificial prospective calculation.²

These impossibilities, which are at once betrayed by the very composition of the speech about the future, are confirmed when one simply asks, "Could Jesus thus speak?" Without staying to test the singular and quite unusual citation from the book of Daniel, or the views of Judaism, Christianity, heathenism, the Sabbath, the temple and temple desecration, adopted in the speech, it is enough simply to ask, Could he be such a speaker about the future?³ At the close of a great life it often happens,

---

¹ Matt. xxiv. 2 and 15.

² The members of the triplet: (*a*) Matt. xxiv. 6; Mark xiii. 7 (retardation of Luke, in respect to Matthew, in Luke xxi. 9); (*b*) Matt. xxiv. 14 fin. (omitted from Luke and Mark), then verse 15; (*c*) Matt. xxiv. 29, curtailed in Luke xxi. 25 (comp. similarly 9, 28, 31) and Mark xiii. 24 (comp. 29). On the other hand, renunciation of calculation and certainty (after Zech. xiv. 7; comp. Deut. xxxii. 34), Matt. xxiv. 36, 42, and parallel passages; comp. Luke xvii. 24 sqq. The limitation of Matt. xxiv. 36 to the narrowest measure of time (R. Hofm. p. 33), or to the mere succession of events (Press. pp. 587 sq.), has been thought "trivial" by Neander, p. 499. Comp. also Weizs. p. 551. On the other hand, Volkmar (p. 539) attains to the new wisdom that Mark has fabricated the passage against the Apocalypse, with the calculations of the future in which he is yet so essentially at one! The Son of Man's ignorance stands— as Volkmar still appears not to know, although the question has been decided for years (comp. above, I. p. 138)—not merely in Mark, but also in Matthew. He thinks the narrators of Jesus' being born of a virgin—a spectre he always keeps before him, as if the story of the virgin-birth had painted a God—have not ventured to insert this passage (p. 544)!

³ Where else is such a citation from a particular book to be found, as in Matt. xxiv. 15 (Dan. ix. 27), whether we take it as spoken to the readers of Daniel or to the readers of this apocalyptical speech based upon Daniel? Comp. Dan. xii. 4 sqq.; Rev. xxii. 18, xiii. 18. Colani, p. 201. Weizs. p. 124. Citations like that in Matt.

and is often supposed to happen, that prophecy exhibits itself and raises the departing spirit, that in its immortality has projected itself into the future, above the bounds of its earthly existence.[1] This may be; yet it is, in the first place, certain that Jesus could not possibly find, in those last feverish moments, the time and the repose minutely to consider the course of the future and to exhibit it in a most exact register of events, classified in a triplet of stages and of progressive intensities. It is, in the second place, certain that the proclaimer, the representative, of unanxious rest in the bosom of God, and the preacher of the inscrutable dispensations of God, never gave himself up to calculations about the future, not even in the province of the mazes of Jewish Messianic belief, and least of all in the province of the great heathen world-politics.[2] It is certain that the strict and sober refuser of signs from heaven, though he might in his grand manner—as this speech itself gives it—detect the historical signs of the times, and connect his second advent with the dreadful catastrophe of Israel, could not possibly speak of miracles in the sun, moon, and stars, and of a "heavenly sign" of the Son of Man, unless he were no longer himself, but merely a Jew.[3] It is quite as certain that, with the humanly limited knowledge which we have always found in him, he could not look through and beyond the external events of the coming years and decades. In fact, what would he not have foreseen if we confine ourselves only to the points upon which the predictions of the speech have been verified, and cover with silence that which did not come to pass—the desecration of the temple, the non-destruction of

xix. 4 are very different, do not admonish the hearers to read, but assume that they have read.

[1] Comp. the farewells of Jacob, Joseph, Moses, Joshua, Simeon, Paul.

[2] Matt. xxiv. 6 sq. The repeated genuinely Jewish and Jewish-Christian warnings against pseudo-Messiahs (xxiv. 5, 11, 23 sq.; comp. the same at least twice in Mark xiii. 6, 21 sq., once in Luke xxi. 8; comp., on the contrary, Luke xvii. 23 against Matt. xxiv. 24) show a too great anxiety on the part of Jesus himself (comp. above, I. p. 65, V. pp. 123 sq.), and a conception of the Apostles as unstable children. Weizsäcker (p. 552) most definitely: Jesus uttered no apocalypse.

[3] Comp. only Matt. xxiv. 29 sq. with xii. 39, xvi. 1 sqq.; Luke xvii. 20.

Jerusalem, the flight from the city, the miracles of the false prophets, the second advent soon after these catastrophes ? It seems he would have foreseen the false Messiahs of the wilderness under the emperors Claudius and Nero, and whom, in spite of their very ridiculous character, he would have taken *au serieux;* the contemporaneous famines and earthquakes of the Roman empire; the wars of the Romans and the Parthians; perhaps even the sanguinary downfall of the Roman dynasty of the Julii; the interregnum under Galba, Otho, Vitellius; and last, the accession of the iron Flavii to the imperial throne. He would have foreseen the horrible administration of the Zealots in the Holy Land; the sufferings and the examinations of Peter and Paul before the Agrippas, father and son, before Felix and Festus; perhaps the baptism of blood of the young Church in general at Rome and at Jerusalem.[1] We can quickly escape from all this perplexity, from this extensive knowing and this extensive non-knowing, not by the assumption of a medley in Jesus' divine-human or even purely human seer-gift, but by the assumption of a late authorship belonging to the boundary-time of knowing and non-knowing, and by a glance at the restless attempts of the later Jews and Jewish-Christians to calculate future events, attempts which, as the fruit of the pioneer in that direction, the book of Daniel, are so tangibly placed before us in the books of

---

[1] The Fragmentist (pp. 184, 201 sqq.) speaks derisively of the unfulfilled predictions. On the other hand, Paulus, Fr., De Wette, and in part also Meyer and others, speak in the interest of the real, but not purely supernatural, prophesying of Jesus. With regard to what was fulfilled (ex eventu: on which comp. the Roman ridicule of Josephus, *B. J.* 3, 8, 9), I briefly refer—as well as to Baur, who admitted the non-fulfilments down to the destruction, but, on the other hand, by transposing the Gospel of Matthew to the time of Hadrian (about A.D. 134), found everything clear (*Kanon. Ev.* pp. 605 sq.)—to Karl Köstlin's adoption of the destruction under Titus as the limit, in his *Synopt. Evang.* pp. 18 sqq., 113 sqq.; Hilg. *Zeitschr.* 1868, pp. 50 sqq.; Hofm. p. 35. Meyer, in his Commentary, has confined himself to denial of the points of similarity; whilst others, as Krabbe, R. Hofmann, lay stress thereon as evidence of prediction. Bunsen (pp. 444 sq.) indeed found the migration of the nations and the oracle not yet exhausted. The only thing capable of refutation in Köstlin was the ascription of the horror of the destruction to the murderous band of Zealots and Sicarii in the temple, when mention had already been made of a $\mu\epsilon\mu\iota\alpha\sigma\mu\acute{\epsilon}\nu\eta\ \pi\acute{o}\lambda\iota\varsigma$, Jos. *B. J.* 4, 5, 2.

Enoch and Ezra, the Ascension of Moses and the Sibylline Books, and in the Revelation of John. That it was not Jesus, but this Judaism, which arranged and linked together those signs of the future, is shown chiefly in the similarity—just here surprising—of many of these predictions, and, for example, in the fact that only zealous Jewish-Christians, and by no means Jesus, could object to fleeing on the Sabbath, or could anxiously dread a desecration of the temple by heathen idolatrous worship.[1]

This piece of writing, therefore, is to be ascribed unquestionably, not to Jesus, but to a Jewish-Christian who lived towards the close of the apostolic period, and who, in view of the impending catastrophe of the temple and of the holy city, dedicated to Christians and Jews the revelations, counsels, and consolations of Jesus, and did this evidently at once in writing and

---

[1] Similarity of description of the coming of the day of the Lord in the Old Testament. Joel ii. 10 sqq., 30 sqq., iii. 15; Isaiah xiii. 4 sqq.; Jer. iv. 23 sqq.; Ezekiel vii. 2 sqq., xxxii. 7 sqq.; comp. Book of Enoch i. 80. Fixed times and calculations (ha-et ba, karob, ad kez), Joel ii. 1; Isaiah xiii. 6, 9, 22; Ez. vii. 2, 6 sq.; Hab. ii. 3; particularly Daniel vii. 12, 22, viii. 17 sqq., ix. 26 sq., xi. 27, 35, xii. 13. The ὠδῖνες, Matt. xxiv. 8 (Woes), are the chabalim, cheble hammashiach, calamitates M. (Lightfoot, pp. 319, 454), bitter with sweet fruit, chiefly out of Micah iv. 9; Is. lxvi. 7 sqq. Only as time of extremity, Hosea xiii. 13; Is. xiii. 8; Jer. xiii. 21, xxii. 23. Comp. Schöttgen, II. p. 550. Berth. pp. 43 sqq. Of the later literature, comp. upon Matt. xxiv. 6 sq., 4 Ezra xiii. 31: ἄλλοι ἄλλους λογίσονται καταπολεμεῖν, πόλις πόλιν καὶ τόπος τόπον καὶ ἔθνος κατ᾽ ἔθνους κ. βασιλ. κατὰ β. Soh. chad. f. 8, 4 : bella in mundo excitabuntur, gens erit contra gentem et urbs c. urbem. *Beresh. Rabb.* 42, f. 41, 1 : si videris regna contra se invicem insurgentia, tunc attende et adspice pedem Messiæ. On verse 19, Schöttgen, p. 211. On verses 20, 22, Lightfoot, p. 365; Schöttgen, p. 212. On Matt. xxiv. 21, as well as Dan. xii. 1, *Mos. Assumpt.* 8: cito adveniet in eos ultio et ira, quæ talis non fuit in illis a sæculo usque ad illud tempus. Comp. Ex. xi. 6; Ez. xvi. 16; 1 Macc. ix. 27. On Matt. xxiv. 12, 4 Ezra v. 2: πληθυνθήσεται ἡ ἀδικία ὑπὲρ ἣν εἶδες νῦν καὶ ὑπὲρ ἣν ἤκουσάς ποτε. Comp. in general, Lightfoot, pp. 363 sqq.; Schöttgen, II. pp. 509 sqq.; Bertholdt, p. 48; Gfrörer, I. ii. pp. 195 sqq. Strauss, 4th ed. II. p. 348; Hofmann, pp. 37 sqq.; Hilg. *Zeitschr.* 1868, pp. 52 sqq. Only not exactly a use of Ezra (Hilg.). How could Jesus (xxiv. 20) find the flight on the Sabbath open to objection (which Mark xiii. 18 drops out), when his principle and his practice in the conflict about the Sabbath, Matt. xii. 1 sqq., were so liberal? How could he, notwithstanding Matt. xxi. 13, entertain anxiety about the temple, which lay more remote from his consciousness in general; and how could he, after Luke xiii. 1 and Matt. xxii. 21 (in spite of Matt. xx. 25), ascribe to the Romans this shameful deed (see above, I. p. 308), which was not perpetrated until *after* *Caligula* (A.D. 39)? Comp. the similarity in 2 Thess. ii. 4.

not orally.¹ It is plain that he wrote before the destruction, nay even before the investment of Jerusalem, therefore before the spring of A.D. 70, since, in accordance with the prediction of Daniel, he feared only a heathen desecration of the temple in the manner of Antiochus or Caligula, and counselled Jews and Christians, in the face of this horror, to migrate from Jerusalem and Judæa, and to await upon the hills the speedy redemption of the immediately returning Messiah.² The more exact point of time is visibly the approach of the storm of war from subjugated Galilee towards Jerusalem, and—if we listen to Matthew in particular—the perpetration of the sanguinary and shameful deeds of the revolutionary party at Jerusalem after the spring of A.D. 68, with which deeds was certainly connected the increasing persecution of the Christians.³ It is probable that the Easter

[1] A purely Jewish, not Jewish-Christian writing, the existence of which Colani (*Les Croyances Mess.* p. 208) asserted, Weizsäcker (pp. 121 sqq., 551 sq.) accepted (on the ground of the similarity of Matt. xxiv. 22 with Barn. 4, an Enoch-Apocalypse; comp. Book of Enoch 80); on the other hand, Pfleiderer, *Jahrb. deutsche Theol.* 1868, pp. 134 sqq., rightly again supposed it to be written by a Jewish-Christian, since the core of it is Christian (29—31, also 15—22).

[2] Flight, Is. xiii. 14. Hills, Ez. vii. 16; Gen. xix. 17. Frequently it is assumed that the writer had overlived the destruction of Jerusalem; thus—after Credner—Strauss, Baur, Köstlin, Hilg., Volkmar. On the other hand, Colani, Weizs. and Pfleiderer recently, have rightly combatted this. The desecration of the temple (comp. above, I. pp. 64 sq.; recently also Pfleiderer, *l. c.*), assumed by the author on the ground of Daniel ix. 27 (comp. Hilg. p. 53), did not actually come to pass, and just as little did the subsequent flight out of Judæa. Strauss, 4th ed. II. p. 350, passes over this instance with the remark that the author had incorrectly made Daniel refer to the destruction of the temple, and indeed also of the city. Hilg. still abides (1868, p. 53) by this unfortunate exposition, as if he could explain ἑστὼς, which (above, I. p. 65; comp. Bunsen, p. 444) can be made to refer only to the sacrifice to the standards under Titus. Hilg. also speaks of a pouring of the wild soldiery (of whom, after Paulus, Hofm. p. 40, Schenkel, p. 257, Volkmar, p. 542, think, in connection with βδελ. ἐ.) out from the destroyed city over the country; wherefore then everything in Judæa was to flee to the hills. But this outpouring of the soldiery is not historically attested. With the εὐθέως (see R. Hofm. p. 28) of Matthew, the secure support of his fidelity in contrast to what was traditional, and which Volkmar, p. 546, does not argue away with his careless verdict, Hilg. (p. 54) well compares, *Mos. Ass.* 7: ex quo facto finientur tempora, momento finietur cursus, quando horæ IV venerint. To this I add c. 8: cito adveniet ultio, &c.; 10: protinus vindicabit illos ab inimicis.

[3] The Galilean war was at an end in the late autumn of A.D. 67 (*B. J.* 4, 2, 5); from that time Jerusalem was (*B. J.* 4, 3, 1), as it knew itself, the point aimed at,

oracle of Jesus, which this witness brought into circulation, appeared as a pamphlet, not as part of a Gospel; for the seriousness of the situation required it to be so and not otherwise, and the whole, regarded both externally and internally, gives the impression of mastership in this apocalyptic province and of seclusion. And, finally, it is possible that it coincided with that oracle which, according to ancient testimony, admonished the Christians of Jerusalem before the war to go out of the city, and induced them to retreat to Pella in Peræa. It must, however, be admitted that the ancient account in Eusebius points rather to a new special revelation of God or of Christ, than to a publication of an earlier utterance on the Mount of Olives.[1]

and from the beginning of the year 68 (B. J. 4, 7, 2, comp. 4, 4, 5 sq., shows Easter) accumulated the horrors of the Zealots and Goëtes (B. J. 4, 2, 1) specially described by Matthew. Matt. x. 23 shows also the persecution of the Christians, which in such a time (as also in that of Bar-Kochba's, Justin, *Ap.* I. 31) were very natural (above, p. 53, note 2), and gave occasion to the migration of the Christians. Matt. x. 23 does not say that the Apostles shall not have finished their mission to Israel before the Messiah comes, but in their flights they shall not have exhausted all the cities before the Messiah shall make an end of the distress. The flight of the *people* (Matt. xxiv. 20, comp. 32) began in the spring of A.D. 68 (B. J. 4, 6, 3). The higher classes went as early as the autumn of 66 (B. J. 2, 20, 1). We are forbidden to think of Easter or of July A.D. 69 (Matt. xxiv. 7) by Matt. xxiv. 20.

[1] Comp. Eus. 3, 5; above, I. p. 68, note 3. Colani, *Croy. Mess.* pp. 208 sq., and Pfleiderer, p. 141, assume the identity of Matt. xxiv. with that oracle in Eusebius, evidently simpler and more original than the Revelation of John. Even Volkmar, p. 542, allows it to be used by his doctrine-inventor Mark. Köstlin's doubt of the identity (p. 119) is based upon the above noted distinction, which, however, may be dependent upon the inexactness of the communication of Eusebius. I must here add that if this pamphlet-apocalypse (against above, I. p. 68) probably belongs to the spring of A.D. 68 (see previous note; Colani and Pfleiderer think of A.D. 67, Pfleiderer the latter end of 67), as afterwards the great Johannine Revelation belongs to Easter, A.D. 69, the composition of the original Gospel of Matthew *before* the destruction loses *somewhat* in probability. It would then have to be assumed that it was written (comp. xxiv. 29) soon after this destruction (comp. xxiv. 15, 22), and perhaps already with reference to the Apocalypse (in xxiv. 30; comp. Zech. xii. 10; Book of Enoch i.; see above, I. p. 67, note 4; much more certainly in Luke xxi. 24, &c.), but at any rate before A.D. 72 (xvii. 24). To the εὐθέως (with somewhat longer space, Heg. ap. Eus. 2, 23; Justin, *Ap.* I. 32) would Matt. then have given retardation, not only by the already earlier verses 21—25, but also by the— by *him* introduced—verses 26—28 (Luke xvii. 23). The most extreme limit for the rise of this Gospel would thus be A.D. 70 72 (above, IV. p. 331). But does not xxiii. 35 point, again, *distinctly* to A.D. 68, and not to the later horrors (B.J. 4, 6, 1; 4, 9, 8 sqq.; 5, 1, 3 sqq.); and could the author, even if he were deriving his material from a source the text of which

Whilst the whole of the farewell address thus appears to resolve itself into nothing, we must not, on the other hand, hide the fact that the seer of the seventh decade, whose oracle our Gospels have incorporated, could scarcely have lacked all historical support justifying him, not only in disclosing coming events in God's name, but also in placing in the mouth of Jesus this enlarged and extended future. It is also a fact that a part of this historical glance at the future by Jesus lies before us in the announcement of the fall of the temple made at the thoroughly appropriate and scarcely altogether fictitious halt of observation on the Mount of Olives. We possess the right, nay the duty, of ascribing to Jesus and to *his* Easter, whatever in the great speech that is otherwise historically well attested, whatever happily corresponds to his certified manner of thinking and speaking, and whatever is in harmony with the situation in which he spoke. In this we have the additional support of the evidence of an imperfect and artificially effected welding of these most ancient passages with the copious additions of the editor.[1] This being admitted, we shall first of all recognize as the production of Jesus the two chief detail of the tableau, the destruction—not the desecration—of the temple, and the second advent of the Messiah as the redeemer of the people after the divine judgment executed upon the tower and the lords of the tower. Indeed, in the definite formulæ of the second advent before the then existing generation had passed away, of the saving of the nation in the midst of the fall, and of the sending forth of the angels by the Son of Man, we shall welcome already well-known genuine points of view and

he wished to preserve as much as possible, in the exact moment of the non-fulfilment (xxiv. 15 sqq.), put the erring prediction in the mouth of Jesus? Here all logic ceases, whilst sound logic perceives that later writers, farther from the events, could do this more easily. Finally, what stands in the way of the assumption that the Evangelist, *writing in the summer* of A.D. 68 (xxiii. 35, xxiv. 20; comp. *B.J.* 4, 5, 2—5) incorporated the little apocalypse which had just appeared into his work?

[1] Reference has already been made, above, p. 233, to such imperfect connections, both formal and material. And what is in detail more striking than the conversion of the temple *destruction*, Matt. xxiv. 2, into a *desecration*, xxiv. 15, perhaps an abasement similar to, yet different from, that in Rev. xi. 1?

expressions of Jesus.[1] The sufferings of the Apostles as the immediate successors of Jesus were also a familiar topic with Jesus, though without knowledge and prediction of the details. From this dark and pessimistic glance at the present, from this solemn and clear look into the future, they could not be altogether absent; nay, thrown into a new form and gilded with hopeful glances towards the Father, these predictions are too characteristic to allow the interpolation of isolated later facts to justify a doubt of the whole.[2] Just as credible is the beautiful and remarkably apposite Easter parable—certainly not the cunningly devised work of a later author—of the putting forth of leaves by the early fig-tree, which pointed to the approaching harvest. The same is true of the self-conscious and noble saying that the predictions of Jesus would be more enduring than heaven and earth.[3] Just so, finally—the genuinely human and the limited becoming lofty, uncertainty and the unsolved obscurity of the future becoming prophecy—a complete genuineness lies in the saying about the ignorance even of the Son as to the time and the hour, and in the saying about the sudden thief-like surprise of a heartless humanity by the lightning-like outburst from heaven of the second advent.[4] These are the fundamental lines, or at least the fragments, of an address about the future, which we would gladly piece together, combine into one body and clothe with flesh and blood, were we not perplexed by the thought, not only that more than one calculation of probability does not work out correctly, but also that the individual sentences perhaps belong to different times and occasions, and that the individual points of view, the illegibility and the legibility of the future, appear to directly exclude each other, at least from the unity of

---

[1] Matt. xxiv. 2 and 30 sq., 34. Comp. also xvi. 27, xiii. 41, and (respecting the *nexus* of the second advent with the catastrophe of the world) xv. 13 sq., xxi. 13, 33, 41, xxiii. 33, 38 sq., xxiv. 28, xxvi. 64. Comp. above, IV. pp. 284 sqq.

[2] Mark xiii. 9—13 and parallel passages, with interpolations, upon which see also below, p. 243, n. 3. The place of this passage is to be sought here (and not Matt. x. or Luke xii.) so much the rather because all the Synoptics are agreed about this position.

[3] Matt. xxiv. 32—35. [4] Matt. xxiv. 36, 42—44 (51).

one and the same hour. The case is not, however, so bad.[1] The Mount of Olives' station may in general pass as reliable. And the single tangible *momenta* of the speech, betraying their unity through the forced connections of the later apocalyptist, adapt themselves to each other without needing any violence. Thus the delineation of the outline of future things—whose figures the limitation and the humility of Jesus could not exhaust, whose exact relation to the final end the departing Master could not measure—follows in a perfectly natural and genuinely human way the confession of the ignorance of the Son of Man concerning the day and the hour; and then comes the admonition to watchfulness against the incalculable epoch of the commencement of the kingdom of heaven.[2]

On the basis of these considerations, the course and contents of the actual speech of Jesus may have been the following. After the brief and solemn prediction, spoken on the way over the Mount of Olives, concerning the temple and the stones of the temple, Jesus sat down probably on the summit of the Mount—as Mark rightly has it—just opposite to the eastward-looking temple hill.[3] Jesus' terrible prediction the more powerfully impressed the souls of the disciples the more the simple

---

[1] Weizs. also (pp. 549, 551 sq.) regarded as portions belonging to Jesus, fig-tree, ignorance, thief-like coming, survival of the Apostles and of the current generation. He even recognizes the warning against false Messiahs and the preaching to the world. The admission (p. 126) is, however, peculiar, that Jesus himself perhaps made use of an apocalyptic Book of Enoch, in which Matt. xxiv. 22 (comp. Barn. 4) was contained. See above, p. 238, n. 1. He is also reminded of the Book of Enoch by the well-known Papias-tradition of the vines (above, I. p. 39). On the other hand, how much will Weisse and even Schenkel accept as original, it is true with symbolical interpretation! Volkmar (p. 549) is able to save only Matt. xxiv. 35, 42; but also the certainly later Mark xiii. 37.

[2] That Jesus gave forth something concerning the course of the future (and indeed not merely the prospect of the survival of the contemporaries, Weizs. p. 552), certainly follows from the sign of the fig-tree; and as concrete objects we can see only the persecution of the Apostles and the destruction of the temple. But the less he saw of detail, and the less he was able sharply to delineate the sequence even of the destruction of the temple and the second advent, the more could he speak of things that could not be calculated and of surprises, of which, in the face of the sharp delineations of the apocalyptist, he could not possibly say more.

[3] Matt. xxiv. 3; Mark xiii. 3.

Galileans had admired the temple, and the more they—despite all that had taken place—had bound up their faith and their pride with the sanctuary of the nation. Their reflections found voice in a question. The most intimate, i.e. the Twelve, according to Mark's individualizing description the two pairs of brothers, went to Jesus and said, "Tell us, when shall this come to pass?"[1] The answer appeared to be irrelevant, but in reality it was most relevant and most needful; it pointed to the last insolent deeds of the lords of the sanctuary who would not be overthrown but with the overthrow of the temple itself. "Take heed to yourselves before men," said Jesus; "for they will deliver you up to councils, and in their synagogues they will beat you. But when they deliver you up, be not anxious how or what ye shall speak; for it shall be given you in that hour what ye shall speak; for it is not ye that are the speakers, but the Spirit of your Father who speaks in you. And a brother will deliver a brother to death, and a father a child, and children will rise up against parents and cause them to be put to death. And ye will be hated by all for my name's sake; but he that endures to the end shall be saved."[2] In the depressed and solemn mood which came over him, he saw the immediate future of his disciples in the gloomiest light, saw it just as the prophetic pictures had long since presented it to him—nay, he saw it darker than it really was when it came. And as the temple spaces and the lords of the temple,

[1] Mark xiii. 3, in the correct sequence of position: Peter, James, John, Andrew. Quite erroneously, Luke allows the possibility that persons from among the people, as it were the nation itself, asked xxi. 7, as in fact the whole speech appears to be delivered in the temple before the people. How often has the late Luke thus anti-Jewishly generalized! The question itself is—as most critics see (Hofm. p. 17; Schenkel, p. 250; Weizs. p. 549)—the most simple in Luke xxi. 7, enlarged in Matt. xxiv. 3; but Mark xiii. 4 again combines.

[2] Mark xiii. 9—13; Luke xxi. 12—19; Matt. xxiv. 9—14 (x. 17—23). Comp. the parallel opening of the apocalyptist, Matt. xxiv. 4; and Paulus, III. i. p. 343. Luke is manifoldly periphrastic; Matt. and Mark force in the mission to the world. Comp. above, p. 233, n. 4. There may be a doubt about the trials—given by all three Gospels—before kings and governors (procurators), before whom testimony is to be borne (comp. the alteration of Luke xxi. 13); but can Jesus have thought of a trial before such a tribunal whilst John and himself experienced nothing of the kind? He could, in his position, the most readily think of a procurator, but not of Antipas or of the not yet existing king Agrippa.

with his daily danger and the morrow's threatened violence, floated before his mental eyes as the place and the instruments of his own path of suffering, so also in reference to his disciples he thought of synagogue and temple judgments; and he could only console them, as he consoled himself, with the presence and aid of the Father, and with the path of patience that led to Messianic glory.[1]

"But then," continued he, after the distress of those days, when their measure shall be filled and the blind leaders shall have fallen with the blind into the pit, "then shall they see the Son of Man coming upon the clouds of heaven with power and great glory.[2] And he will send out his angels and gather his elect from the four winds, from one end of the heavens to the other.[3] But learn a parable from the fig-tree. When its branch begins to become tender and it puts forth leaves, then ye know that the harvest is near. Therefore ye also, when ye see all this, know that it is near, at the doors.[4] Verily I say unto you, this generation shall by no

---

[1] The passage Mark xiii. 12 (Matt. xxiv. 10) suggests the similar passage Matt. x. 35, which is based on Micah vii. 6, and belongs to Galilee. Above, IV. p. 318; V. p. 51. Interesting parallel from A.D. 68, Jos. *B.J.* 4, 3, 4: τὴν καθ' αὑτὸν ἕκαστος σωτηρίαν ἠγάπα. Treachery, *ib.* 3, 8, 1.

[2] Matt. xxiv. 29 sq. and parallel passages. As the eschatological predictions in verses 15—28 either are not genuine or belong elsewhere, as also the eschatological colouring of verses 29 sq., is untenable, the connection of the parts of the speech of Jesus is here for the most to be restored only by *hypothesis*.

[3] Mark xiii. 26 sq. (Matt. xxiv. 30 sq.) has already been attacked by Weisse (I. pp. 594 sq.) with veritable passion. Such a strange vagary, such a phantasm, such an expression of the most narrow-minded superstitious belief in Daniel, could not have come from the mouth of Jesus; he may have thus spoken in a symbolical sense, but without attaching to the words a literal meaning, which later men (as early as the Apostles) first attached to them. Similar views in Hase, Schenkel, and most recently Volkmar, the champion of the great sober man against such distasteful distortion. But see above, IV. pp. 285 sqq. With the expression in Matt. xxiv. 31, comp.—besides Matt. xiii. 41—Deut. iv. 32, xxx. 4; Ps. xix. 6; Ez. vii. 2. If any one thinks suspiciously of Matt. xxv. 32, let him not forget x. 23, xiii. 32, 41.

[4] Scarcely from Ez. vii. 10 (the rod blossoms); comp. Hosea ix. 10; Book of Enoch, v. 1. The early fig (bikkure) comes into leaf at Easter, the harvest is at the end of June. *Ben Seb.* in Wetst. p. 503 : ab exortis foliis ad ficus CXXX days. "The blossoms lie hidden in a fleshy covering, which appears on the old branches (in Palestine in the middle of March) and ripens to fruit before the leaves appear (Pliny, 16, 49)," Winer. Comp. Lightfoot, p. 320.

means pass away until all this has come to pass.[1] The heavens and the earth shall pass away, but my words shall by no means pass away.[2] But concerning that day and the hour knows no one, not even the angels of the heavens, nor the Son of Man, but the Father only.[3] Watch, therefore, for ye know not what day your Lord comes. But observe this, that if the master of the house had known in what watch of the night the thief would come, he would have watched and would not have suffered his house to be broken through. Therefore be ye also ready, for in the hour in which ye think it not, the Son of Man comes."[4] And then he

---

[1] The idea γενεά (Hebrew, dor) quite falsely applied, from Origen until Lange, to the Christians in general, from Calov until Dorner to the Jews, by Jerome to the genus hum. In truth it designates the period of a human generation; so that most critics think of 30—40 years; Baur, with his followers (chiefly to justify the date of the passage under Hadrian), of 100 years. It allows narrower or wider limits; e.g. 100 years, Gen. xv. 16; comp. however Irenæus, 5, 30, 3. Plutarch, *De Def. Orac.* 11, speaks of such as reckon the γεν. to 108 years or even to only one. Herodotus (2, 142) and Heraclitus (in Plut. *l. c.*; comp. Thuc. 1, 14) assume 30 years (Herodotus about 33: γενεαὶ τρεῖς ἀνδρῶν ἑκατὸν ἔτεά ἐστι; Heraclitus the round number 30). On the other hand, Censorinus (3rd cent.), *De Die Nat.* 17, at any rate gives his own opinion emphatically (qui annos 30 sec. putarunt, multum videntur errasse), and defines the sæc. = γενεά as spatium vitæ longissimum. It may be that the estimate of 100 or 120 years is derived from the estimated length of the human life (Varro, *Ling. Lat.* VI. § 11: seclum spatium annorum centum vocarunt, dictum a sene, quod longissimum spatium senescendorum hom. id putarant); the assumption of a generation at any rate favours the usual smaller number. In the Gospels (Matt. xii. 41 sq., xxiv. 34), there can be no doubt it was meant that not merely the so-called longævi, among whom Baur classed the Apostle John, Ignatius, Symeon, Quadratus (comp. Heges. ap. Eus. 3, 32: παρεληλύθει ἡ γενεά, namely, of the eye-witnesses [after Trajan]), but a not small part of the contemporaries would survive unto this future; although, again, other passages (Matt. xvi. 28), based on Jesus' words or on modified traditions of them, point only to the remains of such a generation. Comp. Baur, *Jahrb.* 1849, p. 316; Zeller, 1852, p. 299. Above, IV. p. 286.

[2] Comp. the saying about the Law, Matt. v. 18 (of God, Is. xl. 8), and the remarks thereon, above, III. p. 300. Our passage speaks only of the prediction, not of the teaching, of Jesus.

[3] The mention of the Son of Man as not knowing, is not only in Mark, but also in Matthew on the authority of the oldest MSS., Sin., Vat., Bez., It., also Irenæus, 2, 28, 6 (comp. Tischendorf), whereby Volkmar's remark is set to rest (p. 544), that those who mentioned the virgin-birth did not venture to predicate such ignorance. Rather would Mark (above, I. p. 124) have ventured upon the assertion still less than Matthew, had it not been handed down! On the knowledge and ignorance of the angels, Schöttgen, p. 213. God alone knowing, Deut. xxxii. 34; Zech. xiv. 7.

[4] Matt. xxiv. 42 sq., where, after rejection of the interpolation verses 37—41, verse 42 admirably fits on to verse 36; and what follows to the end of the chapter is

gives to the parable the most useful application, in order to show to the disciples their mission as servants, and their obligations of oversight and provision in the future community. "Who, then, is the faithful and understanding servant, whom his lord has set over his household, to give them food in due season?[1] Blessed that servant whom his lord, when he is come, shall find so doing. Verily I say unto you that he will set him over all his goods. But if that evil servant says in his heart, My lord delays his coming, and begins to beat his fellow-servants, and eats and drinks with the drunken, then will the lord of that servant come in a day when he does not expect it, and in an hour when he is not aware of it, and will cut him asunder and appoint his portion with the hypocrites: there shall be wailing and gnashing of teeth."[2]

so well connected, and is so much in harmony with the parallel passages, that no one has a right to close with verse 42. In Luke we have a corresponding passage, xii. 35—40 (conglomerate of sayings in a later formation), especially verse 39, and yet the passage is also presupposed in general in xxi. 34 sqq., as also in Mark, who in xiii. 34 sqq. gives a kind of synthesis of Matt. xxiv. 43 and Luke xii. 38 sqq. Picture of the thief, Joel ii. 9.

[1] Comp. Proverbs xxxi. 15. On the "then," Volkmar (p. 546) remarks that it is to be explained only from Luke xii. 42, as afterwards the wicked servant from Luke xii. 45. But how can we (comp. next note) find the opening in Luke, verse 41, older, or overlook the greater difficulty of the expression of Matt. xxiv. 48 as compared with Luke xii. 45?

[2] Matt. xxiv. 45—51; comp. the somewhat later form in Luke xii. 41 sqq.—similarly attached to Luke xii. 35—40, as in Matthew to xxiv. 42—44—after which comes the later addition xii. 47 sq., which may treat of the relation of Jewish Christianity to Gentile Christianity. Evidently Luke xxi. 34 sqq. presupposes the same section also in the eschatological speech. The parable-form in Mark is a synthesis of Matthew and Luke; the later date is shown at once in xiii. 33, 35, 37, then also in the unfortunate medley of the Apostles' work (by day) and their night watch, of which alone, according to the context, mention should have been made. In the parable of Matthew and of Luke, mention is made simply of the responsible position of all the Apostles in relation to other believers, not of a supremacy of Peter, or of a substitution of John in Asia Minor for the martyr who died in A.D. 64, or even of the bishops as the successors of the Apostles, as Hilgenfeld, 1868, pp. 56 sq., thinks. As little is the wicked, beating servant, whose portion is among the hypocrites, Paul, the foe of the Jewish-Christians, but every perverse disciple of Jesus. Only not everything derived from unhistorical tendency-soil! The cutting asunder ($\delta\iota\chi$. Ex. xxix. 17) with saw (2 Sam. xii. 31) or sword (Susanna, 59), Hebr. shisseph, 1 Sam. xv. 33 (LXX. σφάττω, Vulg. in frusta concidit), and gasar (also batak, batar, nittach), 1 Kings iii. 25 sq. Also Rabbis: corpus dissecatur (baka, in the judgment), Schöttgen, p. 216. Comp. Luke xix. 27.

B.—AT BETHANY.

According to all appearances, the evening of the 12th of April and the following Wednesday were spent in the quiet of Bethany. As early as Tuesday evening, Jesus announced to his disciples, with solemn, incisive brevity, "Ye know that after two days is the Passover, and the Son of Man will be delivered up to be crucified."[1] Only Matthew has this last announcement of the Passion; but when we note the exactness and the reliability of these very communications concerning the Passion, we can console ourselves for the fact that Luke and Mark, having mentioned the same point of time, immediately pass on to what is weightier to them, to the resolves of the enemies, with the report of which Matthew also has accompanied that last declaration of Jesus. In a certain sense, this prediction of death is indeed the most credible, not only because it is the simplest of them all, but also because Jesus must *now* grasp his fate, and because he must *now* signify it to his adherents.[2] The utterance of Jesus by no means gave expression to a certainty that the enemies were at that moment proceeding to make their attack, or that the day of his Passion would be exactly the Passover-day. He had a sure presentiment of nothing more than that the opening of the Feast would mark the beginning of his catastrophe, and that the mode of his death would be that of the Roman cross. He was sure of the former, because his opponents had only postponed their onset, because he himself had completed the breach, and finally because his retreat and the climax of the stream of festival

---

[1] Matt. xxvi. 1 sq.; Luke xxii. 1 (indefinitely, Easter draws nigh). Mark xiv. 1 has the definite statement of the time, like Matt.

[2] Above, I. pp. 71, 102, 119; IV. pp. 268 sqq. Luke xvii. 25 has an announcement analogous to this. The natural character of the present formula is striking, particularly in contrast to the wealth of words in Matt. xx. 18 and parallel passages. All details are lacking (except the cross, which Matthew alone already has, xx. 19), even the resurrection. Nothing is said of the impression produced on the disciples, as in xx. 19, Mark x. 34. The wisdom of the most recent critics has discovered that the passage is unhistorical just because it is so important to Matthew.

visitors—which was at the same time the climax of his opponents' feeling of strength—necessarily encouraged his foes. And he believed he should die on the cross, because he plainly saw that his opponents would and must adopt the course of a regular indictment, because the procurator was on the spot, and he knew him to be mistrustful and cruel, a despiser of men, a friend of executions, acquainted with and jealously watchful of the people and their leaders.[1] Such reflections could not now be absent from the mind of Jesus, for he was always gifted with a circumspect and reflective sagacity. And still more strongly would he feel the immediate presentiment which is wont, often so inexplicably, to accompany the decisive points of men's lives; and with the personal presentiment would be connected the religious, which would cause him now to believe in a redemptive connection, through Divine Providence, of his death with the ancient sacred cult of the blood of the Paschal Lamb.[2]

On this day the thoughts and words of Jesus would naturally turn afresh to the future of his disciples, to their forlornness as well as to their task of untiring waiting and assiduous toil in the name of their Lord. The most important of these speeches has been preserved to us. The relationship between its contents and the address on the Mount of Olives has led to the two being mixed up in all kinds of ways, and that not only by Matthew, who, according to his wont, brings all the addresses about the future into one day, but partially also by Luke and Mark, nay, already by the author of the Mount of Olives' oracle himself. A speech of such a kind, by no means so well placed as here, is preserved by Luke and Matthew, by the former in the neighbourhood of the Galilean entry, and by the latter in the Mount of Olives' oracle.[3] "The days will come," said Jesus, "when ye

---

[1] Above, I. pp. 266, 304 sqq., II. p. 400.   [2] Matt. xxvi. 26 sqq.

[3] Luke xvii. 22—37 is a speech so natural, practical, and original in its ideas and in its pictures, and so admirably self-consistent, that it is undoubtedly to be used as a speech by Jesus. Comp. already Schleier., *Luk.* pp. 215 sqq., 265 sqq. The best locality, however, is (see particularly verse 37) Jerusalem; for the want of order and the transpositions of Luke are well known, although he is here not far from the right

will long to see one of the days of the Son of Man, and ye will not see it.[1] If therefore they say to you, Lo! he is in the desert, go not forth; lo! in the chambers, believe it not.[2] For as the lightning goes from the uprising and shines to the downsetting, so will be the advent of the Son of Man.[3] And as it came to pass in the days of Noah, so will it be also in the days of the Son of Man. They were eating, drinking, marrying, being given in marriage, until the day that Noah went into the ark, and the flood came and destroyed them all. Even so, also, as it came to pass in the days of Lot: they were eating, drinking, buying, selling, planting, building; but the day that Lot went out of Sodom, it rained fire and brimstone from heaven and destroyed

---

point, as he places the speech near the entry. Only the connection with the spiritual present kingdom, Luke xvii. 20 sq., is unfortunate. Above, IV. p. 13, note 1. Matthew, in the speech about the future, violently inserted from this speech xxiv. 17 sq., 26—28, 37—41. Luke took xxi. 21. Mark took xiii. 15 sq. But without doubt the original oracle had itself—as the three Gospels can show—adopted Matt. xxiv. 17 sq., Luke xxi. 21, Mark xiii. 15 sq., although the original connection and the fuller development are in Luke xvii. 31. Perhaps also that part of the oracle which stands in Matt. xxiv. 23, Mark xiii. 21, is in its original place only in Luke xvii. 23, at least in its original sense (see below, note 2).

[1] Jemot hammashiach, Lightfoot, p. 552. Recalls Matt. ix. 15.

[2] Salvation out of the desert was the watchword of the false prophets, above, II. p. 229, V. p. 123. When the temple was taken by the Romans, the Zealots begged from Titus leave to go into the desert, Jos. *B. J.* 6, 6, 3. Moses also expected out of the desert, Wetstein, p. 503. The chambers (Matt. vi. 6) = Messianic retirement, ἄγνωστος, Justin, *Trypho*, 8; above, II. pp. 254, 297. The whole sentence reminds one of Luke xvii. 20 sq., where Jesus denies to the kingdom of heaven the material coming which he, however, now in his catastrophe, claims. Luke himself has in xvii. 23 (also Mark xiii. 21) a more indefinite expression than the concrete one in Matt. xxiv. 26. But Matthew and Mark (perhaps also the author of the oracle himself) have *quite erroneously* referred these words to false prophets instead of to Jesus.

[3] This splendid figure has close analogies. In general, the glory of God appears in lightning and thunder; comp., besides Ps. xviii. 14 sq., especially Ps. lxxvii. 18, and Job xxxvii. 3. It is not exactly said that the advent itself will be marked by a display of lightning (Matt. xxiv. 30); comp. Numbers xxiv. 17; Matt. iii. 2; Luke i. 78; and Rabb.: lux Messiæ, Berth. p. 204; lux nomen Messiæ, Lightfoot, p. 635; above, II. p. 87); only the suddenness (Matt. xxiv. 43; Rev. iii. 3; 1 Thess. v. 2) and the staggering vehemence are directly expressed. Certainly δόξα, Matt. xvi. 27, will be there. On the sign of the Son of Man (signa redemptionis, above, p. 216, n. 3), Matt. xxiv. 30, comp. different explanations in R. Hofm. pp. 50 sqq., who, however, brings in even the fable of Joseph ben Gorion, 6, 53, about an appearance of a splendid form of the Son of Man above the Holy of Holies at the time of the catastrophe.

them all. In the same measure will it be in the day when the Son of Man is revealed.[1] In that day, he that shall be upon the house, let him not come down to fetch the utensils of his house; and he that is in the field, let him not turn back to fetch his cloak. Remember Lot's wife. Whosoever seeks to gain his life will lose it; and whosoever loses it will gain it.[2] I say unto you, in that night two will be upon one bed, one will be taken and the other left; two men will be in the field, two women together at the mill, one will be taken, the other left."[3] "Where, Lord?" asked the chilled and astonished disciples. "Where the carcass is, there will the eagles be gathered together."[4] He again spoke, as allusively, reticently, mysteriously as on the previous day, of the

---

[1] Luke xvii 26—30. Evidently more original than Matthew; comp. here xxiv. 37, 39. Noah, Gen. vi. 1 sqq. Lot, Gen. xix. 1 sqq. The continuous character of the sinful worldly life might be concluded from Gen. vi. 2—7, 11—13, vii. 1, then especially xix. 5 sqq., 14. Comp. 1 Peter iii. 20. The two examples also connected by the Rabbis, Wetst. p. 777; comp. 2 Peter ii. 5 sq. The carelessness, *Jalk. Rub.* f. 29, 1: homines tempore diluvii viventes rapinam et injuriam exercuerunt, peccarunt et peccare fecerunt, usque dum catarrhactæ cœli se aperuerunt. Schöttgen, p. 213. The description of the facts as in Luke xiv. 18 sqq.; Matt. xxii. 5. Schöttgen, pp. 175 sqq. Above, p. 173, note 1. If it be asked how Jesus, after giving such definite signs of the future (temple), could assume such a sense of security, such a lack of anxiety on the part of men, help towards an answer can be obtained only by supposing that in the actual speech of Jesus the εὐθέως, Matt. xxiv. 29, did not exist, the fall of the temple did not immediately bring in the end.

[2] Luke xvii. 31—33; Matt. xxiv. 17 sq., and the par. passages. Lot's wife (Gen. xix. 26) evidently well connects this little section with the previous one. The eschatological speech, Matt. xxiv. 18, has the concrete picture of the cloak in addition (against Luke xvii. 31). To preserve life, Gen. xix. 17, 20; Matt. x. 39, xvi. 25. Jewish watchword, above, IV. pp. 280, note 2, 281, note 1. The perverted watchword in the time of the war, *B.J.* 4, 3, 4; see above, p. 244, n. 1. Comp. with Luke xvii. 33, the eschatological saying, Matt. xxiv. 13, Luke xxi. 19.

[3] Luke xvii. 34 sq. (bed, mill); Matt. xxiv. 40 sq. (field, mill). The difference may be connected with the fact that Luke places the advent in the night (as also Matt. xxiv. 43; Mark xiii. 35; also by the Rabbis, the last part of the night, Wetstein, p. 503). Similar pictures by the Rabbis, Wetst. p. 214. On the mill, Ex. xi. 5.

[4] Luke xvii. 37. In Matthew unskilfully attached, xxiv. 28. The passage after Hab. i. 8 (comp. Job xxxix. 30). As symbol of judgment, Hosea viii. 1; Jer. iv. 13, xlviii. 40, xlix. 22; Ez. xxxix. 17 (Rev. xix. 17), xvii. 3; Deut. xxviii. 49. On the other hand, Ex. xix. 4 is not to be referred to here (Meyer). The πτῶμα also suggests the πολυάνδριον (field of the dead) which Antiochus wished to make of Jerusalem, 2 Macc. ix. 4, 14. Among the classics, Seneca, Ep. 46: si vultur es, cadaver exspecta! Mart. *Epigr.* 6, 62, 4: cujus vulturis hoc erit cadaver? Comp. Wetst. p. 502.

catastrophe of the fatherland. He did not mean Rome and Israel, he meant himself as the spoil-taker in the physical and moral ruin of Israel.[1]

In this speech he showed at large, in a forcible and earnest manner, the inexorable law of separation which he had already in Galilee proclaimed for the terrestrial development of his kingdom, and which was to accompany—only with still more of energetic application — the irrevocable decision of his second coming. He now gave this law a special application to the narrow circle of his disciples, showing to them—this time in distinction from yesterday to each of them according to their peculiar characters—their missions, their prospects, their gains.[2] He stimulated them by hoping that the majority of his servants would do good brave work, and that their work would receive a final blessing. He alarmed them by drawing the picture of a servant upon whom punishment and perdition would necessarily fall. Matthew, and after him Mark—so far as he can here come under our notice at all—have on the whole rightly placed, in connection with these farewell sayings, the parable-like passage about the servants to whom money was entrusted. Luke, with a distinctly unhistorical view, has placed it before the entry.[3]

---

[1] The Roman eagle was thought of by Lightfoot, Wetstein, and others, as well as R. Hofm. p. 47; but it contradicts the context. Rather (since nesher and ἀετὸς by no means forbid it), on account of the carcass, we are to think of the carrion vulture or the golden vulture, than of the eagle (Paulus, III. i. p. 390; comp. Winer, Grimm, Furrer). Still much worse is the old explanation of the carcass, as referring to men and believers (Christ and the Church). The correct explanation by most modern critics, comp. Hilg. p. 54.

[2] The parable, Matt. xxv. 14, has a similarity to that in Matt. xxiv. 45. On this very account it scarcely, as Matthew now gives it, belongs to the same day. The former treats of the relation of the Apostles as such to the community, the latter of the particular work done by each individual Apostle.

[3] Matt. xxv. 14—30; Luke xix. 11—28, where the parable is brought forward and placed before the entry of Jesus, which is thus treated as a departure. Mark xiii. 34 is evidently a brief working up together of the different parables in Matthew and Luke (thief, Matt. xxiv. 43, Luke xii. 39; master of the house in the night, Matt. xxiv. 45, Luke xii. 42, 36—38; the Apostles, Matt. xxv. 14, Luke xix. 11). Does not this contraction correspond perfectly to the treatment of the speeches in Mark (above, III. p. 17, &c.)? And has not the violence of the combination of business transactions and night-watches been already shown?

That the nucleus of the parable, which has its parallels also among the Rabbis, is primitive and genuine, is to be inferred, apart from the Gospels, from the saying of Jesus, much quoted by the most ancient writers of the Church, "Be good, faithful bankers!"[1] Thus, from his glance at the tables of the money-changers in the temple courts, he had, notwithstanding the repugnance which he felt towards them, extracted an illustration for his kingdom of heaven. The activity of the money-changers, their indefatigableness, the profits derived from their transactions, must have been to him prototypic of the activity that should be exhibited in the higher work of the kingdom of God. It is true there are some very noticeable differences in the narrative. Besides the reports in Matthew and Luke, that in the Gospel of the Hebrews, in the form it had assumed in the fourth century, is also at our service.[2] There is a difference in the number of the servants, the amount of the money entrusted to them, the kind of use to which the money was put, and the reward. It might be inferred therefrom that Jesus himself had contributed nothing to the parable besides the brief saying about the bankers, the very saying which our Gospels have omitted; and that the so contradictory parables developed out of this saying have been the artificial work of later writers and not of Jesus. In their main points, however, the different narratives agree; and a closer examination shows that the divergences of Luke and the Gospel of the Hebrews, already open to question through suspicions otherwise aroused against these sources, are a work of arbitrary fabrication.[3] The oldest form is therefore without

---

[1] Γίνεσθε τραπεζῖται δόκιμοι, Clem. *Hom.* 2, 51, &c. Above, I. p. 37. Hilg. *N. T. ex. Can.* IV. p. 27. A late Jewish parallel in *Soh. chad.* f. 47, 2: a king gives three servants a deposit (pukdana, pakdan, Heb. pikkadon). The first custodivit, the second perdidit, the third commaculavit, partem alteri custodiendam dedit. When he returns he asks for his deposit. The first laudavit et præfectum domus s. fecit (neeman beto). The second ultimo supplicio affecit. The third is kept in prison until information is given concerning his accomplice. Schöttgen, p. 217, comp. p. 198.

[2] Eus. *Theoph.*, Greek by O. F. Fritzsche in the *Monatsschrift d. wiss. Vereins* in Zürich, 1856, pp. 56 sqq., epitomized also by Hilg. *N.T. ex. Can.* IV. pp. 17, 26.

[3] Luke xix. 11 (above, p. 65) is as little (comp. Strauss, Meyer, Weisse, II. pp. 127 sqq.) original (Neander, p. 504, who believes in two parables; further, Holtzm. p. 202)

doubt to be found in Matthew. We need not here repeat all the details of the well-known parable. Each one of three servants of a lord who is travelling into a far country receives a sum of money proportionate to his ability, to his mental capacity for engaging in business transactions. One receives five talents or 30,000 francs, the second two talents or 12,000 francs, the third one talent. The first and the second double their capital, the third does nothing but bury his talent, excusing himself with the plea that he acted thus out of sheer dread of the severity and insatiable avarice of his lord, who in fact, on returning, can answer that he ought on this account to have put out the money to interest instead of merely taking care of it. The two good and faithful servants, who had been faithful in little, are set over

as its occasion. This is shown by the ten servants (rather a picture of the twelve Apostles) against the three of Matthew, the smaller amount given to the servants (to each one a mina = 100 drachmæ; Matthew, talents = 60 minæ, 6000 drachmæ), because an ἐλάχιστον (Matt. ὀλίγα) will have been assumed; by the colourless equality of the distribution (to each one mina, Matt. five, two, one talents); by the great increment of the amount entrusted to the servants, indeed artificially a ten-fold increment (= number of servants) or five-fold (Matt. two-fold); and finally by the corresponding reward, ten and five cities, comp. Schöttgen, p. 198. Besides, there are arbitrary insertions, *e.g.* verse 25. Above all, the violent introduction of the relation of the lord going to a far country to the Jewish nation instead of only to the servants, which two points of view are extremely loosely combined; and the punishment of the rebellious Jews (in Matt. the punishment of the three servants) unintelligibly limps in the rear. The Gospel of the Hebrews, also, gives nothing original against Matthew, in its three servants, whose obligations are, moreover, too compendiously treated. The first servant increases his possession (ὕπαρξιν: but this is not exactly the one equal talent which Hilgenfeld by interpolation gives to all three) and is accepted; the second hides the talent and is censured; the third, as a reprobate, wastes his possession with harlots and pipers, and is thrown into prison. Hilgenfeld says this is in the first place simpler, in the next place better, more many-sided, than the narration in Matthew, where there are two servants almost identical, and where the dissolute servant is, in order to screen the Gentile Christians (wherefore does not Luke xv. screen them?), converted into the second, the one who keeps the original amount. On the other hand, again, Volkmar (p. 175) thinks the dissolute one has become the third in Matthew. Is it, then, more probable that Jesus was deceived in two-thirds of his servants than in one-third—that he should assume as probable the dissoluteness which in chap. xxiv. he treats only as a possibility? Finally, does it seem half reasonable that the lazy Jew was only censured by Jesus; and does it not appear very narrow-minded and fanatically Jewish that *only the Gentile* is punished? Moreover, the Gospel of the Hebrews is the later Gospel, though perhaps older than the more detailed parallel, Luke xv. 11 sqq.; comp. above, I. p. 104, note. Volkmar, it is true, represents that the pearl of Luke has been "broken to pieces" by Matthew, as well as by the Gospel of the Hebrews.

much, and are allowed to participate in the joy of their lord;
the third is cast into the outer darkness, his capital given to the
first, because, according to the popular adage, "to him that has
shall be given, that he may have abundance; but from him that
has not, shall be taken even what he has."[1] Jesus—or the parable
—by no means meant to make these servants represent the Jews
or the Gentiles, but great and small, active and lazy, apostles;
and it is a sign of the genuineness of the parable that neither the
history of Peter nor that of Paul, who "wrought more than all,"
appears to be in any way interwoven.[2]

We must doubtless regard as much later and less original
several other speeches in Matthew and Luke which, attested by
only single authorities, found a lodgment either in this connection or elsewhere. There are descriptions of waiting for the Lord,
of the second advent, of the judgment, in which the apostolic or
post-apostolic time expressed their sighs, their longings, their
hopes. The waiting is depicted in the Matthew-parable of the
ten virgins, in the Luke-parable of the widow and the unjust
judge; the judgment of the world, in the conclusion of the farewell speeches in Matthew and in the conclusion of the same
Evangelist's Sermon on the Mount. The parable of the five wise
and the five foolish virgins, who waited in the night for the
bridegroom, and only half of whom took a gladsome part in the

---

[1] The third servant in Matthew buried the money, the third in Luke hid it in sudario, upon which *Ketub.* f. 67, 2 : R. Abba pecunias in sudario ligavit illudque post se rejecit, ut pauperes invenirent. Cavedoni, *Bibl. Numism.* p. 146. Faithful in little, næœman bakethannim (Schöttgen, p. 217), comp. *Shem. R.S.* II. : Deus nunquam res magnas largitur hominibus, nisi eos prius per res parvas exploraverit (*e.g.* Moses and David), Wetst. p. 510. The sum, though great in itself, was small for a king (comp. Matt. xviii. 24). He that has, comp. Matt. xiii.; above, IV. p. 130. Also *Soh. chad.* f. 75, 4 : quic. addit, illi plura adduntur, qui demit, illi plura demuntur. *Tanch.* f. 38, 1 : Deus, si videt hominem, in quo spir. sap., illum sap. implet. Schöttgen, p. 218. Into the joy, *Shem. R.* XVIII. : veniet in gaudium filii mei. Wetst. p. 510; comp. Schöttgen, p. 218.

[2] 1 Cor. xv. 10. Hilg. (1868, p. 58) understands the first servant, who increases the money, to represent the Jews that believed in Christ, those who added a belief in the Messiah to their attachment to the Law; the second, who buries the money, he takes to be the unbelieving Jews; the dissolute servant of the Gospel of the Hebrews is the Jewish-Christians.

marriage because five lacked oil, is constructed on the basis of Oriental marriage customs, in accordance with which the bridegroom and his friends appeared at night in the bride's house, sometimes to be ceremoniously received in the house of the wedding by the bride and her companions who met him with torches, as Matthew supposes, and sometimes to conduct, amid glitter of lamps and shouts of jubilation, his bride into his ancestral house.[1] Well constructed as is the parable—the elements of which can be detected in Luke, perhaps in their genuine words—it is very inappropriate, in this application, to the lips of Jesus. The picture of the virgins, the picture of the sleeping of the whole of the virgins, the picture of the heedlessness and uselessness of a full half of those that waited,—these pictures by no means apply to the disciples—the servants of the previous parables—who alone in the first instance were addressed. They apply better to the later community, the bride of Christ, which consisted only to the half of those that were wise, nay, in consequence of the long tarrying of the Lord it consisted of none but sleepers, awaking only in the midst of the positive signs of the second advent.[2] The companion piece is the picture in Luke

---

[1] Wedding ceremony in the house of the man, 1 Macc. ix. 37 sqq.; Tobit xi. 20; comp. R. Solomon, below. In the house of the bride, Judges xiv. 10; comp. Song of Sol. iii. 4 sqq. In Matthew it is evident (xxv. 1, 10, comp. Meyer) that the house of the bride is meant, of course, for the returning Messiah comes back to his community. The matter is thought out very circumstantially by Bleek: the scene is laid first at the bride's house, *then* at the bridegroom's. At the marriage ceremonies the friends of the bridegroom are present (παρανύμφιοι υἱοὶ νυμφῶνος, Matt. ix. 15; John iii. 29; comp. 1 Macc. *l.c.*, Hebrew merëim, Judges xiv. 11; Talm. shoshbanim), but also the companions of the bride, Judges xi. 37; Song of Sol. iii. 11. In Matthew, the virgins come to the foreground as representatives of the community. Judges xiv. 11, thirty friends are mentioned; R. Solomon, in *Chelin.* 2, 8, speaks of ten torches; Lightfoot, p. 368; Wetst. p. 507. Ten was the minimum of a Passover-lamb company, of a Pharisaic or Essene assembly, of a synagogue, of a marriage or funeral procession, *ib.*; Friedlieb, p. 53. Above, I. p. 383, note 2. The remark of the already mentioned R. Solomon is interesting: mos est in terra ismaelitica, ut sponsam ducant e domo patris sui in domum sponsi ferantque ante eam circiter decem baculos ligneos, in cujusque summitate vasculum instar scutellae habentes, in quo est segmentum panni cum oleo et pice. His accensis facem ei praeferunt. Torches of honour, see Schöttgen, p. 88.

[2] The elements of the parable, Luke xii. 35—37. Volkmar (p. 190) looks for them in Mark ii. 19. Doubt neither in Neander, p. 506, and Bleek, II. p. 385, nor in Weisse,

256 THE FAREWELL.

of the widow who compels justice against her adversary from the judge that was destitute of all fear of God and of all regard for men.¹ It is the forsaken community of Jesus that cries day and night to God for vengeance against its enemies, and must eventually be heard. This parable betrays its late date by its distinct reference to the necessities, the impatience, the lukewarmness of a later age, and by the crude wrangling with God, and the crude comparison of God to a sinful man which is developed in the thoroughly Ebionite spirit of the late parable of the unjust steward.²

In the description of the judgment of the world by Jesus, Matthew, or probably the Gentile-favouring editor of Matthew, has given a fine conclusion to these speeches about the future.³ Coming in his glory, with an escort of all the angels, the Son of Man will take his seat on the throne of glory, and as a shepherd divides the sheep from the much meaner goats, he will separate the assembled peoples of the earth, from whom the Christians are expressly distinguished as exempted from judgment.⁴

II. p. 125. Christ the bridegroom, comp. Matt. ix. 15, John iii. 29, 2 Cor. xi. 2, Rev. xix. 7, 9 ; in the Old Testament, God and Israel, above, IV. p. 40, note 1. Comp. the analogy in *Pirke Abot*, R. Eliezer, c. 41, where Moses awakens the Israelite camp : surgite a somno vestro, venit sponsus et quæret sponsam, ut eam in chuppam introducat. Et sponsus egressus est in occursum sponsæ, ut scil. daret ipsis legem. Schöttgen, p. 216. Kimchi mentions, on Is. lxv., a saying of R. Johanan ben Zacchai, who invited his servants without fixing a time : sapientes se ornarunt, stolidi abierunt ad opera sua. Thus some went ornati, the others sordidi (Matt. xxii. 11), with whom then the king was angry. Lightfoot, p. 369. The awaking in prospect of the second advent, Rom. xiii. 11 sqq. Most critics do not question the genuineness of the parable ; on the other hand, Strauss, *New Life of Jesus*, Eng. trans., I. p. 352. Volkmar, pp. 190, 545.

¹ Luke xviii. 1 sqq.; comp. R. Johanan in *Tanch*. f. 15 B : nemo hom. singulis horis defatigare debet Deum. Schöttgen, p. 305.

² Above, I. p. 100, note. In the earlier Gospel, Matt. xxv. 24, it is only the wicked servant who thus designates his lord. Lukewarmness of a later time and stimulation by a touching word of Jesus, Luke xviii. 8.

³ Matt. xxv. 31 ; comp. above, I. p. 83.

⁴ That the Christians have an exemption from judgment, stands very plainly in verses 40, 45 ; for the brethren of Jesus are different persons from the judged, good or bad, the conversion of whom to Christianity is nowhere related. To Hilgenfeld (comp. his *Ev*. p. 104, and *Zeitschrift*, 1868, p. 59) belongs the credit of having emphatically established this ; assent of Weizs. p. 553, Volkmar p. 546 ; and earlier

Some he will place on his right, others on his left, and then in his character of king he will invite the former, as the blessed of his Father, to inherit the kingdom prepared for them from the creation of the world, but will send away the others as accursed into the eternal fire prepared for Satan and his angels.[1] To the astonishment of the former, he will give as the grounds of his sentence the deeds of feeding, giving drink, sheltering, clothing, sick and prison visiting, done to the Christians, to the brethren, to the clients of Jesus; and in reply to the protesting humility of the righteous, who object that they have done no such deeds to him, he will support his sentence by maintaining that what they have done to the least of his brethren they have done to him.[2] He will then justify his decision against the condemned in a similar way. He will roundly cut short their exculpatory appeals to the impossibility of such services to his own person, by pointing to their lack of love towards his poor brethren. Though this delineation is captivating in its finely-conceived pictures, with its liberal Jesus-like proportions, and with its remarkable tolerance even for the Gentiles, and though there is little doubt that Jesus in some way claimed for himself as the returning Messiah the judgment of men, nevertheless the creative or at least the formative hand of a later generation is unmistakably

---

thus Keil, Olsh., Baumg.-Cr. Others, since Lact., Jerome, have thought of a judgment upon Christians only (Neander, Bleek, Meyer upon all Christianized Gentile nations); others, again, as Calov, Kuinöl, Fr., De Wette, have thought of an absolutely universal judgment, the dead in part not excluded. The exemption of the Christians, Rom. vi. 2; Rev. xx. 4; comp. Matt. x. 32, xii. 41. Separation of sheep from goats, after Ez. xxxiv. 17. Comparatively small value of latter, Luke xv. 29; Gen. xxxviii. 17.

[1] Right, left, Luke i. 11; Mark xvi. 5. Essenes, above, I. p. 376, note 3; comp. V. p. 50, note 3. *Soh. chad.*, f. 45, 2: datur dextra, datur etiam sinistra. Dantur Israelitæ et gentiles (at the exodus of the Israelites from Egypt), paradisus et gehenna, mundus hic et mundus futurus. Schöttgen, p. 219. Seven things before the creation: lex, pœnit., *paradisus, infernus*, thronus, templum, nomen Messiæ, *ib.* Devil in hell, above, II. p. 317, note 1; Rev. xx. 2, 10.

[2] *Ialk. Rub.* f. 13, 2: unicuique exponet opera ejus; illi vero stabunt et mirabuntur. Similar approval of deeds of mercy to the poor, to the sick, to pilgrims at whose right hand God stands, and whom God sends, Schöttgen, p. 220. Comp. Proverbs xix. 17. The least, Matt. xviii. 6, x. 42. Above, III. p. 252, note 1; IV. p. 336, note 2.

to be detected here.¹ This speech tacitly assumes, if not the Christianizing of the whole of mankind, at any rate the diffusion of the confessors of Jesus over all parts of the earth; whilst Jesus has not—at least until now—publicly uttered a word about such a diffusion, or indeed about a mission to the whole world.² It assumes a time in which the opinion had been formed that Christians—why not also non-Christians?—can minister to their absent and invisible Head in his suffering and persecuted members, and by such ministrations can even acquire an interest in the future kingdom.³ These conceptions appear to be altogether late productions of the apostolic time. Nay, we should be compelled—especially in view of the liberal conception of heathenism which makes the better spirits among the heathen the elect of God from eternity—to ascribe them to the second century, if we could not assume that the author had introduced Jesus' strikingly strong benediction of the heathen with the idea that he was describing a judgment upon Christianized heathens, and not upon heathens in their natural state, as his source had originally understood it.⁴ Any one who is still inclined to doubt

¹ Judgment of Jesus, Matt. xvi. 27, xiii. 41, &c. Above, IV. p. 295, note 1. But never expressly upon all peoples. Also many traces of a final judgment of God, *l. c.* This is what is correct in Weizsäcker's uncertainty, p. 553.

² Passages such as Matt. xxi. 43, xxiv. 14, have fallen away; and Matt. v. 13 sq., viii. 11, xii. 41, xiii. 38, 41 sqq., xxiv. 31, contain at most obscure intimations.

³ 1 Cor. viii. 11 sqq.; Rom. xiv. 15, 18; comp. Barn. 19; Hermas, 2, 8; Clem. *Hom.* 3, 69; Ignat. *Eph.* 10, &c. Imprisoned, Rev. ii. 10, xiii. 10; Heb. x. 34. Lucian, *De Morte Per.* 12. With respect to non-Christians, note the milder opinion of the apologists of the second century (comp. already John iii. 21, x. 16); on the other side, note the protection which to their own loss they often afforded to the Christians in the Roman persecutions. As prelude thereto, see the opinion of the heathens in Rome upon Nero's persecution, A.D. 64, Tacitus, *Ann.* 15, 44. Eus. 4, 15; 5, 1; 6, 41; 10, 8, &c.

⁴ Particularly on account of the emphatic recognition of good men, Neander (p. 508) declines to think of mere heathens, and erroneously thinks of a separation between true and impure Christians. The conception most readily arrived at would be that in verses 40 sqq. only the *poor* (Luke vi. 20; James ii. 2) or *martyrs* (Rev. ii. 10, vi. 9, vii. 14; *Hermas*, 1, 3, 1 sq.|; 3, 8, 2 sq.; 3, 9, 28; Tert. *An.* 55) are exempt from judgment. But Bleek (II. p. 390) believed in a disarrangement of the original form of the parable by the Evangelists; only he conceived that originally a judgment upon the confessors was described, and afterwards a general judgment. But before a man brings in Matt. x. 32 (which Bleek does not), x. 40—42 lies much nearer.

should examine the titles which Jesus is made to give to himself: Lord of all angels, judge and final judge of all nations, and then repeatedly the king—"the king will say." These are titles he was not accustomed to bear, titles which he was accustomed to give to God; but they are titles of reverence, such as the community laid with emphasis at the feet of the glorified one.[1] Finally, it is to be noted that this speech appears nowhere else; while, on the other hand, the elements of its composition—a composition which in many points has a dual character, and has plainly grown by successive additions of the actual words of Jesus, together with insertions from the Old Testament—are easily to be detected.[2] Still another judgment address, placed by Matthew at the close of the Sermon on the Mount, belongs to the province of the same later compositions. The saying about the false prophets of the future appears to be entirely a new construction of the words of rejection which Jesus spoke against the Pharisees; and the repudiation of those who by using the name of Jesus had become prophets, miracle-workers, exorcists, and would in the future judgment attempt to justify themselves by their works, evidently rests upon a later reconstruction—not directed exactly against the Apostle Paul—of the words of rejection uttered by Jesus against the people with which Galilee and Luke have made us acquainted.[3]

Thus whilst much here falls away, much nevertheless remains,

[1] Lord of the angels, but not exactly of all (this is God's attribute, Book of Enoch, 5, 39 sq.; Rev. iv. 4; Jude 14), Matt. xiii. 41, xvi. 27; king, only God, v. 35, xxii. 2 sqq. God the final judge, x. 32, &c. Paul and the Apocalypse describe Jesus as king; but also John i. 49, xviii. 37.

[2] It is based simply in part on Matt. xvi. 27, in part still more on x. 40—42; comp. also xxiv. 31. Weisse (II. p. 132) similarly decides, with a doubt as to the original character of the piece; also Weizs. (p. 553), who seeks, but does not produce, a foundation for it in the sayings of Jesus. From the Old Testament, Ez. xxxiv. 17 (separation of sheep from goats); Is. lviii. 7; Ez. xviii. 8 (compassion); Proverbs xix. 17. Volkmar (p. 546) is inclined to derive the speech from Mark xvi. 16, Rev. xx. 4—15, 4 Ezra vi. 3 sq. (orient. rec.).

[3] Matt. vii. 15—23, comp. xii. 33 sqq.; Luke xiii. 25. Hilg. and Köstlin are inclined to think of Paul. But theoretical and practical vagaries existed among both Jewish Christians and heathen Christians; and was Paul *par excellence* a miracle-worker? Let but Matt. xxiv. 24 be thought of!

not only as genuine utterances of Jesus in these last days, but also as the revelation of his self-consciousness and his consciousness of the future. The persecuted, rejected Messiah calculates upon the eternal validity of his person and his cause. The world that opposes him will lie at his feet, must come to him, await him, bow before and do homage to him.[1] His self-consciousness has been justified, and his expectation has been crowned with victory, though everything has not been so fulfilled as was the downfall of the temple. In particular, his return as conqueror and as judge has not come to pass as he pictured to himself and to his followers. And because the issue has been different, the ancients improved upon his sayings, and the moderns have attempted subtle expositions of them. It is, however, as we long since saw, a fact above all objection, that Jesus in thoroughly genuine words held out the prospect of his return to the then living generation and to the then living disciples; and that Peter and Paul and the community lived for decades and centuries upon this belief.[2] There is also nothing more certain than that he, standing on the ground of a human self-consciousness, could find only this and no other adjustment of the difficulties of the situation, if he would connect the salvation of the world not only with the spiritual truths which he taught, but also with his own person and with his own Messiahship. It is equally certain that, from the same human standpoint, the catastrophe of Jerusalem must appear as the terminus in which his Messiahship upon earth should attain to honour and power.[3] He may be charged with human error, but his is a noble and beautiful humanity: first he humbly admits his own limitations, then he adopts a well-considered belief, not in a speedy act of divine vengeance and restoration, but evidently in a slow and lingering evolution of the downfall of Jerusalem. In the

---

[1] Not only Weizs. (p. 553, note), but also Volkmar (p. 549), recognize this main fact.

[2] Above, IV. pp. 285 sqq.

[3] Volkmar, *l. c.* quite rationalistically: he could be certain that *spiritually* he would be for all time the teacher and redeemer, the judge and king (king ?). See *Ausbruch gegen eine hist. realist. Auffassung*, p. 550.

third place, he carries in his hand like a banner of victory the great historical justification, the proof of facts, that he thought of himself not too grandly but too meanly, too humbly when he found a second advent necessary. The idea which he had planted in the world, and to which he had given an incarnation in his historical appearance, was great enough to rise again and survive in the minds of his disciples, nay in the world-mind itself, and to become the measure, the power, the light of universal history, a breaker in pieces not only of the stones of Jerusalem, but of all the rocks of Jewish and heathen resistance, and a builder of the New Jerusalem, whose walls should embrace all countries and islands and seas.

Wednesday evening (the 13th of April) closed with a beautiful tribute of homage at Bethany, and with a most memorable declaration. Jesus was reclining at table with his disciples in the house of his host, Simon the leper.[1] This man, whom Matthew and Mark plainly point out as the host at whose house Jesus sojourned, has been already referred to in discussing the entry into Bethany.[2] He could hardly be leprous at this time—it does not appear to have been at all the intention of the Gospels to give prominence to a fearlessness on the part of Jesus in entering this house. Simon had been leprous and had been healed, plainly not by Jesus, for if so this fact would have been handed down with the other incidents connected with Bethany. But the severe illness, which may have left its traces in his countenance, procured for him in the mouths of the people the name which distinguished him from the numerous other Simons, "Simon the leper."[3] The meal which introduced the

---

[1] Matt. xxvi. 6; Mark xiv. 3, comp. Luke vii. 36, 40; John xi. 2, xii. 2 sqq.

[2] Strictly one might find in Matt. and Mark, as in Luke, merely the host of a meal; but Matt. and Mark distinguish between sojourning in a house and merely taking a meal there.

[3] It is by no means to be concluded that because a man was called "leper" he was then suffering from the malady (on the contrary, Bleek, Meyer, Volkmar). Nor is it to be concluded that Bethany was the home of the lepers of Jerusalem (comp. Grätz,

ovation, apparently an evening banquet, at which the disciples of Jesus were present, and to which it was wished to give a festive conclusion, presents nothing striking.[1] It may appear peculiar that at such a critical position of affairs a meal of a festive character should have been offered to and accepted by Jesus. But the full seriousness of the situation was recognized by Jesus alone, scarcely by his company of disciples, and least of all by his adherents at Bethany. Moreover, the house was that in which Jesus was sojourning, and it was possible for him, even at such a solemn hour, nay at the very dawn of the crisis, and in fact by way of farewell, to be once more genial and familiarly cordial with his friends. Important as the table-talk must have been, none of it has been preserved to succeeding ages; but what happened at the close of the meal put everything else out of view at the time, and to-day compensates for what is lost.[2]

There entered a woman who was evidently neither one of Jesus' Galilean friends nor the wife or relation of the host, since the recollection of such a fact could not have been lost. She must have been a woman of Bethany, a noble part of the small Jerusalemite harvest which, in these few days, in the days of his intense earnestness, of his bitterness, of his struggle, had ripened to him under the sparse yet still brilliant and warming beams of Galilean sunshine. With a small alabaster bottle of most costly spikenard oil, the best and most highly valued gift she had, the woman came behind Jesus, broke off the slender neck of the

---

III. p. 240 sq.; see above, p. 127, note 1), because such diseased persons were not allowed in the city (Jos. B. J. 5, 5, 6). Meyer, with many of the Fathers (comp. Friedlieb, p. 27), groundlessly thinks of healing by Jesus. Least of all are we to think, with Cornelius a Lapide (Friedlieb, l. c.), of a family name, similar to the Roman name of the Claudii.

[1] Matthew and Mark speak of a meal ($\dot{a}\nu a\kappa\epsilon\tilde{\iota}\sigma\theta a\iota$, $\kappa a\tau a\kappa$.), Luke and John of a meal to invited guests. In honour of Jesus, John. Matthew and Mark do not exclude this. Festive meals were as a rule about the second hour (8 p.m.), Jos. Vita, 44; B. J. 1, 17, 4. The noon meal ($\delta\epsilon\tilde{\iota}\pi\nu o\nu$ $\mu\epsilon\sigma\eta\mu\beta\rho$.) was considered only as breakfast ($\check{a}\rho\iota\sigma\tau o\nu$), comp. Luke xiv. 12.

[2] Most critics, by following John (xii. 1), escape the difficulty caused by a festive meal falling almost immediately before the Passion. Thus even Schenkel, Bib.-Lex. III. p. 295.

vessel, from which the ointment could flow only drop by drop, and poured the whole full stream of the deliciously fragrant Indian oil without stint upon his head.[1] This was an act of personal homage such as he had never before received, though the anointing of the head of guests, particularly of illustrious teachers, with oil and costly substances was not at all unusual, in spite of being considered effeminate by men of sterner tastes. It was an act without words, and yet it spoke louder than any words; it was a genuinely womanly act in its delicate display of outward self-sacrificing service, and yet a deed worthy of a man in its boldness towards Jesus and his companions at table, and in saving the honour of the nation whose Messiah she anointed while Jerusalem stood off coldly and heartlessly and failed to understand him.[2] As he—although not, as Renan thinks, an ambitious man—was receiving with silent emotion the honour whose dispenser he well knew and the significance of which he more profoundly interpreted than did the woman, there began to show itself among the disciples—not among the guests generally,

[1] Matt. xxvi. 7; Mark xiv. 3. Pliny, 13, 3: unguenta optime servantur in alabastris, odores in oleo. 36, 12: lapidem alabastriten vocant, quem cavant ad vasa unguentaria, quoniam optime servare incorrupta dicitur. The narrow neck, 9, 56. The breaking, see Friedlieb, *Archäol. der Leidensgesch.* 1843, p. 33. Wichelhaus, *Komm. zur Leidengesch.* 1855, pp. 71 sq. Wetst. p. 515. Paulus, I. ii. p. 768. Matthew has μύρον, *i.e.* aromatic anointing oil in general, finer than ordinary oil, hence in special use by women, Xenophon, *Symp.* 2, 3; Luke vii. 46. It was as a rule compounded of several substances, particularly myrrh, unguentorum mixturæ, Pliny, 13, 2; 29, 8. Mark gives oil of spikenard: nardus indicus, principale (regale) in unguentis (less costly syriacum, Phœniceum, gallicum, creticum), Pliny, 12, 26; 13, 2. Mark speaks of genuine (πιστικὸς) spikenard, as opposed to pseudonardus, Pliny, 12, 26. Fritzsche's (also Cas. and Bez.) derivation from πίνω = potabilis, obsolete. It means reliable, genuine. Plutarch, *Pelop.* 8; Artemidorus, *On.* 2, 32, 66; 3, 54.

[2] Comp. Luke vii. 46 and *Bab. Ketub.* f. 12, 2: nonne mater tua effudit pro te (in nuptiis tuis) unguentum super capita Rabbinorum? Lightfoot, p. 456. Among the Greeks and Romans, Plato, *De Rep.* 398 A; Martial, *Ep.* 10, 19, 20; Petron. *Sat.* 65. Comp. Wetst. p. 515, and Winer, articles *Gastmahl* and *Salbe.* Therefrom, and also from Ps. cxxxiii. 2, Bunsen, p. 390 (who accuses Matthew and Mark of error), might have learnt that ointment was poured upon the head without fear of "soiling the clothes." It is, however, correct that this custom prevailed more among the Babylonian Jews (Pliny, 13, 1: Persæ madent unguento) than among those of Jerusalem, and that at Jerusalem the maxim was established, *Hier. Berac.* f. 11, 2: indecorum est discipulo sapientum, olere aromata. Lightfoot, p. 457; comp. above on the Essenes, I. p. 375.

as Mark gives it—the pedantic criticism of men who, with the shallow wisdom of acquired ideas, censure an unusual and uncomprehended fact of a higher character, confine and crush in the mould of abstract moral doctrine the outburst of a true and deep feeling.[1] "Why this lavish waste, evaporating in a moment?" whisper they, like the Roman Pliny. "For this might have been sold for much"—for more than 300 francs, it is said in Mark— "and given to the poor."[2] In an incomparable manner Jesus rebutted this, and to make amends for the censure he at once let the praise which he had at first hidden in his soul flow forth in a full stream. "Why trouble ye the woman?[3] She has performed a beautiful work upon me. For ye have the poor always with you, but me ye have not always. For in that she poured this ointment upon my body, she did it to my burial.[4] Verily I say unto you, wheresoever this gospel shall be preached in the whole world, shall be told also what this woman did, as a memorial of her."

Thus mildly, but firmly, did he correct the hasty and indeed

---

[1] Renan, 15th ed. p. 385 : It was sought by redoubling external marks of respect to overcome the indifference of the public!

[2] Pliny, 13, 4 : hæc est materia luxus cunctis max. supervacui. Margaritæ enim gemmæque ad heredem tamen transeunt, vestes prorogant tempus, *unguenta illico exspirant ac suis moriuntur horis*. Immediately after : exceduntque quadragenos denarios libræ. Comp the prices in chap. 2, and in 12, 26. Also by the Rabbis, 300 denarii. Lightfoot, p. 457.

[3] Greek, usually πραγμ. παρ. Wetst. p. 516. Hebrew, hithriach, mathriach ethammelech. Schöttgen, p. 224.

[4] Thus Matthew and Mark. The same is the sense of the Received Text in John xii. 7. But the genuine text also, "Let her alone, that she may observe this against the day of my burying" (comp. ix. 16, xv. 10), regards her action as an anticipation of a pompous burial, and the explanation, "Leave her alone, that she may preserve it (the remainder of the pound) for my burial" (Meyer; also Bunsen, p. 440), is weak and trivial. After the head of the vessel had been broken off, this was no longer possible; certainly Venturini (p. 402) is wrong in thinking it was only the remainder of the oil used in anointing Lazarus. Wichelh. (p. 95), again, says that she had withheld it (τετήρηκε) from her brother! The artificial expression, however, points clearly to the view of the author, which was, in the already mooted question of the second century as to the τηρεῖν or the μη τηρεῖν of the Jewish Passover by the Christians, to pronounce for the τηρεῖν, not of the Passover-day, but of the day of Jesus' death or that of his burial. According to John, indeed (see below), the day of anointing is the picture of the day of burial, the Saturday before the burial Saturday.

arrogant disciples. He upheld the ministering to the poor which he himself had preached; but he was far removed from the iron consistency which is the foe of what is good, and which converts one good principle into a tyrannical obstacle in the way of a second and equally justified good. Not only poverty, but his own person was to be honoured and cherished, for he was more than the poor, and he would not be with them much longer. With equal modesty and thoughtfulness, he made it apparent that in another situation, at another time, notwithstanding he was what he was, he would have declined the merited honour, would have left the money to be used for the poor; but he now accepted the act as a farewell greeting, as a work of love which might be held to have reference to his burial, and, in the intention of the woman, was done more or less consciously with such a reference. He here at once fully and tenderly justified the woman, and in the midst of the festive company pointed solemnly to his death, which he saw close at hand, and which would lack, not an honourable sepulchre, but—as was easy to be foreseen—the customary and coveted ministrations of love, yet, because of the previous attention paid to him by the woman, would not entirely lack them, as Socrates had wished.[1] His last words triumphed over death and the grave and his fall. It is true he neither said nor knew anything about a rising again of his weary body;

---

[1] Socrates (why has this not been quoted ?), Plato, *Phædrus*, 115 A : δοκεῖ γάρ δὴ βέλτιον εἶναι λουσάμ. πιεῖν τ. φάρμ. κ. μὴ πράγματα ταῖς γυναιξὶ παρέχειν, νεκρὸν λούειν.—An over-scrupulous criticism might conclude that the utterance under consideration was afterwards invented in order to make amends for the factual subsequent non-anointing of the corpse of Jesus. In point of fact, Strauss, in 1864 (*New Life of Jesus*, Eng. trans., II. p. 297), not yet in 4th ed. I. pp. 733, has taken hold of this point. But this invention could not well originate with Mark the poet, since he ascribes to the Galilean women an intention to anoint which was rendered superfluous by the resurrection of Jesus (xvi. 1). But as to the supposition of its invention (in fine, by Matthew, as by Mark), how can Strauss imagine that the Christians, who believed more than did Strauss in the resurrection of their Lord, and thought more about that than about his death, should have painfully missed his anointment, and have invented this anointment story? If Jesus necessarily thought of his death, if he necessarily thought of a sepulture without honour, he would speak just as he spoke. And in reality he did not at all intimate that the anointing of his corpse was excluded, but only that it was now superfluous.

but he knew that his gospel would take its course through the world, and would preserve from oblivion not only himself, but even the woman who had paid the last duty to his body. And as every one of the few words at the Bethany guest-table must necessarily be golden, he quite incidentally, and as if accidentally, introduced into his very last utterance, not only the firm and sure faith in his future, but also the—by us longingly coveted—avowal of his universal mission, of his conquest of the world. This faith in his universal mission was already shown in obscure outline in the Sermon on the Mount; Galilee matured it, so far as that he there included in his prospect the belief of the heathen world; and Jerusalem perfected it. The utterance at Bethany is the only quite reliable saying of Jesus' last days concerning the world-wide course which he saw opened to himself and to his cause. This utterance goes so far as to show that he was not merely conscious of being a light to the world, and saw the Gentiles coming in a wider sense than—as in Galilee—that of superseding the Jews, but that in a calm vision of the distant future he saw the universal spread of the gospel, the preaching of the glad tidings broadening out from the Holy Land to the nations of the earth. But here also there is no exaggeration. He said nothing about the entering of the Gentiles instead of the Jews into the kingdom of God; and he did not say that his twelve disciples were to be the Apostles of the nations. He knew only this—that the Gentiles as well as the Jews would hear the truth, and that the message of truth would pass beyond the boundary of Israel to the nations of the world, though he was still as careless by whose instrumentality this was to happen as he was about the preservation of his own personal history. It was Jerusalem that had at last led him to this knowledge. The fact that his people rejected him evidently did not induce him on his part to reject his people, whose Messiah he was and still wished to remain; but it led him to relax the rigidity of the national idea which fettered his Messiahship, and, as far as it was possible in his historical situation and necessary to his historical dignity, to give effectual expression to the universal character of his mission, a character which from the beginning had been in contention with the national one.[1]

Criticism, while throwing suspicion upon this incident, has in truth only condemned itself. It is as incorrect to talk of supplementary and invented prophesyings, as of disturbances of the context and of the tendencies of Gentile-favouring editors. The latter is refuted by the fact that Mark, who did not know the edited form of Matthew, nevertheless possesses the passage as well as Matthew; the former is refuted by the easy conceivability of the sorrowful and ingenuous utterance about the sepulture, and by the humility—intelligible only in Jesus, but not in a late inventor—that keeps silence concerning the resurrection. In particular, prejudice rather than sound judgment is shown by overlooking the signs of antiquity and genuineness just there where an open eye can only admire the unique coincidence of the most concise form, and of an overflowing yet not overloaded wealth of meaning.[2]

[1] Comp. above, III. p. 55, IV. pp. 84 sqq. A commission of the Apostles to preach to the Gentiles stands only in Matt. xxviii. 19 (not v. 14, viii. 11, x. 5, 18, xxiv. 14).

[2] Hilg. has attacked this little incident, in his *Ev.* p. 104, and in his *Zeitschrift*, 1868, p. 62, first as an addition of the Gentile-favouring editor, then as that of the Evangelist. His chief ground is the break in the context of xxvi. 5 and 14. Comp. Köstlin, p. 73. Even Meyer, in the interest of the attempt to prove the secondary character of Matthew in contrast to John, could welcome this present from the enemy; whilst Volkmar (p. 559) is pleased to allow the applicability of Hilgenfeld's remark to Matthew, but not to Mark, the Pauline didactic writer to whom the interruption of a principal action by interludes is allowed. Holtzmann (p. 95) rightly finds no introduced incident. In fact, how can one speak of a rupture of the context in either Matthew or Mark, when the action of Judas in verse 14 is not brought about by the plan of the hierarchs, and is actually an interference with that plan (verse 5)? Since that plan and Judas' action are thus mutually independent, it is far better that something historical lies between and softens the antagonism of things that are partially contradictory and are not in any way brought into harmony. For by the pause, verses 6—13, an altered development is made possible, even though a participation of Judas in the dissatisfaction at Bethany (according to the fourth Gospel) is not to be thought of. It is also worthy of note that this fourth Gospel evidently presupposes the order of sequence of the meal at Bethany and the treachery of Judas, *i.e.* the representation of Matthew and Mark.—A further objection to this incident (apart from Strauss's suspicion, mentioned above, p. 265, note) can lie only in Jesus' words about a universal Gospel (comp. thereupon Wichelh. p. 104); and even Bleek is willing to admit at least

The Bethany meal is to be retained only in the form of the oldest tradition, in that of Matthew and Mark, not in that of Luke and John. Luke transposes this festive meal to another time, to other surroundings. In his Gospel it occurs in Galilee, in the lifetime of the Baptist, and in the time of the first great struggles with the Pharisees. The host Simon is a Pharisee; the majority of the guests belong to the same party; the anointing woman is well known in the town as a gross sinner, but is certainly not Mary Magdalene. Her deep penitence and her love; the wetting the feet of Jesus with her tears and drying them with the luxuriant waving hair with which she had been wont to allure her wooers, but with which she now, like a servant-maiden, serves the man of her faith; then the kissing his feet; and finally, that which she intends to be specially distinctive, the humble anointing, not of his head, but of his feet, with the oil from the alabaster vessel: all this becomes the subject of a conflict with the Pharisees.[1] The host says in his heart, "If this were a prophet!"

that the expression "*this* Gospel" belongs only to the composition of the Evangelist. I would refer to Matt. xxiv. 14. But Jesus has sufficiently spoken of the good message of the kingdom, Matt. xi. 5 (xxiv. 14; Luke iv. 18, xvi. 16; Mark i. 15); and if he had already regarded his work as cosmical, could he not now give special emphasis to this attitude? And though we should dispute as to whether Jesus said "in the world" or "in the whole world," the chief point is still the uninvented simplicity and greatness of the utterance (comp. Weisse, I. p. 599), the genuineness of which finds its culmination in the fact that no fiction-writing Evangelist has been able to give the *name of the woman*, notwithstanding the strong provocation to do so. Volkmar naturally believes the incident to be unhistorical. The homage-paying woman is the Church. And the protesting Apostles?

[1] Luke vii. 36 sqq. The anointing of the feet is, in accordance with the position of the person, an act of greater humility (therefore not because the head of Jesus—according to 1 Sam. x. 1—was already anointed by God, Volkmar, p. 559). To wash the feet of guests with water or oil was customary, Luke vii. 44, *Menach.* f. 85, 2, whence it appears that servant-maids did it. Yet in *Hier. Peah.* 1, the mother of a Rabbi imposes upon her son, on the authority of Ex. xx. 12, the duty of foot-washing. Anointing the feet with choice oil was indeed commonly held to be effeminate, and the Israelitish women were accused of anointing their shoes out of coquetry, Lightfoot, p. 653. Athenæus, 12, 78, in Wichelh. p. 81. Strauss, 4th ed. I. p. 743. Comp. Essenes and Pharisees, above, p. 263, n. 2. It is not the fact, however, as W. says, that only the effeminate and the debauched could do it; from oil to ointment is but a step. In the woman, the uncovered head was held to be indecent: *transgreditur legem, si prodeat in publ. capite aperto.*, Lightfoot, p. 515. The unbinding of the hair, however, was held to be disgraceful, *Sot.* f. 5, 1: sacerdos solvit capillos uxoris

But Jesus confutes him by the parable of the two debtors, both of which had their debts remitted, the one with his five hundred francs, the other with his fifty. The Pharisee himself is compelled to lay down the principle that the greater the forgiveness, the greater should be the love. Jesus then points out to him the instances of less and of greater love: from the Pharisee he received on coming in no water, no kiss, no oil for his head; from the sinful woman he has received tears, kisses, ointment! "Her many sins are forgiven, because she has loved much; but he to whom little is forgiven, loves little!" He dismisses her with express forgiveness, and the guests are astonished at the forgiver.[1]

From the earliest times it has been debated whether this is the incident which occurred at Bethany, or another. And because John comes with an anointing by Mary, many have assumed that there were three or, reckoning Mark's account as a distinct one, four anointings, and three or four anointing Marys, since a mistaken acuteness has found in the sinful woman of Luke, Mary Magdalene.[2] On the other hand, Tertullian, and a little later

---

suspectæ. It sometimes occurred in mourning and in sorrow, comp. 3 Macc. i. 9. The women of the Germans passis crinibus flentes implorarunt, Cæsar, *B. Gall.* 1, 51. Here it was done in grief and in humble servitude. Magdalene was very arbitrarily thought of by the ancient Church (Greg. M. *Hom.* 25), because of Luke viii. 2 (of course also John xii. 3), comp. Deyling, *Obs.* III. p. 291. Recently (against J. D. Michaelis) Paulus, I. ii. p. 766, who makes her first dissolute, then a demoniac; Lange, II. p. 730, and in Herzog, article *Mar. Magd.*

[1] The forgiving is here represented in a fine and elastic manner; on the one hand it is, in ideal anticipation, prior to the deed of love; on the other hand it is actually communicated after that deed. On the contrary, Meyer and others have given a violent interpretation of it; and Weisse (II. p. 142) has spoken of confusion. Luke was not thinking of Gal. v. 6.

[2] Origen upon Matt. 77: multi quidem existimant, de una eademque muliere IV ev. exposuisse. He is for three (or four) women, (1) Luke, (2) Matthew, Mark, (3) John. Quite correctly on this ground, Chrys., Theoph., and last (16th century) Faber Stapulensis, assumed three anointing Marys. On the contrary, the West (with exception of Irenæus, 3, 14, 3) readily identified the incidents: Tert. *Pudic.* 11, and then Ambrose, Augustine, Gregory the Great. The mistake was, that this Church with increasing emphasis found both in Luke vii. and John xii. the (particularly in France) highly revered Magdalene. At present, most critics are in favour of the identity of the incidents in Matt., Mark, and John (against which Lightfoot protested, following Origen,

the contemporaries of Origen, and later still Gregory the Great at the head of the Roman Church, with perfect justice assumed the identity of these two, nay, of all these incidents. And an earlier writer than Tertullian, Luke himself and indeed the other Evangelists support this, since each has but one incident, whilst Luke in particular forbears to relate an incident at Bethany, because he has already given it. How could there be a four-fold or even only a two-fold repetition of an anointing which the Lord himself, in his great encomium, has dignified above all plainly as a *unique* incident? The great similarity is evident in spite of the points of difference. Both here and there a festive meal, a host Simon, a number of guests, a homage-paying woman with ointment in an alabaster vessel, a protestation against the woman, a vindication by Jesus. The greater simplicity, however, belongs to Matthew and Mark: the homage-paying woman is no notorious character out of the dark side of society; the homage paid is more intelligible, more unobjectionable, more natural; the action, together with the utterances, briefer, more condensed, marked by a greater degree of unity. The contrast of the Pharisee and the sinful woman is evidently a source of pleasure to the author, and is drawn with a considerable outlay of artistic effort. The circumstance as a whole calls to mind Jesus' intercourse with publicans and sinners, which evoked the antagonism of the Pharisees. It also calls to mind the entrance of publicans and harlots into the kingdom of heaven instead of the Pharisees. The parable recalls the two debtors in Matthew; the astonishment at forgiveness, the paralytic; the sending away the woman in peace, the

---

Jerome, and Chrysostom). On the other hand, many hold Luke vii. to be a different incident (the person being the same: Augustine), Olsh., Neander, Winer, Tholuk, Lücke, Hase, Krabbe, Wichelh., Bunsen, De Wette, Meyer. The correct opinion held by Grotius, Hug, Schleierm., Ewald, Strauss, Bleek, Baur, Hilg. Bleek, however (II. pp. 112 sqq.), makes a marvellous attempt at harmonizing the accounts, and frees the sinful woman of Luke (as already Schleierm. *Luk.* pp. 111 sqq.) from all stain which, *e.g.*, Meyer affixes to her lewdness. The remote Luke is held to have inferred it only from vii. 48. The Johannine account is preferred, from a sense of obligation, by Neander, Meyer, Bleek, Ewald, Bunsen, and others; and Wichelh. (p. 62), angry at the evil eye of criticism, indulges heartily in harmonizing.

woman with the issue of blood.[1] Hence it is to be assumed that the incident in Luke is in the main a later production, not due to his invention, but the contribution of his Ebionite source. That source was fond of artificial combinations, and was marked by indifference to chronological arrangement, by controversies with Pharisees, by disputes at table, by the antithesis of Pharisees and publicans or sinners. And one might almost suppose that Jesus' apparently depreciative utterance about the poor was purposely dropped out, while the sinful woman was purposely introduced as one who was at the same time poor in contrast to the rich Simon, like the widow that gave her all but was ashamed before the rich. If the question of the existence of an historical remainder be left open, that remainder may be sought above all in the natural parable and in the words of Jesus, "He to whom much is forgiven, loves much." These are words which, quite independently of the anointing incident borrowed and imitated from Bethany, might have been at some time uttered in view of the self-renunciation of sinners or of an individual sinful woman, and in antithesis to the aristocratic coldness of the righteous Pharisees. And these words, in their paradoxical connection with the apparently quite contradictory conclusion of forgiveness as a reward of rich love, were extremely profound and completely true to nature, yet almost beyond the invention of lesser spirits.[2]

Nearer to the old account than Luke stands the report of the anointing given in the latest Gospel. The author, as it seems, was at first inclined to hasten over this incident; and when he does subsequently give it, he hands down only a mosaic, composed, with much adroitness and subtlety, of details from Matthew and

[1] Comp. Matt. ix. 11, xviii. 23, ix. 2, 22 (Luke viii. 48), xxi. 31.

[2] Just so Weisse (II. p. 142) holds fast the parable, only he finds some confusion in the above views. But how much illustration lies in Luke viii. 2, x. 40, xix. 8 sqq.? Also above, p. 269, n. 1, and my Sermons, II. pp. 328 sqq. On the other hand, Bunsen (p. 391), not being able, and that correctly, to assent to Schleiermacher's and Bleek's cleansing of the sinful woman, found in Luke vii. the remains of an actual narrative of a sinful woman—mixed up with the occurrence at Bethany—in which only tears, not ointment, flowed or was wiped off.

still more from Mark, with only traceable allusions to Luke.[1] In John's Gospel also the meal takes place at Bethany and in the last days of Jesus, yet not quite near to the end, but on the day before the entry into Jerusalem, six, not two, days before Easter. The house is not expressly said to be that of Lazarus and his sisters; yet everything suggests this, while nothing leads us to think of a Simon. Lazarus reclines at table with Jesus; Martha serves; Mary appears with a pound of ointment, anoints the feet of Jesus, dries them with her hair, and the house is filled with the aroma of the spikenard.[2] Only Judas the betrayer raises an objection in the circle of the disciples. He thinks the ointment might have been sold for 300 francs and given to the poor. It is not in behalf of the poor that he thus speaks, but as the bearer of the sacrifice-box which he is in the habit of robbing.[3] He is refuted in the same way as in the old account; yet the reference to the sepulture is less simple, and not only too artificial, but unintelligible. It is probably an allusion to what, in the freer view of the second century, would have been the correct ceremonial at the burial of Jesus.[4]

The false assumption of the eye-witnessing Apostle has, in this representation, again discovered the relatively correct form.[5] Here we have at last found the right house, the right woman, the right disciples; and when with a lively faith we fill in

---

[1] John xii. 1 sqq. John xi. 2 can be explained only by supposing it was the author's original intention to omit this passage altogether. Otherwise it would have been soon enough in xii.

[2] As was remarked by Origen on Matt. 77, Mark xiv. 5, by giving the price, gave the weight—a pound. Comp. above, p. 264, n. 2. On the filling of the house, Origen on the Canticles, ed. Lomm. XIV. p. 429: replevit omnem hujus mundi domum ac totius eccl. domum.

[3] On this assumed box, see above, III. p. 347. Wich. p. 90, thinks it was an alms-box (since Origen thus names the almoner of the church).

[4] The question in the second century (not for the first time in A.D. 170) was the $\tau\eta\rho\epsilon\tilde{\iota}\nu$ and the $\mu\dot{\eta}$ $\tau\eta\rho\epsilon\tilde{\iota}\nu$ of the Jewish Passover-day. The striking $\tau\eta\rho\epsilon\tilde{\iota}\nu$ (comp. above, p. 264, n. 4) may allude to that, and the sense then is: leave her alone, that she may observe the (my) festival upon the day of my sepulture or the day of my death. See Eus. 5, 23 sq.; and below, p. 274, n. 2.

[5] See above, p. 270, note.

the names from the others, the Bethany pedigree is said to be made out.¹ It has also been easy to find in the incident in Luke traces of the Johannine Bethany-homage, i.e. the anointing, not the head, but the feet, and the drying them—moistened, not with tears, but with ointment—by the hair of the woman who was performing the act of homage; although in this remarkable humiliation—the anointing the feet and wiping them with the hair—probability is in favour of the penitent of Luke and not of the Johannine friend of Jesus.² But even apart from general Gospel criticism, we are led to a different conclusion by the report itself. The latest Gospel has utilized to the very letter the late Mark; and even the quantity of the ointment—a pound—is inferred from Mark's calculation as to its cost.³ It has without doubt also utilized the earlier Luke, and particularly two passages in Luke, the one where he describes the sinful woman, the other where he describes the two friends of Jesus in the Galilean village, Martha the hostess and Mary who sat reverently at his feet.⁴ That the fourth Gospel also borrowed Lazarus from Luke is shown by the resurrection of Lazarus, on which occasion the family trio have already appeared, Martha and Mary especially exhibiting the same diversity of character as at the festive meal and in Luke.⁵ New features, doubtless neither old nor original, are the transformation of the house of Simon—who according to the naive harmonists was the father or the brother-in-law of Lazarus—into that of Lazarus, the conversion of the nameless or the sinful woman into Mary, the undefined quantity of ointment into a pound, the nameless disciple

---

¹ See the fables, below, p. 274, n. 1. How harmonistically have Ebrard, Wichelh., Bunsen, and even Bleek, laboured in this province! According to Bunsen (p. 390), the Synoptics have confused the Johannine account.

² An extreme self-humiliation might indeed befit the pious adherent (against Volkmar, p. 560), but it would much better befit the penitent woman.

³ John xii. 3 and Mark xiv. 3; John xii. 5 and Mark xiv. 5.

⁴ Luke vii. 37, x. 38 (see above, I. p. 104, III. p. 151, V. p. 87). The relationship of the adulterous woman in the spurious passage in John to the sinful woman in Luke was discussed above, pp. 165 sqq.

⁵ Above, pp. 79 sqq.

into Judas the betrayer,—whereby we may very plainly see that no Evangelist would have forgotten the betrayer if that betrayer had in fact in these last moments troubled Jesus and the woman. Moreover, the words of Jesus would have been far too mild for the one whom he knew to be his betrayer.[1] The sixth day before Easter, which John mentions instead of the second, stands closely related to the reminiscence of the historical entry day of Jesus, with which it is sought to bring the meal into connection. The subtle author probably attempted to indicate that if Jesus was anointed to his burial on Saturday the 8th of Nisan, at Bethany, the next Saturday would naturally be the sad and solemn day of Jesus' sepulture.[2] Thus we have here artificially constructed narration, and not history. Those who object to this must remember that, with the loss of the resurrection of Lazarus, the house of Lazarus and the wonderful excitement of an association at table of the raised man and Jesus are irretrievably lost also. It is therefore quite worthless to interest oneself in the possibility

---

[1] Whilst formerly the penitent in Luke and the friend of Jesus in John (to the profit of the former and to the prejudice of the latter, Bleek, II. p. 113; above, p. 270, note) were identified and placed under the name of Magdalene, recently Ewald, Bleek, and others, have brought together the Simon of the Synoptics and the three members of the family in John. Ewald, as several Fathers (above, p. 84, n. 1), found in Simon their old, now deceased, father; Bleek (after Paulus), the (according to P. deceased) husband of Martha! On the other hand (following ancient precedent), Renan, Wich., Bunsen, and others, are content to find in Simon the host, in Lazarus the guest. But Judas has been retained, not only by Paulus and all the defenders of John down to Renan, Bunsen, Wichelh., but even by Schenkel.

[2] The proximate purpose of the definition of date in xii. 1 is the definition of the day of entry, which also, according to Synoptic tradition, fell about a week before the catastrophe. Since the author wished to preface the entry into the city by a short rest at Bethany, partly in order to give new prominence to the place which had become important through Lazarus, partly in order to give the Jerusalemites time to come out to Jesus, he very appropriately fills up the time by introducing the meal, as he did not wish to come back to Bethany again. Thus it was that, for the sake of the symbolism of the death, he fixed upon the sixth day before Easter for the meal. The sixth day before the 14th of Nisan, before the Friday and the day of Jesus' death (according to John), is the 8th of Nisan, Saturday, the same day of the week as the burial day of Jesus. Volkmar (p. 560) reckons the day as Sunday, therefore the same day of the week as the resurrection; but the sepulture has nothing directly to do with the resurrection, and it is well known that in John we must not reckon from the 15th of Nisan, but only from the 14th.

that the village of Martha and Mary mentioned by Luke, who so often incorrectly mixes up dates and places, was after all no other than the Bethany of John.

C.—AT JERUSALEM. THE LAST SUPPER.

The Thursday—in the later Christian mediæval language called Green Thursday—the 14th of Nisan, the day of the Passover lamb (the 14th of April), dawned, and brought with it the seven-days' Passover festival.[1] Two fundamental ideas, which seem to have gradually coalesced, dominated this festival. It was the festival of the divine passing over (pesach, old Aramaic and Greek pascha) of the people in Egypt, perhaps originally—as in the customs of other nations—an expiatory festival connected with the spring equinox. To this had attached itself, since the settlement in the Holy Land, the agrarian celebration of the beginning of the time of harvest.[2] The opening of the festival placed the two fundamental ideas at once prominently in the foreground. On the 14th of Nisan the lamb was slain, its blood and its fat dedicated to God, and its flesh eaten by the sacrifice-guests on the beginning of the 15th. Again, in the night of the 15th—16th the first barley was cut, and in the morning, after having been ground, was brought with oil and incense before the Lord. In early times the Passover sacrifice was evidently celebrated by every head of a household at his ordinary place of abode, as is indicated by the sprinkling of the door-posts and lintels of the

---

[1] The name (dies viridium, comp. pascha floridum for Palm-day) is differently explained. We may think, not of the Passover herbs, but of the green spring food. Might not also the antithesis of the Lord's Supper joy (dies lucis) and the hebdomas nigra lie therein? The German name Easter, according to Bede, from the Anglo-Saxon goddess of the light of spring, Eostre; *Karfreitag*, dies lamentationum. Comp. Steitz, in Herzog, articles *Pascha* and *Grosse Woche*.

[2] On the original expiatory signification of the festival, comp. later the executions at Jerusalem, and particularly above, II. p. 399, note 2. On the name πάσχα (Aramaic, Herzog, *l.c.*; Targ., Rabb. pis-cha), Buxt. p. 1765. Gesenius, *Hdw.* II. p. 372. Wichelh. p. 5.

house with the lamb's blood. But from the days of Hezekiah and Josiah it was connected with the temple and Jerusalem. A remnant of the universal priesthood remained to the people in the right possessed by heads of households to slay the lamb even though it necessitated a breach of the Sabbath when the festival fell on one, and in the sacrificial meal which gathered together the household as such.[1] The festival was held to be so sacred and was so profoundly venerated that, notwithstanding the difficulties of travelling in the spring, thousands, nay millions, of Israelites streamed towards Jerusalem, the seat of it, from all parts of the world; the non-observance of the festival was indeed threatened with death.[2]

On the morning of the festival day, the disciples went to Jesus with the question, "Where wilt thou that we make ready for thee to eat the Passover?"[3] They took it for granted that Jesus would observe the sacred rite; and since he had in these last days been looking forward to the festival with longing, the observance of it would already have been spoken about, even though Jesus carelessly delayed, or seemed to delay, making any detailed arrangements, and though no one had thought at all of providing a Passover lamb on Sunday the 10th of Nisan, according to the old rule of the Law which was obsolete.[4] The disciples' question left it open to Jesus to decide where he would like to eat the Pass-

---

[1] 2 Chron. xxx. 1 sqq., xxxv. 1 sqq.; Ex. xii. 7. Comp. generally Winer and Herzog, *Pascha*. Pascha breaks the Sabbath, Lightfoot, pp. 373, 458. ἱερωσύνη παντὶ τῷ ἔθνει, Philo, *Vita Mos.* 3, 29; comp. my *Gesch. Chr.* pp. 18, 72. Above, I. p. 349.

[2] Above, I. p. 303. Ex. xii. 15, 47; Numbers ix. 13.

[3] Matt. xxvi. 17; Mark xiv. 12. On the other hand, in Luke xxii. 7, Jesus first makes general arrangements, and then asks the disciples about the place.

[4] Longing of Jesus, Luke xxii. 15. The day of selection, Ex. xii. 3. Obsolete, according to *M. Pesach.* 9, 5 (Steitz, in Herzog, *Pascha*, XI. p. 141). Jesus had not been quite careless; he had perhaps already privately engaged a place, see below. Jesus' tardiness in this weighty matter has long been found objectionable, comp. Gabler, in his *Theol. Journal*, II. v. pp. 441 sqq. Strauss, 4th ed. II. p. 381. Now also Volkmar (p. 562), who finds it a sign of a non-historical character. He holds, indeed, that Mark is no biographer, but a doctrinal narrator of the pre-arranged death-bed!

over lamb. Without doubt they thought of Bethany, since the immediate neighbourhood of Jerusalem, at least as far away as Bethphage, had the right to eat the Easter lamb outside the city, a right based on the subtle theory of connections of locality, but which was also in harmony with the domestic character of the festival, and had reference to the over-filling of Jerusalem.[1] But Jesus chose Jerusalem, although for two days he had kept away, and although in taking this step he had to fear the violence of his foes.[2] In this remarkable resolve might be read the intention of provoking the attack of his foes, of finally bringing on a crisis to his intolerable position, or the hope of attaining his end, not certainly by the help of the festive-tempered people, but by the help of God. The general mood of Jesus, however, has pointed not to hope, but to resignation; and his quiet, private entry into Jerusalem shows that he sought neither the violence of his foes nor the miraculous arm of the Father. His choice of Jerusalem rested simply upon the wish to celebrate the sacred rite at the legal festival locality, and in the midst of the people who were similarly engaged and to whom he still desired to belong. And he wished to give to the solemn rite which *he* was secretly intending to establish, a higher sanctity by its performance in the neighbourhood of the temple, in the city of the Great King, in the city where the people of God assembled, in the city of prophetic testimony. "Go into the city"—said he to the disciples, two of whom, according to Luke Peter and John, he selected as his messengers—"to such an one, and say unto him, The Teacher says, My time (he meant his death) is at hand; I will make the Passover at thy house with my disciples;" or according to another account: "Where is the chamber, that I may eat

---

[1] Lightfoot, p. 198, whence it appears that the lamb had to be slain in the temple, but could be eaten in B. Comp. above, p. 134, notes 1 and 2.

[2] Volkmar (p. 561) thinks that Jesus had been in conflict with his adversaries until Wednesday (why not until Thursday?), and had incensed them; and that the breaking off of the struggle in the Gospels is the *schema* of the writers! With reference to the final attack, there should be added to IV. p. 274, note 2, that even Neander (p. 486) thought of the employment of Sicarii against Jesus.

the Passover with my disciples?"[1] It is thus evident that he indicated to them, and that not obscurely, a distinct name which afterwards escaped memory, the name of a reliable and well-to-do adherent at Jerusalem, in whose house he could with certainty expect to find a room at his disposal, notwithstanding the overcrowded condition of Jerusalem, a person of whom indeed, according to one reading, he had previously and in secret engaged a room.[2] If any one wishes for a name, the one most readily to be thought of would be that of Joseph of Arimathea, the former disciple and the friend at Jesus' death, were it probable that tradition would here have forgotten the man that it did not forget elsewhere.[3] This view would apply at least to Matthew; while in Luke and Mark tradition was compelled to combine with the inclination to make a mystery of the miracle, a tendency not only to conceal the name, but also to set aside all well-known names.

These unquestionably obscure accounts, which are at once put to the blush by the simple, clear, sober words in Matthew, represent Jesus as speaking to his disciples in the manner of a clairvoyant prophet, just as in the case of bespeaking the animal on which to ride into Jerusalem. "Go into the city, and there will

---

[1] Matt. xxvi. 18 (disciples in general, whereon Volkmar makes merry); Luke xxii. 8 (Peter and John); Mark xiv. 13 (two disciples, as many times elsewhere). The first form of Jesus' words in Matthew, the second in Luke and Mark. A certain one, Hebr. peloni almoni. Make=asah, Joshua v. 10; comp. Xen. *Hell.* 7, 4, 28: ποιεῖν Ὀλύμπια. The time is not that of the Passover solemnity; perhaps—as has been readily assumed—Jesus had ante-dated that by a day (Kuin. and others); nor is it the Messianic manifestation (Ewald). Comp. Wich. p. 228.

[2] According to Luke xxii. 11 and Mark xiv. 14.

[3] Ewald (also Lichtenstein, *L. J.* p. 394) thought of the house of John Mark, Acts xii. 12. Erasmus and since him Bleek and Meyer have assumed that Jesus mentioned the name. Kuinöl thought he did not name him (lest Judas might find him out); according to Fr. the disciples already knew who he was. According to Theophylus, and also Wichelh. (p. 226), the man was unknown and himself knew nothing of the matter; and Jesus sent in faith in the Almighty Father, who could open to him a large room! The sentence, *Schol. Luc. vit. auct.* 19: τὸ δεῖνα εἰώθασιν οἱ παλ. λέγειν—ἐπὶ τῶν συγκρύπτειν τι βουλομ. τῇ ἀοριστίᾳ τοῦ ὀνόματος, does not altogether apply. Wetst. p. 516. Even Olsh., II. p. 385, found in Matthew's narrative simply nothing miraculous (as Strauss, 4th ed. II. p. 383); Weizs. (p. 559) also thinks of a friend's house, but speaks of a secret arrangement.

meet you a man carrying an earthen pitcher of water.¹ Follow him, and where he enters in say unto the master of the house, The Teacher says, Where is my room, that I may eat the Passover with my disciples? And he will show you an upper chamber, large, spread with cushions, and furnished; there make ready for us."² As to this communication, we shall be equally perplexed whether we see a miracle here or none.³ In the former case, it would have to be assumed that Jesus when at a distance saw men walking about in Jerusalem, detected the right one out of thousands, the right servant, the right master, the one favourable to him and just then at home, the right room,—in fact, that he saw everything, pitcher, house, cushions, and the owner's sentiments. Nay, more; the miracle must extend from Jesus to the disciples; for in the bustle of the festival city, to detect the right pitcher-bearer among the multitude of pitcher-bearers who would be fetching water for washing utensils and the hands of the guests, could be only a matter of accident or of miracle.⁴ In the other case, there would have to be assumed an arrangement made by Jesus with the Jerusalemites, not only as to house and room and table, but also as to the sending out of a

[1] Hewers of wood and drawers of water the most menial of servants, Deut. xxix. 11; Joshua ix. 21. Wichelh. (p. 230) indulges in fancy as to the locality of the well.

[2] Luke xxii. 10; Mark xiv. 13. Volkmar (p. 563), following Luther's erroneous translation, explains ἐστρωμένος = square-stone chamber, the chamber of the Sanhedrim,—this or such a high-priestly room was placed at Jesus' disposal. One can talk like this when one likes to indulge in poetry. From the time of Homer (Wetst. p. 672; Wichelh. p. 232), the Greeks said στρωννύειν κλίνην (sternere triclinia), comp. Acts ix. 34; and the κλίνη, indispensable at this meal (see below) and (below, p. 280, n. 5) placed at the disposal of the guests, is pointed to by Matt. xxvi. 20; Luke xxii. 14. If any one will force in the meaning of stones, there were in Jerusalem ἐστρ. enough, exclusive of the lishkat haggasit, e. g. the temple courts, the palaces, the better houses. Prophetic knowledge, e. g. Samuel's concerning Saul, 1 Sam. x. 2 sqq., to which Strauss, 4th ed. II. p. 385, and Wichelh., p. 226, appeal. But who would think, with Volkmar, p. 562 (after Strauss), that Jesus, like Saul, was on the road to kingship or to high-priesthood!

[3] As formerly Schulz, Schleier., Weisse, Wich., Ewald, could prefer the narrative of Luke and Mark, so now again Holtzmann, pp. 96, 203. Volkmar, p. 568 : to the prosaic it is much too wonderful! For Matthew, rightly, Theile, Strauss, Meyer, Bleek. The superiority of Matthew dawns even upon Weisse, I. p. 600. Others attempt to give a natural explanation of Luke and Mark (Olsh., Neander).

[4] Above, I. pp. 108, 124, 170; II. p. 303; III. pp. 271 sq.

servant with a pitcher; and in point of fact, some have already seen in this an eloquent sign of the anxious situation, and of the well-weighed and cautious action of Jesus with respect to his foes and his betrayer.[1] To others, this solution of the difficulty will be still more objectionable than the untenable miracle. Jesus is dishonoured rather than honoured by ascribing to him this secret cunning and this triviality of previous arrangement; and it would remain to be explained why the arrangements should have been made in this mysterious manner, when the sending of trusted disciples with definite instructions as to man and house would have effected the same end, and that yet more quietly and privately.[2] It is plain that the tradition included a miraculous knowledge; and the sign of the man bearing a pitcher came in appropriately because he symbolized the preparations for the solemnization of the festival, to which, e.g., the washing of hands was indispensable; perhaps also because he symbolized, in a half-Johannine way, the transition of Jesus from the Jewish water to the wine and blood of his own last supper.[3]

Thus we shall do best to abide by the simple account of Matthew. In the first place, then, Jesus was announced, and with him his twelve disciples.[4] It may here be mentioned that it was customary to allow to strangers the use gratis of the necessary room, with articles of furniture, especially with cushions and tables; in return for which it was usual to leave behind the skin of the Passover lamb and the earthen vessels that had been employed.[5] Further, it was the custom for the family circle that

[1] Thus Gabler, Paulus, Kuinöl, Kern, even Neander (p. 526). Comp. Strauss, 4th ed. II. p. 383.

[2] We could only assume that Jesus, in the unavoidable presence of others (as Judas), would be compelled to speak this obscurely, or that he could not rely upon the silence of even his most trusty followers if he gave direct commissions and names.

[3] Comp. above, IV. p. 210. Volkmar's exposition, based on 1 Sam. x. 3, see above, p. 279, n. 2.

[4] Volkmar (p. 570) justifies to himself the fable that Jesus partook of the last supper *with a part* of his disciples.

[5] *Bab. Jom.* f. 12, 1; *Megill.* f. 26, 1 : traditio est, non mercede conduci domos Hierosolymis, quia propria non erant. — Recepit ergo paterfam. ab hospitibus coria sacrificiorum. Abai dixit : hoc etiam inde discas, moris fuisse, ut quis relinq. vas

gathered together to eat the lamb, to be composed of from ten to twenty definitely enumerated persons.[1] Jesus, together with his disciples, represented a family; indeed, he had always assumed the character of the head of a household, and had acted as such in the breaking of bread at their common meals. The number of heads at his table stood about midway between the usual extremes. The wider circle of disciples and the Galilean women were left out, not only on account of the number, or of the non-necessity of the participation of women, but also because Jesus wished to have around him only his own household, his most intimate disciples, that he might say and give to them the last that he had upon his heart to say and give.[2]

Whilst these things were taking place at Bethany, Jerusalem was not idle. The two opposite movements—the turning of Jesus towards Jerusalem and his sorrowful celebration of the Passover, and the plots of the hierarchs against Bethany and Jesus—must, by a remarkable accident, have coincided to the day and almost to the hour.

The Gospels of Matthew and Mark relate that, on the last day but one, or the last day, before Easter, on the 12th or the 13th

---

fictile atque etiam corium sacrif. s. hosp. suo. Wetst. p. 516; comp. Lightfoot, p. 376. *Ab. R. Nat.* f. 9, 1 : nec dixit quisq. prox. suo : non inveni clibanum, in quo assem Pascha meum, vel non inveni lectum, in quo recumbam. Lightfoot, p. 186. A part of the strangers (Winer) may have celebrated the Passover under tents.

[1] Jos. *B. J.* 6, 9, 3 : οὐκ ἔλασσον ἀνδρῶν δέκα. πολλοὶ δὲ καὶ σὺν εἴκοσιν ἀθροίζονται. Similarly Jon. on Ex. xii. 4 (minus quam decem, quantum ad comed. agnum satis). *Pesach.* f. 64 ; 2 *Ech. R.* 1, 1 : non est P., in quo numerentur ultra decem. R. Chila dixit : etiam XL, etiam L ; fil. Caparæ : imo C. Wetst. p. 517. *Gem. Pesach.* c. 5 hal. 3 : si mactant pro non numeratis, profanum est. Lightfoot, p. 377.

[2] The women, Lightfoot, pp. 379 sq. Whilst, however, *e. g. Hier. Pesach.* f. 37, 2, mentioned the wine as the joy of the festival for all, even women and sons, *Bab. Pes.* f. 109, 1, gave prominence to fine clothing as that which had the most attraction for them. According to the Gemara, the women were not obliged to eat the Passover; the Karaites distinctly excluded them. Thence is in part explained the absence of the Galilean women. According to the Gospel of the Hebrews, James, the brother of Jesus, was present at the last supper: jurav. Jac., se non comesturum panem ab illa hora, qua biberet calicem domini. Even Hilg., *N. T.* IV. p. 27, *Zeitschrift*, 1868, pp. 63 sq., admits the doubly unhistorical character of this remark, since James was no Apostle, and at that time was not a believer; but it took its rise in the spirit of the Palestine church, which made James equal to the Apostles.

of April, Jesus' opponents held a final consultation against him.[1] The Gospels favour the former day, that is, the Tuesday on which Jesus closed his ministry at Jerusalem with the reckless candour of his "Woes" pronounced against Pharisees and Scribes, and then hastily withdrew to the Mount of Olives. The consultation would have been most appropriately held on this day: the unparalleled demagogic attack of Jesus united the hierarchs by arousing their instinct of self-preservation, and on this very day it could be best decided whether proceedings should be taken against the disturber before or after the festival. The fourth Gospel, which places two decisive sittings of the Sanhedrim at the time of the raising of Lazarus and of the re-entry of Jesus into Bethany, need not here be noticed.[2] Matthew reports now in detail a meeting of the high-priests and elders of the people in the palace of the high-priest Caiaphas (his proper name was Joseph), whose initiative John also mentions. Luke in his brief notice is silent as to this; and Mark still more inexcusably never mentions the name of Caiaphas, and finds it enough to speak of high-priests in general and Scribes.[3] Neither this earlier account

[1] Matt. xxvi. 3; Mark xiv. 1.   [2] John xi. 47, xii. 10 (comp. below).
[3] Matt. xxvi. 3 (erase γραμμ.); John xi. 49. Luke xxii. 2 and Mark xiv. 1 have only high-priests and Scribes (hence the introduction of the latter in Matthew); yet Luke at least mentions Caiaphas, iii. 2, Acts iv. 6. Caiaphas, originally called Joseph, Jos. *Ant.* 18, 2, 2: ὁ καὶ Καϊάφας; 18, 4, 3: Ἰώσηπον τὸν καὶ Κ. ἐπικαλούμενον. Matt. says only λεγομ., which (as καλουμ.) may refer to the name (ii. 23, ix. 9, xxvi. 14, 36, xxvii. 16, 32 sq., 57), and surname (i. 16, iv. 18, x. 2, xxvii. 17). The surname, not according to usual acceptation (also in Hausr.) = Kepha (like Peter), but = Kajepha (kajeph naphshi, *Targ.* Ps. lvii. 7; Buxt. p. 1024). Paulus, *Ex. Hdb.* III. ii. p. 463 (followed by Fritzsche, Meyer, Grimm), quotes the subst. kajepha (depressio), *Targ.* Prov. xvi. 26 (Buxt. *ib.*). Verb kuph, comp. kaphah, kaphaph, subst. kaph, signifies to bend, to press down. Jost. I. p. 332 (comp. *ib.* I. p. 404), thinks of the town Chaipha. Noack's fancies, p. 245. Comp. Wichelh. p. 49. The time of Caiaphas, above, I. p. 266 (even Grimm, A.D. 25—36!). In deference to Luke and John, recent critics depreciate Caiaphas in favour of Annas, in comparison with whom he was of no importance, and remained high-priest so long only because of his insignificance. Thus Langen, p. 230; Hausrath, p. 411. Αὐλή here is not court (Vulg. atrium, recently Meyer, Friedl.), which certainly is the meaning in Matt. xxvi. 69; Luke xxii. 55; Mark xiv. 66; but, according to late usage, Athenæus, *Deipn.* 4 (but comp. Odyss. 4, 74), house or palace; comp. Esther vi. 4; Matt. xxvi. 58; Mark xiv. 54, xv. 16; John xviii. 15. Luke xxii. 54 plainly enough puts οἰκία for it; and again Matt. xii. 29 substitutes οἰκία for the αὐλή of Luke xi. 21.

nor the urgency of the occasion requires us to think of a full gathering of the Sanhedrim. It was rather an informal assembly of the leading men among the high-priests, Scribes, and rulers of the people, such as we see meeting together and arriving at decisions in various critical circumstances down to the time of the last Jewish war.[1] The point of greatest moment was, that now the antagonistic parties, and at their head the highest spiritual dignitaries, acted in unison. That Sadducees and Pharisees were acting together is shown, on the one hand, by the fact, which is certain notwithstanding the obscurity thrown over it by the Gospels, that Caiaphas the high-priest, and his father-in-law, and perhaps at that time still more influential man, Annas, were both Sadducees; and, on the other hand, by the credible report of Luke and Mark that Scribes, factually Pharisees and Sadducees, were present. Indeed, John also represents high-priests and Pharisees as acting together in the Sanhedrim after the raising of Lazarus.[2] This complot of the parties is rendered intelligible by what had previously occurred, chiefly by the last address of Jesus, which, notwithstanding its predominant application to the Pharisees, nevertheless disavowed respect for any of those who sat in Moses' seat, for any of the Scribes, and repudiated all faith in the durability of their God-opposing rule.[3] The coalition of Sadducees and Pharisees, most of all the appearance in the front line of action of Sadducees holding the highest offices, and infamous on account of their reckless severity and cruelty, portended the speedy downfall of Jesus, unless a divine miracle interposed between him and his foes.[4]

[1] Comp. Jos. *B. J.* 4, 5, 4; *Ant.* 17, 6, 3: 'Ιουδ. οἱ ἐν τέλει; 20, 8, 11: οἱ προὔχοντες; 20, 1, 1: ἄρχ. κ. πρῶτοι; *B. J.* 2, 12, 5 sq.; 2, 15, 2; 2, 17, 5: οἱ δυνατοὶ σὺν τοῖς ἀρχιερεῦσι. Also 2, 14, 8; 4, 3, 5, and *Ant.* 20, 10: ἀριστοκρατία ἡ πολιτεία. Similarly Paulus, *Ex. Hdb.* III. ii. p. 462.

[2] John xi. 47. The party attitude of Caiaphas, *Gesch. Chr.* p. 239. My article *Annas*, in *Bib.-Lex.* I. p. 135. The same view held by Renan, Holtzmann, Hausrath.

[3] Matt. xxiii. 1 sqq.

[4] Comp. also above, I. pp. 359, n. 1, 364, n. 2. *Gesch. Chr.* p. 239. It should be observed how the Talmud connects the spoliation of the chanujot (houses) of the sons of Hanan (Annas), three years before the destruction of Jerusalem, with the law-

And yet—a sign that Jesus was still feared by his opponents—even the powerful Sadducees, generally so contemptuous towards popular movements, were this time very cautious. When Caiaphas "the oppressor," the most influential and the ablest of the high-priests, who in an almost incredible manner had succeeded in retaining his high position for seventeen years under the emperor Tiberius, under two procurators, and particularly under that closely allied hyæna, Pontius Pilate,—when Caiaphas assembled the heads of the people in his palatial house within the precincts of the temple, it was the unanimous opinion that the person of Jesus must be seized and that he must be put to death.[1] The account in the fourth Gospel represents the councillors as giving way to despair under the overwhelming impression of the Bethany miracle (therefore much too early, in truth weeks before the entry), and as yielding with lamentation to their fate—viz. that every one would believe in Jesus, and that then Rome would take away the temple and the nation—until finally Caiaphas, erroneously called the high-priest of the year, with more than Sadducean sternness and violence, though at the same time with an all too tender consideration for the value of a human life, convicted his colleagues of both want of courage and of ignorance. This account, however, evidently contradicts not only the earlier sources, but also all the facts, by endeavouring to discover in the anxiety of the Sanhedrists and in the vigorous counsel of Caiaphas, who would have one man die for the nation, involuntary and miraculously, nay—in an impossible way—even divinely arranged predictions of the actual future, on the one hand of the downfall of Jerusalem in consequence of the guilt of shedding the blood of Jesus, on the other of the salvation of Israel and of the world through the death of Jesus.[2] But though it was unanimously

lessness of the sons of Annas (quia facta sua stabilierunt super verba legis), Lightfoot, p. 409. Their arbitrary conduct, *ib.* p. 502.

[1] More in detail upon Caiaphas' house, when considering the narration of the sitting of the Sanhedrim, Matt. xxvii. 1.

[2] John xi. 47. That Caiaphas is thrice said to be high-priest for the year doubtless betrays an erroneous view of the duration of Caiaphas' term of office, or of the high-

AT JERUSALEM. THE LAST SUPPER.

resolved that Jesus should be put to death, it was nevertheless found necessary to proceed with extreme caution. In the first place, his opponents wished to get possession of him by strategy, that meant now to come upon him secretly; in the second place, they apparently wished to postpone, not only the execution, but the whole action to the end of the festival, when the festival guests were gone, therefore for a whole week.[1] Thus no one thought of hindering Jesus from appearing before the people, if he would venture to do so, on the chief day of the festival, the 15th of Nisan, especially as there was no longer any reason to fear him.[2] They plainly thought of being able to rely upon the people of Jerusalem; any leaning towards Jesus, any inclination to disturbance, was looked for, and that rightly, only among the strangers, above all among the Galileans.[3] The risk involved in delay was at any rate less than that involved in too great haste. There was no longer any reason to be anxious in the interval about any immediate success of Jesus among the masses;

---

priests in general, xi. 49, 51, xviii. 13. If it had been mentioned but once, it might have been explained as an indication of the significance of that year. But why does it occur in xi. 51, xviii. 13? John was mistaken here as much as he was about the name (in truth the surname) of Caiaphas. Thus Bretsch., Strauss, Baur, Weisse; on the other hand, evasions even in Krabbe, p. 425. Comp. Strauss, 4th ed. II. p. 361. And he might mistake, because the Herods and the Romans often allowed the high-priests to remain in office only a year, from Easter to Easter. Comp. Jos. *Ant.* 18, 4, 3; 18, 5, 3, and above, I. p. 266. Lightfoot, p. 668. *Vajikr.* 189, 1: cum pontif. cœmerent nummo, abbreviati sunt anni eorum. That the high-priests enjoyed divine revelation corresponds better to the Old Testament than to the Johannine conception of Judaism, although, according to Jos. *Ant.* 3, 8, 9, the oracular character of the high-priests had ceased for two hundred years (he means since the death of John Hyrcanus, B.C. 107). Better that one should die, see parallels in Wetst. p. 919. Unconscious prophecy: vaticinata est filia Pharaonis et nesciebat, quid vaticinaretur. *Shem. R.* 1.

[1] "Not at the festival" was explained by Neander and Ewald, in opposition to all the expositors (comp. also Hase, p. 231; Krabbe, p. 453), as referring to an intention to carry out the purpose before the festival. Thus now also Hausrath, p. 444. An execution before the festival proper is indeed described by John. Wieseler, *Syn.* p. 367: apprehension not on the scene of the festival! Comp. on the passage, Matt. xxii. 15; Acts xii. 4.

[2] Hausrath, p. 444.

[3] Tumults at festivals, see above, I. pp. 254 sqq., 267. Also Wetst. II. p. 514. Incorrectly, Tert. *Ap.* 21: cum ingens multitudo deficeret.

and there was no danger of his escaping, since he could be apprehended and thrown into prison either in Jerusalem or at Bethany towards the close of the festival, or after the festival on his journey back to Galilee, or even in Galilee itself.[1]

But whilst Jesus' opponents were thus deliberating and resolving in Jerusalem, and, influenced not by magnanimity but by pusillanimity, were granting him a week's respite, deliberation and resolving were going on at Bethany, by which the plans of his foes were both supported and thwarted. Those plans were thwarted not by Jesus, not by the band of his friends and adherents, but by a spirit of darkness whose secret deliberations aimed at the same end as the consultation of his mortal foes.[2] The plot was devised by one hitherto an adherent, and, more than that, by one who was not a novice, by one who did not belong to the outer circle of disciples, but—the worst feature of all—by one of the old and most intimate circle of disciples, one of the twelve Apostles, Judas the man of Kerijot.[3] The fact of his betrayal of his Master is so unexpected, so incredible, so horrible; it so alarmingly threatens not only belief in all human fidelity, but also in the dignity and greatness of Jesus, in his knowledge, his judgment, his sagacity, most of all in the force of the impression he produced and the powerful influence of his love; it is so beset by the scorn of foes, led by the venomous Celsus, who exalts the discipline of a robber band at the expense of the attachment of the disciples to Jesus, that it would be greeted as the removal of a heavy weight from the heart of Christendom if it could be proved, what some have attempted to prove, that the betrayal by Judas never occurred, that it was a fiction of Christian fancy personifying in Judas the Jewish people with or without the inclusion of the Apostles, and desiring, by

---

[1] Schleier. (p. 417) thinks Jesus might have been able to save himself by retiring from Jerusalem.

[2] Ewald's representation (p. 531) is too strong: Jesus could not be seized until recourse was had to treachery.

[3] All the Synoptics lay stress upon "one of the Twelve." Matt. xxvi. 14; Luke xxii. 3; Mark xiv. 10.

the removal of Judas from the number of the twelve Apostles, to gain a place for the Apostle of the Spirit, Paul, in the sacred apostolic choir.[1] But unfortunately it is not possible to construct historical evidence for this bold and in truth fantastic supposition, a supposition which was afterwards somewhat modified even by its author.[2] It is true that the obscure story of Judas is veiled in enigma and partly in untenable myth. It is true that it is not certain whether Paul knew of a betrayer, whilst it is certain that both he and the Revelation of John even to the end spoke of twelve, not eleven, Apostles to whom Jesus appeared after his resurrection. All this, however, is easily explained; whilst, on the other hand, there exists the unanimous testimony of all the Gospels, as well as of the sources of the Acts of the Apostles, which bear witness to the election of a twelfth Apostle in the place of Judas; and the Christian invention of such a shameful stain upon an Apostle and upon the twelve Apostles, of such a terrible ground of accusation against Jesus, is not for a moment to be thought of.[3] In order to decide here

[1] Origen, Con. Cels. 2, 12 : στρατηγὸς μὲν ἀγαθὸς καὶ πολλῶν μυριάδ. ἡγησάμ. οὐδεπώποτε προϋδόθη, ἀλλ' οὐδὲ λῄσταρχος πονηρὸς κ. παμπονήρων ἄρχων.

[2] Unfortunately there is nothing to be made of Old Testament parallels, not even of Ahitophel, of whom Volkmar thought (2 Sam. xv. 31, xvii. 23). Comp., on the other hand, 2 Sam. xvi. 23, xvii. 1, 14. Volkmar, *Rel. J.* pp. 260 sqq. Quite recently, ib. *Ev.* pp. 554 sqq., where, however, the historical character of the man and of his rôle of betrayer (whether traitor to Jesus or to the earliest Church!) are admitted. But he could not have belonged to the specially chosen, to the "Twelve ;" and since such a betrayal would prostitute both the disciple ("a more than knavish person, a brutal caricature") and Jesus (rationalistic desperation of exposition), since moreover this help was not needed for the apprehension of Jesus, Judas was essentially only the type of the Judaism that put Jesus to death, and Mark in particular shows that this traitorous Judaism existed in all the Twelve. Strauss (*New Life*, Eng. trans., I. p. 376) has rejected this hypothesis, which is still thought much of by its author, but is approved (see below) and further developed by a Noack alone; it is rejected also by Hase, p. 232, and Mangold, article *Juda*, in *Bib.-Lex.* III. p. 429. We may call it fantastic and ill-digested, since a personification of Jewish treachery (comp. Acts ii. 23, iii. 13) does not lead to the forcing of the man into the number of the Apostles, the delineation of apostolic unfaithfulness does not involve the unification of the Apostles in one man, or at least in a betrayer.

[3] 1 Cor. xv. 5; Rev. xxi. 14. Of course the honourable title of the Twelve does not cease because one of them falls, particularly since his place is supplied, Acts i. 16 sqq. Is not Philip still called one of the Seven in A.D. 59, though Stephen had long

with full conviction, it is merely necessary to remember that the first Gospel writings containing an account of Judas came into existence only a generation after Jesus, during the lifetime of many old witnesses and even of Apostles; and also that all the Gospels as well as the Acts of the Apostles take pains, by illustrations out of the Old Testament, by explanations concerning the foreknowledge of Jesus, in a word by every possible means, to place the betrayal by Judas, the horrible dark spot, in a better, in an endurable light. In fact, the Gospels and the Acts take what would have been foolish and ridiculous pains in this respect if the matter were nothing more than a fable which had been "poetically" constructed as a rod of correction, a fable which, with the outlay of but little courage and reflection, must have been indignantly repudiated in a very different manner from other unhistorical incidents, such as, e.g., Luke knew how to discover.

The question how Judas came by his project can no longer be answered with certainty, though many, from the Evangelists downward to the recent times, have attempted with various arguments to find an explanation.[1] Unfortunately, scarcely anything is well attested except the naked fact of the betrayal, all details in the narrative, whether of the deed or of the end of the man, being mere surmises of individuals or late and obscure myths. Moreover, it is the case with Judas as with most of the Apostles: of his early discipleship not a single feature is reported which would in any way throw light upon his personal character

---

since finished his course, Acts xxi. 8 ? Does not Paul speak of the Twelve in A.D. 58, though the elder James had been dead since A.D. 44 ? In 1 Cor. xi. 23, there is still to be found a trace of the betrayal, since the precise statement of time, "delivered up *in the night*" (notwithstanding Rom. viii. 32), applies not to God, but rather to the human betrayer; thus not only Grimm and Mangold, but also Hilg. 1861, p. 316, explain it: night of betrayal. In support of the testimony of the fourth Gospel comes the Acts, i. 16, ii. 23.

[1] Comp. the collection of the views of antiquity, in Winer, article *Juda*. Strauss, 4th ed. II. pp. 363 sqq. Hase, pp. 231 sqq. Very reticent as to the motive, Strauss, and Weisse, I. pp. 450 sqq. The conceivableness of the act, A. Schweizer, *Dogm.* II. p. 144.

and the secret motives of his inner life.[1] The Gospels agree with the Acts of the Apostles, in representing him as having taken money, or as having been influenced by the prospect of a money reward, for his treachery. But whilst in Luke and Mark the money is promised him after his delivery up of Jesus, Matthew and subsequently John with much less probability represent him as bargaining to get money beforehand.[2] However, the two narrations which give this latter view are decidedly unhistorical. Matthew, or more correctly his editor, in detailing the transaction of Judas with Jesus' foes, and in giving Judas' question as to the amount of the payment for the betrayal, has in a very self-evident manner merely fabricated a fulfilment of prophecy. John, again, in describing the immediate occasion of Judas' resolve—namely, his vexation on account of the anointing at Bethany, which deprived him, the dishonest cash-keeper, of the rarely or never received sum of 300 francs, as well as on account of the correction administered by Jesus, which at the same time wounded his ambition—has narrated things found in no other source, things which have no other value than that of a skilful, surprising, and yet not reliable combination based on the two circumstances in Matthew, viz. that Judas bargained for money, and that he began his treachery after the Bethany meal.[3] Indeed, apart from

[1] It is remarkable that Judas' deed is not more fully handled in the apocryphal Gospels; either this dark side of the apostolate was avoided, or the main facts were found to be described with sufficient exactness in the Gospels, particularly in John. On the other hand, many accounts were in circulation as to the end of the traitor (see below). Concerning his youth, the Arabic Gospel of the Infancy, 35, says that Judas was the victim of a biting madness (comp. his kiss!), which in the lack of other substances to bite caused him to bite himself. Judas' mother went to Mary and her child; Judas, sitting by the right of Jesus, sought to bite him, but not being able to do so then struck him on the right side, making the child weep. Immediately the devil fled from Judas in the shape of a mad dog. It was in his right side that the Jews, moved by the same devil, after wounded Jesus.

[2] Luke xxii. 5; Mark xiv. 11; Matt. xxvi. 15; John xii. 6, xiii. 29; Acts i. 18.

[3] John xii. 4 sqq. To this adheres, e.g., Schleier. pp. 414 sqq.; whilst even Hase (p. 232) and Neander (pp. 517 sq.) differ from it. That John's conjecture is erroneous is to be seen from the facts that the Synoptics, while mentioning the objections of several disciples to the extravagance at Bethany, were not able to mention Judas, and that Jesus himself, even according to John, answered the disciples on that occasion with extreme moderation, and by no means combatted the vice of ambition (Neander, p. 517).

these arguments, the mercenary motive of Judas, in any form in which it can be presented, gross or refined, throws no adequate light upon the transaction.¹ A man who in association with Jesus imposes upon himself the sacrifice of temporal goods, who finds a satisfying compensation for what he has lost in the unanxious character of this living in common and in his hopes of the future, certainly could not so easily give way to the mean motive of pecuniary gain. Nay, if we accepted this commonplace motive, it would not be Judas alone who would be disgraced, but Jesus also who chose as a disciple a soul so fundamentally base, and in fact persisted in tolerating a notorious thief as cash-keeper.² In the same way the motive of wounded ambition disappears. This motive is to be found only in John; elsewhere it is not visible; for in the little disagreements among the disciples it is not Judas but the favourites, Peter and the sons of Zebedee, who manifest ambition. And if such a madness of passion on account of the mildest censure in the world is not altogether unworthy of the circle of Jesus, how is it to be explained that Judas sought merely the death of Jesus, and not also that of his rivals among his fellow-disciples, and particularly of the detested favourites?³

---

[1] It is remarkable that not only the many who will not give up the money, on account of the Gospels (Bleek, Ewald, Meyer, Krabbe, Wichelh., Mang., also Weizs., p. 562, who refers to Matt. xxv. 24), but even Strauss and Renan have defended this view, which is vigorously combatted by Theile, p. 63; Hase, p. 232; Neander, pp. 516 sqq., and Weisse, pp. 450 sqq. Strauss (4th ed. II. pp. 366, 380) still finds this (*New Life*, Eng. trans., I. pp. 375 sq.) more plausible than any of the ideal explanations. Renan (15th ed. pp. 394 sq.) puts the case thus: Judas did not covet money for himself (he would have gained more by remaining with Jesus), but he was rather an economist than an Apostle; he thought Jesus cost the company too much. Goldhorn had already (in Tzschirn. *Memor.* I. ii. pp. 152 sq.) converted him into a St. Crispin. Again, others have thought that Judas wished by his treachery to save his life and money. Henneberg, *Komm. über Leidensgesch.* pp. 32 sq.; recently also Lange, II. p. 1173.

[2] To Schleirm. also (p. 416) this is too much for Jesus and the fellow-disciples of the thief; it must therefore have been only an "inference" of John's. Similarly Neander, p. 517.

[3] This hypothesis rests simply upon John xii. 4 sqq., xiii. 26 sq., and is advocated by Kaiser, *Bibl. Theol.* I. p. 249 (also in Klopstock's *Messias*), recently by Wichelh. pp. 127, 132; also by Renan (15th ed. p. 394), who speaks of ruptures in the society, wounded self-love, and of the anger of the Apostles against the economist.

Those who do not admit the avarice and ambition of Judas to be his motives, will perhaps look with favour upon a second mysterious explanation, which Luke first offered and John afterwards adopted, namely, the temptation of Satan.[1] This certainly involves a renunciation of all explanation of this transaction by ordinary human motives. But when the motives are in fact so very inconceivable, recourse to obscure superhuman powers may be the more readily made; and the initiative of such powers, whatever effect those powers produced in the human soul, whether avarice, or ambition, or malicious destructiveness, saves both Teacher and disciple from harsh reproaches, and creates for the downfall of Jesus a not merely hateful but grandly tragical and truly cosmical background, which in quite recent times has called forth the lively interest of a philosophical thinker.[2] But if the earlier Gospels know nothing of this entering of the devil into Judas, and if Jesus here in plain words, as on other occasions, throws the blame of the crime upon the man Judas and upon him alone, are we to accept from less ancient sources a report which is clearly connected with later Ebionite and Jewish-Christian views of the devil and of Antichrist, as well as with the tendency in the direction of an unhistorical glorification of Jesus?[3] This last tendency is most strikingly impressed upon the Gospel of John. Whilst Luke, the predecessor, speaks simply of an entry into Judas of the devil that prompted him to treachery, John distinguishes between an inspiration of the devil and an entry of the devil, and represents the latter as not taking

---

[1] Luke xxii. 3; John xiii. 2, 27. Comp. the Arabic Gospel of the Infancy, quoted above, p. 289, n. 1.

[2] Daub, *Judas Iscariot, or the Bad in relation to the Good*, 1816. Comp. Ullm. p. 136; Mangold, article *Juda*, Bib.-Lex. III. p. 430. Also Olsh., Ebrard, Ullm., even Weisse, have spoken of the most extreme diabolical wickedness. Weisse, p. 451: thoroughly wicked motive, no better incentives.

[3] Comp. Matt. xxvi. 24; Luke xxii. 3; John xiii. 2, 27, comp. xii. 23, 27, 31, xiv. 30, xvii. 12. It is noteworthy that Luke gives expression to the dualistic idea of the Ebionite Gospel, John to the idea of the immanence of the Antichrist (instead of the eschatological Antichrist). The Gnostic Antichrists of the first Epistle of John stand as it were midway between the two.

place until Jesus assented to it when he handed to him the sop at the last supper and required him to do at once what he was intending to do. In the interval between Jesus' handing to Judas the sop and his uttering the words, Satan entered in. Besides this diabolic causation, a divine one appears in the Acts of the Apostles and to some extent even in John's Gospel, according to which the Son of God binds and unbinds the devil. The divine appointment which wills the death of the Son in order to give to mankind the redeemer through blood from sin and punishment, needs an instrument and provides it. This divine appointment is a bright conception against the gloomy power that wishes to rule man and to snatch the world out of the hands of God. And how often do we, in distress and sorrow and amid the inscrutable mysteries of existence, take refuge in this divine appointment? Yet no; we know of a divine appointment which permits wickedness, but none that is the author of wickedness for a good purpose.[1]

A semi-historically credible explanation of Judas' conduct can be arrived at only by bringing together the sparse historical facts and the historical probabilities of the situation. We thus obtain, in the first place, a sure impression that Judas, whatever may have been his behaviour in the beginning, was throughout Jesus' career to the close, like the other disciples, a trusted and self-denying companion of Jesus, even in those Galilean journeys of flight which none but the Twelve shared with Jesus. He therefore had a prospect of participating in the twelve thrones.[2] This impression is by no means affected by the conscious efforts of the

---

[1] Acts ii. 23, comp. iii. 13—18. Similarly Olsh. II. pp. 458 sqq.; see Strauss, 4th ed. II. p. 369. Also Ullm. p. 138. Akin to this view is that which makes Judas a willing instrument of this higher will, see below, p. 296, n. 2.

[2] Wichelhaus, p. 125 (comp. Krabbe, p. 459), lays stress upon the rights of Judas, the thrones, the blessed because of the seeing eyes, in order to show the horrible character of the sudden fall of him who was not predestined to salvation. On the other hand, Mangold (*Bib.-Lex.* III. pp. 426 sqq.) applies everything possible—the parable of the weeds and the wheat, the corrupt fishes, the non-wedding garment, the saying about offence—as warnings from Jesus to Judas. Weisse (II. p. 112) has thus applied the wedding garment, Weizs. (p. 562) the unfaithful servant.

fourth Gospel to exhibit him as a disciple who had been unfaithful from the beginning, and whose real character had all along been discerned by Jesus, as a disciple therefore who was self-called, to his own personal hourly torment, to the desecration of the holy cause, and also to his own ruin.[1] A fact totally opposite to a former voluntary self-renunciation is now shown by the progress and completion of the betrayal. When Judas spontaneously, without any instigation from without, goes to the hierarchs and offers them as prey the person of Jesus, when he subsequently remains as a designing hypocrite in association with Jesus, listens to his sayings, even accompanies him to Jerusalem,—when, finally, he volunteers the sign of betrayal, the kiss, and with cruel resoluteness steps up to Jesus to greet him as Rabbi and to kiss him, he shows himself to be determined and able, and at the same time to be a man who has broken through all the restraints of respect, of piety, of esteem and love, and has passed over to the most cold-blooded contempt or to the intensest hatred.[2] In such a case, it becomes once more quite evident that this detestable conduct is very poorly explained by motives that would have their rise in mere avarice, or ambition,

[1] John vi. 70, comp. ii. 24 sq. This absolute knowledge of Judas by Jesus (held not only by Wich., p. 133, but also by Weisse, though without knowledge of the betrayal, p. 452), was too much for Strauss, 4th ed. II. pp. 367 sqq., and even for Schleierm., pp. 440 sq., comp. *ib.* p. 320. Whilst other conservative theologians endeavour to exhibit in Judas as Apostle at least a struggle between good and evil, a possibility of moral victory had he possessed great spiritual capabilities (comp. Neander, Ullm., Olsh., Krabbe, Wich., Press.), Schleierm. held that the discipleship of Judas was intelligible only on the assumption that the choice of the Apostles did not depend absolutely upon Jesus, but upon those who came to him. *Luk.* p. 88; *L.J.* pp. 320 sq. The preponderance of evil from the beginning is most distinctly assumed by Ullm., *Sündl.* p. 136; yet he makes ἐξ ἀρχῆς, John vi. 64 (Neander, p. 516), mean (Wich. p. 132) not from the beginning, but only from an early period. The Synoptics, on the other hand, do not show the knowledge of Jesus until the last evening, Matt. xxvi. 24.

[2] Inner apostacy, Schweizer, II. p. 144. External influence, *ib.* p. 145; and see below, p. 295, n. 2. Pressensé, p. 435, rightly speaks of a strong, passionate nature. Intelligent, worldly, violent, Hase, p. 233. Strength of character even in doing wrong, Weisse, p. 451. Lavater, comp. Wich. p. 128, speaks of his terrible elasticity, of the remains of apostolic greatness (Niemeyer, *Charak.* I. pp. 85 sq.). Neander, p. 522, speaks of his practical talents.

or even fear of suffering, since no such motives would really suffice to produce such a cruel uprooting of all traces of reverence. The conviction is irresistible that such a treatment of the Master can rest only upon the completest estrangement in the inmost consciousness of the disciple from his Master. According to the probabilities of the situation, this deeply penetrating rupture could have only two causes, the one or the other of which, or both united, brought about a radical revolution in the man's spiritual life. One was disappointment in the Messiah, who had excited the most gigantic expectations but had fulfilled none of them, who no longer wrought miracles, so that even the fear of his miracles passed away, who neither attracted the people nor smote his opponents, who withdrew from the public gaze, spoke sometimes of his own death, sometimes of the sufferings of his Apostles, sometimes, it is true, of the prospects of the future, but they were prospects which vanished like a jingling of words, like a hollow dream, in the presence of the actual reality.[1] The other was a growing respect for the men who sat in Moses' seat, who still extorted reverence, to whom belonged the temple with its marble splendour, with its treasures and its consecrated gifts, with its sacrifices, with its priests and Levites without number, and to whom the nation paid obedience and homage in the persons of the thousands, nay millions, that crowded to the Holy City and thronged the temple courts, whilst Jesus with his Twelve, insignificant and powerless, passed out of sight.

It is not to be denied that, under the pressure of these weighty facts, a profound crisis was possible among the adherents of Jesus. To those adherents the proud Jerusalem, the strong impression produced by which was felt and heard of on Jesus' retirement to

---

[1] Disappointment on these grounds is spoken of by most recent critics, Schleier. pp. 263, 440 (also Neander, Bleek, Mangold, Volkmar); Schenkel, p. 266; Hausrath, p. 444; particularly Ewald, pp. 531 sqq., who points out the general indefiniteness of the situation which was a source of temptation to all; on the other hand, Neander, p. 522, quite overlooks the special character of the situation. It is interesting that John's Gospel (xiv. 22) has ascribed this materialistic Messianic tendency to the other Judas.

the Mount of Olives, became in and of itself a place of temptation, and that both because of the collapse of the cause of Jesus and because of the so sudden, so violent check and suppression of the just now most highly-wrought expectations.[1] And while it must be regarded as one of the most notable indications of the spiritual greatness of Jesus that the crisis went no further, that from his still weak and materialistic followers the course which things were taking did not evoke a loud "But, why?" that apostacy did not make havoc among the Apostles, and that the one apostate was compelled to tread his dark path alone and silently, without even attempting to weaken the fidelity of his fellow-disciples, who stood firm and defiant as a strong wall, it is at least intelligible, and it reflects no dishonour upon Jesus, that one out of twelve fell, one whose preponderantly materialistic mode of conception and whose coarsely vigorous mode of action prevented him from preserving in the trying circumstances of the moment the equilibrium of his inner attachment to the person of his Lord. Moreover, it may be that a native of this southern district—as was this one alone among the Apostles, whether we look for Karijot in a southerly or in a northerly direction—became the subject of a burning mental struggle under the immediate influence of relations and friends; or the force of his old associations with the sanctuary of Israel was powerfully revived; or, finally, the legal-material pietistic tendency slumbering in the nature of the Judæan burst forth afresh under the excitement of the festival surroundings.[2] Such considerations

[1] Comp. Matt. xxiv. 1. The crisis in John vi. 66—71.

[2] Comp. above, III. pp. 276, 392. To the two places called Kerijot (LXX. Καριώθ) there mentioned, and of which only the more southerly had generally been taken notice of, there is now to be added a middle one, south of Bethlehem and Herodium, Khureitun (Kiepert and Van d. Velde). Matt. and John have Ἰσκαριώτης; Mark and Luke, Ἰσκαριώθ. In Cod. D and It. through all the Gospels, Σκαριώτ, Σκαριώτης, ἀπὸ Καρυώτου (D always in John, Sin. in vi. 71), Carioth, Scarioth, Scariothes (a). On Ish Keriot, comp. also Ish Jerush, in *Pirke Abot* and Talmud. Bleek, I. p. 418. On the fantastic explanation, Origen on Matthew, 78: exsuffocatus (also interesting parallel of the two Judases). Noack, p. 235, mentioned the Moabite Keriot. Olsh., II. p. 458, was led by Gen. xlix. 17 to think of the tribe of Dan.—Neander, p. 522, holds a preceding negociation by the Pharisaic party possible. A. Schweizer (*Dogm.*

will help us to form a juster estimate of even this crime, though we may not defend it or exculpate the "brave honest man." And whilst thus the criminal is raised from the brutish monster to the man who errs in a question of truth, the Master himself is again relieved from odium, and the dark incident of the betrayal is as a whole lifted above the level of a foul and repulsive scandal to that of a phase in the great human conflict between light and darkness, between truth and error.[1] Others have in other ways sought for higher motives in this catastrophe. But those who have ascribed to the apostate a belief in a miraculous power of Jesus which would necessarily protect Jesus from the consummation of his opponents' deed of violence, or in a power of Jesus which at the challenge of a hostile attack would be aroused to put an end to the fatal truce, and would with the assistance of the people and in connection with a festival insurrection effectually establish the Messiahship; or those who, following the precedent of the ancient Gnostics, would acknowledge Judas' efficient assistance in bringing about the redemptive death and the victory of Christian truth;—such have invented nothing that is noble, but only an impossible, a more or less unworthy and positively childish fancy.[2]

II. p. 145) suggests that perhaps Judas was previously acquainted with individual Sanhedrists. Hausrath, p. 444, thinks that Judas had always held an isolated position among the Apostles, and that on that account the second Judas was, for distinction's sake, called Lebbæus, the cordial.

[1] The brave man, in Schmidt, *Bibl. f. Krit.* III. p. 165 (Venturini explains himself differently). Comp., however, even Lavater, p. 248. More than knavish, a brutish caricature, Volkmar, p. 555.

[2] Belief in the miraculous power of Jesus, Theophyl., Lightfoot, Heum., Bahrdt, Niemeyer, Schmidt. The driving of Jesus into action, Thiess, Liebe, Goldh., Paulus, Winer, Theile, Hase, G. Schollmeyer (*Jesus u. Juda*, 1836). According to Paulus, *Hdb.* III. p. 351, and *L. J.* I. ii. p. 200, Judas wishes to save Jesus by a rising of the people, especially of the strangers. Comp. Hase, p. 233. The direct opposite is Henneberg's "Attempt to save Life and Money in the Shipwreck of Jesus," p. 245. Refutations in Neander, pp. 519 sqq.; Bleek, II. p. 399; Strauss, 4th ed. II. pp. 376 sqq. But the simple refutation is the terrible audacity of the man. Judas' attempt to bring about the redemptive death, view of the Gnostics, Irenæus, *Hær.* 1, 3, 3; 1, 31, 1; 2, 20, 1 sqq. Tert. *Præscr.* 47. Origen upon Matthew, 78. Epiph. 38, 3; comp. Strauss, 4th ed. II. p. 373; Wichelh. p. 128. Noack (*Gesch. Jesu*, 1870, pp. 230 sqq.) has recently fallen back upon the Gnostic opinion that Judas (Lebbæus,

Judas quickly executed his purpose. The sources agree in reporting that the betrayal was conceived and settled in the interval between the consultation of the opponents of Jesus on the 12th of April and the sending of the disciples on the 14th to make arrangements for the Passover meal. This report is in essential harmony with the facts, since Judas' proposal led to a change in the plan of the opponents, whilst on the other hand the execution of the conspiracy on the evening of the 14th, as well as Jesus' previous pointing to the betrayer in the course of the Passover meal, show that the conspiracy was arranged in the course of the 13th or early on the 14th. Matthew and Mark, however, give a still more detailed account. According to them, Judas' plan to betray is connected, directly or indirectly, with the Bethany meal, therefore with the late evening of the 13th or the early part of the 14th, most probably—as Matthew would lead us to think—with the late evening, since the work of darkness would be favoured by night, and Jesus missed none of his disciples on the morning of the 14th.[1] Though the Bethany meal offered little that was calculated strongly to excite the passion of the betrayer—of which John alone, and without ground, speaks —it was nevertheless, in the view of the disciple, the crowning point of Jesus' inaction and retirement, and of his resignation to death and the grave.[2] If Jesus had finished his career, if there was nothing more to expect or to hope for, if the much-vaunted Messiahship was entirely relinquished, then the time was come for Judas to finish his work, to close the old account, and to shape the new project. The report of the fourth Gospel does not shut out this intimation of the older sources. Certainly it is

the bosom-son) did Jesus the pleasure, the loving service of bringing him to the wished-for and honourable death by involving him in the Samaritan rising, and by leading him into fellowship with the Samaritan deceiver.

[1] Comp. the fine words in John xiii. 30. Among recent critics, Venturini (p. 416) has found probable an agreement with the hierarchs as early as the entry; Ewald (p. 534), such an agreement for several days before the betrayal. Matt. xxvi. 16 does not necessarily indicate a series of days.

[2] Schleier. (p. 416) surmises that the mention of sepulture gave the immediate impulse to Judas.

possible for us to assume, according to John, that Judas initiated the work of the betrayal on the evening of the last supper, after Jesus had challenged him and after the devil had actually entered into him, and that the execution of his work immediately followed its initiation. But it is quite as possible that John passed over the preparatory stages which according to the other sources were undoubted facts, and that he regarded the execution itself as being, in contradistinction to them, the consummated work of the devil. Indeed, the mention of the plan of betrayal which Judas carried with him to the last supper, as well as the connection of the betrayal with the incident at Bethany, plainly show a general agreement with the Synoptic account.[1]

In the secrecy of the early night, whilst Bethany went to rest, Judas took the road down from the Mount of Olives to the temple. Whether he still had to struggle within himself we do not know; the defiant obduracy which he exhibited the next evening scarcely permits us to believe in any protest of his heart at the last moment. Indeed we may conjecture that he, detecting in Jesus the false prophet whom Moses had beforehand described together with his genuine follower and fulfiller, would nerve himself to his work by repeating the saying: "When the prophet speaks in the name of the Lord and nothing comes to pass, then has the prophet spoken presumptuously, *therefore be not afraid of him!*"[2] At the time of the festival, when the people were going to and fro from early in the morning until late in the evening and even in the night, it would still be possible to get admittance to the outer court. The temple guard of priests and Levites, learning that he had important matters to communicate, directed him to the head authorities of the temple of whom Luke expressly speaks. These procured him access to

---

[1] John xiii. 2, 26—30. Also Lightfoot (p. 381) and the majority of recent critics connect John with the Synoptics. On the other hand, Strauss (4th ed. II. pp. 364 sqq.) thinks that, according to the fourth Gospel, Judas made no advances to the opponents until the last evening. Comp. Lücke, II. p. 484. On the other hand, with justice, Krabbe, p. 454.

[2] Deut. xviii. 22, comp. 15.

the chief priests, at any rate to Caiaphas, who may have been present or was sent for, or perhaps the secret visitor was taken to Caiaphas' palace.[1] Judas, with cold-blooded deliberation, announced his willingness and his ability to deliver Jesus into their hands. A gleam of joy and satisfaction, visible even in the dim lamplight, lit up the countenances of the hierarchs. They easily convinced themselves that this man was one of the disciples, and that he was in earnest. They hastened to seize the good opportunity without delay, and without regard to the resolution previously arrived at. The chief thing was to get possession of Jesus, and this possession Judas could effect without causing a commotion, in secrecy, and in the absence of the people, whose presence at the apprehension was especially to be avoided. The details of the plot could not yet be arranged, since Judas himself was not in a position to know what would be the next movements of Jesus; but upon this they were agreed, that Judas should take advantage of the next opportunity and make it known to those whose commission he was executing, and they on their part would await his call in a state of readiness.[2] Thus they parted for this time, after the new friends had held out to their accomplice, besides their laudatory recognition of the serviceableness of his good work, the prospect of a money payment for the sale " of the righteous."[3] That they did this, and that he accepted it without protest, was a fitting conclusion of the covenant. The hierarchs showed upon what they relied—upon violence and corruption; Judas accepted the mean estimate of

---

[1] The gates were closed towards evening (περὶ δείλην), particularly the inner, Jos. B. J. 6, 5, 3, but also the outer, Ant. 18, 2, 2. At the Passover, however, they were opened by the priests to the people at midnight, Ant. 18, 2, 2. Any one who announced himself at the door earlier would also be admitted, because there were dwellings in the courts. And whoever, e.g., announced the new moon, could gain admittance at any time. On the chief officers of the temple (Luke xxii. 4), see below, the apprehension.

[2] Matt. xxvi. 16; Luke xxii. 5, 6; Mark xiv. 11. Luke and Mark mention the joy, as well as the promise of money. The serviceableness of the act, Ewald has well emphasized, p. 534. Lightfoot (plainly also Schleier. p. 416) thinks that Judas had decided to deliver up Jesus immediately after the celebration of the Passover, p. 381, which is quite against the text.

[3] Sale of the righteous, Amos ii. 6.

his patrons by yielding to base motives, whilst he had meant to take the field only on higher grounds. We here make no use of the copious account of Matthew, for reasons which have been in part already stated. That Judas went abruptly to the hierarchs with the base question, "What will ye give me, and I will betray him to you?" and they then and there weighed to him thirty pieces of silver or shekels, i.e. about 90 francs, the double of what Herod the Great bequeathed to each of his guards,—this is not only opposed to the simpler account of the other sources, but it is an evident and intended imitation of the thirty pieces of silver which—according to his own figurative description—were weighed to the prophet Zechariah by his people as the paltry wages of a prophet, in truth a beggar's fee.[1]

The hierarchs had not long to wait. On the very next day, it happened that Jesus was to be found in Jerusalem. On the morning of that day (Thursday, April 14) we left the two messengers of Jesus in Jerusalem, engaged in the preparations for the Passover meal, according to the directions and in honour of their Master.[2] A number of miscellaneous details they might well leave to the hospitality of the host and hostess, who had already given sufficient evidence of their goodwill by granting the use of the commodious festival-room. To them would also be left the duty of removing the leaven out of the house and room, a ceremony which was carefully begun on the evening of the 13th by the light of tapers, and was completed at noon on

---

[1] Matt. xxvi. 15. As evidently Zech. xi. 12 sq. is used (comp. Matt. xxvii. 3, 9) where ἔστησαν (jishkelu) = weighed, the often favourite exposition, they promised, settled, promised it (Vulg. constituerunt ei, thus also Fr.), is impossible. To weigh to, also in Jeremiah's purchase of land, xxxii. 10. Thirty shekels the wages paid to God's shepherd by the people, Zech. xi. 12 sq. Also the price of a slave, Ex. xxi. 32. Lightfoot, p. 376. Fifteen shekels and some barley for an adulteress, Hosea iii. 2. Herod's fifty drachmæ, $Ant.$ 17, 6, 5. According to Origen on Matt. 78, the thirty shekels represent the years of Jesus. The shekel, four Attic drachmæ (a drachma a little less than a franc), $Ant.$ 3, 8, 2; more exactly (comp. Winer) $3\frac{1}{2}$ drachmæ, therefore 30 shekels about = 90 francs. Reckoning a shekel as four drachmæ, the amount would be 104 francs. Hase (p. 233) finds a small payment conceivable (without defending Matthew), since Jesus could be otherwise tracked.

[2] Matt. xxvi. 19. See above, p. 280.

the 14th. To them would fall the duty of baking, in the early morning, the pure unleavened *mazzot*, the cake of wheaten meal, as well as the preparation of the *charoset*—the thick batter of fruit flavoured with vinegar and cinnamon—and the bitter herbs. These were all reminiscences of the distress in Egypt, and, still further back, symbols of the solemn festival expiation and purification.[1] On the other hand, the disciples themselves, according to law and custom, undertook the purchase, slaughter, and preparation of the unblemished male lamb of the first year. There is nothing said anywhere of the presentation of a special festival sacrifice, of the so-called *chagiga* in cattle or small animals, which indeed was not required on this day.[2] The festival ceremonial began in Jerusalem at noon, while in Galilee all business was stopped through the whole morning.[3] At about 2 p.m. the blowing of horns called the people to the temple, which on account of the multitude of participants in the festival could be entered only by divisions of the people, by three consecutive divisions. The head of the house or his servant—in this case, therefore, the two disciples—took the lamb, when they did not then and there purchase it in the court, and bore it, with a knife fixed in the wool or attached to the horn, on their shoulders to the temple court, which was specially adorned for the occasion with bright-coloured carpets and was at once closed again. There

---

[1] The usages based on Ex. xii. 1 sqq. (particularized in the tractate *Pesachim* and in Maim.), see Lightfoot, pp. 376 sqq., 458 sqq.; Paulus, *Hdb.* III. ii. pp. 482 sqq.; Winer and Herzog, *Passah*. Friedl. pp. 38 sqq. Langen, *Die letzten Tage Jesu*, 1864, pp. 147 sqq.; also Wichelh. *Komm. zur Leidensgesch.* 1855, pp. 106 sqq., 247 sqq. Mor. Kirchner on the Jewish Passover and Jesus' last meal, 1870. The unleavened bread was referred to the haste of the exodus from Egypt, charoset (=pulmentum, Buxt. p. 831, made of pounded dates, figs, grapes, nuts, almonds) and the bitter herbs (lettuce, celery, parsley, cress, horse-radish) were referred to the clay and the bitternesses of Egypt. Certainly these materials were originally connected with the idea of purity at the feast of expiation.

[2] The choosing of the lamb (properly on the 10th of Nisan) and keeping it until the 14th (on the bed of the head of the house), Friedl. p. 43. Chagiga (Buxt. p. 707= festival, festival offerings, sacrif. festi) were held to be necessary only for the 15th, not for the 14th. Friedl. p. 49.

[3] Friedl. pp. 41, 45.

the priests inspected the animals and ascertained the number in each Passover-meal company.[1]

In consequence of the multitude of persons bringing sacrifices, these regulations were not punctually observed. We learn incidentally that the names of the heads of houses—e.g. that of Jesus—were not written down, but that the number of persons keeping the festival was subsequently calculated from the number of kidneys of the lambs.[2] About 2. 30 p. m. the evening sacrifice was slain and an hour after was laid upon the altar. Then the triple trumpet-signal of the priests and the choral singing of the Levites, the so-called "Hallel," gave the sign for the slaughter of the lambs, which took place between 3 and 5 p. m.[3] The heads of houses themselves or their commissioned servants generally slew the lambs; the priests stood in two long rows, with great silver and golden lipped bowls, in which they received the blood of the animals, and passed it through the hands of others until it reached the altar, at the foot of which it was poured out.[4] The lambs, hung upon the iron hooks of the walls or pillars of the court, or else upon a staff between the shoulders of two men, were then flayed and disembowelled, the tail, the fat, the kidneys, and the liver, consigned to the altar, and the rest, wrapped in the skin, was carried from the temple hill to the house, towards evening, as soon as the last division had finished operations.[5] When evening fell, the carcase was skewered crosswise through the length and across the forepart of the body with dry pomegranate sticks, and cooked in the ground in a specially-prepared earthen pot-oven without bottom. At sunset, when the stars rose and the beginning of the 15th of Nisan was announced by

---

[1] Comp. Lightfoot, p. 376, &c. The place of the head of the house taken by a servant, *Pesach*. 8: dicit quis famulo: macta mihi Pascha. Lightfoot, p. 459; Friedl. p. 46. Inspection, Lightfoot, p. 377; Friedl. p. 47. The carrying=hirkib, Lightfoot p. 377. The knife, *ib*. p. 458.

[2] Above, I. p. 303.

[3] Lightfoot, p. 376; Friedl. pp. 46 sqq.; Kirchner, p. 15.

[4] *L. c.*   [5] Friedl. p. 48; Kirchner, p. 16.

the sounding of trumpets from the temple hill, the meal could begin.[1]

In the evening, when it was dark, Jesus, leaving his retirement at Bethany, appeared in the city and in the well-lit house of his host, with his disciples, from among whom not even Judas was missing.[2] According to the later Jewish custom, he reclined upon the ground, which was covered with cushions, carpets, or mats, he himself occupying the middle place and his disciples being on either side of him. They thus expressly illustrated the view that while the ancient custom of standing signified the servitude in Egypt, the later custom of reclining signified the liberty won even for the poorest in Israel.[3] One cushion generally sufficed for three guests, and was thence called a *triklinion*; we have therefore to imagine four cushions arranged in a semicircle in order to make the usually round and low footstool-like table accessible to all.[4] The position of each individual was such, that supporting himself on his left hand, he had his right at liberty to use in eating and drinking; the feet were stretched out behind. Jesus lay upon the single cushion in the middle—this was the place of honour; of his two neighbours, the one, lying above, therefore again in a place of honour, was at his back, the other at his breast. Thus conversation was somewhat difficult: if Jesus wished—to abide by the description of the fourth Gospel—to converse with John, who lay at his breast, John would have to turn himself; if with Peter, then Jesus would have to turn from left to right.[5]

But these are the least important questions. It is a matter of

[1] Si tenebræ oboriebantur, exibant et assabant, Paulus, III. ii. p. 483; Friedl. pp. 50 sq.; Kirchner, p. 17; Herzog, p. 148.

[2] Matt. xxvi. 20; 1 Cor. xi. 23 (night); comp. Friedl. p. 50. Volkmar (p. 570) thinks only a part of the disciples were present. According to Venturini, Jesus had breakfasted sadly in the morning with his mother.

[3] *Hier. Pes.* f. 37, 2: mos servorum, ut edant stantes, ut nunc comedant recumbentes, ut dignoscatur, exiisse eos e servitute in libertatem. *Bab.*: record. libertatis. *Hier. Pesach.* 10, 1: etiam pauper in Isr. non comedat nisi inclinatus. Wetst. p. 517.

[4] Lightfoot, p. 377.

[5] *Ib.* He thus explains the positions of John and Peter in John xiii. 23 sq.

much greater moment that we can obtain no distinct picture of the course of the meal. In the Jewish authors, from the Talmudists down to Maimonides, we have exact descriptions of the Passover meals, although contradictions are not wanting, and the literal likeness of the celebration in the days of Jesus and by Jesus is questionable. In the Christian Evangelists, on the other hand, we have, besides brief allusions to the Passover celebration itself by Jesus, a detailed narrative of only the remarkable addition which Jesus made to the Passover meal in *his* last supper.[1] But how they were both connected, how the supper was accommodated to the Passover meal, how far it retained or abbreviated or supplanted the latter in its ceremonies and in its compass, we have no certain account. As a consequence, many various suppositions have been made, which differ so widely, that while some critics have thought of an observance by Jesus of the whole Jewish ceremonial, and an introduction of the supper at the close of the Jewish celebration, others have thought of a setting aside of the latter at its very commencement, and yet others of a direct and undivided unity of old and new.[2] However, if we are never able to arrive at a certainty upon this point, we may rejoice in the fact that the second, the decisive act, the Christian supper, has been described to us by the pens of four writers, three Evangelists and the Apostle Paul, this last being the earliest witness to and the faithful reporter of the tradition of the Apostle Peter. By these it has been described in a detailed manner, though not without difficulties and contradictions in small details.[3] Indeed, a careful treatment of the existing

---

[1] Even between Hillelites and Shammaites it was disputed, *e.g.*, whether the wine or the day was to be blessed first. *Pesach.* 10, 2; Lightfoot, p. 378.

[2] The first, *e.g.* Friedl. p. 64, Langen, p. 153, Meyer, pp. 492 sqq., Wichelh. p. 252; the second, Fritzsche and others, who place the introduction of the new features at the customary breaking of bread; the third, Hilg. *Ev.* p. 214; *ib.* 1868, p. 63. Similarly, Volkmar, p. 568.

[3] Matt. xxvi. 20 sqq.; Luke xxii. 14 sqq.; Mark xiv. 17 sqq.; 1 Cor. xi. 23 sqq. Comp. Rev. iii. 20. A critical comparison and general estimate would lead us too far. Some have preferred Matt. and Mark; others, Luke; others, John, who gives however no Passover-meal and last supper, but only an ordinary meal, xiii. 2 sqq. (see below),

AT JERUSALEM. THE LAST SUPPER. 305

scanty material still remaining as to the Passover meal might succeed in procuring for us better-established assumptions concerning the early part of the celebration.

Among the Jews the Passover meal had the significance of a joyful festival. Every one looked forward to it with longing; and the morning meal was curtailed in order that a good appetite might be brought to the Easter lamb and the unleavened bread.[1] Even Jesus opened the ceremony in a joyous mood. It is true there was sadness mingled with the joy; for while he was glad to be able to eat this *last* meal, he was sorrowful at the prospect of the separation. "With yearning," said he, "have I desired to eat this Passover with you; for I say unto you that I shall not eat it again till it is perfected in the kingdom of heaven."[2] With

---

on which account Schleier. (p. 420) expresses himself somewhat sceptically, and the negative criticism naturally rejects all the testimonies, even that of Paul. Renan holds that much more was soon made of the last transaction of Jesus than it originally signified, as only metaphorical expressions and the custom of breaking bread lay at its foundation (15th ed. pp. 312 sqq.). Strauss, respecting the testimony of Paul, in his first "Life of Jesus," 4th ed. II. pp. 421 sqq., now finds him no longer certainly reliable, *New Life*, Eng. trans., I. p. 389; to which Volkmar (pp. 565 sq.) follows with a decided negative, making, with indifferent foundation, the assertion that Paul was absolutely wanting in the capacity to report objectively; hence here only the Passover-meal with a part of the disciples remains, to which has been added the later use of the Church and Paul's subjective belief. Paulus had already furnished a precedent, since he found at least the repetition of the transaction (Paul, Luke) unhistorical, but derived from the later Christian ritual, III. ii. p. 527. Thus now also Wittichen, *Idee des Menchen*, p. 175. Weizs. p. 554, correctly: the transaction belongs to the most certain! Comp. on the different accounts, especially Paul's, my essay on the "Last Supper in the Meaning of the Founder," *Jahrb. für deutsche Theol.* 1859, pp. 63 sqq.

[1] *Hier. Pes.* 37, 2 : necesse est, ut homo exhilaret uxorem s. et filios ad festum. At quomodo exhilarant? Vino. According to *Bab. Pes.* 109, 1, also clothing (children, wheaten bread and nuts), Lightfoot, pp. 379 sq. Comp. Herzog, XI. p. 147.

[2] Luke xxii. 15 (Gospel of the Hebrews: μὴ ἐπ. !), comp. Matt. xxvi. 29. It is difficult in general to prefer Matt. and Mark to Luke, and *vice versâ*, since each part has its superiorities (comp. Bleek, II. p. 409); evidently, however, in Luke the introduction is most faithfully narrated (Neander, p. 530), and there is no ground for Volkmar's (p. 568) objection (Hilg. *Ev.* p. 214 ; *Zeitschrift*, 1868, p. 63) that Luke as a Pauline writer makes a distinction between the Jewish Passover and the Christian ordinance, that he wishes to show two acts (Ewald, p. 547, rightly asserts the contrary). The ἐσθιόντων of Matt. and Mark, and the μετὰ τὸ δειπν. of Paul and Luke, show that the institution of Jesus assumes the preceding essential completion of the Jewish Passover, as indeed it is impossible to suppose that Jesus would really neglect the fes-

these words he lifted from the table with his right hand the first cup of red wine which a disciple had filled.[1] It was usual to fill the quart cup with three parts of wine and one part of water poured into the wine at table, in order to make an agreeable drink.[2] The customary blessing of the first cup consisted of the words: "Praised be thou, Lord our God, thou King of the world, thou that createst the fruit of the vine!"[3] After he himself, supported by his left hand, had drunk as the custom was, he passed round the one cup, which he lifted up as an eloquent sign of the unity of his community. "Take it," he said, "and divide it among you; for I say unto you that I will no more hereafter drink of the growth of the vine, till I drink it new with you in the kingdom of my Father."[4] Through a long series of significant

tival custom.—The addition, "before I suffer" (Luke), is to be ascribed to the writer; on the other hand, the mention of not eating (Luke) and drinking any more (Matt., Mark) is more appropriate to the beginning of the transaction (Luke) than to the end (Matt., Mark), where Jesus has already proceeded to the institution for the disciples (against Meyer, and Bleek, p. 409). The fulfilling in Luke is not accomplishment (Matt. v.), but completion, without more exact definition (Bleek, II. p. 408: eternal celebration of the spiritual redemption, comp. Wich. p. 274).

[1] *Hier. Pesach.*: præceptum est, ut vina rubido (jain adom, comp. Gen. xlix. 11; Prov. xxiii. 31) præstet id officium, Lightfoot, p. 380. Lifting up, Lightfoot, p. 384.

[2] Size of the cup of glass, metal, &c., several finger-lengths, Lightfoot, p. 380. Quart (rebiit): quartana vini italica (3 cyathi, 6 conchæ, 12 mystra, spoons) ib. quarta pars aquæ, *Pes.* 108. Wetst. p. 518. Paulus, III. ii. p. 529. Friedl. pp. 54, 63. Gloss. on *Bab. Ber.* 50, 2: vinum eorum strenuum (strong) erat admodum, Lightfoot, p. 380. But sapor et adspectus vini must remain. *Bab. Pes. ib.* Also undiluted wine allowed, *ib.* As to the shape, comp. the sacrifice-cup on coins, round-cup on pedestal, or bag-shaped with constricted neck, as among the Greeks. In the houses of the rich we may think of silver cups, above, I. p. 359.

[3] Lightfoot, p. 378. Friedl. p. 54. Baruch ha-bore et-peri ha-gephen.

[4] Luke xxii. 17. Probably a two-fold intimation of the end, according to Luke xxii. 16 and Matt. xxvi. 29, Mark xiv. 25. The Gospels (including Luke xxii. 17, notwithstanding διαμερ.) assume one cup; the late Rabbis speak of a cup for each, which the head of the house blesses in his own, Lightfoot, p. 378. Comp. Paulus, *l. c.* p. 513. Friedlieb, p. 63. Langen, pp. 149 sq., 185. Hence Maim. (Lightfoot, p. 378) speaks of an *ebibere* of the head of the house, which does not occur in Jesus' meal. According to the requirements of each, there was (Maim.) more or less water added, Friedl. p. 63. The smallest quantity of wine which each individual might take was half an egg-shell. Paulus, *l. c.* Probably at the time of Jesus the ordinary custom was simpler; in fact, such a number of cups might not be found in every house. It is to be assumed that the one cup was repeatedly filled in the course of the meal. That Jesus himself drank is implied in Luke xxii. 18, Matt. xxvi. 29 (Origen, *Con. Cels.* 1, 70); Jerome, Aug., Chrys., and others, represent him (according to Matt.) as drink-

AT JERUSALEM. THE LAST SUPPER.

ceremonies, of which the Gospels make no mention, they slowly approached the festival meal. The table was brought forward bearing the various kinds of food, including the lamb already cut into pieces. The company then ate with thanksgiving the bitter herbs, and also, after praising God who had created the fruits of the earth, the sweet red batter, into which was dipped herbs and pieces of bread about the size of an olive. The table was then pushed back, and there followed the mixing of the second cup, instruction concerning the Passover meal, the singing of praise, the beginning of the so-called Hallel (Psalms cxiii. cxiv.), and finally the second cup circulated round the room.[1] A last and very significant solemnity formed the transition to the meal itself, after the table had been in the mean time again brought forward. The head of the house took two of the round loaves, broke one, laid the broken pieces upon the unbroken loaf, and repeated the words of thanksgiving: "Praised be He who brings forth bread out of the earth!" He then wrapped up a piece of bread in the herbs, dipped it in the sweet batter, and praised God the Eternal King who had sanctified Israel through his commands and had commanded *that* meal. Having eaten the piece of bread, the head of the house, after a fresh prayer, then proceeded to partake first of the lamb.[2] The unrestricted part of the transaction, the meal itself, now began. Every one ate and drank at will, following the patriarchal custom of the East of putting the fingers in the common dish.[3] For Jesus, the main point was to

ing of the eucharistic cup. The early expositors, and also Olsh., Rückert, De Wette, Baumg.-Cru., thought he had not yet drunk. On the contrary, rightly, Bleek, II. p. 408, and now also Meyer. On the not drinking any more, Strauss, 4th ed. II. p. 425, makes the remark: not exactly in the next days, but only before the next Passover, would the tarrying in this pre-Messianic dispensation end for Jesus! On the drinking anew, Bleek, p. 409: glorified spiritual drink!

[1] Chiefly according to Lightfoot, pp. 378 sq.; Paulus, *l. c.* p. 511; Friedl. pp. 54 sqq.; Wichelh. pp. 247 sqq. Meyer, *Matth.* pp. 492 sq. The formula: Bened. sit, qui creavit fructum terræ. Difference as to Hallel, Lightfoot, p. 459.

[2] Benedictus sit ille, qui producit panem e terra. B. tu, dom. Deus noster, rex æterne, qui nos sanctif. præc. suis, &c. Lightfoot, p. 379. Plate-like, thumb-thick bread-cake.

[3] Matt. xxvi. 23; Lightfoot, p. 379.

pass from the legal transaction—which he may have abridged in some of its details, particularly the repeated washings—to himself.[1]

He had come to the city with a presentiment of his impending fate. On the way to the city, however, his suspicion that infidelity lurked within the circle of his most intimate companions was strengthened to certainty, not by the solemn warning of a friend such as Joseph of Arimathea, but by his observation of the whole bearing of the traitor-disciple, now of his silence, then of his forced cordiality, scarcely however of any confusion in his manner.[2] Some mistrust may be felt as to the report of the Gospels that Jesus knew his betrayer. Harmonious as the Gospels are in the main fact, they differ remarkably in the details, and there is a strong contrast between the simple account of Luke and the highly coloured one of Mark, still more that of Matthew, and most of all that of John.[3] And were they not all, Luke included, interested in removing from Jesus any stigma arising out of the betrayal by a disciple? They could not accomplish this better than by representing Jesus as knowing of the betrayal, nay, as supernaturally knowing and even willing it, by making him point with his finger to the apostate and at the same time announce the necessity of his downfall and the inexpiable guilt of the delivering him over to that downfall. Yet it is here

[1] Washing of hands, especially after the first cup, then before the breaking of bread, Lightfoot, pp. 378 sq.

[2] Information from without was thought of by Paulus, *L. J.* I. ii. p. 205: shortly before the sitting down, Jesus learnt that in that night, &c. Also Neander, p. 523. Strauss (*New Life*, Eng. trans., I. p. 388; comp. *ib.* II. pp. 318 sq.) does not think of the bearing of Judas; at most, Jesus might have been warned by a secret adherent. Thus also Volkmar, p. 570. But we know nothing of such a circumstance; and the whole behaviour of Jesus makes the impression of a distrust springing up within him. Strauss and Volkmar also admit that Jesus saw that his crisis was coming on. Comp. below, the prediction of the denial in the coming night. Similarly Ewald, p. 541. Weizsäcker, p. 562. A. Schweizer, II. p. 144.

[3] Luke xxii. 21—23; Mark xiv. 18—21; Matt. xxvi. 21—25; John xiii. 18—30. Scepticism, especially in Strauss (the passage was afterwards put in the mouth of Jesus, perhaps on the basis of the Old Test. [Ps. xli. 9; John xiii. 18]), 4th ed. II. pp. 410 sqq., *New Life*, as quoted in previous note. Volkmar, pp. 563 sqq. Weisse, p. 452: at least he did not designate Judas personally.

not simply a question of renouncing a tradition which has a strong testimony in its favour, which in the form it possesses in Luke and approximately also in that of the other two Synoptics is given quite irreproachably in the primitive words of Jesus, in vivid and by no means Old Testament style, with a characteristic outburst of passionate excitement, and is capable of being naturally explained as easily as the ordering of the festival room.[1] If, for instance—and this is the main point—the betrayer was really present, as he was (though nothing or at least no precise details are reported of his coming and going), because only thus could he act the spy upon his Master's movements, then—even assuming the greatest cunning on the part of the unfaithful disciple—it would be to think meanly and contemptuously of the searching and penetrating mental glance of Jesus, which is no novelty of yesterday to us, to suppose that the countenance of the criminal was not transparent to him who in Galilee had discerned the heart of Peter, of the paralytic, of the publicans, and who in Jerusalem had anxiously noted the weakness of his disciples; nay, who above all others had read the heart of men and of mankind.[2] Jesus was not able to conceal and to suppress the feelings which agitated his soul, even though he thereby hastened that breach in the festival joy from which he could not after all save the disciples. He owed it to himself, to his disciples, to the mutual confidence which existed between them and which was again to exist, to give expression to his suspicion, to his grief, to his indignant amazement. And perhaps the spoken words were

[1] John (xiii. 18) first quotes the passage from the Psalms (xli. 9). The Acts (i. 16 sqq.) does not refer to this fact, but to the prediction of the downfall of Judas. If Old Testament passages were wanted, Obadiah i. 7 and Micah vii. 6 might have been quoted; indeed, Jesus had applied the latter passage, Matt. x. 36. That no thought of such an application occurred to these Evangelists is itself an evidence of the simplicity and antiquity of the tradition. Comp. the remarkable similarity of Matt. xxvi. 24 and xviii. 6 sq.

[2] The Synoptics assume that Judas was there with the other Apostles; as to his going away (perhaps at the general breaking-up of the party) they are silent; on the other hand, John (xiii. 30) makes Judas leave before the others. Remarkable are the anxieties of Jesus concerning his disciples before Gethsemane, *e.g.* in the parables of the servants, Matt. xxiv. and xxv.

the means of clearly discovering whether he was in error or not; it was perhaps also the way to call back the brooding or half-decided disciple from the path of crime.[1]

Whilst, therefore, the eating was still going on—as Matthew and Mark rightly show, against Luke—Jesus surprised the disciples by the sudden words: "Verily I say unto you, the hand of my betrayer is with me at the table.[2] The Son of Man goes as is written of him; but woe to that man by whom the Son of Man is delivered up; it were good for that man if he had never been born."[3] The disciples were grieved, and began to cry one after another: "But it is not I, Lord?" Thus cried eleven in the consciousness of their fidelity, of their—in this respect spotless—innocence, an innocence to which even the bare thought of such a possibiility had never occurred. The voice of the twelfth reluctantly chimed in. Jesus was silent. His observation of the demeanour of the unfaithful one had strongly confirmed him in his suspicion, yet he could not renounce and thrust

---

[1] What is correct in the Johannine representation (xiii. 27) is, that Judas then definitively yielded to the devil. Certainly, if Jesus so prostituted him, as John represents, he was to a certain extent irresponsible.

[2] Matt. xxvi. 21; Mark xiv. 18. In Luke xxii. 21, it is after eating the Passover and immediately after the institution of the Lord's Supper; and since here (which Volkmar, p. 568, does not see) the indecorum begins that Judas remains at the Lord's Supper, Paulus, Olsh., Lücke, Neander, Friedl., Wichelh., Langen, Press., and others, have preferred first John, and then Matthew and Mark. Luke simply would not divide the transaction, whilst the two others had not given the former part of it, and therefore could well put this scene before the Lord's Supper. If Luke—according to Hilg. and Volkmar—had proceeded to separate the two transactions, the Jewish and the Christian, he would (just then) have been able to introduce this scene before the Lord's Supper. John (xiii. 18) places the scene after the beginning of the eating and after washing of feet, but before the last farewell, when Judas was no longer present. In so far, what Bleek says (p. 406)—that John, like Matt. and Mark, sets the announcement of Jesus in the beginning of the meal—is not quite correct. Ewald, p. 551, following Luke : at the end of the whole meal.—The words above according to Luke; on the other hand, Matt., Mark, John : one of you will betray me. Since these authors then bring "the hand upon the table" again, Luke is here evidently simpler. The word betray is not wanting to him, but Jesus spoke it only once.

[3] Matt. xxvi. 24; Mark xiv. 21; Luke xxii. 22. This expression frequent among the Jews: thoph lo (nuach lo), asher lo nibra (lo jitbare, lo ba [jaza] baolam [laolam], leor haolam). Bux. p. 1316. Lightfoot, p. 378. Schöttgen, pp. 83, 225. Comp. Matt. xviii. 6 sq.

AT JERUSALEM. THE LAST SUPPER. 311

out even the son of perdition; he therefore mentioned no name and gave no sign, and even refrained from any significant glance of his eye.[1]

This indistinct intimation on the part of Jesus very naturally did not satisfy the evangelical tradition. The exalted character and the glory of Jesus in contrast to the dark betrayal must be fully manifested by a clear designation of the sinner who was to pursue his course with the knowledge and the consent of Jesus. Thus the hand over the table, of which Luke had spoken, and by which Jesus did not intend to exhibit a sign by which the traitor might be known, but simply to make evident the horrible character of a betrayal by a table-companion, became in Matthew, Mark, and John, an actual sign of the guilty one. Certainly the utterance of Jesus in Matthew, which is in response to the urgent questions of the disciples, "He who has dipped his hand with me in the dish," might have been the actual original answer with the meaning that he wished to designate no one in particular, but simply to lay emphasis on the reality and the heinousness of the deed that was to be perpetrated by one of the circle of festival associates, in the same sense as Mark's descriptive narrative makes him say, "One of the Twelve will betray me."[2] But since, after those words of Jesus, Judas alone put the repeated question, "But it is not I, Rabbi?" it is sufficiently shown that *he* was the one dipping in the dish, and that Jesus intended to make him known as the traitor. In fact, the question of Judas is expressly and straightway answered by Jesus, "Thou hast said it."[3] In Mark, no question is proposed by Judas, and none is answered; but mention of the dish is there, and speaks as plainly as the most direct indication would do. This utterance

---

[1] Particularly according to Luke xxii. 23; Matt. xxvi. 22, &c. According to John xiii. 22, the disciples only looked at each other, though afterwards Peter and John asked the question. Paulus (p. 573) could not credit Judas with the boldness to ask such a question. Also Holtzmann, p. 203. This opinion justly applies to Matt. xxvi. 23—25, but not to xxvi. 21 sq. See also above, p. 293. Weisse's correct remark, above, p. 308, n. 2.

[2] Matt. xxvi. 23. [3] Matt. xxvi. 25.

in Mark must as such contain within itself a sign, because it cannot possibly be the mere repetition of the expression of abhorrence, which, according to Mark, Jesus had already uttered: "He that eats with me will betray me;" and because it cannot possibly refer to one then dipping, instead of one who had already dipped, as stands in Matthew, without the particular disciple who at that very moment stretched his hand toward the dish with Jesus being at once known as the man in question.[1] This making known the betrayer, which Matthew and Mark endeavoured to exhibit, has become in John, on the strength of the two Synoptics, a most obvious and palpable fact, and a most forcible testimony to the knowledge and power of Jesus, on which the disciples might rest their believing glance.[2] Jesus here speaks of the betrayer with a triple repetition; the disciples look at each other and are distressed as to who is meant. Then Peter makes a sign to the disciple who was beloved by Jesus and, lying to his right, rested upon his breast: "Ask who it is of whom he speaks?"[3] "Lord, who is it?" the favourite now asks of Jesus plainly. "It is he," answers Jesus, "to whom I will give the piece of bread which I dip in the dish." And lo! he gives it to Judas, and at once the devil enters into Judas, upon which Jesus urges to make haste, and Judas goes away. "And it was night."

All these narrations, circumstantial as they are, are unhis-

---

[1] Mark xiv. 19. Kuinöl, Henneberg, Hitzig, Weisse, Holtzmann, understand the words in Matt. and Mark quite generally, as the similar ones in Luke; but even Strauss, 4th ed. II. p. 415, finds that these two authors make the original and perhaps neutral words refer definitely to Judas. Quite ludicrous attempt at harmonizing the Gospel accounts in Kuinöl on Matthew, p. 707. Strauss, *l. c.* p. 413.

[2] John xiii. 21 sqq.; comp. the statement, xiii. 19, which, as Strauss also saw, *l. c.* p. 371, clearly shows the tendency of the author. But Sieffert could prefer John, pp. 147 sqq.

[3] The triple intimation (after what had already been given in vi. 70), xiii. 10, 18, 21. The mode of reclining, above, p. 303. But comp. also Wich. pp. 111 sqq. If, according to Lightfoot and Wich., Peter had the place of honour above Jesus, while John that below him, then Peter and John could not see each other without turning towards each other. But perhaps Peter lay upon another cushion where he could see John.

torical. Luke is much the simplest. In Matthew, the question of Judas—to have the audacity to put which, after the cursing of the birth of the traitor, he must have been a devil—and the confirmation by Jesus, have been forced into the text; in Mark, Judas' undisturbed continuance in eating, which then became itself a sign against him, is an absolute impossibility; and the Johannine report is nothing more than the artificial and at once apologetically tendency-supporting conclusion, based on these untenable previous accounts.[1] This picture is vivid and profound: the unfaithful disciple is designated and not designated, for only the favourite, and perhaps Peter, are admitted to the secret, and the betrayer is apparently so little publicly exposed, that the other disciples quite misunderstand the last requisition addressed to Judas, for they imagine it has reference to commissions for purchases for the festival. And what is still more significant, it is only by the will and act of Jesus, who ceases to guard the unfaithful disciple, that the latter is given over to the devil, whose victim, whose Antichrist he becomes, and then proceeds to commit his nocturnal crime.[2] But this individualization is completely dissipated by the confuting silence of the other sources, and by the impossibility that Judas should have continued to eat, or that Jesus, contrary to the usages of the table, should—after the Catholic-Lutheran fashion at the Lord's Supper—have thrust the sop into his mouth.[3] Moreover, when examined more closely, it is found wanting in delicacy in so many respects: in that intentional giving of prominence to those privileges of the favourite disciple which put an end to the actual equality of the disciples; in the exposure of Judas by Jesus, at least to John and Peter; and lastly, in the misuse of

---

[1] In Matthew we can erase xxvi. 25 without any injury to the text.

[2] Comp. the τηρεῖν, xvii. 12, and the perfect power of the Son of God, x. 18 and xviii. 6 sqq.

[3] John xiii. 26 speaks certainly only of a reaching forth to him, which was possible in itself. Paulus, III. ii. p. 507; Wich. p. 108. The intentional character of the conversion of the taking (Matt., Mark, Luke) into a giving, lies, however, on the surface. His taking would be unbecoming (as the kiss); *Jesus* must be the actor.

power to a prostitution, as well as in the harsh dismissal of Judas.[1] The earlier account is certainly more tender in every respect; and even the apparent harmony of John with the earlier, nay with the earliest account, in the persistent want of clearness in the minds of the disciples concerning the betrayer, only brings again into view this author's old offence of caricaturing the disciples' want of understanding. If Jesus had disclosed who was the betrayer to John, the latter must have understood or surmised the meaning of Jesus' words, "What thou doest, do quickly!" And if Jesus had in such a striking manner drawn John's attention to Judas, not one of the listening disciples could have misunderstood the dark secret that concerned Judas, whilst not one could have happened upon the idea that Judas was sent out in the middle of the night to buy something.[2] Let us not forget one thing more. Only a moment before this happened, Jesus had referred to the passage in the Psalms, "He who ate bread with me, has lifted up his heel against me."[3] If Jesus had really thus spoken, the obtuseness of the disciples, who saw with their own eyes the bread given to Judas, would be beyond comprehension. But there is no doubt that Jesus did not thus speak, since even Matthew, the most zealous appealer to ancient prophecy, knows not a syllable about it; while, on the other hand, John, in quoting this passage, has at the same time brought in an only apparently apposite fulfilment of prophecy in the giving of the bread to Judas. One of the Evangelists—Mark—had anticipated John in this, making Jesus say, "One of you will betray me; he who eats with me." Thus the passage in the Psalms may already have been present to Mark's mind; and if it had been present to the minds of all the Evangelists, the doubt

---

[1] Thus also Weisse, II. p. 277. Would not this also apply to John xiii. 18?

[2] Schleier., p. 417, found here the hint that Judas should now fetch his assistants. The late purchasing might remind us of the carelessness of Jesus (Matt. xxvi. 17) or of the disciples (xvi. 5). But who would make purchases near midnight, especially when, according to the Synoptics, the festival-day had begun (Levit. xxiii. 7; Numb. xxviii. 18; comp. Ex. xii. 16)?

[3] Psalm xli. 9.

AT JERUSALEM. THE LAST SUPPER. 315

would have been inevitable that the whole Judas scene, the table
and dish scene, owed its existence simply to the conversion of
the passage in the Psalms into a fictitious incident.[1]

As Jesus refused to give any further information concerning
the betrayer, the meal was continued, though certainly in a
depressed mood and with a doubly damped joyousness, because
the unknown betrayer still remained.[2] This serious mood was
acceptable to Jesus himself. This seriousness, the betrayer, the
impending death, made a bridge by which to pass to the transaction which was more to him than the Passover, and which
without doubt he had reflected upon during the last days, and
before he knew of the betrayal. He now proceeded to this, using
the privilege which, notwithstanding the restraints of the celebration, left to the head of the house considerable freedom in the
explanation and exposition of the rite, and considerable scope in
the conduct of the regular meal.[3] Whilst they were still eating,

[1] Comp. above, p. 309.

[2] From the time of the ancients, critics have been in doubt whether Judas was
present at the Lord's Supper or not, Wichelh. pp. 256 sqq. The Fathers, the Scho-
lastics (comp. Langen, pp. 165 sq.), the Lutherans, even the Reformers (comp. Zw.,
Calv., Butz., Bez.) are preponderantly of opinion that he was present; of recent
critics, e.g. Lightfoot, Bengel, Hofm., Strauss, Ewald. Most recent critics, however,
following Musculus, Piscator, Gomarus, Byn., are led by a general feeling of fitness to
believe that he was absent, Paulus, Olsh., Neander, Tholuk, Lücke, Bleek, Kahnis, De
Wette, Meyer, Friedl., Wichelh., Langen, Pressensé. Volkmar also (p. 569) expresses his
repugnance to the assumption, only he directs his anger merely against Matthew. If
we look to the evidence of the Gospels, we find that neither of the Synoptics favours
the going away of Judas; Luke evidently assumes his presence, only he renders this less
striking by making the institution of the Lord's Supper precede the declaration of the
betrayal (Luke xxii. 21), comp. above p. 310, n. 2. John xiii. 30 gives a departure
of Judas, but not before the Lord's Supper, about which John's account contains nothing;
on the other hand, it makes him go after the completion of the washing of feet (the
representative of the Lord's Supper), which Jesus performed upon the betrayer also
with a full knowledge of what the latter was about to do. According to Strauss, 4th
ed. II. p. 411, John gave the departure of Judas in order to introduce the conspiracy
then (on the other hand, see above, pp. 297 sq.). The reason is rather the complete
absolute severance, the handing over to the devil. The actual presence of Judas is
made more probable by Jesus' considerately refraining from naming him, and by the
absence of anything special in the distribution of the elements of the Lord's Supper; it
is postulated, moreover, by the fact that the betrayal was only thus possible.

[3] Paulus, and recently Strauss, Weizs., Holtzm., Holsten, have thought of the mood
of the moment induced—according to Paulus—by the breaking of bread. Even

though towards the end of the Passover meal, he took afresh, with solemnity as at the beginning of the transaction, one of the round plate-shaped loaves, gave thanks in the usual manner, broke the bread, laying the pieces as before upon an unbroken loaf, and then, without eating or drinking any more himself, said to the disciples: "Take, eat; this is my body which is given for you; this do in remembrance of me."[1] With this solemn act he ended the eating of the Passover. It is improbable that the material enjoyment of the terrestrial food was continued; the holy ceremony could not have been thus covered without losing its sanctity, and even the disposition to eat must have ceased. On this account it is to be assumed that Jesus carefully chose the moment when the eating was about to cease. Either the

Strauss, 4th ed. II. p. 426, gives the possibility of previous consideration. If any value is attached to Luke xxii. 15, 19, as well as generally to the long-cherished reflections of Jesus on the necessity and value of his death, the transaction must be held to have been premeditated.—With regard to the point of time of the transition, the essentially correct view is in Bleek, p. 410, Meyer on Matthew xxvi. 26; on the whole, also Paulus, p. 513, and Wichelh. pp. 256 sqq. Divergent views, above, pp. 304 sq. Friedlieb and Langen think of the emptying of the fourth cup.—With regard to the relative freedom of action, comp. the—in part quite unrestrained— declarations of the head of the house (Friedl. p. 55), and also the harmless continuance of the meal, cœnam protrahit, hoc vel illud edens bibensve, prout lubet. Lightfoot, p. 379.

[1] Paulus thought here of the last breaking of a piece of bread by the head of the house at the close of the meal (p. 513), which, however, belongs to a late custom; whilst Fritzsche would connect the act with the first breaking. Factually Jesus connected it immediately with nothing. The breaking of bread among the Jews, baza, chalak. The formula seh guph (corpus) hapesach, does not exist among the Jews; but Maimonides speaks of an eating of the guph hapesach. Lightfoot, p. 559. See Schöttgen, pp. 226 sqq. Paulus, p. 525. The formula of Jesus: Take (Matt., Mark), eat (Matt.); body given (Luke) for you (Paul, Luke); remembrance (Paul, Luke). Comp. my essay, 1859. The command to do it in remembrance, the institution, has in particular been questioned (Weisse, Holtzm.): Jesus was too modest (Kais., Stephani); the Christian overseers have spoken thus later (Paulus); it has risen up among the Christians through the annual Passover and the meals of the Essenes (!) (Strauss, *New Life*, Eng. trans., I. p. 390). Could not this opinion be supported by the fact that the Acts of the Apostles knows only of Jesus' breaking bread, and of no saving significance of his death? But the testimony of Paul (formerly recognized with its details also by Strauss, 4th ed. II. p. 426) decides. Volkmar would regard as original only, "This is my body, my blood" (p. 565). Weizs. p. 557: "Take, eat, this is my body." According to Holtzmann, the "eat this" is only liturgical (pp. 96, 204). On the other side, Gess (p. 147) harmonizes most beautifully by making Jesus say alternately, "for you, for many."

lamb was all eaten, and it only remained for the head of the house and the guests to eat the last morsel, of the size of an olive, which had to be done after the distribution of the bread of remembrance, as after that last morsel no one might eat anything more; or Jesus, towards the close of the meal, set aside the legal prescription as to the last morsel, and substituted for that this last loaf of bread.[1]

According to the Jewish ceremonial, the eating was followed by a third and fourth, seldom by a fifth cup, and between the third and fourth it was customary to sing the second part of the great song of praise, the Hallel (Psalm cxv.—cxviii.).[2] When, according to the four accounts which lie before us, Jesus, after the meal was over, having caused a cup to be filled, offered thanks for it, and, elevating it in commemoration of his death, presented it to his disciples, it is uncertain whether he had first exhausted all the cups allowed in the legal meal, therefore whether he was then consecrating the fifth cup to his death, or whether he devoted the third to this purpose.[3] The latter supposition is more than probable. There could be unity and coherence in Jesus' institution only through an immediate connection of the cup of remembrance with the bread of remembrance, otherwise the two elements of his transaction would be split apart.[4] Moreover, the accounts of Paul and Luke say that this cup followed the eating, they meaning by the eating not the complete Passover celebration to the fourth cup, but of necessity

[1] Lightfoot, p. 379. Every one ate at the last and had to carry away the taste of the lamb with him, Paulus, p. 517.

[2] Lightfoot, pp. 380 sq.

[3] Friedl., Langen, Meyer, think of the fifth cup, Jesus having necessarily gone through the whole ceremonial. It is seldom supposed to be the fourth cup (yet see Paulus, p. 529, against Langen, p. 153); on the other hand, very commonly among the ancients and in modern times the third cup. Comp. Lightfoot, p. 380. Thus also Hilg. Volkmar (p. 563) knows of only three Passover cups!

[4] Not without some plausibility, Bleek says (II. pp. 410, 413) it may be assumed from the Gospel and Paul that the eating still proceeded, and that there was therefore an interval between the two parts of the institution. In truth the sources say nothing on this point, and the grounds on which the representation in the text rests preponderate. Langen (p. 178) is also for the immediate connection.

simply the eating of the Passover lamb, in the course of which it must have been that the new bread of remembrance was distributed, since after the end of the eating of the Passover lamb nothing more might be eaten.[1] Finally, Paul expressly calls Jesus' cup of remembrance the cup of blessing, a designation which was given by the Jews to the specially solemnly-handled third cup, the so-called *kos haberacháh*, and to that exclusively. There is no conceivable reason why Paul should have thus designated the fourth or fifth cup, particularly as he very evidently supplements the Jewish designation by the Christian, " the cup of blessing which we Christians bless."[2] But if any one is suspicious of a celebration by Jesus which does not completely satisfy the letter of the ordinances, let him remember—if he has forgotten Jesus' freedom with regard to the ordinances—that the very institution of the bread and wine of remembrance was both in letter and in spirit a breach of the ordinances, nay of the law, a conscious and unconscious exaltation of the new religion above the old.[3] Thus then Jesus, taking hold with both hands of the third and specially holy cup, the cup which the Jews regarded as the solemn offering of the head of the house to his household, then elevating it with his right hand, he gave it to his disciples, and as he looked round upon the company he broke the profound silence by saying with impressive earnestness, " Drink ye all of this; for this is my blood of the covenant, which is shed for you; this do, as often as ye drink, in remembrance of me."[4]

[1] 1 Cor. xi. 25; Luke xxii. 20.

[2] 1 Cor. x. 16. The Jews also called it in full kos birchat hamas(z)on (cup of blessing of the food), Lightfoot, p. 380. Comp. Bux. p. 657. Wetst. II. p. 142. The solemnity (particularly the covering of the head of the chief of the house, and the general stillness), Lightfoot, *ib*. and p. 348. Even Paulus, besides the fourth cup, goes back to the third ; but the two could not be connected. The arguments of Meyer and Langen against the third cup are weak.

[3] Schenkel, pp. 270 sqq., speaks too strongly of a breach with the theocracy (also in Luke xxii. 16), Weizsäcker of acting independently of the law.

[4] *Bab. Berac.* f. 51, 1: velat se et considit; sudarium expandit in caput suum. Poculum accipit manu utraque, at dat in man. dextram, elevat a mensa, oculos in illud figit; sunt, qui dicunt, *dono* impertit suis. Drink ye all, Matt.; Mark secondary

Through all the Christian ages, since the days of Paul and John, for two thousand years, the faith and love of Christians have been exhibited in the task of showing the force and meaning of the act of Jesus which he prescribed in remembrance of himself, and which, even without any such prescription, he would have made historically immortal for every feeling man who saw in it the heart of Jesus and the breath of his love for all.[1] It may be admitted that this faith and love have often, in the obscurity in which at any rate this transaction is involved, far overstepped the boundary, and in the defence of their facts, or at least of their assumptions, each of which involved a question in the theology of redemption, they have lost themselves in the passion and zeal of their warfare. For mere dogmaticalness, mere uncharitableness, without higher interests, have never ruled in the Lord's Supper controversies which began in antiquity, were carried on in the Middle Ages, and culminated in the Reformation time between Luther and Zwingli. And though we may be thankful that the Reformation, by its conflicts and still more by its principle of the sole authority of the Bible and of free study of the Bible, has released us from one-sidedness of opinion and from the heat of the controversy, at the same time it must nevertheless be admitted that the real and extraordinarily great mysteriousness of the subject itself explained and excused the errors and the confusions of the centuries.

Whilst the Last Supper institution of Jesus was brief and unostentatious, a simple appendix to the broad basis of the Passover ceremonial, it was solemn and mysterious in form and great and profoundly significant in substance. However, a sober examination of the facts and of Jesus' words at once frees

(notwithstanding Meyer and Holtzm.), thus also De Wette and Bleek. My blood of the covenant, Matt., Mark, against Paul and Luke: this cup of the new covenant in my blood. Which is shed for you, Luke (against Matt. and Mark: which is shed for many; Matt. adds: for the remission of sins). Remembrance, in Paul; Luke, only in the first member.

[1] 1 Cor. x. 16 sqq., xi. 26 sqq., comp. John vi. 51 sqq. More in detail below, when considering its meaning.

us from the very mysterious interpretations which have prevailed from Justin Martyr in the middle of the second century, down through Lanfranc, Luther, the Catholic and the Lutheran Churches, the interpretations, namely, that represent Jesus as having distributed his veritable body and blood at the supper, and teach that the bread and wine are now changed by the words of the priest or the words of the institution into the actual body of Jesus, or that Jesus is offered to the faithful and veritably enjoyed by him together with the elements.[1] Formerly men wrote long works upon these questions. We now know that the phrase "This is," can mean here, as in hundreds of other cases, only, "This signifies my body." We know that the Apostle Paul himself extorted the same meaning when he spoke only of the eating of the bread, not of the body, and when he made Jesus say of the wine cup, "This is the new covenant in my blood," and not, "This is my blood." We know that the eating and drinking of human flesh and blood—a savage custom of Paganism, forbidden by the Jews—could never, beautifully as its real character might be disguised, belong to the religion of Jesus, to the religion of culture and of humanity. And the very thought of it was excluded by Jesus when he made bread, not flesh, the material substratum of his ceremonial. We know, finally, and this is the end of the controversy, that Jesus, neither when living nor when dead or glorified, was in a position to distribute his material body and his actual blood to be eaten and drunk, unless he was a magician, which he was not, or unless he—to speak more mildly—was able by divine power to perform not only the

---

[1] Already Justin, *Ap.* 1, 66 : τ. εὐχαριστηθεῖσαν τροφὴν, ἐξ ἧς κατὰ μεταβολὴν τρεφ. αἱ σάρκες ἡμῶν, ἐκείνου τοῦ σαρκοποιηθέντος Ἰησοῦ κ. σάρκα κ. αἷμα ἐδιδάχθημεν εἶναι. Similarly Ignatius, *Sm.* 7; Irenæus, 4, 18, 4 sq., &c. Recent literature : D. Schulz, The Christian Doctrine of the Lord's Supper, 1824 (second ed. 1831); Ebrard, The Dogma of the Lord's Supper and its History, 2 vols. 1845 sq.; Kahnis, Doctrine of the Lord's Supper, 1851 ; Dieckhoff, Evangelical Doctrine of the Lord's Supper in the Time of the Reformation, 1854, I. Very particularly, L. J. Rückert, The Lord's Supper; its Nature and its History in the Ancient Church, 1856 (comp. Baur, *Theol. Jahrb.* 1857, pp. 533 sqq.). Other treatises are mentioned, *e.g.* in Hase, p. 237, and in my essay.

impossible, but that which was repugnant to nature, which again he could not do, because he was not God, and because God himself could not thus act.¹ The meaning of this transaction was therefore a very simple one; it was, as Weizsäcker rightly and beautifully says, Jesus' last parable.² "This is my body, my blood," means, The broken bread is a symbol of my body; this red wine, this "blood of the grape," is a symbol of my blood; just as he said in the parable, the sower is the Son of Man, is a symbol of the Son of Man.³ This was not, however, the whole, the complete meaning; and those who give the palm to the exposition of those words by the Reformed Church may yet find themselves in a position, with reference to the whole transaction, to ascribe to their predecessors and contemporaries of that Church, not the correct exposition, but a presentiment of the correct one.⁴ The words give the impression that Jesus had something more in view than merely to exhibit before the guests a striking symbol of his body broken and slain for the salvation of the disciples. They give the impression of a present, of a gift, of which, singularly

---

¹ My essay on the Lord's Supper in the Sense of the Founder, pp. 84 sqq. Ewald (p. 547) suggests the lamb's flesh instead of the bread in case the meal was (which he does not believe) a Passover meal. In case of a partially Capernaumite view of the Lord's Supper, it would fare badly with Aberle's ingenious hypothesis (*Kath. Quartalschr.* 1859, pp. 585 sqq.; comp. Hilg.'s *Zeitschr.* 1864, pp. 425 sqq.) that the Synoptics, particularly Matthew, aimed at refuting the Jewish and heathen reproaches of Christian abominations by their detailed account of the Lord's Supper.

² Weizsäcker, p. 559.

³ Thus as early as the Reformation period, Zwingli, *Subsid.* p. 343 : quis tam tardus erit, ne dicam hebes aut pertinax, ut non videat, *est* hoc loco pos. esse pro *significat*. Particularly strong against a more positive conception, 12th Feb. 1531, Zw. Buc. VIII. p. 580: dati, dati, dati corporis in cibum animæ sacramentum, symbolum dedit. Paulus, III. ii. p. 523 : this torn and broken bread *is* my body, resembles it. P. 530 : to me it is as if I saw my blood in this cup. Similarly Rückert. Even Neander, Bleek, and the majority of the accommodating theologians no longer shun this symbolical explanation.—As Jesus spoke Aramaic, he would say hu (seh or sot or den, dehu, dek, ha) guphi (corpus) or bisri (basar, besar=caro), Paulus, p. 519. Bleek, p. 412. The formula among modern Jews : this is the bread (hu lachma), which our fathers ate in Egypt, Paulus, p. 525. Langen insists upon retaining this formula (pp. 174 sqq.) against Schöttgen's evidence of its later date.—Blood of the grape, Gen. xlix. 11 ; Deut. xxxii. 14.

⁴ But even Strauss (4th ed. II. p. 422) says: to translate "this signifies" is to think too little and too soberly.

enough, Judaism speaks, and which he in a fresh manner in this solemn moment consecrates to his own. And this gift lies, first, in the emphatic and authoritative mention of the salvation of the disciples as the end of his approaching death; and, secondly, in his handing over, in connection therewith, to the heirs of salvation, the emblems of that salvation, not merely to be gazed upon, but to be taken and enjoyed. He therefore in the most formal, the most tangible, and the most assuring manner, deposited in their hands and sealed in their persons, not only the symbol, but the thing symbolized, which was to be to them the possession of the saving death and its fruits. This is the gift of the Lord's Supper, this is the real body of the Lord's Supper, with which the Church consoled herself, and the confession of which, even in the Reformed Church, was renewed in particular by Butzer, Œcolampadius, and Calvin, though without sufficient avoidance of the rocks of that materialistic mode of conception of Catholicism and Lutheranism, the overcoming of which was the special mission of the Reformed Church. No body, no blood was given, or could have been given, in a natural or supernatural way; but in a purely spiritual manner, by the word accompanied by the emblem, could the claim to the efficacy of the operation of that death, which was consummated in the broken body and the outstreaming blood, be imparted to the disciples. And the love of Jesus has its monument, not merely in the fact that he died with such thoughts of salvation, but also in the fact that in the last agitated and quickly fleeting hours of his life he did not forget to say and to give to his own, as the secret of his cross and as the pearl of their future, that which in the agony of his passion and of his death his mouth would no longer be able to offer them.[1]

---

[1] This is the fundamental thought in my essay on the last supper, the thought to which I would still draw attention, instead of the exceedingly vague definitions of recent times as to spiritual and spiritual-corporeal enjoyment (Neander, Bleek, Jul. Müller, Meyer, and others). Meyer's *Komm.* and Beck's *Dogm. Gesch.* 2nd ed. 1864, p. 425, have not rejected this; Weiz. p. 557, Schenkel, p. 278 sq., Gess, pp. 147 sq., have similarly expressed themselves; Pastor Dr. Bodemeyer in his Illustration of

But the transaction of Jesus at the last supper is doubly important. It possesses an importance in itself; and at the same time it throws the clearest light forwards upon the death of Jesus, and upon the intention and the self-consciousness with which Jesus firmly and resolutely went to meet it. Jesus' account of the character and significance of his death, given by himself at the last supper, must now be looked at more closely. He has said so little concerning the meaning of the dark fate which awaited him, and this little is again so uncertain or even so strongly contradicted, that we yield ourselves up with the greatest satisfaction to the detailed, primitive, unassailable, most genuine testimony of the last supper, as to a guide and light-bearer in the dark mystery of his last fate and of his mental attitude towards that fate.

In point of fact there are only three utterances that are at all rich in references to Jesus' end—one in Galilee, one on the way to Jerusalem, and finally that at the last supper in Jerusalem. All three are of the most credible kind and all three are mutually corroborative, the last being, however, on account of its surpassing reliability, its clearness, and its definitive position, the king of the three. There is, however, a certain initial contradiction. On adopting the conception of the Passion, in the Galilean Cæsarea Philippi, Jesus recognized the path of suffering, which the facts of his situation disclosed to him, altogether as the personal obligation imposed upon him as means and way to glory: through death to life, through humility to exaltation, through sacrifice to

the Doctrine of the Lord's Supper by Dr. Keim, in *Stud. u. Krit.* 1860, pp. 382 sqq. has made an attack of no worth; critical remarks by Meyring, in *Luth. Zeitschrift*, 1867. Volkmar declares to us that *practically* not much depends upon whether the last supper factually had this meaning. Thus ends the scepticism to which Strauss, yielded in a comfortless way (*perhaps* it was so, and Jesus might anticipate that *perhaps* his body would soon be broken, *New Life*, Eng. trans., I. pp. 388 sqq.), at least with the assertion that all would be well without the words of Jesus. Schleiermacher's scepticism, which attacked at least the appointment of a permanent institution, started essentially—as in other cases—from John; finally he satisfied himself against John by assuming that the disciples (except John) had at any rate understood the words of Jesus as a command, pp. 418 sqq.

reward, through loss of life to the Messianic throne. And he proclaimed the same way of self-denial to his disciples, through self-denial the conquest of judgment and glory.[1] But in his conversation with the sons of Zebedee, near Jericho and Jerusalem, a new direction of the thought of Jesus was announced; we pass rapidly over it because the new conception found its full expression where we now stand, in the solemnity at the last supper.[2] The conversation with the sons of Zebedee is properly the connecting link between Cæsarea and the last supper. His starting-point is the personal obligation and its performance, as at Cæsarea; he imposes it upon himself and upon the sons of Zebedee to drink the cup of suffering as the bitter transition to the throne of the Messiahship. But, in his instruction of the jealous Twelve, to whom he preaches humility, he passes unnoticeably and almost without preparation to the new proposition that converts the personal performances and the acquisitions in the path of pain into a sympathizing philanthropic acting and suffering for others: "The Son of Man is not come to be ministered unto, but to minister, and to give his life as a ransom for many." As if the egoism of the disciples was needed to strip even him of any remnant or of any appearance of self-seeking, as if the looking back upon his life of ministry to men, which he opposed to the self-seeking of the disciples, forced him to regard the close of his life as a link in the great chain of his ministrations for others instead of for himself, he here placed his death under the point of view of a conquest of the Messiahship, under the new aspect of a saving of men from the burden of their debts, from the punitive justice, from the judgment of God. With the idea of a "ransom for many," which the Passover suggested to him, he represented his death as an atoning sacrifice which was to be presented to God on behalf of many, and would win from God remission of human guilt, remission of the divine punishment of imprisonment and condemnation, therefore protection,

---

[1] Above, IV. pp. 243 sq., 279 sqq.   [2] Above, pp. 51 sqq.

AT JERUSALEM. THE LAST SUPPER.

forgiveness, grace, for the many through the fall of one.[1] And now came the last supper with the double peculiarity that the initial personal standpoint had completely disappeared, while the philanthropic conception of the purpose of his death was in truth redoubled. For as soon as Jesus' attitude towards men as an atoning sacrifice was made prominent in the repeated "For you" with which he accompanied the distribution of the symbolic bread and the symbolic wine, Matthew not incorrectly explained it as "For your sins;" and the resemblance to the sacrifice of the Passover lamb—though the latter was no atoning sacrifice at all in a strict sense—readily suggested the idea of atoning and cleansing efficacy.[2] But the new designation of the death of Jesus as a covenant sacrifice now received a still greater emphasis than the idea of an atoning sacrifice, nay, it absorbed the latter into itself. "This is the blood of the covenant," said Jesus, when he caused the cup to circulate among the disciples. He thereby not only brought his death into a suggestive relation to the Passover lamb, with the blood of which had been connected the protective passing over, the saving, nay the covenant of God with the ancient people, the covenant which was afterwards ratified and completed at Sinai in a formal covenant sacrifice; but he also gave to his dying as such a higher, an affirmative, a truly edifying significance. In the spirit of his teaching, he offered, in the place of a merely Jewish remission and absolution, the seal of the peace and of the filial relationship which was henceforth to exist between God and man. And since the Old Testament, notwithstanding the covenant and the covenants, had never attained to the filial condition or to the kingdom, he followed up the ancient and obsolete covenants with the divine

---

[1] Above, p. 55. Gess, pp. 117 sq. Comp. in the farewell addresses in John xvii. 19: ἁγιάζω = consecro me sacrificium (the corresponding Hebrew for sacrifice, hikdish).

[2] *Gesch. Chr.* p. 92, note 2. That the ὑπὲρ ὑμῶν of Paul and Luke is to be preferred to the περὶ (ὑπὲρ) πολλῶν of Matt. and Mark, follows from the restriction of the transaction to the Twelve, and from the endeavour of Jesus to guarantee *to them* the blessing of this death. It is different in Matt. xx. 28, where he speaks more objectively.

covenant of accomplishment; in truth, although he did not use
the word, which was first used by Paul, he gave the *new*, more
correctly the real, the true covenant, which crowned and perfected
into reality the beginnings, the prophecies, the prototypes of
Mosaic times, without on that account threatening the validity
and the truth of the law or of the prophets.[1]

Rich as are the relations which Jesus lends to his death, and
which he, though in scant and parsimonious words, discloses to
us in the moment when his departure seems suddenly and enig-
matically to stand dark and indefinite before him and us—a
sign how profoundly he reflected even upon matters about which
he was silent—yet we cannot speedily dismiss from our minds
two grounds for question. In the first place, how could he
thus uneasily, unsteadily, one might say with such hasty and
feverish groping, pass from one point of view to another? And
in the next place, when he finally found external and internal
rest in his thoughts expressed in the last supper, and went to the
cross with the serious purpose of obtaining atonement and covenant with God, not, it is true, for the race, but for his own, for his
disciples, adherents and believing followers, had he the power to
accomplish that which he purposed, and was he commissioned
to do it either by God or in virtue of those eternally valid
principles to which his life-ministry had been devoted?

The first question is easier to answer than the second. It
is the genuine humanity of Jesus which expresses itself in his
restless struggling after light, even in the night and in the dark

---

[1] The covenant sacrifice, Ex. xxiv. 1 sqq. The new covenant only in Paul and
Luke; merely covenant in Matt. (where the reading should be τὸ αἷμά μου τῆς
διαθήκης, and καινῆς should be struck out) and Mark. Baur (*Theol. Jahrb.* 1857,
pp. 551 sqq.) has derived the whole expression of new (erase that!) covenant even in
Matt. from the initiative of Paul. Volkmar (p. 567) adopts this, and ascribes to the
Pauline Mark the disinclination to adopt the καινή of his master. Weizs. (p. 557)
rightly holds it fast (which we are doubly determined to do, since we know no dependence of Matt. upon Mark or Paul). Only into this "covenant" no one should introduce
the dissolution of the ancient religion, as Weizs. Schenkel, see above, p. 318, n. 3.
That is a much too definite and too modern Christian opinion of the Old and New
Testaments, an opinion which Jesus' very able resort to a parallelizing of his sacrificial
death with the Mosaic covenant sacrifice by no means justifies.

question of the death which was as certainly as incomprehensibly about to befall this Messiahship. And in truth it is not only a human step, it is a glorious advance which stands before us in the process of Jesus' conception of the Passion. From the necessity of death for his personal mission he passes to the discovery of its importance for men. How could it be otherwise, when his whole life served men, than that his death also should serve them, not only indirectly because he would then become their Messiah, but directly because he would sacrifice himself for them? From the discovery of the atoning efficacy of his death, he passes on to the recognition of its covenant-establishing power. How could it be otherwise, when the aim of his life, the goal of his self-consciousness and the motive force of his effectual self-communication and mediation were the blessings of oneness with God, and of divine-human regeneration of the world, instead of a mere blotting out in the divine register of guilt? But in order to understand how he began to foster in his soul the ideas of sacrifice which he had not previously possessed, and the Old Testament prototypes of which he had treated almost with indifference by his Galilean utterance, "Mercy, not sacrifice," we must not imagine that the sacrificing Jerusalem would revive to him that vanished world of sacrificial faith, for he would rather feel repelled by the sacrificing Jerusalem, and his sacrificial intention was firmly established before he reached Jerusalem. Besides the fate which was coming to him and which awoke the first thought, the prototype of the Passover lamb evidently influenced him more than the utterances of the prophets, for it seemed to him a divine providence that his journey, his passion, and his dying coincided with the primitive ceremony which had called Israel to be the people of God. And how many resemblances would he soon discover between the past and the present! Formerly the Passover lamb diverted the judgment of God from Israel: now again a divine judgment was imminent, the Messianic judgment of the nation, at the thought of which he, in the conflict of his infinite faith in divine grace with his equally strong faith in divine righteousness, trembled for his weak and sinful disciples.[1] Of old the Passover lamb initiated the communion of the people and God, the victorious exodus, the glorious entry into the land of promise. Now there stood in view a greater future, a greater entering in than that into the promised land, the coming of the kingdom of heaven with its Messiah, the end of the promise, the beginning of the fulfilment. The introduction and the ratifying of the new passing over, of the new era of covenant, was the new Passover lamb, the sacrificial death of the Messiah. Indeed, we may imagine Jesus to have reflected that, as of old immediately after the bloody sealing of the covenant, Moses and Aaron ascended to the God of Israel and looked upon his form; even so, and in a yet higher way, he was called to enter into the presence of God after he had completed his sacrifice, an expectation which, as we know, was certainly to him on other grounds already incontestable.[2]

Measured by the profoundest ideas of the Old Testament and of the teaching of Jesus himself, this sacrificial purpose appears —if we confess the truth—rather as a relapse into obsolete opinions which were then being resuscitated in the contemporary dissolution of Judaism and Paganism, than as striking out a fresh path of higher and the highest truth.[3] This sacrifice ranges itself in the category of blood sacrifices, and as such has already been discarded by the Old Testament. For the law disapproved of human sacrifices, and the prophets ridiculed animal sacri-

---

[1] Comp. Matt. xvi. 26.   [2] Ex. xxiv. 8 sq.

[3] Exaggerated Jewish estimate of sacrifices, comp. above, I. pp. 302 sqq.; comp. also Paul and the Epistle to the Hebrews. Human sacrifices, comp. Cæsar, Pompey, Octavian, Nero, Hadrian, M. Aurelius, Commodus. Dio. C. 43, 24; 48, 14, 48; 69, 11. Suet. *Ner.* 36, 38 (Dio, 63, 14). Tacitus, *Ann.* 15, 47. Aurelius Victor, *Cæsares*, 14. Marcus Aurelius, see Capitolinus, *M. Ant.* 19. Commodus, see Lampridius, *Comm.* 9. Comp. Peregrinus' burning himself alive, Lucian, *De Morte Peregr.* 1, 2, 20 sqq.; also the cruel cults of the Phœnicians, Carthaginians, the people of Asia Minor, Gauls, and the taurobolians and criobolians, who were Roman citizens. Plutarch, *Superst.* 13. Tacitus, *Ann.* 14, 30. Philostratus, *Vita Apoll.* 7, 11. Porph. *De abst.* 2, 27. Capitolinus, *V. Pertin.* 4. Lampr. *A. Sev.* 60. Spart. *Nig.* 6. The Christian apologists, Tert. *Ap.* 9. Euseb. *Scorp.* 7. Minuc. 30, &c. Examples of pagan self-immolations, Wetst. I. p. 458, II. p. 46.

fices.¹ He could not make the forgiveness of God dependent upon blood, nor even upon the intercession of Noah, Abraham, Moses, Daniel, and Job, but upon the gracious disposition above, which lets even the sinner live, and upon reformation and righteousness upon earth.² It was upon this foundation that Jesus based his preaching of grace, which made the paternal love of God infinite, and His forgiveness, even of loads of sin, without bounds. It was his greatest satisfaction to exhibit the goodness, the immensity of the heart of God, who, in mercy to the penitent that asked but offered nothing, freely remitted millions of sins.³ On the other hand, he was at the same time a zealot for works, for human performances, and in the spirit of the Old Testament he insisted upon the presentation of actual, serious, moral human righteousness as the true means of compensation before the throne of God.⁴ Thus the purpose of Jesus does not rise to the level of his own knowledge and of that of the prophets. There is no necessity for us to consider whether he, with his sacrifice, even if he was the absolutely pure and not merely the purer than others, could perfectly, without requiring any indulgence on God's part, satisfy the demands of divine righteousness upon the world or even only upon his adherents, and that after the Old Testament itself had finally renounced the idea—which, along with that of animal sacrifices, was so popular in antiquity —of human substitutes and representatives, and had made the cause of every man depend upon himself, his repentance and righteousness, and upon God.⁵ But Jesus' purpose is explicable

---

¹ Levit. xviii. 21, xx. 2, comp. Gen. xxii. 2, 12. Jeremiah xix. 5 (against the burning of the children to Baal): " which I neither commanded nor spake of to them, nay it never came into my heart." Against animal sacrifices, *e. g.* Isaiah i. 11, lxvi. 3; Amos. v. 22; Micah. vi. 6 sqq.; Jer. vi. 20; Ps. l. 8; Prov. xv. 8.

² Comp. only Ezekiel xiv. 14—20, xviii. 23—32, xxxiii. 11; Ps. xlix. 7.

³ Matt. xviii. 21 sqq.

⁴ Matt. v. 20, vi. 33. At least with and after forgiveness, vi. 14, xviii. 35.

⁵ The well-known question, discussed from the time of Anselm down to the present. Acceptilatio? The idea of the substitute, *Gesch. Chr.* p. 207. Even Noack, p. 220. Strongly rejected, with special reference to Abraham and Sodom (Gen. xviii. 23 sqq.), even in view of Noah, Daniel, and Job, Ez. xiv. 14 sqq. Yet the idea of the melizim (luz), Job xxxiii. 23, or, as the Talmud says, of the intercessors (sannigor, Buxt. p. 1509,

from the circumstances, from the imminent death which according to God's will was the legitimate martyrdom of a witness to the truth, of *the* witness to the truth, and which in the imagination of men involuntarily clothed itself in Jewish conceptions as soon as an attempt was made to describe its character and value. And Jesus' purpose is best and most fully explained out of his heart, and it rises to the level of his heart. He made a strong effort to procure for the world a benefit out of his death. He wished to perform for men a deed such as he in his faultless moral energy demanded of himself as of them, a deed performed even in his passion, even under the eye of God, to whom he would present a human performance. With the ardour of a pure self-forgetting love he sought the salvation of his brethren, and was so moved by his sympathetic view of their defects as to doubt that which was to him most certain, the divine grace, and to place himself in a representative position before the judgment. These acts of will, which were accompanied by all the holy zeal, all the bravery and love of the Son of Man, and finally even by the faith in the love of the Father to the Son and to the sons, by all the old thoughts of his Galilean spring,—these acts of will give to his purpose its moral worth and its eternal truth before God and before men, even though the conception upon which they are based or which accompanies them, viz., that of the necessity of a divine propitiation in this way, was not entirely free from error.[1] These acts of will chain humanity to the cross of its

Greek συνήγορος), or of the Paraclete (peraklith, Buxt. p. 1843), is still retained by Philo (see above, I. p. 323; Grimm, p. 331). Comp. the reconciler, Ecclus. xlv. 16, 23. The blood of purifying, 4 Macc. vi. Comp. 1 Cor. iv. 13, xv. 29; 2 Kings iv. 10 sqq.; Rom. ix. 3; Phil. ii. 17. Wünsche, pp. 17 sqq.; Delitzsch, *Hillel*, pp. 34 sq.

[1] *Gesch. Chr.* pp. 206 sqq. In order to reconcile the old (Matt. vi. 12, v. 45, xviii. 27 sqq.) and the present standpoint of Jesus, we must not forget (1) the performances even to the hyperbole of satisfaction which he had required (xvi. 24—26); (2) the adjustment which he kept in view between God and man even after men had entered into the filial relationship (Matt. vi. 14 sq., xviii. 15, xii. 36, xviii. 3). The essential distinction, however, remains that he had formerly taught a grace in the main unconditional on the only conditio sine qua non of Matt. vi. 14, whilst he now held that grace to be conditioned by the great sacrifice. We cannot think of finding a mode of reconciliation by saying that he intended his sacrifice to apply only to the guilt

tender-hearted friend, of its powerful representative, of the defender of its honour, even now when so many have renounced the old conception. And that old conception itself has made it possible to millions, with the intellectually mighty and yet Jewish-thinking Apostle Paul at their head, to believe not only in the bottomless depth of their sinfulness, but also in the redemptive attitude of Jesus, in the paternal will of God, and in an end of the sacrifices. For the great majority of men are not able to believe in ideas and spiritual truths, but are able to believe in facts in which those ideas and truths have become visible. And we might almost believe that Jesus had in view this very majority, this need of weak men burdened with old and new sins, since he so evidently intended, not mainly to give something to God, but to give in the last supper a pledge to men, in the first instance to his friends whom he loved with a genuinely human love, and then—according to the broad and yet correct view of Paul—to *all*, even to *those* sinners for whom no one else in the world would sacrifice himself.[1]

In the Lord's Supper, Jesus not only explained his death and in a certain measure testamentarily made it over to his disciples and to us, but with an earnestness proportioned to his own estimate of this death and of this testament, he took precautions that it should be remembered in every age, nay, that it should

contracted after entering into the filial relationship. On the other hand, a continual oscillation between the standpoint of grace and that of Jewish satisfaction can be established (above, III. p. 115, n. 3).

[1] *Gesch. Chr.* p. 92. Holsten's objections (*Zum Evang. des Petr. und Paul*, p. 177) to the latter representation are overthrown by the fact that in the last supper at any rate *only* the effort to comfort men is prominent, not the influence upon God, which is postponed until the cross. That I have not intended to exclude the idea of ἱλαστ. to God, every word both formerly and now must show. The above representation, however, as a whole reminds me again of Holsten's opinion (p. 179) that the last supper transaction of Jesus—which, in contradiction to Strauss and Volkmar, he definitely holds fast—was only a thought of the moment. To him it is a transitory moment, to me it is the last definitive self-consciousness.—Noteworthy difference between 1 Cor. xi. 24 and 2 Cor. v. 15; Rom. iv. 5, v. 6—8. Reconciled by Matt. xviii. 14, xx. 28. Rom. v. 7 is primarily applicable to the death of Jesus, and verse 6 only in connection with verse 7, since he (in a genuinely human way) dies for the godless only as for the partially or potentially good. But Paul again places himself on the ideal height of Jesus, Rom. ix. 3.

become a strong, dominant, and striking foundation-stone of the community he left behind. In requiring the repetition of this transaction, Jesus incontrovertibly—for the facts here are too certain for the doubts of the most recent critics—referred to the certainty of his departure, to the necessity of organization among his little society, to their essential distinction from the great Jewish society within which they stood and within which they were at first to abide—a fact that altogether excludes an imitation of the meals of the Essenes.[1] The remembrance of the Lord, of his death, of the covenant sacrifice by which he founded a new world, he wished to elevate to the keystone of the meetings of his followers, and thereby, without any definite limitation in detail, to guard against a relapse into the purely Jewish character, a relapse from which the Jewish-Christian community, as is well known, scarcely escaped, and so far as they did escape were saved chiefly by retaining their Master's breaking of bread.[2] That we know of this will of Jesus, and that the Lord's Supper has been perpetuated until our days, we owe in a notable manner almost exclusively to the Apostle who was not present, and who wrote as it were at a distance that account of the Lord's Supper, the exactness of whose details, derived from the mouths of eye-witnesses, compensates for the fact that the writer was not himself an eye-witness.[3] Only Paul, and Luke after him, have not merely the two elements, but also the addition of Jesus: "This do in remembrance of me; this do, as often as ye drink, in remembrance of me." And it is scarcely to be questioned that in consequence of these words of Jesus, the Apostle Paul, in

---

[1] Above, p. 316, n. 1. Comp. I. p. 383. *Gesch. Chr.* p. 16. Hilg. thinks of the Essenes day and night. Comp. Strauss, quoted above, p. 316, n. 1.

[2] Acts ii. 42; 1 Cor. x. 16 sqq., xi. 20 sqq.

[3] It is still disputed whether Paul claims an immediate divine revelation, or refers to a mediate hearing through Peter and others. The former has been held by Calov, Bengel, Flatt, Olsh., De Wette, Osi., Jul. Müller, and even Rückert. The latter by Süsskind, Schulz, De Wette, Neander, Strauss, Hofm. Meyer makes a poor attempt at combining the two: mediately (because not παρά, but ἀπό, distant reference), and yet a revelation, namely, by intimation of the Spirit or of an angel, or by ecstacy! Exegesis scarcely leaves a doubt that the second explanation is the correct one; comp. also 1 Cor. xv. 3, and my essay, pp. 68 sq.

his exposition of the Lord's Supper, was led to throw the chief emphasis upon the memorial character of the transaction that stood between the departure and the return of Jesus, upon the announcement and the confession, within the community and in a certain measure to the ears of mankind, of the death of Jesus that was brought to pass for the benefit of men, although a mysterious element, obscurely expressed, was by no means absent from the Apostle, and—again an incentive to the repetition of the transaction—has been by the Apostle afresh imposed upon the church.[1]

The only point open to question is the mode in which, according to the will of Jesus, this transaction should be repeated. It is evident that he as little thought of a mere repetition on the anniversary of the eve of the Passover, as of such a literal repetition of the words by which he instituted the ceremony as gradually became the use of the church. By requiring a repetition, "as often as ye drink it," he evidently sought to sanctify by this custom every common meal of the disciples. By bidding them "do this," he required primaily only the transaction itself, the breaking of bread and the circulating of the cup with a regard to him and his last meal, and not the literal repetition of the words by which he had accompanied those acts.[2] And if there were any doubt here, a glance at the apostolic church would bring the

---

[1] 1 Cor. xi. 26. The uncommonly difficult question as to wherein Paul or John sought the mystery of the last supper, we may leave to the exegesis of 1 Cor. x. and xi. and John vi., and to New Testament theology. Comp. my essay, pp. 107 sqq., although there are many things there that need modifying. In general, Paul and John stand nearer to each other than is usually believed; John stands upon Paul. The latter has the idea of a real κοινωνία of man with the body and blood of Christ (1 Cor. x. 16, comp. i. 9; 2 Cor. xiii. 13; Phil. iii. 10), not only through subjective disposition (1 Cor. xi. 24, 26), but through objective appropriation of the elements of the sacrifice meal of Jesus, the bread and the cup of the Lord (ix. 13, x. 16—21), by which mysteriously a personal union is effected with him, the second Adam, in his passion and resurrection, or with his spirit, the spiritual manna of the wilderness (x. 3), the miraculous effect of which, again, is the unity of the body of the church (x. 17, comp. with x. 3 sq., xii. 13, also vi. 17; 2 Cor. iii. 17). On the other hand, 1 Cor. xi. 27, which is to be explained by verse 26, needs no mysterious exposition. In John vi. it all amounts to the participation in the πνεῦμα. See below.

[2] Matt. xxvi. 29 does not apply merely to the Passover cup.

question to a decision. The Acts of the Apostles knows simply of a daily breaking of bread in the congregation in Jerusalem, to which custom the words of institution would the more certainly be wanting because the congregation in Jerusalem did not ascribe any saving efficacy to the death of Jesus until they came under Pauline influence. But even to the Apostle Paul, the still older and more trustworthy witness, the upholder of the sacrificial death and of the mystery of the last supper, the frequently recurring Lord's Suppers of the Christians completely coincide with the remembrance of the death of Jesus, and nothing is said to show that there followed these meals, as a distinctive ceremony, either the breaking of his bread, or the circulating of his cup, or the repetition of his words.[1] It is simply the separation which occurred centuries later between the love-feast and the Lord's Suppers, the fruit of persecution and of the degeneracy of the love-feast, as well as of the gradually developed and increasingly mysterious views of the Lord's Supper, which has led many to carry back into primitive Christian antiquity a distinction which was very far from existing then at all.[2] The fact of the later separation of the two transactions, and ultimately of the complete abolition of the Lord's meals or love-feasts with their abuses early denounced by Paul and with their manifold unprofitable features, might certainly give rise to the supposition that Jesus had set up an institution which did not contain within itself the conditions of universal practicability, which was not adapted to all circumstances, being planned, as it were, too modestly, and with a view to meet the requirements of a small community, not of a universal church. Common meals, such as Jesus ordered to be kept up in

[1] Acts ii. 42, 46, xx. 7; 1 Cor. xi. 20 sqq. That in the speeches of Peter at Jerusalem, given in the Acts of the Apostles, a recognition of the saving significance of the death of Jesus is essentially lacking, is well known, and is shown equally by Lechler as well as by Holsten.

[2] The second century, from the letter of the younger Pliny to the Epistle of Jude, and to Justin, Ignatius, and Tertullian, even also the third century (Eus. 6, 43), show no certain trace of the division. First in the times of Chrysostom and Augustine the love-feasts appear partly as something separate, partly as something obsolete; Gieseler, K.G. I. ii. p. 299.

memory of him, could be continued only so long as twelve or a few more came together, but not the hundreds and thousands of a Corinthian congregation or of a modern church. This objection would, however, be precipitate. The modern congregations could meet together at a meal of remembrance, in order to satisfy the command or the anticipation of Jesus, as well as they can to celebrate the Lord's Supper. Moreover, just as he himself held this first meal only with his most intimate friends, he has in truth not excluded the festive meetings of families and friends for the purpose of talking about his life and his death; and when we examine closely we see that he has in reality determined nothing with regard to the size or the frequency or even the detailed customs of the assemblies, treating these things in his grand manner as of secondary importance in comparison with the main point.[1]

With the institution of the last supper, the farewell evening of Jesus at Jerusalem, as narrated by Matthew and Mark, is at an end. On the contrary, in Luke the conversations are still spun on; and much as is here doubtful, several correct reminiscences are not to be overlooked. Of the four conversational fragments which Luke exhibits, there is not one which might not, at least with great probability, be transferred to another period.[2] The controversy among the disciples and the admonition to mutual ministration occur in the same form, according to the two other sources, in the incident of the ambition of the sons of Zebedee at Jericho, an incident which Luke has there passed over. The promise of the table in the kingdom of God and of

[1] The above does not render unjustifiable the striving after a feasible approximation to the institution of Jesus; to which belongs above all the retention of the Green Thursday, whose prerogative has even recently been sacrificed by fools to the Friday, even where the ancient custom had been preserved, e.g. in South Germany imperial towns; next the use of the very words of Jesus; and finally the "taking" by the communicants, who are not to be condemned to have the wine poured into them like children. Comp. my essay, pp. 115 sqq.

[2] Luke xxii. 24 sqq. In general, Strauss, Ewald, De Wette, and Meyer, thus express themselves; on the other hand others, Sieff., Paulus, Olsh., Neander, also Bleek, even Ewald in single instances, here find welcome points of contact with John.

the judgment-seats, hangs together with the words addressed to Peter on the journey to Judæa. The word of warning to Peter, as well as the admonition to be armed, belongs evidently, as the subject shows and as the other accounts betray, to the departure from Jerusalem to the Mount of Olives.[1] The present position of these conversations is condemned not only by the evidence of the other testimonies, but also by the insupportableness, nay the unworthiness, of the childish dispute in the solemnity and seriousness of the moment, and finally by their great want of connection. And are the great promises to the persistently faithful disciples in their place between the correction of jealousies on the one hand, and the great impending test, nay, the prediction of the apostacy, on the other hand? Or the charge to purchase swords, after the announcement of the shameful apostacy? That many disconnected things are here found together can be explained. The author or his sources wished to give longer farewell speeches. The table of the kingdom of heaven did not badly join on to the announcement of the completion of the Passover solemnity in the kingdom of heaven; while the admonitions to humility were strikingly apposite to the act of ministering which Jesus had just performed at the last supper. At any rate, these passages are not to be treated in a depreciatory manner; they contain what is peculiar, and they are in their place at the place. Indeed, something like the first speech may have been uttered at the table of the last supper itself. We are at once reminded of that addition to the last address to the Pharisees in Matthew, which is so little appropriate there, because it contains in itself a private conversation of Jesus with his disciples, that was thrown together with the correction of the Pharisaic longing for the title of Rabbi, simply by the association of ideas.[2] But this speech is appropriate on this quiet evening, if we admit that the ambition

---

[1] Comp. Luke xxii. 24 and Matt. xx. 24; Luke xxii. 28 and Matt. xix. 27; Luke xxii. 31, 35, and Matt. xxvi. 31 sqq.

[2] Matt. xxiii. 8—12. Comp. above, p. 201.

AT JERUSALEM. THE LAST SUPPER.

of the disciples depicted by Luke, and excited either by the kingdom in sight or by Jesus' preference for individual disciples, might disturb the sacred exaltation of the evening; and we have a great right to bring that very speech in Matthew hither, because the contents, sometimes to the letter, resemble the speech in Luke, particularly in the requirement of mutual ministration.

The speech in Matthew shows us, to our gratification, that there was no question of jealousies; and to our still greater gratification, that the Lord, who at the last supper organized a part of his community, by no means allowed the last weighty hours to pass by without final words of preparation for the living organs of his community. "Be ye not called Rabbi," he said, "like the Pharisees; for one is your teacher, but all ye are brethren. And call no one father upon the earth, for One is your Father, the heavenly. And be not called leaders, for one is your leader, Christ. He that is the greater of you will be your servant.[1] For who is greater, he that reclines at table or he that serves? Is not he that reclines at table? But I am in your midst as the servant.[2] But he that shall exalt himself will be made low, and he that shall humble himself will be exalted."[3] With unspeakable excellence he compressed into these brief words the meaning of his last meal, the confession of faith and the brotherly principle of his community, consolation and teaching to those whom he left behind.[4]

[1] The titles Abi, Rabbi, Mori, see above, III. p. 15, V. pp. 206 sq. Rab or Sar (Isaiah xliii. 27, comp. Buxt. p. 2534) would best correspond to the title $\kappa\alpha\theta\eta\gamma$. As a curiosity it may be mentioned that Osw. Myconius in Basel refused to take the doctor's degree merely on account of this word, upon which Carlstadt had already laid stress (Jäger, *Karlst.* p. 277). Hagenb. *Oekol. u. Myk.* p. 341. At most a doubt may arise as to the title "Christ." The title due to the author, Matt. xi. 2; Mark ix. 41.

[2] This according to Luke xxii. 27. This passage is appropriate to the whole Passover meal, at which Jesus had served his own, part of the time standing; as R. Gamaliel II. served, standing, the three Rabbis, whereupon R. Joshua, appealing to Gen. xviii. 8, answered: invenimus majorem, qui ministri officio functus est. *Kidd.* f. 32, 2. Wetst. p. 458.

[3] Comp. Ez. xxi. 26, &c. Rabbis, in Schöttgen, p. 198; Wetst. p. 482.

[4] The brotherliness already in principle in the Sermon on the Mount.

338   *THE FAREWELL.*

We may be allowed to make one more conjecture. The evening of the last supper might have yet another addition about which all the Evangelists are silent. According to Matthew, and evidently also according to Luke, Jesus instituted baptism as the second visible sign of his community, after his resurrection, at the moment of his separation from earth and from his own.[1] By being placed in the history of the resurrection, baptism shares, as an institution of Jesus, all the doubts that gather round these last incidents themselves. And yet baptism—as is shown by the practice of it by the Apostles and by Paul, and the equality with the last supper given to it by Paul—must be plainly referred back to the initiative of Jesus, however unhistorical may be the practice of it by Jesus from the beginning of his ministry, as described in the fourth Gospel.[2] Is it not possible, nay probable, that the Gospels have removed the institution of baptism from its original place to a later date, wishing to exhibit him who was ascending into heaven as the Lord of heaven and earth, therefore as the legitimate possessor of the nations, and therefore as the ordainer of baptism for all nations?[3] The institution of baptism evidently belongs to the last part of Jesus' career, to the time when he acknowledged John to be the sent of heaven and his baptism as a work of heaven, i.e. after Jesus had reached Jerusalem.[4] Again, it evidently belongs to *that* point of time when Jesus, at Jerusalem, busied himself with the final organization of his community, with the constitution of their peculiar new customs in distinction from the old, with appointing the symbols of the completed covenant, and with the handing

[1] Matt. xxviii. 19, comp. Luke xxiv. 47; Acts ii. 38. Spurious appendage of Mark xvi. 15.

[2] Acts ii. 38, &c.; Gal. iii. 27, &c.; especially 1 Cor. x. 2—4 (baptism and Lord's Supper in Old Testament); also xii. 13. Will any one ascribe the initiation to the Twelve, who were so very dependent upon the "Teacher"? John makes Jesus baptize iii. 22, iv. 1. The expression in iv. 2 is certainly such that it may quite as well point to 1 Cor. i. 17—according to which Paul represents baptism as performed by subordinate deacons—as to the fact that the disciples did not practise baptism until later. The introduction of baptism by the Baptist, above, II. pp. 239 sqq.

[3] Matt. xxviii. 18 sq. points to this.   [4] Matt. xxi. 25.

over of the fruits of his death. If this is correct, then the institution of baptism would best fall on this evening; it would be the second symbol, and it would be the work which the Apostles as the new teachers, who nevertheless were but brethren in their relation to each other and to the fellowship of salvation, were to prosecute. He would scarcely ordain at once the baptism of all nations, as the apostolic time proves to a certainty and as is later to be shown; but without an exact definition of the terms, he would ordain the baptism and forgiveness of penitents, believers, those that were ready to become disciples, those who would live according to his life and commands, and would prepare the way for his return.[1]

The fourth Gospel offers yet another addition to the last supper evening, and that the greatest of all. Jesus' farewell to his Twelve is carried through five long chapters, the introduction of that second chief division of the Gospel which is devoted to the glory of his death.[2] The farewell on the Mount of Olives and that at Jerusalem are in a free manner used as a foundation, and echoes of these last sayings, of the sayings of Jesus in general as reported in the previous Gospels, are scattered here and there. Thus the mention of persecutions and the comforting with the Holy Ghost point to the Mount of Olives, the admonition to mutual ministrations in obedience to the one Lord and Teacher points to the sayings at the last supper, while the promise of re-union points to both farewell addresses.[3] In truth, however, a new and richly organized world of revelations is based upon the older material. First we have the last meal without the Passover lamb but with the accompaniment of the washing of feet—the emblem of mutual ministration and of the new commandment of love received by the young community —and the designation of the betrayer, with the thrusting out of whom into the covenant with Satan begins the glorification of

[1] Comp. Acts iii. 19 sqq.   [2] John xiii.—xvii.
[3] John xvi. 2, 32 sq., xiii. 13 sqq., 35, xiv. 3, 16, 18, &c. Comp. the announcement concerning Judas, xiii. 2, 10, 21; concerning Peter, xiii. 36 sqq.

the Son of God who is to triumph in his passion.[1] Then there are the last sayings, the consolation at departure, which is afforded by the announcement of the necessity of Jesus' death for the building up of the community, by the promise of a new comforter, the Spirit, nay of the glorified self-revealing Son himself, and by the prospect of a victorious conclusion of the world-conflict. Finally, after the grand words, "In the world ye have tribulation, but be of good cheer, I have overcome the world," there is the high-priestly committal of the present and the future community, consisting of Jews and Gentiles, into the hands of God.[2] The tone of the sayings becomes more and more exalted until we reach the last prayers, exhibits both the consciously victorious divine hero, for whom there exists no question of personal and arduous sacrifice but only a work of bearing witness to the world, and the tenderly loving, anxiously careful, sadly pathetic earthly life-companion, nay friend, of these disciples.

This tone of triumph, this tone of affection, this divine-human bearing, without the Jewish colours, customs, imaginations, and calculations that have grown so strange to a later age, and possessing the breadth of a glance over the whole world, will ever fall with a magical power upon the human soul which would hear the passion-anticipating Lord speak yet once more richly and grandly and intelligibly and warmly to it and to all the faithful of the future whom he must have seen in spirit. But these sayings are not historical. They are the outpouring of a Christian spirit who raised his feelings, his faith, his thoughts, his wishes and his hopes, as high and made them as great and as lofty as he had power to do, and then transferred them to the soul and

---

[1] John xiii. 2—30.

[2] John xvi. 33 and xvii. The full historical character was not upheld by Lücke and Neander, nor now by Ewald, p. 555, and Weizs. p. 554, although Weizs. at the same time very strikingly speaks of the *essential harmony* of these farewell speeches with the Synoptics. It should be added, for curiosity's sake, that whilst Bretschneider's *Probab.* very strongly challenges these speeches, especially chap. xvii. (Weisse, II. pp. 294 sq., is still more zealous against the altogether unhistorical chap. xvii.), Paulus, in *L. J.* I. ii. p. 165, could think that John had written out these speeches perhaps on the next day!

AT JERUSALEM. THE LAST SUPPER. 341

the lips of the Master upon whose breast he in spirit was lying. Hence we do not enlarge this history by a detailed consideration of these farewell addresses, and we simply relegate them to the exegesis of this Gospel. For—to refer to only a few points— these farewell addresses know no Mount of Olives, no prediction of the future of Jerusalem, and of the return of the Son of Man; they know no Passover evening, no last supper evening, and no institution of the symbols of remembrance, which, much further back, at the Galilean Easter, are arbitrarily and obscurely alluded to, but are nevertheless betrayed.[1] The history of the betrayer is arbitrarily transformed; and instead of the festival evening, an ordinary meal is arbitrarily introduced, into which the last supper cannot be interpolated by the most persevering art, and at which there took place a washing of feet as impossible as it is unattested. This latter incident is only an imitation of the foot-washing and foot-drying by Mary, and a plastic realization of the genuine words of Jesus in Matthew and Luke concerning the ministering Lord, just as the interminable farewell address exhibits an elaboration of the long speeches in the earlier Gospels, particularly Luke.[2] Thi Jesus, fearless,

[1] John vi. 27 sqq., with those truly subtle paradoxes which estranged the Galilean people and the outer circle of disciples; (1) he is the bread from heaven, vi. 35; (2) his bread is his flesh which he gives on behalf of the life of the world, vi. 51; (3) it is his flesh and his blood which he offers to be eaten ($\tau\rho\omega\gamma\epsilon\iota\nu$ to bite) and to be drunk, in order thereby to dispense life, eternal life. These paradoxes were ultimately (in vain) relaxed in the sayings, vi. 61—63, which were again obscure, but the more probable meaning of which is, that (1) his ascension should remove the idea of a consumption of his body or his corpse (truly no exaggeration but a removal of the offence); (2) that his flesh would not be profitable, but only his spirit; (3) that this spirit was throned in his words (comp. verse 68). Taking all together, Jesus had spoken only figuratively of the appropriation of his flesh, he had in reality spoken of the appropriation of his person (vi. 57), but in the sense that reference was made first to the Spirit as alter ego of Jesus (vi. 63, comp. 56 and iv. 14, vii. 38, xiv. 16, &c.), secondly, to the proceeding of the Spirit out of the death of Jesus (vii. 39, xvi. 7, xx. 22). The similarity of this view with the Pauline one is illustrated above, p. 333, n. 1. It is Alexandrianism in Christianity.

[2] The washing of feet, xiii. 2 sqq. (slave's work, comp. Friedl. p. 64, yet see the beautiful example of the Rabbi's mother, above, p. 268, n. 1 [Paulus, I. ii. p. 729], generally before the meal, Luke vii. 44, *but here in the midst of it*, John xiii. 2, 4, 12, 23), is evidently developed out of Matt. xx. 25 sqq., and still more Luke xxii. 27 (thus Strauss, Baur, Schölt., while Weisse, II. p. 274, will base it upon the Johannine utter-

victorious, speaking long and oratorically at the moment of the greatest tension and when the need of being prepared for defence was the most frightfully urgent, is only the dogmatic Son of God of the later confession. The much-promised Spirit, the indwelling of all divine powers in the community, the unity of the Church, the equality of believers with the Son of God, the kingdom of God in heaven instead of upon earth—all this is the Christian philosophy and the Christian Church of the second century. Not a particle can be broken away from the whole. But the

ance, xiii. 10); on the other hand, the defenders of the fourth Gospel seek rather in Luke the slight trace of what is exactly narrated in John (even De Wette, Bleek, Ewald, Meyer). After the washing of feet, which followed the (Passover) eating (comp. xiii. 2 and Ewald; according to Wichelh. not until the next day), or even preceded it (Paulus, Friedlieb, Langen), there followed the last supper; but, again, concerning the interpolation of this into the Johannine account there exist the most diverse views (most after xiii. 30, others after 32, others 33 sq., others 38, Bengel, Kern, Wich., Röpe, after xiv. 31, comp. Strauss, 4th ed. II. pp. 404 sqq., and Meyer, chap. xiii., close). Weizs., p. 556, saw at least that this transaction of the washing might belong to another evening, and he is right so far that Jesus did not overload his disciples with symbols at the close, but is certainly incorrect in holding both. The suspicious circumstance that the historical last supper is set aside, while on the other hand the washing of feet—quite invisible in the old sources—is introduced, has been met in different ways. The last supper, in his time—opp. Synopt.—already an established custom (Krabbe, p. 468), John would have assumed as having been long known and described (Paulus, Olsh., Lücke, Neander, Bleek, Ewald); or Jesus had virtually instituted it in Galilee (Casp. pp. 133 sq.; Gess, pp. 59 sq.), assertions which Schleier. (p. 420) put to the blush by his greater seriousness. Further it is said, the washing was not repeated, because it was not instituted as a special transaction (Neander), because it was the special act of Jesus (Ewald, Hase), or because it was the sentiment, not the act, that was postulated (Meyer): so much the more occasion for the supplementary narration of John (Neander, p. 526; Krabbe, p. 466). Quite against xiii. 14 sq., certainly correct, in that the pedilavium (not in specific sense, 1 Tim. v. 10) cannot be proved until Augustine's time (Merz, *Herzog*, IV. p. 630). These weak attempts at defence show how untenable is the whole Johannine account. And if John himself is so economical as not to give Jesus the credit of both washing and last supper on the same evening, and if he has evidently suppressed the really historical last supper and substituted for it the quite unattested washing, those are justified who admit neither the suppressor instead of the suppressed, nor both, but who dismiss the suppressor. This is done by Fritzsche, Strauss, Weisse, Baur, Hilg., Scholten, Volkmar; whilst A. Schweizer formerly (*Joh.* pp. 164 sqq.) defended the foot-washing, Weizs. half-accepted it, Renan will rather admit it than the last supper authenticated by later men out of the plain table-customs of Jesus; and finally, Noack (p. 233), the saviour of the fourth Gospel, finds it better proved than the last supper. Weisse, II. p. 272, has, with special energy, censured the theatrical character of the transaction. On the other hand, Hase, p. 235. On John xiii. 10, comp. Origen, t. 32, 5 sq. Scholten, p. 292.

signature of unhistoricalness, visible to every eye, lies in the violent act of destroying the last supper evening. This is an act of violence pardonable only on account of the fact that the author, breathing in Gentile-Christian freedom and yet still in an atmosphere of mystery, wished, despite all the ancient accounts, to believe and to celebrate, not a Jewish, but a genuine and complete Christian Passover. Thus developed to him the unhistorical history that Jesus ate no Passover lamb, but himself ended as the veritable, the one permanent Passover lamb, on the Passover day itself, a day before his actual death.[1]

[1] Comp. above, I. p. 174. In a remarkable manner, Strauss, 4th ed. II. p. 408, thought of John's non-acquaintance with the scene of the institution ! Weisse, II. p 276, thought of the absence of these portions in the delineations of John !

www.ingramcontent.com/pod-product-compliance
Lightning Source LLC
Chambersburg PA
CBHW071016240426
43661CB00073B/2325